Communications and Report Writing for Law Enforcement Professionals

FOURTH EDITION

Jeffrey S. Rosnick

Dianna McAleer

CONTRIBUTOR
Sergeant Brenda McGillvray

emond ▪ Toronto, Canada ▪ 2016

Emond Montgomery Publications Limited
60 Shaftesbury Avenue
Toronto ON M4T 1A3
http://www.emond.ca/highered

Printed in Canada.

We acknowledge the financial support of the Government of Canada.
Nous reconnaissons l'appui financier du gouvernement du Canada. Canada

Emond Montgomery Publications has no responsibility for the persistence or accuracy of URLs for external or third-party Internet websites referred to in this publication, and does not guarantee that any content on such websites is, or will remain, accurate or appropriate.

Publisher: Mike Thompson
Managing editor, development: Kelly Dickson
Developmental editor: Sarah Fulton
Director, editorial and production: Jim Lyons
Production editor: Laura Bast
Copy editor: Mike Kelly
Permissions editor: Lisa Brant
Proofreaders: Andrew Oliveira, Cindy Fujimoto
Indexer: Paula Pike
Cover and text designer: Tara Wells
Typesetters: Tara Wells, Chris Hudson
Cover image: Thinkstock/Getty Images

Library and Archives Canada Cataloguing in Publication

Rosnick, Jeffrey S., author
   Communications and report writing for law enforcement professionals / Jeff Rosnick, Dianna McAleer, Brenda McGillvray (contributor). -- 4th edition.

Revision of: Communications for law enforcement professionals / John A. Roberts. -- Toronto: Emond Montgomery Publications, 2003.
Includes bibliographical references and index.
ISBN 978-1-77255-020-7 (paperback)

   1. Communication in police administration--Textbooks.   2. Police reports--Textbooks.
I. McAleer, Dianna, 1962-, author   II. McGillvray, Brenda, author   III. Title.

HV7936.C79R68 2016   808'.066363   C2015-907394-4

Thanks to my dedicated colleagues for their comments and insights: Linda Whetter, Don Vail, Dave Sinclair, Duncan Lucas, and Barbara Norell. I am indebted to John A. Roberts for bringing me on board and teaching me so much, and for personal support, I must thank Nancy Sullivan, my partner in crime.

—Jeffrey S. Rosnick

Thanks to my colleagues and friends at Algonquin College for keeping me on my toes and on track: Jack Wilson, Kevin Mallory, Melissa Gabriele, and Michael Watters. Thanks to my family, Ian, Sarah, and Robin Patrick, for their encouragement and constant support.

—Dianna McAleer

Brief Contents

Detailed Contents vii

Preface xi

About the Authors xii

Acknowledgments xiii

PART I   Communication Skills

1   The Importance of Communications in Law Enforcement   3

2   Effective Listening   19

3   Spelling and Workplace Vocabulary   39

4   Writing Foundations and Grammar   63

5   Polishing Your Writing   103

6   Emails, Memoranda, and Letters   123

7   Research Skills   143

8   Essay Writing   165

9   Speaking Effectively   191

PART II   Report Writing

10   Introduction to Report Writing   221

11   The Notebook   241

12   Report Writing   263

13   General Occurrence Reports   277

14   Supplementary Reports   299

15   Witness Statements   319

16   The Crown Brief   337

17   The Written Communication Test   367

Glossary   383

Index   387

Detailed Contents

Brief Contents v
Preface xi
About the Authors xii
Acknowledgments xiii

PART I

COMMUNICATION SKILLS

1 The Importance of Communications in Law Enforcement

Learning Outcomes 3
The Communication Process 4
Communicating in a Multicultural Society 5
Communicating with People with Mental Health
    Challenges 8
Communicating with People with Disabilities 10
Understanding Language and Semantics 11
    Vocabulary Considerations 11
    Connotation and Denotation 11
Communicating Effectively in Groups 13
Chapter Summary 14
Key Terms 14
Review and Reflection Questions 14
Additional Exercises 14

2 Effective Listening

Learning Outcomes 19
Introduction 20
Your Listening Profile 20
    Quiz 1 Analysis 21
    Quiz 2 Analysis 21
    Quiz 3 Analysis 22
Nine Rules for Effective Listening 23
    Rule 1: Decide to Listen 23
    Rule 2: Avoid Selective Listening 24
    Rule 3: Give Acknowledgment and Feedback 24
    Rule 4: Ask Appropriate Questions 25
    Rule 5: Look for Non-Verbal Cues 27
    Rule 6: Listen with Your Whole Body 28

    Rule 7: Separate Fact from Opinion and Propaganda . . . 28
    Rule 8: Control Your Emotional Response 29
    Rule 9: Make Notes 29
    Some Additional Principles for Practising Effective
        Listening 30
Barriers to Effective Listening 31
Memory Techniques 32
Drawing It All Together 32
    Community Interaction 33
    A Word on Following Instructions 33
Chapter Summary 38
Key Terms 38
Review and Reflection Questions 38

3 Spelling and Workplace Vocabulary

Learning Outcomes 39
Introduction 40
Improving Your Spelling 41
Useful Spelling Rules 41
    Rule 1 41
    Rule 2 43
    Rule 3 43
    Rule 4 44
Plurals 44
Word Problems 48
Canadian Spelling 56
Chapter Summary 60
Key Terms 60
Review and Reflection Questions 60

4 Writing Foundations and Grammar

Learning Outcomes 63
Introduction 64
    Grammar Pre-Test 64
Grammar Essentials: Sentences 70
    Subject 70
    Verb 71
    Subject–Verb Agreement 74
    Sentence Fragments 77

Run-On Sentences 80
Modifiers 82
Pronoun References 85
Parallel Structure 88
Correlatives 89
Grammar Essentials: Punctuation and Capitalization . . . 91
Commas 91
Apostrophes 93
Periods 96
Question Marks 96
Exclamation Points 96
Quotation Marks 96
Semicolons 97
Colons 97
Capital Letters 98
Voice 100
Chapter Summary 101
Key Terms 101
Review and Reflection Questions 101

5 Polishing Your Writing

Learning Outcomes 103
Introduction 104
Clichés and Slang 104
Clichés 104
Slang 106
Jargon 107
Subjectivity and Objectivity 108
Connotative Language 109
Avoiding Bias 109
Fact Versus Inference 110
Being Precise and Concise 113
Being Precise 113
Being Concise 113
Points of View: First Person, Second Person, and
   Third Person 115
Points of View and Their Uses 115
Active Voice and Passive Voice 117
Chapter Summary 121
Key Terms 121
Review and Reflection Questions 121

6 Emails, Memoranda, and Letters

Learning Outcomes 123
Introduction 124
General Purposes 124
On Social Media 124
Emails 125
Specific Purposes 125
Is That Email Necessary? 125

Format 125
Style 125
Replying 127
Formatting and Attaching Documents 128
Memoranda 128
Specific Purposes 128
Format 128
Style 129
Letters 129
Specific Purposes 129
Format 130
Style 130
General Principles for Correspondence 134
Content 134
Tone 134
Readability 134
Spell Checks 134
Writing Strategies 134
The "You" Approach 134
Direct and Indirect Order 134
Chapter Summary 141
Key Terms 141
Review and Reflection Questions 141

7 Research Skills

Learning Outcomes 143
Introduction 144
Using Appropriate and Credible Sources 144
Note Taking 145
Writing a Summary 146
Changing Direct Speech to Indirect Speech 148
Counting Words 149
Sample Summaries 150
Writing a Paraphrase 151
Methods of Paraphrasing 152
Avoiding Plagiarism 153
In-Text Citations in APA Style 154
Reference Lists in APA Style 156
Citing Sources in MLA Style 158
Additional Resources for Using APA and MLA 161
Chapter Summary 163
Key Terms 163
Review and Reflection Questions 163

8 Essay Writing

Learning Outcomes 165
Introduction 166
Purpose 166
Audience 166

Paragraph 167
    Types of Paragraphs 172
Essay 173
    Getting Started 174
    Outline 175
    Thesis Statement 175
    Organizing the Essay 177
    Writing the Introduction 178
    Body of Essay or Support Paragraphs 180
    Transitions 180
    Writing Strategies 181
    Conclusion 184
    The First Draft 185
Research Paper 186
    Finding the Facts 186
Chaper Summary 189
Key Terms 189
Review and Reflection Questions 189

9 Speaking Effectively

Learning Outcomes 191
Introduction 192
    Community Outreach 192
    Academic Presentations 192
Effective Oral Presentations 193
    Purpose 193
    Selecting a Topic 193
    Narrowing the Topic 194
    Conducting Research 195
    Preparing Your Presentation 195
    Organizing Your Presentation 197
    Building the Mechanics of Your Presentation 198
    Answering Questions 198
    Overcoming Nervousness 199
    Using Visual Aids 199
Non-Verbal Communication 202
    Visual Elements 202
    Vocal Elements 203
    Spatial Elements 204
Impromptu Speaking: Say What You Mean, SIR 205
A Last Word About Oral Presentations: Don't Read . . . 206
One-on-One Communication 206
    Dealing with a Difficult Person 206
    Conferencing with Peers 207
Applications of Speaking Techniques 208
    Testifying in Court 208
Chapter Summary 218
Key Terms 218
Review and Reflection Questions 218

PART II

REPORT WRITING

10 Introduction to Report Writing

Learning Outcomes 221
Introduction 222
The Report Writing Trail 222
    Sample Scenarios 223
Types of Reports 224
    Notebooks 224
    General Occurrence Reports 224
    Supplementary Reports 224
    Arrest Reports 224
    Crown Briefs 224
    Additional Reports 225
The Report Writing Process 225
Who Will Read Your Reports? 227
    Supervisors 227
    Other Personnel at Your Service or Agency 228
    Other Enforcement Agencies 228
    People Involved in the Prosecution Process 228
    Insurance Companies 228
    Media 228
Following a Case 228
    Background 228
    Notebook Entry 228
    General Occurrence Report 230
    Supplementary Reports 230
    Summary 231
    Sample Reports for a Private Enforcement Agency 233
Chapter Summary 240
Key Terms 240
Review and Reflection Questions 240

11 The Notebook

Learning Outcomes 241
Introduction 242
Questioning to Obtain Information 242
    Effective Questioning 242
    How to Ask Questions 243
Note Taking 244
    Tips on Note Taking 245
    Tips on Taking Complete Notes 245
    Use of Notes in Court 249
    Diagrams in Notes 249
Guidelines for Notebook Entries 253
Chapter Summary 261
Key Terms 261
Review and Reflection Questions 261

12 Report Writing

Learning Outcomes	263
Introduction	264
Parts of the Report	264
General Rules for Report Writing	265
Organization for Writing Reports	266
Report Outline	267
Composing the Report	268
Facts in Issue	270
Common Errors in Report Writing	271
From Notebook to Report	271
Chapter Summary	276
Key Terms	276
Review and Reflection Questions	276

13 General Occurrence Reports

Learning Outcomes	277
Introduction	278
When Is a General Occurrence Report Required?	279
The Cover Page	280
The Narrative	280
Sample General Occurrence Report	281
Sample Cover Page	282
Sample Narrative Page	284
Reporting Information—Reviewing Key Concepts	287
Chapter Summary	297
Key Terms	297
Review and Reflection Questions	297

14 Supplementary Reports

Learning Outcomes	299
Introduction	300
Supplementary Reports for Further Investigative Actions	300
Linking Reports	301
Arrest Report	303
Documenting an Arrest	306
Warrants	307
Sample Arrest Report	307
Statement from Accused	309
Exercises for Supplementary and Arrest Reports	312
Niagara Regional Police Service Reports	315
Summary	316
Key Terms	316
Review and Reflection Questions	316

15 Witness Statements

Learning Outcomes	319
Introduction	320
Taking a Witness Statement	320
Questioning a Witness	322
General Rules for Taking a Witness Statement	322
On Procedure	324
Motor Vehicle Accident Statement	324
Niagara Regional Police Service Reports	331
Chapter Summary	336
Key Terms	336
Review and Reflection Questions	336

16 The Crown Brief

Learning Outcomes	337
Introduction	338
Rules of Disclosure	338
Contents of the Crown Brief	339
Writing the Crown Brief	339
Title Page or Cover Page	339
Introduction	340
Witness List/Synopsis	340
Summary	340
Witness Statements	341
Reviewing a Sample Crown Brief	341
Chapter Summary	365
Key Terms	365
Review and Reflection Questions	365

17 The Written Communication Test

Learning Outcomes	367
Introduction	368
The Instructions	368
The Fact Sheet	371
The Essay	376
Points to Remember	376
Chapter Summary	381
Review and Reflection Questions	381

Glossary	383
Index	387

Preface

The fourth edition of *Communications and Report Writing for Law Enforcement Professionals* has been expanded to offer more comprehensive coverage of both general writing strategies and specific law enforcement writing strategies. In Part I of the book, new chapters include Polishing Your Writing; Emails, Memoranda, and Letters; and Research Skills. In Part II of the book, the material on report writing has been greatly expanded to include separate chapters: General Occurrence Reports, Supplementary Reports, Witness Statements, and The Crown Brief.

This fourth edition continues to offer scenarios and exercises that are applicable to a variety of law enforcement agencies, and that cover bylaws, corrections, security (including airport and transit), border control, and policing. New exercises appear throughout this edition, and many scenarios carry over from one chapter to the next to provide a sense of continuity. The new "In the Field" box features provide practical examples for students.

Notable changes to specific chapters are described below. Chapters 5, 6, 7, 14, 15, and 16 are new to the book.

- **Chapter 1: The Importance of Communications in Law Enforcement.** This chapter has been expanded to include material on communicating with people with mental health challenges and people with physical challenges.

- **Chapter 5: Polishing Your Writing.** This new chapter covers avoiding errors such as using clichés and slang, using jargon sparingly, and editing for bias and subjectivity.

- **Chapter 6: Emails, Memoranda, and Letters.** This new chapter brings together material from three appendixes in the third edition to provide an integrated discussion of these topics. The chapter addresses the specific issues related to electronic communications and social media in a law enforcement context.

- **Chapter 7: Research Skills.** This new chapter combines the research material from the third edition with expanded material on finding and using appropriate sources, avoiding plagiarism, and summarizing and paraphrasing.

- **Chapter 13: General Occurrence Reports.** This chapter offers expanded material on general occurrence (or incident) report writing and includes more sample reports and new exercises.

- **Chapter 14: Supplementary Reports.** This new chapter provides expanded material on supplementary reports and includes new exercises that link to exercises in Chapter 13. Through a series of reports, including the arrest report, the chapter emphasizes how a criminal case is built.

- **Chapter 15: Witness Statements.** The expanded material in this new chapter addresses critical questions about identifying and questioning a witness. This chapter provides detailed samples of statements. Exercises and scenarios are included.

- **Chapter 16: The Crown Brief.** This new chapter expands on the Crown brief material in the third edition and includes a new sample Crown brief and additional exercises.

About the Authors

Jeffrey Rosnick is a professor in the School of Communications at Mohawk College.

Dianna McAleer is a professor in the Police and Public Safety Institute at Algonquin College.

Acknowledgments

Thank you to the reviewers of the fourth edition: Amy Bjerknes, St. Lawrence College; Calum Cunningham, Fanshawe College; and Randy Hamelin, St. Clair College.

Thank you to the outstanding crew at Emond who have made this edition successful: Sarah Fulton, Kelly Dickson, Mike Kelly, Laura Bast, Jim Lyons, Cindy Fujimoto, Andrew Oliveira, and Mike Thompson.

Thank you also to Sergeant Brenda McGillvray who wrote the "In the Field" box features and provided invaluable advice on police procedural matters.

PART I

Communication Skills

1 The Importance of Communications in Law Enforcement

LEARNING OUTCOMES

After completing this chapter, you should be able to:

- Recognize barriers in the communication process.
- Communicate respectfully with people from many cultures and with people who have physical or mental health challenges.
- Explain the value of choosing appropriate vocabulary for your intended audience.
- Describe the challenges of communicating as a member of a group.

The Communication Process

You speak, listen, watch, use body language, and write to interact with others, all of which can be considered methods of communicating.

Communication involves more than one person. Even when your attempt to communicate feels quite unsuccessful, the person you're addressing does *receive* your communication. But perhaps he or she is not listening, or is not responding appropriately, or is not responding at all. In other words, your message isn't getting through, even though it's being received. No response, or an inappropriate response, is a form of feedback to your message. A traditional diagram used to illustrate this is set out in Figure 1.1.

FIGURE 1.1   Communication Theory

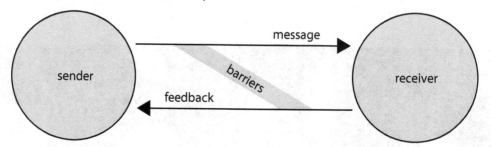

The person speaking, writing, or gesturing (the sender) sends a message to another person (the receiver). The receiver gives feedback to show that the message has been received and how the message has been received.

When someone doesn't respond to your communication or responds inappropriately, there are reasons for this breakdown; they are called *barriers to communication*. Possibly the receiver can't hear your message clearly; possibly the receiver doesn't agree with what you said and doesn't want to tell you so; or possibly the receiver is unable to respond for another reason. For example, your environment may be unsuitable for effective communication. Think of how difficult it might be to communicate with the victim of a hit-and-run accident in the following conditions: people around you are discussing the accident, it's raining, sirens are wailing, it's late at night, the victim is injured, and witnesses are trying to get your attention. These environmental factors are all barriers to communication, and they make it difficult for you to obtain the information necessary to do your job.

The complex and challenging nature of communication with victims, witnesses, and suspects requires law enforcement personnel to

- take responsibility for the communication
- withhold judgments
- show respect
- be **empathetic**
- tolerate **ambiguity**
- look beyond the superficial
- be patient
- recognize their own biases

Empathetic means being able to understand and be sensitive to another person's feelings or responses to experiences even though you may not have had similar feelings or experiences yourself.

Ambiguity is vagueness or uncertainty.

- be flexible
- send clear messages.

Other situations involve different barriers to communication. Specific problems may occur, for example, when you are dealing with people who don't speak English or who have physical disabilities or mental health challenges.

Communicating in a Multicultural Society

Immigration to Canada has increased significantly over the last 25 years, and close to 25 percent of the total present-day Canadian population was born outside of the country. Therefore, law enforcement personnel in this country must frequently communicate with people whose first language is not English, and it is essential that they be able to communicate in any cultural environment. Law enforcement officers, in particular, must be able to obtain information quickly, accurately, and in a non-threatening manner, regardless of their environment.

Q: How can you communicate effectively in a multicultural environment?

- Speak slowly and **enunciate**.
- Face the person and speak directly to him or her, even when using a translator.
- Avoid concentrated eye contact if the other speaker is not making direct eye contact.
- Do not use **jargon**, **slang**, or **idioms**. Use short, simple sentences; pause between sentences.
- Supplement your spoken words with visual cues such as gestures, demonstrations, and brief written phrases.
- Give numerous breaks.
- Respect the silence that persons whose native language is not English need to formulate their sentences and translate them in their minds. Be patient as they do so.
- Check the other speaker's comprehension by having him or her repeat your words and instructions, and remember to summarize frequently yourself.
- Provide positive feedback.
- Don't speak louder; it won't help, and it's insulting.

Non-verbal methods of communication are also important in a multicultural environment. It is helpful to remember the following:

1. An officer's body language and non-verbal messages can override his or her own words in high-stress and crisis situations, especially for people whose first language is not English. Imagine, for example, if at the scene of a house fire you are

---

Enunciate means to pronounce clearly.

Jargon refers to words or expressions that are commonly used by a select group of people and would usually be unfamiliar to others. Some better known examples include the use of *stat* in a hospital environment, or *10-4* between radio users.

Slang refers to an informal, common, but technically incorrect use of words. An example would be the use of *hanging out* to mean being somewhere for a while with no particular purpose.

Idioms use language, usually figuratively, to express something in a creative way. Some common examples include "Cat got your tongue?" and "Hit the books."

asking the homeowner to calm down while you are speaking very quickly, pacing, sweating, and speaking very loudly. Your words would have little effect; instead, your mannerisms would have a more influential effect.

2. Different cultures have diverse ways of communicating stress, confusion, and uncertainty; a person who is silent and nervous and seems to be uncooperative may in fact simply be confused by the questions being asked.

3. Careful gestures and non-verbal cues from the officer can help the non-English-speaking person understand the verbal message and reassure the person that you are making every effort to have a mutually successful communication.

Officers should learn to avoid gestures or physical behaviour that another culture might find offensive or taboo. For example, the law enforcement officer should understand

- when touch is appropriate and when it is inappropriate
- what different cultures consider to be a comfortable physical distance between two people
- what the protocols are governing eye contact in different cultures, and what is meant by eye contact or lack of eye contact
- how facial expressions are affected by culture
- what the inappropriate and appropriate gestures are for a particular cultural group.

IN THE FIELD

You and your partner are responding to a 911 call for a domestic violence incident between a husband and wife. Neighbours reported hearing a female voice screaming for help and described the sound of a fight in progress coming from the living room area.

Upon arrival, you speak with the married couple, Mr. and Mrs. Ming. You notice that the husband is doing all the talking. "Officers, we were just wrestling, and there was shouting coming from the TV, and it was on too loud. We are OK here and don't need any help, right dear? Thanks for coming."

As you glance at Mrs. Ming, you notice that her eyes are lowered to the ground while she nods "yes" in agreement.

Your partner says, "Fine, we are done here then. No report required," and he turns to leave. You feel uneasy about this and ask your partner to stay with Mr. Ming while you talk to Mrs. Ming in a separate area where you can have a candid and private conversation with her.

Your partner replies to your request by saying, "She deserves what she gets if she won't let us help her. I don't believe her anyway; she won't even look us in the eye and that means she has something to hide."

You request an interpreter to attend while you question Mrs. Ming. She reluctantly reveals a history of domestic violence dating back three years. She advises that the violence has been increasing since her husband lost his job and reveals some bruising and broken skin on her back where he struck her repeatedly with the TV remote. Mrs. Ming reveals that she is afraid of police and indicates that her husband regularly threatens to have her deported.

What are some of the barriers to communication faced by Mrs. Ming? How have cultural differences been misunderstood here? What were some of the non-verbal signs of communication used in this example?

Below are examples of gestures and behaviour that people from other cultures could find offensive:

- In Canada, direct eye contact is thought to indicate honesty and reliability, whereas shifting one's gaze away is thought to indicate the opposite; however, in Latin America, direct eye contact is thought to indicate a challenge or aggression, and shifting one's gaze away from a questioner is often used to indicate respect.

- In Canada, it is customary to smile for introductions and to indicate a friendly attitude even between strangers; however, in Japan, a smile is used as a polite expression of a range of emotions, from shame to anger. In Germany, smiles are reserved for family and friends.

- In Canada, we use the "OK" sign to indicate a positive response; however, this is a vulgar sign in some countries, including Turkey.

Also, be aware of problems that may arise from semantic differences across cultures and dialects. A single word within a language can have different meanings and nuances depending on its cultural context, and the way something is said is often more important than the words used. Remember, too, that law enforcement officials are viewed differently from culture to culture.

It is interesting to note that many police services now have a diversity component as part of their officers' yearly evaluations. Regular diversity training is also offered. This is useful and necessary as we welcome new populations of immigrants into our country. The Hamilton Police Service officer evaluation form includes a section relating to diversity. It's also important to take note that one of the core competencies a Canadian police candidate must demonstrate in order to be hired is the proven ability to work with a diverse population.

EXERCISE 1 » Communicating in a Multicultural Society

1. Divide into groups of four and take 10 to 15 minutes to discuss the following:

   a. Share a time when you experienced a miscommunication due to a cultural difference. How have you adapted your communication style as a result of this experience?

   b. How can you prepare yourself to be an effective communicator in a multicultural environment?

   Assign one member of your group to ask the questions and keep the conversation on track (this includes encouraging all members to contribute), one to record your findings, one to introduce your group members to the class (for #2, below), and one to share the findings with the class.

2. Reconvene as a class and have each group take turns sharing its findings.

3. Individually, write a list of cultures you identify with. Don't stop at country of origin, but think about such things as provincial or regional culture; leisure-activity culture; political, philosophical, or religious culture; and so on.

4. Meet and greet: Circulate around the room and try to find people who share the cultures you listed. Put first names beside the shared culture, and try to get at least one name beside each.

Communicating with People with Mental Health Challenges

Diversity in Canada is not limited to culture. Due to our increased understanding over the last several decades of the complexity and range of mental health illnesses, we now realize that systematically institutionalizing people with mental health challenges is not a solution (a positive trend). We also are faced with the very real crisis of not having enough supports in place for those dealing with mental health challenges (a negative trend). The Canadian Mental Health Association estimates that about 20 percent of the population will "experience a mental health illness in their lifetime" ("Fast Facts About Mental Illnes," n.d., http://www.cmha.ca/media/fast-facts-about-mental-illness/).

This means that as front-line workers, you will be communicating with individuals living with mental health issues. Among their challenges can be their ability to communicate effectively with others.

Q: How can you help facilitate communication when interacting with people who have mental health challenges?

- Be aware of your environment: Would it be useful to move to a quieter spot with fewer distractions?
- Be patient and allow for extra time.
- Understand that any hallucinations, illusions, or fears are very real to the person experiencing them.
- Watch your use of humour and figurative speech.
- Do not lie or assume the person cannot grasp the situation (mental illnesses don't necessarily affect a person's cognitive abilities).

EXERCISE 2 » Communicating with People with Mental Health Challenges

1. In groups of four, have a discussion about what you know about mental health challenges. Use the news media, television and film, and personal experience to discuss such things as symptoms, attitudes, misconceptions, and risk factors.

2. As a class, have a large group conversation using these questions:
   a. What are some common misconceptions about mental health challenges?
   b. How does the media portray people with mental health challenges?
   c. What are your concerns about communicating with people who have mental health challenges?

3. In pairs, come up with effective communication strategies you could use for the following scenarios:

   a. You are dispatched to the scene of a conflict in a public park. A citizen has called to report seeing two young people yelling at an older female. When you arrive, you see a woman on a park bench being yelled at by two young men. You hear one man say, "You crazy weirdo. Give me back our Frisbee. It's not an alien spacecraft!" You hear the woman respond with, "The voices told me to save you. I took the space disc to save you. You must leave this place before they exit the disc and attack your neurons."

      What would you do?

   _____

   _____

   _____

   b. You are working as a mall security guard and are called by a store manager to help with an unruly customer. When you arrive at the store, the owner immediately starts talking to you in an agitated manner. He points to a customer who is standing in front of a key-chain display and demands that you remove the customer before he takes physical action. As you approach the display, you see a man who is talking to himself while rapidly rearranging the key chains. You hear him say "red before green, L before M, do not let yellow near pink."

      What would you do?

   _____

   _____

   _____

   c. You are giving a bicycle safety talk to a class of grade 4 children. As you proceed with your talk, you notice a boy who is talking to himself and making elaborate hand gestures. He has drawn the attention of the children around you.

      What would you do?

   _____

   _____

   _____

   d. You are a transit security officer trying to explain to a teenage boy that he cannot bring his large pet snake onto the bus. He tells you the snake is his best friend, and it keeps him out of danger. He also says the snake is writing a book about the bus adventures the two are having, and it is critical the snake be allowed on the bus.

      What would you do?

   _____

   _____

   _____

4. Get together with another pair and share the ideas you came up with for effectively resolving the above communication challenges.

Communicating with People with Disabilities

Advances in assistive technologies and increasingly enlightened attitudes about accessibility have made it possible for people with physical disabilities to lead independent lives in the community. But people with physical disabilities still face many challenges, and it is critical that they can count on law enforcement professionals to be mindful and considerate when communicating.

> **Q: How can you help facilitate effective communication with people who have physical disabilities?**
>
> - *Recognize the existence of a disability.* People with disabilities may often use gestures to draw law enforcement officers' attention to their condition; they would prefer that their disabilities not be ignored.
> - *Understand the nature of the disability.* Some disabilities impair a person's ability to formulate and send a message; other disabilities impair a person's ability to receive and understand a message. Understanding the nature of the disability allows law enforcement officers to understand the barriers to communication and to shape their own efforts at communication accordingly.
> - *Be resourceful in attempting to establish communication.* For example, written notes are often the best way to communicate with a hearing- or speech-impaired person.

EXERCISE 3 » Communicating with People with Physical Disabilities

This exercise should take 30 to 45 minutes to complete.

1. a. In pairs, brainstorm to create a list of communication challenges people with physical disabilities could possibly face.

   b. For each challenge you identify, provide a solution that could help overcome the challenge.

2. Get together with another pair and compare lists.

3. In your group of four—and referring to both lists—choose five challenges with their solutions to write a document you could use for a training handout for newly hired law enforcement professionals.

Understanding Language and Semantics

Vocabulary Considerations

As a law enforcement professional, you must be comfortable communicating with a wide variety of people: schoolchildren, elderly people, high-ranking officials, and the media, to name a few. Interviewing a child about a crime she witnessed requires a different communication style than you'd use to interview a store owner who witnessed the same crime. Your words need to be tailored to reassure and get the most from each witness.

For example, if you said to a store owner, "Can you tell me when you think the bad man came into the store?" you might offend her. Likewise, if you said to an eight-year-old witness, "When did you first take note of the perpetrator's entrance into the establishment?" you might confuse her.

The English language is colourful and complex, and we often employ synonyms (words that mean the same as other words—for example, "inquire" is a synonym for "ask") to make our communication more interesting. Consider, for example, the word "walk": You can stroll, saunter, sidle, or slink. Fiction writers choose words for maximum effect. Law enforcement officers must also pay attention to their word choices. If you love the English language and enjoy finding "just the right word" when conversing with others, you might consider using the simplest approach while at work.

Think about the differences in meaning for these questions:

> **When did you first notice the suspect walking away from the scene?**
>
> **When did you first notice the suspect sauntering away from the scene?**
>
> **When did you first notice the suspect slinking away from the scene?**

Connotation and Denotation

The **denotation** of a word is its dictionary meaning. For example, the words *house* and *home* both mean a dwelling place. The **connotation** of a word refers to any additional impression the word carries with it. For example, when we think of home, we can think of comfort, love, and warmth. Those adjectives do not appear in the dictionary definition of *home*.

Think of the words *childlike* and *childish*. Both have similar definitions, but which word seems to have a more positive meaning? Words that have high connotative meaning are also value-laden and should be avoided if possible.

Denotation is the dictionary meaning of a word.

Connotation refers to any additional impression the word carries with it.

EXERCISE 4 » Understanding Language and Semantics

1. In pairs, come up with as many synonyms as you can for the word *said*.

_____

_____

_____

2. Have one person in the class go to the board, and using the words generated by each pair, write a master list of all synonyms the class came up with.

3. Read each scenario and the question that follows. Circle the most appropriate word from the choices in brackets by considering the person being interviewed.

   a. You are called to the scene of a bicycle theft. A bike had been left in front of a convenience store, and as the bike owner—a 13-year-old male—was exiting the store, he witnessed a suspect get on the bike and pedal away.

      You question the youth: What did the (perpetrator, thief, bad guy, suspect, thug) look like?

   b. You are dispatched to the home of a woman who reported a garbage can fire on her street. When you introduce yourself to her, you realize she is a recent immigrant and is just learning to speak English.

      You question the woman: When did you first (register, see, check out, take note of) the fire?

   c. You are patrolling a neighbourhood and come across an elderly man who seems to be in distress. He tells you his dog has gotten off its leash, and he can't find the dog.

      You question the man: Has your dog (run away, taken off, split, vamoosed) before?

   d. A well-known defence lawyer is questioning you on the witness stand. She asks you to describe any outstanding characteristics you noted on a suspect you interviewed.

      You reply, "He had a large mole on his right cheek and he (was heavily inked on his arms, had sleeve tats, had tattoos covering both arms)."

4. In groups of four, discuss the connotations that make each of the following word pairs seem more negative or positive:

   thrifty/stingy

   cunning/intelligent

   slim/skinny

   chef/cook

   vagrant/homeless

   fragrance/smell

   curious/nosy

   cop/officer

Communicating Effectively in Groups

Communicating is often a one-on-one situation. As was seen in the illustration of the communication process at the beginning of this chapter, a sender sends a message, a receiver receives the message, and the feedback indicates how much of the message was absorbed, understood, and accepted.

There are many situations, however, when you will be communicating with more than one person. After all, law enforcement is a group effort, and you will work with investigators, forensic specialists, civilian personnel, members of other law enforcement bodies, and court personnel, to name a few. These people are members of your group. When mixed messages are sent among members of the group, or when various members interpret a message differently and fail to assist one another in the communication process, confusion usually ensues—another communication barrier.

Q : How can you ensure that you do your part to be an effective communicator in a team environment?

- Adopt a clear, simple communication style that you use consistently.
- Be sure that messages you send to multiple people or groups are identical.
- Do not hesitate to ask for clarity when needed.
- Be open and transparent with information as appropriate.
- Solicit feedback to ensure that you are being understood.

EXERCISE 5 » Communicating Effectively in Groups

1. The telephone game: Have ten volunteers go to the front of the room and stand in a line. Hand the first person a written message. That person whispers the message into the ear of the second person. The second person then relays the message by whispering the message he received into the third person's ear, and so on until everyone has received the message.

2. The last person tells the class the message she received. The first person then reads the message he was handed.

3. Class discussion: How different were the two messages? What are some factors that may have caused the changes in the message?

CHAPTER SUMMARY

Everyone communicates, but the effectiveness of the communication process varies. Effectiveness is reflected in the types of feedback given and depends on how well the barriers to communication between sender and receiver are overcome. Law enforcement officers must be effective communicators. They must understand that certain barriers to communication, such as language differences, mental health challenges, physical disabilities, and working in groups, present challenges.

These challenges may seem overwhelming, but a genuine desire to communicate effectively using common sense, respect, an informed approach, and a willingness to adapt will ensure that as law enforcement professionals, you will overcome communication barriers.

KEY TERMS

ambiguity, 4

connotation, 11

denotation, 11

empathetic, 4

enunciate, 5

idioms, 5

jargon, 5

slang, 5

REVIEW AND REFLECTION QUESTIONS

1. What steps can you take to ensure good communication with newcomers to Canada?

2. What steps can you take to ensure good communication with people with physical disabilities or mental health challenges?

3. What are some effective ways law enforcement professionals could learn to communicate better with a certain cultural group?

4. In what ways do law enforcement services benefit from respectful communication with the communities they serve?

5. What can you do now that will improve your communications skills in preparation for your career in law enforcement?

ADDITIONAL EXERCISES

EXERCISE 6   »   Exploring Personal Space

Divide the class into pairs. Have the pairs face each other at a distance of about 1.5 metres. Ask one person in each pair to move gradually closer to the other. Have students monitor the effects of this exercise, particularly noting when they feel the other stepping into their "personal space."

EXERCISE 7   »   Identifying Cultural Differences in Communication

The chances are good that your class consists of people from a variety of cultures. Have a class discussion on the variety of cultures in your class, and ask classmates from different cultures to volunteer information about their own cultures. What are some of the cultural differences in communication you found?

EXERCISE 8 » Understanding the Power of Words

Law enforcement officers must be effective communicators. Consider the phrase "Words have power." As a class, discuss the different meanings this phrase might have in a law enforcement context.

EXERCISE 9 » Evaluating Your Group Work Strengths and Weaknesses

Law enforcement officers must learn to work in teams. Group work is an essential way for you to learn teamwork skills. Use this brief quiz to identify your strengths and weaknesses. Rate yourself on a scale of 1 to 5 for each question (5 = I strongly agree; 1 = I strongly disagree). Compare answers with a partner, and discuss the reasons for them. Think about how you might improve in areas you are weak.

1. I am good at word processing.
2. I am a good presenter.
3. I am good at organizing people.
4. I am good at generating discussion.
5. I am good at keeping notes.
6. I know how to use presentation programs, such as PowerPoint.
7. I like to lead and inspire others.
8. I do my share.
9. I expect others to carry me along.
10. I expect to have my way.
11. I ask others what they think.
12. I am not afraid to disagree.
13. I am willing to take the time to solve problems.
14. I generally wait until the last minute to finish a project.
15. I need deadlines to focus my attention.
16. I practise presentations before I give them.
17. I do better working in groups.
18. I enjoy group work.
19. I have had bad experiences working in groups.
20. I want to learn to deal with group work.

EXERCISE 10 » Understanding the Challenges of Communicating in a Different Culture

The Problem

What is it like to undergo questioning from an officer who doesn't understand your culture?

The Setting

You've been hired by a large multinational company, which is expanding its operations in Komanistan. You will be living there for one or two years, but you haven't had much to do with the local culture. You know you are experiencing culture shock.

Part A: Questioned in Komanistan

One night, you are walking in town with your guide, who suddenly darts into a shop and leaves you waiting on the street. While standing there, you witness a case of theft. A man grabs a woman's bag, throws her to the ground, and runs off. A security officer appears on the scene, and the woman points at you.

The remainder of the scenario is presented below and divided into numbered parts. For each part, determine how you would feel and what you would be thinking.

1. The security officer is running toward you and shouting at you. He is using many Komani words you don't understand.

2. You look around for your guide, but you don't see him. You're on your own. Suddenly, you realize everyone is staring at you.

3. You call your guide's name, hoping for assistance. Immediately, two older men come up to you and begin speaking in loud, agitated voices. They are waving their hands in the air. What are they talking about?

4. Now the security officer steps toward you so that he is almost nose to nose and says, "Passport!"

5. You glance around at the faces of the men who were staring at you. They are now looking toward the ground.

6. You hesitate, and look directly into the officer's eyes for understanding. Just then, your guide appears and begins arguing with the two agitated men in Komani.

7. You see the officer's expression change. He begins waving one hand at you and another toward his patrol car.

8. Your guide now addresses the officer: "Hi. Sorry about that. What's the problem, officer?" And then your guide looks down while he listens to the officer speak in Komani. Your guide looks surprised. Finally, he looks you up and down.

9. Your guide explains that the officer would like you to come to the station to make a statement as an independent witness to the theft.

Part B: Debriefing

Answer the following questions:

1. What did you learn from going through this experience?

_____

_____

_____

2. How would you adjust your communication behaviour here at home when dealing with a recent immigrant from a different culture?

_____

_____

_____

3. Form small groups and compare your answers with those of your group members.

    a. In what ways are your answers similar?

_____

_____

_____

    b. In what ways are they different?

_____

_____

_____

_____

_____

2 Effective Listening

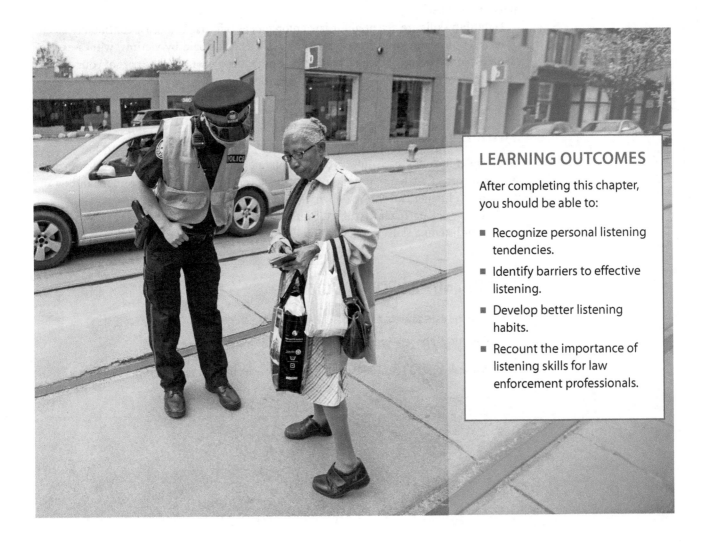

LEARNING OUTCOMES

After completing this chapter, you should be able to:

- Recognize personal listening tendencies.
- Identify barriers to effective listening.
- Develop better listening habits.
- Recount the importance of listening skills for law enforcement professionals.

We have been given two ears and but a single mouth in order that we may hear more and talk less.

—Zeno of Citium

Introduction

"No one listens anymore!"

This is a complaint that many students have heard from their instructors, but is it correct? You sit in class and "listen" to what is being presented—except, of course, when you're looking out the window, or talking to someone, or daydreaming, or not concentrating because the room is too hot or too cold, or when you just don't feel like listening.

So, are you really listening? Are your instructors correct? Do the words go in one ear and out the other?

Listening skills are essential for law enforcement officers. You must continually listen to instructions from your superiors and to what is being said by victims, witnesses, accused persons, lawyers, colleagues, and many other people who will be part of your career. The best place to learn how to listen is in the classroom.

Your Listening Profile

This chapter includes three quizzes to help you rate yourself as a listener. There are no correct or incorrect answers. Your responses, however, will extend your understanding of yourself as a listener and show you where improvement is needed.

These are not particularly difficult quizzes, but your answers will reveal something about your listening skills in relation to others who have done the test.

LISTENING PROFILE » Quiz 1

- Circle the category that best describes you as a listener:

  excellent / above average / average / below average / weak

- On a scale of 0 to 100 (100 being the best), how would you rate yourself as a listener?

  _____

Listening is a complex communication skill and not simply a matter of hearing sound.

Quiz 1 Analysis

- Eighty-five percent of all people questioned rate themselves as "average" or worse. Fewer than 5 percent rated themselves as "excellent."

- On the 0 to 100 scale, the extreme range of all respondents was 0 to 90, the general range was 35 to 85, and the average was 55.

LISTENING PROFILE » Quiz 2

On a scale of 0 to 100 (100 being the best), how do you think the following people would rate you as a listener?

- Your best friend: _____

- Your instructor: _____

- An acquaintance: _____

- Someone in your class: _____

- Your girlfriend / boyfriend / spouse / partner: _____

- Your employer, if you have a job: _____

Quiz 2 Analysis

Most respondents rated themselves highest in the role of listeners to their best friends. In most categories, respondents rated themselves higher than they did in Quiz 1.

What does this tell us? If people are in fact, as most of them suspect, strong listeners in relation to their best friends, it is perhaps because such relationships, unlike others, necessitate good listening. It is interesting to note that most respondents felt that they were seen as poor listeners by spouses and partners. Does "familiarity breed contempt"? The results seem to indicate that respondents talk a lot to their partners but do not listen well.

The implications of all this for law enforcement personnel are startling. The quiz contains no categories for witnesses or victims, but if you assume that your overall listening performance would remain the same in connection with these people, you have to wonder how much information is being missed. What are you hearing? If you are an average listener, what happens to the information you missed, information that ought to appear on, say, a witness statement? Obviously, this information gets lost, and the implications can be serious. Being found guilty of a crime or at fault in a traffic accident can obviously affect a person's criminal record, insurance record, driving record, and employment status. The stakes are high.

LISTENING PROFILE » Quiz 3

Choose one of the following answers for each of the questions below, and score yourself accordingly.

Answer	Score
Almost always	2
Usually	4
Sometimes	6
Seldom	8
Almost never	10

As a listener, how often do you ...   **Answer**   **Score**

- consider a subject uninteresting?

- criticize a speaker's delivery or mannerisms?

- become passionate about something said by a speaker?

- listen only for facts?

- try to outline everything?

- fake attention?

- look for distractions?

- ignore difficult material?

- become antagonistic?

- daydream?

Total _____

At a Lecture, Only 12 Percent Listen

Bright-eyed college students in lecture halls aren't necessarily listening to the professor, the American Psychological Association was told.

If you rang a bell at sporadic intervals during a lecture and asked students to record their thoughts and moods at that moment, you would find the following:

- About 20 percent of the students, men and women, were pursuing erotic thoughts.
- Another 20 percent were reminiscing.
- Only 20 percent were paying attention to the lecture.
- Only 12 percent were understanding what was being said.
- The remainder were worrying, daydreaming, or thinking about something else.

—Paul Cameron, Wayne State University

Quiz 3 Analysis

The lower your score, the weaker are your listening skills. Think about it: If your listening skills are weak, what are you really hearing at your job?

Most of us engage in ineffective listening, an obvious barrier to good communication. People are generally poor listeners, usually out of habit, as a result of lack of attention or interest, or because the message is complex. The following section offers nine suggestions for how to listen effectively.

Nine Rules for Effective Listening

Poor listening habits are the cause of more communication breakdowns than most of us realize; we tend not to think of listening as a communication skill. The first thing to realize about listening is what it's not. First, listening and hearing are not the same thing. Hearing is the physiological event of sound hitting the eardrum. Listening is complex; it involves receiving a message, interpreting the message, interpreting the speaker's feelings, eliminating personal biases, understanding what is being said, and practising other skills, which will be discussed in this section.

When someone else is speaking, usually you are not; there is silence from your side of the conversation. But if you are running over your reply in your mind and just waiting for the other person to finish so that you can jump in, that's not real listening.

Listening is a conscious act, and if you don't practise it actively, you simply cannot communicate effectively.

Rule 1: Decide to Listen

Human beings deal with the noise in their environment by filtering out what doesn't interest them, so that they can concentrate on what does. For example, people who live on busy streets often claim that they don't hear the cars going by. The problem is that we often rely too heavily on this filtering mechanism and end up filtering out messages that we need to hear.

In law enforcement settings, we can't afford to let that happen, so we must actually *decide* to listen and then listen actively, with concentration and intent, using all of the skills that we discuss in this section.

Why should we listen? Here are three good reasons: Listening keeps us informed, listening keeps us out of trouble, and listening makes us appreciated.

Listening Keeps Us Informed

"Nobody ever tells me anything around here!" This cry is usually heard just after someone has found out something that he or she should have known before. This exclamation reflects an attempt to blame others for one's own lack of knowledge. How often, on the other hand, have you heard someone say, "I never listen to anything that anyone says around here"? Make a point of paying attention to what's going on around you—listening to messages and information from your colleagues—so that you will always be well informed. Knowledge is power; the best way to acquire knowledge is to listen.

Listening Keeps Us Out of Trouble

Perhaps you remember your mother saying, when you were quite young, something like, "I've told you over and over not to do that. Don't you listen?" The answer, of course, is that we didn't listen. We didn't realize it at the time, but we had more important things on our minds than instructions from Mom, so the information went, as my mother used to say, in one ear and out the other.

Unfortunately, that situation isn't confined to childhood. Many of us carry poor listening habits into adulthood and the business world. If someone is giving you instructions and you don't listen well, there's a good chance that you won't be able to carry out those instructions properly. Over time, this can be detrimental to your career.

Listening Makes Us Appreciated

One of my best friends in university was very popular. More than once I heard people say that when they were with her, she made them feel as if they were the most important people in the world. They felt that way because she was a great listener. She listened with her ears, her eyes, her smile, her body, her mind—her whole self. When you put that much of yourself into the listening end of a conversation, the other person can't help but admire and appreciate you. Good listeners will often find themselves respected and trusted simply because other people enjoy working with them.

Rule 2: Avoid Selective Listening

Selective listening occurs when we listen only to what we want to hear—we select the message. In law enforcement, as in our personal lives, we can't afford to practise selective listening. The fact that we ignore bad news or uninteresting material doesn't make it go away or become irrelevant. In fact, things may well become worse if we act on just one part of a complex message.

One way we listen selectively is by not listening to all of what the other person is saying. We listen to half a sentence and then, assuming we know what the person is about to say, we respond without listening to the rest. Has anyone ever done this to you when you were speaking? Then you know how annoying it is. "That's not what I was going to say!" is like a dash of cold water in the listener's face, and it is well deserved.

A common cause of selective listening is personal **bias** or **stereotyping** against the speaker. As a customs officer, for example, you may attend a meeting of customs officials concerning procedures to eliminate the smuggling of illegal weapons across the border. While these procedures are being discussed, you overhear another customs officer whisper to another person, "This isn't going to work. We just don't have enough people to handle the inspections." Obviously, someone with this attitude is not going to listen to the presentation with an open mind, and in fact may not listen at all. That's selective listening.

It's also tempting to discount the opinions of people you simply don't like. If you feel yourself switch off when a certain person begins to speak, you are guilty of selective listening. Remember, the information may be valid and useful even if the person delivering it isn't someone you would have over for dinner—so listen up!

Rule 3: Give Acknowledgment and Feedback

You can encourage a speaker through either a verbal or a non-verbal response. A simple nod of the head, a smile, a raising of the eyebrows—these are all forms of non-verbal acknowledgment. They let the speaker know you are paying attention. Remaining silent at the appropriate times also indicates you're listening.

If you prefer to acknowledge the speaker verbally, you might interject encouraging words into the conversation, such as "Tell me more about it," "I didn't know that," or "I understand." Note that this indicates your understanding, not your agreement. Your chance to disagree will come later. You could also ask for clarification, with such expressions as "Are you saying that … ?" or "Do you mean that … ?" You may want to paraphrase the speaker's words, and begin your rephrasing with an expression such as "I hear you saying that . …" We look at the paraphrase in more detail in Chapter 7, Research Skills. These forms of acknowledgment let the speaker know that you understand what is being said. They demonstrate your interest and establish a rapport between the two of you. In a

---

Bias indicates a strong opinion that influences a point of view.

Stereotyping means to adopt an oversimplified idea of a person.

meaningful conversation, each party acknowledges the other's *feelings* as well as the actual words that are spoken.

For example, suppose that a co-worker is complaining about a seemingly trivial matter. She frowns and says angrily, "Why do they have so many rules and regulations? Why do they keep coming up with more? How does the security company expect me to pay attention to all of this paperwork? I almost feel like I need to be a lawyer as well as a loss prevention officer." If you simply agree with her, or say that you don't have a problem interpreting all of the new regulations, you might be missing the point. Respond instead with a statement such as, "This really seems to have upset you." This response opens up the possibility of further conversation. Indeed, you may find that the regulations aren't the problem so much as the fact that she feels overwhelmed with her workload, and is apt to view another piece of paper as the last straw. This is another example of how effective listening could contribute productively to the discussion.

Men and women tend to react differently to this type of acknowledgment. Of course, this is not always the case, but as a general rule, men are often reluctant to discuss their feelings, and are likely to deny them. When responding to a man in this situation, preface your remarks with phrases such as "It seems to me … ," or "Could it be … ," or "I wonder if . …" Women tend to be more direct about their feelings, although you still need to be careful.

It's important to watch the language you use in giving feedback. If you use preliminary phrases such as "My advice is …" or "Your problem is … ," your feedback may not be welcome. You want to tune in fully to what is being said without offering your own judgment or ideas or feelings. If you give speakers the opportunity to talk a problem through, they will often come up with the answer themselves, which is much more effective than having you impose an answer.

Don't downplay a problem. Avoid responses such as "Don't worry" or "That's not so bad." These responses can be perceived as devaluing the speaker's concerns.

Reflective Listening

Reflective listening is a form of feedback that involves carefully rephrasing a speaker's message and returning it to him or her for confirmation, such as in the following exchange:

> *Richard*: **"I'm fed up with issuing speeding tickets and seeing the speeder have the charge dropped in court."**
>
> *Jerry*: **"It sounds as if you're frustrated by not having more convictions. Is that right?"**

That's reflective listening. It isn't suitable for all situations, and you have to avoid merely parroting what the speaker has said, but it can be a useful method of making sure, for example, that you have heard instructions correctly.

Rule 4: Ask Appropriate Questions

Questioning is an important part of the listening process because it helps the speaker convey his or her thoughts. By asking the right questions, you can greatly increase the scope of the conversation, which is the real art of listening. Compare the following modes of questioning:

> *Inspector 1*: "Has Jenny been to work every day this week?"
>
> *Inspector 2*: "How is Jenny doing now that she has a new partner?"

Here we see two different types of questions: **closed** and **open**. Inspector 1 asks a closed question, which means that it can be answered with a simple "yes" or "no." Inspector 2 asks an open question, which means that the other person must elaborate and give information in order to answer it.

If you want to develop and broaden a conversation, start by asking open questions. Then, as the need for confirmation arises, insert closed questions where appropriate. Let's continue with the sample dialogue from above:

> *Inspector*: "How is Jenny doing now that she has a new partner?"
>
> *Sergeant*: "Okay."
>
> *Inspector*: "Do you think she's more satisfied with her job?"
>
> *Sergeant*: "She seems a lot happier."
>
> *Inspector*: "How so?"
>
> *Sergeant*: "She used to take a lot of time off, complaining about headaches and stress. She didn't seem to be very happy. Now, she actually comes in early, is more outgoing than she used to be, and handles her reports quickly and efficiently."
>
> *Inspector*: "And you attribute this to having someone new to work with?"
>
> *Sergeant*: "Definitely."
>
> *Inspector*: "I'm glad we were able to figure out the problem. What else do you think we need to do?"
>
> *Sergeant*: "I think Jenny will be fine. We should look at the rest of our personnel and see if there are similar problems."

You can use both types of questions, closed and open, to broaden a conversation, to clarify or confirm meaning, or to move the conversation in another direction. Below are examples of questions that accomplish these three goals.

Additional information about the effectiveness of questions in law enforcement situations can be found in Chapter 9, Speaking Effectively.

Broadening Questions

> "Mary, you've told us about the new procedure they're using to inspect luggage at the Toronto airport, and it seems to be working well. How do you think we can adapt it to suit our conditions here?"

As you can see, this question calls for an analytical response that will bring in more information and broaden the discussion.

Closed questions limit choices when answering, as in "yes" or "no."

Open questions allow for information and elaboration.

Clarifying or Confirming Questions

> "What do you mean? Are you saying you agree with Doug's assessment?"

By asking questions like these, you give the speaker an opportunity to restate a position and clarify it for others.

Questions That Change the Direction

> "We've discussed in depth your proposed procedure for handling young offenders, and it seems to have merit. Can you tell us what impact it will have on the budget?"

The first sentence brings closure to one part of the discussion, and the ensuing question moves it on to another part.

Do you see how the open-ended questions elicit information, and the closed-ended questions serve to confirm information or opinion? Think about your own conversations. Do you use questions effectively? Questioning is a valid and helpful aspect of listening, so it's important to work on it.

Rule 5: Look for Non-Verbal Cues

Suppose for a moment that you now live in a different place from the one where you grew up, and that you have gone home on vacation. For the first week, you have spent every day and evening with your mother, and you have thoroughly enjoyed her company. Now, an old friend has invited you out for dinner. As you leave, you say, "Okay, Mom, I'm off. I'll probably be at Barbara's place for a couple of hours, so I won't be too late."

Instead of looking at you with her usual cheerful face, Mom looks down at the carpet, her head leans forward and down to one side, and her voice seems to slow down and age 20 years as she says in a world-weary tone, "Oh, don't worry. I'll be fine. Just you go ahead and enjoy yourself, and don't give a thought to me."

This is a classic case of the **non-verbal cues**—body language and tone of voice—being in direct conflict with the spoken words. Mom's non-verbal message is clear: "I don't want you to go, I'd prefer that you not enjoy yourself, and I have no intention of being fine!"

People send non-verbal messages in the workplace all the time, and effective listeners learn to "hear" them. How you decide to respond is not the issue here; the important thing is that you recognize the non-verbal message. Additional information on body language and non-verbal communication can be found in Chapter 9.

Body Language

Interpreting body language is not an exact science. There is danger in interpreting individual gestures and mannerisms according to a fixed set of rules; the meanings of gestures and mannerisms vary from one person to another. For example, we are told that folded arms indicate defensiveness or an unwillingness to be persuaded; however, many people fold their arms simply because it is a comfortable position.

It is important to look at body language *clusters* if you want to interpret body language accurately. If your sergeant stands in front of you with his arms folded and asks for information, it doesn't necessarily mean anything. But if he folds his arms while tapping his foot, frowning, and clenching his teeth, you can be sure that a problem exists.

Non-verbal cues include body language and tone of voice.

What the good listener looks for is body language that seems to contradict the words of the speaker. When words and body language are in direct conflict, the body language is usually a truer indicator of meaning.

Tone of Voice

Have you ever heard a speaker stand up on a platform and begin a speech with the words, "I'm pleased to be here with you today," spoken in a flat monotone that indicated no pleasure at all? You probably noticed that the tone of voice didn't match the words, and you probably believed the tone. Most people would. What did that do for the speaker's credibility? Likely, not much.

Tone of voice plays a larger role in our conversations than we realize. On hearing their voices on a recording for the first time, most people refuse to believe that they sound "like that." People don't realize that they speak in such a flat tone.

Alertness to tone of voice is another tool for evaluating the truth and sincerity of a person's actual words in relation to the real feelings behind them. Ideally, for a message to be clear and uncomplicated, the words, body language, and tone of voice should all be in agreement; in other words, they should all send the same message.

Effective listeners always pay attention to non-verbal cues because they are a vital component of communication.

Rule 6: Listen with Your Whole Body

Picture this: Something exciting happened on your shift today. When you and your partner sit down to dinner, you begin to relate the incident. Your partner doesn't look at you, doesn't say a word, shows no reaction—just keeps eating. Do you feel listened to? Is your partner using the tools of lively listening? The fact is that that person might well be listening, might be taking in every word you say. But is it effective listening? No.

The effective listener not only takes in information but also indicates in many ways that the speaker's message is getting through. If you want to make it clear that you are listening, use your entire body.

First, *look* at the person speaking. Give the speaker plenty of non-verbal feedback: Nod your head, smile, frown, vary your expression to suit your response, lean toward the speaker; the speaker is encouraged to continue because you have made it clear that you're listening.

Using your body also helps you as the listener; if you're active, your attention is much less likely to wander. In other words, by physically indicating to the speaker that you *are* listening, you will actually improve the quality of your listening.

Rule 7: Separate Fact from Opinion and Propaganda

The challenge of this rule is that you must learn to distinguish what is **fact** from what is merely **opinion** or what someone would like you to believe. People colour their words in many ways, which adds to the challenge of effective listening.

"These people are doing it. Why don't you join them?" This is the familiar message of what the advertising industry calls *lifestyle advertising*: A group of happy, laughing adults enjoys a certain brand of beer. The implication, the suggestion, the unspoken message is that if you drink this brand of beer, you too can enjoy this lifestyle. You are encouraged to jump on the bandwagon.

Fact is verifiable and based on evidence.

Opinion is merely a point of view.

We recognize this tactic in advertising, but we don't always notice it in normal conversation. Any time someone is trying to persuade you to do something or believe something, listen carefully for the facts and strip away the opinion.

Another way that facts can be distorted is with biased words and expressions. People sometimes have so much invested in their opinions being accepted that they sound like a circus pitchman in full swing. "This process will revolutionize the way our company operates!" This may well be true, but it may not be the kind of revolution you want. Or it may not be true at all. Learn to strip away the opinion and propaganda and listen for the facts before you respond.

Rule 8: Control Your Emotional Response

We all have **hot buttons**. We all have attitudes and beliefs that make us respond with a quick flash of anger when people raise certain topics in particular ways.

What are your hot buttons? It's important to be aware of them so that you can decide how to react when someone pushes them in a conversation. As a lively listener, you need to take several steps to control your emotional response to what someone says to you.

First, you must recognize your response. When someone says something that makes you angry, what does it feel like? What happens in your body? Usually, one of the first things we notice is a change in our breathing pattern—breathing becomes shallower and faster. Perhaps you find that blood rushes to your face, and you feel heat there. Some people feel a headache suddenly begin; others automatically clench their hands into fists. How do you feel if one of your hot buttons is pushed? Take some time to really think about this, because it needs to be immediately recognizable to you if you want to be an effective listener.

How do you control an inappropriate emotional response? First, acknowledge it to yourself. Then, take a momentary pause and breathe deeply. This will change your physiological state while giving you time to consider what to say. In that brief interval, you can get control of yourself and choose your reaction.

Depending on various factors—the subject under discussion, the identity of the person who has upset you, the purpose of the conversation—you might take one of three paths:

1. *Ignore the comment and move on.* This will enable you to continue the conversation, but it might leave you simmering below the surface.

2. *Mention it and make an issue of the remark.* If the same person constantly pushes the same hot button, at some point you will need to do this just to clear the air. It is possible that the person is pushing your buttons unwittingly and only needs to have it mentioned in order to stop.

3. *Respond in passing and continue the conversation on the right track.* Say something like, "You may be right, but that's not what we're discussing."

An inappropriate overreaction can put an end to any conversation, so you would do well to learn how to control your emotional response.

Rule 9: Make Notes

Notes can be on paper, on a computer screen, or just in your head, depending on the situation. If one of your colleagues is explaining a situation and asking for your help, begin by saying, "I'll just make a few notes as we talk," and make it obvious that you are doing so. The person now knows that you are really listening and paying attention, and the notes

---

Hot buttons are topics that trigger an emotional response based on attitudes and beliefs.

serve as focal points to help you formulate your response. Don't overdo the note taking. It's one thing to make occasional notes; it's quite another thing to write down every word and make the speaker feel as if he or she is being interrogated.

Of course, in order to decide which points need to be noted, you need to take steps we have already discussed: Provide feedback, ask questions, and listen with your whole body. All these practices help elicit information that you can use to take effective notes. Note taking is a vital step in becoming an effective listener.

Guidelines for taking notes in memo books can be found in Chapter 11, The Notebook.

Some Additional Principles for Practising Effective Listening

1. Remember that the listener's job is to assimilate information, understand the information, and act on it.

2. Don't ignore the speaker's silence. Silence is a behaviour that has meaning, and it's often important to discover that meaning. You might try the following question: "You seem reluctant to discuss this matter. What's on your mind?"

3. Organize your perceptions: Decide whether the speaker is angry, unreasonable, or open to advice. Also, recognize stereotypes and prejudices in others. Keep your perceptions provisional.

4. Interpret the speaker in the speaker's own terms, not yours.

5. Get agreement: Summarize what you heard and have the speaker agree to your version.

IN THE FIELD

You are a brand new police officer and you have just finished your required hours with your coach officer. You arrive at the morning parade briefing and receive an assignment to "guard the scene" of a homicide. The homicide occurred overnight, and the firearm is still missing. It appears to be related to a retaliation for an armed robbery arrest.

You report to your staff sergeant to get the details. Also present are a few of your friends from night shift who are animatedly discussing the busy shift they had. They are recounting the homicide scene that was discovered while officers were occupied attending the bank location for the robbery. You are very interested in hearing all of the exciting details of the shift your friends worked. While this conversation is going on, your staff sergeant is providing you details of your assignment.

> *Staff Sergeant*: "You will need to take a cruiser out to guard the scene at a residence at 123 South Street. Park your cruiser where you can see both entrances of the residence and allow nobody to come and go from that location. Forensic investigators will be there conducting their examination of the scene at some point and will be allowed to enter. You will be provided a "crime scene register" to record any persons who enter and exit the scene and the times. Nobody enters without your permission, understood?"
>
> *Recruit*: "Yes, Staff."
>
> *Staff Sergeant*: "Any questions or concerns?"
>
> *Recruit*: "None, thanks."

You arrive and take over the scene from the night shift officers. You record in your duty book the time, and you settle in to "guard the scene." Approximately two hours later, you are approached by a woman who shows you ownership of a vehicle parked in the driveway and states that she needs to move her vehicle to get it outside the police tape or she will be late for work. You try to remember the conversation you had with your staff sergeant, and you recall very little. You remember that you are to allow nobody in or out of the residence and that anyone who does enter or exit is supposed to sign the register. This vehicle is in the driveway, not the residence, and the woman does have the proper ownership, so you allow her to take the vehicle to work. What harm can this do?

Approximately one hour later, detectives arrive with their search warrants and the forensic examination team to conduct their scientific analysis on the scene.

Detective: "Where is the crime vehicle?"

Recruit: "Which crime vehicle? Nobody told me about one."

Detective: "The vehicle that was involved in the robbery and shooting; it was parked in this driveway when we left to write our warrants."

Recruit: "Oh my God, I didn't know it was off limits. I was told only to guard the house and not let anyone enter there. I didn't know the car was involved."

Detective: "The weapon was in the vehicle. The police tape marking the scene included this entire property. The yard, the garage, the shed, and the vehicle. What have you done? Crucial evidence is now lost!"

EXERCISE 1 » Knowing Yourself as a Listener

1. Identify some topics of discussion to which you listen attentively. Why do these topics interest you?

2. Identify some topics that don't usually cause you to listen attentively. Why not?

3. For those topics that don't compel your full attention, develop a list of strategies for listening more attentively to discussion of them.

Barriers to Effective Listening

There are a number of reasons why people don't listen effectively. These barriers to effective listening can affect both the message being sent and the message being received. They include the following:

1. *Lack of interest.* If you're not interested in what's being said, you don't listen, or you listen only to those things that interest you—in other words, selectively—and ignore the rest.

2. *Daydreaming.* Your mind is occupied by something other than what's being said.

3. *Emotional concerns.* You may be emotionally involved in the topic and therefore interested in only one point of view, or you may have recently suffered an emotional or traumatic experience in your personal life that is occupying your thoughts.

4. *Judgmental approach.* You hear what is being said through the distortion of your own ideas, judgments, or feelings. Your biases and prejudices take over.

5. *Environmental and physical distractions.* These include background noise, uncomfortable seating, heat, cold, cramped space, colleagues who talk while you're trying to listen, and many others.

6. *Lack of understanding.* You lack the background needed to fully understand the speaker's topic.

7. *Unclear presentation.* The speaker is discussing the topics in a vague manner and not providing elaboration.

8. *Incorrect interpretation of the message.* You misunderstand the motives behind the message, being unable to interpret others in their own terms.

9. *Lack of retention.* Statistically, we forget more than half of a message immediately, and remember only about 35 percent after eight hours.

Memory Techniques

Lack of retention is a serious barrier to effective listening. Learn to use the following memory techniques, or mnemonics (pronounced "*ni*-monniks"), to increase your retention.

- For a series of things to remember, try an acronym. For example, use the acronym RICE to remember the procedure for treating a minor injury: **r**est, **i**ce, **c**ompression, and **e**levation.

- Another common technique is *chunking*—organizing ideas into groups. For example, a ten-digit phone number is better remembered in a series of three groups of numbers: 293 399 4834.

- Elaborative encoding makes connections between a list of things and our own experience. It is a personal approach to memorization, and works by association. For example, you associate a person with his or her name, address, car, and so on.

- Telling a story (narrative) helps us remember in terms of characters, settings, actions, and more. The story you invent might be realistic or ridiculous; so long as it helps you remember, it doesn't matter. For example, tell a story that focuses on specific aspects of a character (describe a suspect's prominent nose), the setting (exaggerate the cold or heat on the night of the event), or the action (compare the amount of blood at the scene of an assault to a slaughterhouse).

- Making a mental picture is an ancient approach to memory. You can organize key images together in a sort of inner photograph. For example, listening to a list of electronic items and devising a picture in which you can see the items laid out on a table is a good way to give the items a sense of order.

EXERCISE 2 » Identifying Effective Listening

Watch the film *12 Angry Men*. Which rules of effective listening are the characters following? Which are they not following? What barriers to effective listening can you identify? In particular, pay attention to their non-verbal cues, such as body language, and try to identify characters' hot button issues. Summarize your findings verbally or in a short report.

Drawing It All Together

Now that we have identified both the skills involved in effective listening, and some of the barriers to it, we can summarize the steps you need to take to improve your listening skills and also identify the qualities that will enhance these skills:

1. *Pay attention.* The speaker may be saying something you can use to your advantage. **Skill enhancer: *Efficiency***

2. *Concentrate on the message.* The message conveyed is more important than what the speaker is saying. **Skill enhancer: *Clarity***

3. *Hear the speaker out.* Let the speaker finish speaking before you make any judgments. **Skill enhancer: *Objectivity***

4. *Listen for main ideas, principles, and concepts.* Be aware of the large picture. **Skill enhancer: *Perception***

5. *Listen two or three minutes before taking notes.* Do not begin writing immediately. **Skill enhancer: *Ability to conceptualize and summarize***

6. *Relax while listening.* Tension detracts from listening ability. **Skill enhancer: *Self-discipline***

7. *Eliminate distractions.* Distractions are any barriers to listening, such as noise, which will detract from the message. **Skill enhancer: *Decisiveness***

8. *Learn how to listen to difficult material.* Do not withdraw your attention when the factual or the emotional content is difficult. **Skill enhancer: *Perseverance***

9. *Identify your own greatest word barriers.* Word barriers are words or concepts that trigger bias or negative attitudes. **Skill enhancer: *Objectivity***

10. *Make your interpretation skills an asset.* Use the following techniques to assist you:
    a. Anticipate the next point to be made.
    b. Make comparisons and contrasts.
    c. Identify the speaker's evidence.
    d. Practise mental summarizing.

    Skill enhancer: *Resourcefulness*

Community Interaction

Law enforcement depends on not only public acceptance but also its assistance. Institutions reach out to the public for feedback through social media, surveys, tip lines, and so on. In other words, even institutions must listen effectively to do their work properly. Likewise, individual officers need to listen effectively to the general public. Informal conversations can generate trust, produce useful information, and alert an officer to criminal or threatening behaviour. You also send the message that you are listening, and this message itself will be appreciated. As you have learned from this chapter, to listen effectively means to observe body language, ask questions, overcome barriers to listening, and more. Apply these principles during your interactions in the community.

A Word on Following Instructions

As a student, you will find that your assignments grow more complicated as you move through your courses. You are being tested not only on material but also on your ability to follow instructions. This is quite appropriate. One important skill of law enforcement professionals is to follow instructions. Modern law enforcement is governed by complex policies and procedures. The costs for mistakes can range from rewriting a report to losing a case at court. Use the principles from this chapter to help you follow instructions:

1. Listen actively to the speaker, with concentration and intent.

2. Overcome barriers to listening so that you can gather all relevant information.

3. Ask appropriate questions to give your instructor, supervisor, or partner a chance to restate instructions. Don't wait until confusion causes further problems you can't handle.

4. Take notes using a notebook or a mental outline. Instructions will range from simple (filing an expense claim, for example) to complex (a tactical procedure, for example). Break these instructions into a series of steps or a checklist.

5. Use a memory technique such as an acronym or chunking to help you remember the list or steps in a process (see "Memory Techniques" above).

Effective listening is a crucial component of understanding how to properly follow instructions.

EXERCISE 3 » Tracking Your Listening Behaviour

1. For the next five days, pay attention to your listening behaviour. Make note of the times you genuinely try to listen and understand what someone else is saying, and of the times when you aren't listening.

2. Keep a record of this information. For each entry include
   a. the day and time
   b. the people involved
   c. the situation (the topic of conversation, the emotions involved)
   d. the outcome (how your listening style affected the outcome)
   e. your level of satisfaction with the situation.

3. At the end of the five-day period, ask yourself the following:
   a. Which of the listening styles described in this chapter did you use?
   b. In what situations did you use the various styles?
   c. Are you satisfied with your listening behaviour?
   d. What improvements do you need to make to your personal listening style?

EXERCISE 4 » Identifying Barriers to Effective Listening

Case Study

I didn't want to go to work today. It had been raining all weekend, but now the weather was great; it figures that Monday would be warm and sunny. But I had a meeting first thing in the morning, and my supervisor had been on my case to finish a couple of files, so I dragged myself out of bed, thought about calling in sick, realized that I was late, and rushed out of my apartment without stopping for breakfast. At least, I rushed as far as my car; it wouldn't start. I called a cab. The cab came right away, but when I got to the office, I discovered that I didn't have any money with me, so I had to find an ATM to get the cash to pay the cab driver. He was a bit peeved with me, because he had another call waiting. I guess I could have given him a bigger tip, but I didn't like his attitude. It's not as if it's my fault that my credit card was maxed out. I was a few minutes late, and my supervisor, Mary Kim, was already speaking. She always starts on time. She should consider people like me, who have good reasons for being late, and give us an extra few minutes. I had wanted to get to work early, because there had been a big party on Friday night and I wanted to catch up on the gossip. Now I had to sit there for an hour or so until I could find out what went on. So Mary droned on for another 15 minutes. She usually doesn't have anything to say in any case, so I ignored most of her presentation. I was thinking about how, now that I didn't have a car, I was going to get to the bank at lunch hour to pay some bills. I made up my mind to pay attention to the rest of the meeting, but Joel King was making a presentation, and as far as I'm concerned, there wasn't much he could tell me. What a sycophant! Always running up to the boss and asking if there's anything he can help with. It makes me sick! I think he's after my job. And the topic bored me to tears. Something about legal research or new government regulations or something like that. I can't imagine who'd be interested in that stuff. I don't remember much about the rest of the meeting. The room was stuffy; you'd think they could have opened a window. So I guess you could say that, as far as my attention level was concerned, the lights were on, but no one was home. I was catching up on some missed sleep, even though my eyes were open. I should paint some eyes on my glasses so everyone will think I'm awake. But my body was there even though my mind wasn't. That's all that counts in these big law firms.

Activity

Identify the barriers to listening in this case study. For each barrier listed, describe what could be done to overcome it.

EXERCISE 5 » Listening in School

Take a look at the courses you're studying this semester. It is easy enough to determine those in which you are succeeding and those in which you are struggling. Analyze the "good" courses to determine why you are successful in them. Then, decide why you aren't successful or as successful in the others. How can you apply good listening skills to improve your grades? Before analyzing your own case, however, practise on the one that follows.

When I was in university, I had to take a biology course. I couldn't get out of it; everyone in an arts program had to take one science course. My problems were as follows:

1. I didn't like biology; I was an English major.
2. I didn't like cutting up animals.
3. The course was dull, dull, dull.
4. The members of my group all wanted to be biologists.
5. The classroom smelled like a funeral home.
6. The instructor was dull, dull, dull.
7. I had no skills in math or chemistry.

Believe it or not, I didn't do well in this course. Suggest ways in which I could have improved through active listening.

EXERCISE 6 » Listening in Groups: Motivation

1. Select groups, with four to six participants in each group.
2. Appoint one referee per group.
3. Ask each participant to make a list of items—thoughts, feelings, complaints, wishes, plans—that he or she would be willing to share with other group members. It could be a to-do list, a wish list, a "things-that-bug-me" list, a "what-I'd-do-if-I-won-the-lottery" list, or something similar.
4. The referee will collect the lists from each member, shuffle them, and select one. The member whose list it is will be "it" and will speak first.
5. The referee will give each participant two minutes to tell the rest of the group what is on his or her list.
6. The rest of the group, while not being visibly rude, should do their best not to listen to the speaker. Group members can make occasional eye contact, but this should be minimal. The group members might, for instance, concentrate on their own lists as a way of ignoring the speaker. Group members should not speak to each other or to other members of the class.
7. The referee will also ignore the speaker, and will not discourage nervous laughter from the group, attempts to distract the speaker, and the like.
8. When two minutes have elapsed, the referee will select another speaker, and repeat the process until all members of the group have been "it."
9. The referee will then lead a group discussion based on the following questions:
   a. How did you feel when you were "it"?
   b. How did being ignored affect or influence your motivation to continue speaking?
   c. How did being ignored affect your sense of self-esteem?
   d. How do you think others feel when you either don't listen to them or don't give them your full attention?
   e. How do you think your inattention would affect children, adults, or co-workers?
   f. How did you feel when you weren't "it"?

EXERCISE 7 » Listening in Groups: Meaning

Take several minutes to discuss strong feelings, moral convictions, and personal beliefs. Record the findings on the blackboard, on a flip chart, or by some electronic means. Topics may include, but should not be limited to, the following:

- whether to legalize "soft drugs" and invest the tax profits in education and health care
- whether to legalize prostitution (both male and female) and invest the profits in health care and research
- whether to ban all forms of corporal punishment for children (including parental "discipline")
- whether to ban smoking in automobiles
- whether to make licences mandatory for the operation of motorized recreational vehicles such as snowmobiles and motorboats, and whether to restrict these licences to people 16 years of age and older
- whether to stop funding any system of education that is not public (e.g., religious schools, other private schools)

- whether anyone caught with illegal possession of firearms while committing a crime should get an automatic ten-year prison term on top of what the judge imposes
- whether religious institutions (e.g., churches, mosques, temples, synagogues) should be taxed and the profits invested in municipal infrastructures such as roads, sewers, and the like

Having compiled a list of this sort, proceed with the following steps:

1. Select groups of three participants.
2. Appoint one referee from each group.
3. Ask the two others in the group to select a topic from the list (or come up with an alternative) that will produce a disagreement between them.
4. Ask one participant to explain to the other his or her point of view on the topic. Limit the speaker to two minutes and ask him or her to focus on a small number of points. The speaker will be allowed to continue later in the exercise if more points need to be made. The listener may not speak during this discussion or express disagreement by any gestures or expressions.
5. When the speaker's time is up, ask the listener to paraphrase what the speaker has said.
6. When the person who was listening is finished with the paraphrase, ask the person who first spoke, "Is this what you said?"
7. If the person who spoke first agrees that the paraphrase was accurate, the two participants will change roles. The person who listened first becomes the speaker and gives his or her point of view on the topic. Repeat the process.
8. Go back to the person who spoke first, and ask whether he or she has any additional points to make or has a response to the second speaker. Repeat the process.
9. When both participants have finished, ask them to paraphrase what the other one has said.
10. The referee's role will be to keep the discussion on track, to limit the two-minute discussions to a few specific points, to make sure that the listener does not speak or gesture while the other participant is speaking, and generally to maintain order.

Participants can then discuss the feelings and attitudes they had while listening, how difficult it was to listen and not interfere, whether they changed their point of view on the topic after listening to the speaker, and how important it was to listen to the entirety of what the other had to say.

EXERCISE 8 » Listening in Interviews

Assume that you are the investigating officer in the Yaworsky interview described in the first few paragraphs of the "Facts for the Mock Trial" section of Exercise 11 in Chapter 9. Have one person in your class assume the role of Charles Yaworsky. Using the information supplied there, interview Yaworsky concerning the incident. Use some of the questioning techniques described in this chapter and, by practising good listening skills, attempt to find out exactly what happened. The person playing the role of Yaworsky is allowed to make up facts (e.g., "I was checking my cellphone for messages at the time."). He (or she) might also behave as if he were upset by the recent incident, straying off topic into unrelated family problems. Write down the answers while the victim, Yaworsky, is speaking.

CHAPTER SUMMARY

Listening skills are difficult to master because of the various distractions, external and internal, that exist in any listening situation. Understand your own listening habits, and learn how to improve any shortcomings in your personal listening skills. Proper questioning methods will likely result in more useful responses.

KEY TERMS

bias, 24   hot buttons, 29   open questions, 26

closed questions, 26   listening, 20   opinion, 28

fact, 28   non-verbal cues, 27   stereotyping, 24

REVIEW AND REFLECTION QUESTIONS

1. Explain the difference between hearing and listening.

2. What three rules of listening do you think you should focus on to improve as a listener?

3. Why is it important to read non-verbal cues in clusters?

4. What are your hot button issues? How should you control your emotional response?

5. How do electronic devices such as smartphones introduce barriers to listening? What are your strategies for handling these devices when you need to listen?

3 Spelling and Workplace Vocabulary

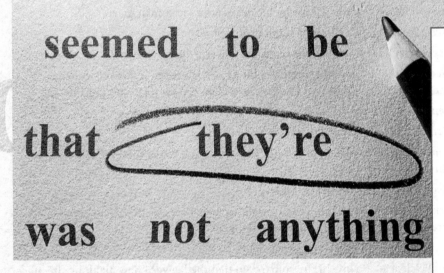

LEARNING OUTCOMES

After completing this chapter, you should be able to:

- Understand the importance of spelling to law enforcement professionals.
- Follow spelling rules.
- Spell troublesome words.
- Increase your personal vocabulary.
- Increase your professional vocabulary.
- Differentiate between words that are commonly confused.

Introduction

Spelling in English is difficult because the language contains so many words that defy the basic spelling rules. In addition, irregular verbs, double *l* words, *ou* words, irregular plurals, possessives, and contractions make spelling a chore.

However, the law enforcement officer must know how to spell. Poor spelling casts doubt on the quality of reports and evidence. Law enforcement personnel are expected to be professionals, and poor spelling brings their professionalism into question. Imagine the following scenario:

> *Defence lawyer*: You state in your notebook that the costumer was standing by the cooler in the convenience store when my client came in to the establishment.
>
> *Officer*: Yes, that's right.
>
> *Defence lawyer*: Can you tell me how you knew he was a costumer?
>
> *Officer*: I'm sorry. I don't understand the question.
>
> *Defence lawyer*: Did you ask the costumer what he did for a living?
>
> *Officer*: No, that wasn't relevant to the interview. However, in his subsequent witness report, he said he was a mechanic and owned his own small business.
>
> *Defence lawyer*: Is this in addition to being a costumer?
>
> *Officer*: Do you mean customer?
>
> *Defence lawyer*: I'm just reading what you wrote. You wrote that the witness was a costumer.
>
> *Officer*: I must have meant customer.
>
> *Defence lawyer*: Do you think there might be anywhere else in this notebook where you wrote one thing and meant another?

It would be clear to anyone in the courtroom that the lawyer knew all along the officer meant customer. However, it is the defence counsel's job to clear her client of guilt. It is within her rights to point out the officer's mistakes, which illustrate sloppy work or poor attention to detail, since these mistakes may create speculation about the possibility of the officer's errors in more crucial areas of the case.

Would you want to be the officer whose poor work led to the dismissal of a case?

In spite of the many spelling irregularities in the language, there are some basic rules. Some of these spelling rules are set out in this chapter. Also included are lists of difficult words to help you discover patterns in the spelling of single words and groups of words.

When you review the principles of good writing, you begin with the study of words and of grammar. This chapter of the book and the next one, therefore, deal with how words are spelled, how grammar applies to good writing, and how words are used in sentences.

You cannot write effectively if you are a poor speller. Poor spelling is the most noticeable of all writing faults. The complaints that schools hear about the writing of their graduates are often concerned with poor spelling.

Improving Your Spelling

If you've always had trouble with spelling, it may seem a daunting task to become a strong speller. Here are some tips that will help you become competent:

1. *Start a spelling journal in which you list words you have difficulty spelling.* You should keep this journal with you at all times, so you can add to it as needed and study from it as time allows. You can use a paper journal or start one on your phone or tablet. Make sure your journal is organized in a way you will find easy to use. It might be best to have several sections to the journal: everyday words, legal terms, workplace words, and so on. Remember to consult the journal often, and ask people to give you spelling tests when possible.

2. *Read more.* It has been proven that regular reading helps with vocabulary expansion and spelling ability. Read what you enjoy, and try to supplement that with reading articles that relate to law enforcement (news magazines, newspapers, and law enforcement magazines, for example).

3. *Study the spelling rules in the following pages of this text.* Really study them. Make sure you understand each rule and can apply it.

Useful Spelling Rules

Because most of us learn to spell by studying and practising one word at a time, you may find that some spelling rules are more confusing than helpful. But these rules apply to thousands of words and therefore may help you avoid many common difficulties. Four useful rules are set out below.

Rule 1

If a word ends with a *y* **preceded** by a consonant (as in *copy* or *try*), change the *y* to an *i* before every **suffix** except *ing*.

copy	+	es	=	copies
copy	+	ing	=	copying
worry	+	ed	=	worried
worry	+	ing	=	worrying
try	+	ed	=	tried
try	+	ing	=	trying
lady	+	es	=	ladies

Preceded means to come before; for example, *a* precedes *b* in the alphabet.

Suffixes are letters added to the end of a word to make a new form of the word; for example, adding the suffix "ed" to *walk* will make *walked*.

150 Troublesome Words

Read this list and cross out the words you have no trouble spelling. Circle the words you know you have trouble spelling. Put a box around words you are unsure of. This will give you a more manageable list to study from. Consider adding the circled words to your spelling journal.

1. absolutely
2. accordance
3. acknowledge
4. acquaintance
5. addressed
6. advertising
7. advisable
8. affectionately
9. all right
10. although
11. American
12. annual
13. anxious
14. apparently
15. appearance
16. appreciation
17. approval
18. approximately
19. arrangement
20. assistance
21. association
22. assume
23. assure
24. attached
25. attention
26. available
27. balance
28. beginning
29. benefit
30. bulletin
31. business
32. campaign
33. cancellation
34. cancelled
35. capacity
36. catalogue
37. certificate
38. circumstances

39. clothes
40. commission
41. committee
42. communication
43. community
44. completely
45. consideration
46. convenience
47. convenient
48. cooperation (or co-operation)
49. correspondence
50. courtesy
51. criticism
52. customer
53. definite
54. description
55. difference
56. disappoint
57. doubt
58. duly
59. duplicate
60. earliest
61. endeavour
62. envelope
63. equipment
64. equipped
65. especially
66. estimate
67. exactly
68. exceedingly
69. exception
70. experience
71. explanation
72. extremely
73. familiar
74. February
75. finally

76. financial
77. foreign
78. forward
79. further
80. government
81. grateful
82. guarantee
83. immediately
84. impossible
85. information
86. inquiry
87. instruction
88. interest
89. invoice
90. judgment
91. knowledge
92. length
93. library
94. material
95. memorandum
96. mention
97. merchandise
98. minimum
99. mortgage
100. naturally
101. necessary
102. necessity
103. occasion
104. occurred
105. opportunity
106. organization
107. paid
108. partial
109. particular
110. permanent
111. planning
112. possibility
113. practical

114. preferred
115. probably
116. proposition
117. quantity
118. realize
119. recommendation
120. reference
121. regretting
122. remittance
123. replying
124. requirements
125. response
126. ridiculous
127. satisfactory
128. satisfied
129. Saturday
130. schedule
131. secretary
132. sincerely
133. specified
134. studying
135. success
136. sufficient
137. suggestion
138. superintendent
139. surprise
140. temporary
141. tentative
142. therefore
143. thoroughly
144. transferred
145. undoubtedly
146. unfortunately
147. unnecessary
148. usually
149. various
150. Wednesday

If the *y* is preceded by a vowel, do not change it (as in *valley* or *honey*).

valley	+	s	=	valleys
honey	+	s	=	honeys

Rule 2

Write *i* before *e* except after *c* or when sounded as *a*, as in *neighbour* or *weigh*.

i before *e*:   brief, piece, belief, chief
e before *i*:   receive, ceiling, deceive, freight, weight, sleigh

Exceptions to the rule:

either, neither, seize, leisure, weird

Rule 3

If a word ends with a single consonant preceded by a single vowel (*stop*, *begin*) and you add a suffix beginning with a vowel (*-ed*, *-ing*, *-ance*), double the final consonant in the two situations described below:

1. The word has only one syllable:

stop	+	ed	=	stopped
trip	+	ed	=	tripped
rub	+	ing	=	rubbing
drop	+	ing	=	dropping

2. The word is accented on the last syllable:

confer	+	ed	=	conferred
begin	+	ing	=	beginning
omit	+	ing	=	omitting
remit	+	ance	=	remittance

Do not double the final consonant if the accent is not on the last syllable (*benefited*, *profited*, *exhibited*).

Rule 4

If the word ends with a silent *e* (*bite*, *use*) and you add a suffix, the following rules apply:

1. Drop the *e* if the suffix begins with a vowel.

bite	+	ing	=	biting
use	+	able	=	usable
desire	+	able	=	desirable
gaze	+	ed	=	gazed

2. Keep the *e* if the suffix begins with a consonant.

use	+	ful	=	useful
achieve	+	ment	=	achievement
love	+	ly	=	lovely
hope	+	less	=	hopeless

These rules have two exceptions:

1. Words such as *noticeable* and *courageous* retain the silent *e* to keep the preceding consonant (*c* or *g*) soft.
2. Words such as *truly* and *argument* drop the silent *e* that follows a vowel.

Plurals

With most words, you simply add *s* to form the plural.

bed	beds
book	books
pipe	pipes

Words ending in a sibilant *ch*, *sh*, *s*, *x*, or *z*, however, add *es* to form the plural.

boss	bosses
box	boxes
bush	bushes
buzz	buzzes
catch	catches
sash	sashes
dress	dresses
fox	foxes

There are two rules for words that end in *y*:

1. If a consonant precedes the *y*, change *y* to *i* and add *es*.

activity	activities
apology	apologies
duty	duties

2. If a vowel precedes the *y*, simply add *s*.

attorney	attorneys
monkey	monkeys
toy	toys

For words that end in *f*, either add *s* or change *f* to *v* and add *es*, depending on the particular case.

belief	beliefs
chief	chiefs
cliff	cliffs
half	halves
life	lives
leaf	leaves
self	selves
loaf	loaves
wife	wives

There are many irregular plurals, some of which are set out below.

ox	oxen
child	children
deer	deer
foot	feet
goose	geese
moose	moose
man	men
woman	women
mouse	mice

There are three types of nouns that end in *o*, and there is a different pluralizing rule for each type.

1. If a vowel precedes the *o*, simply add *s*.

boo	boos
stereo	stereos
radio	radios

2. If the word is a musical term, add *s*.

piano	pianos
solo	solos

3. For all other words ending in *o*, there is no rule. The plurals must be memorized.

echo	echoes
silo	silos
hero	heroes
poncho	ponchos
zero	zeroes
potato	potatoes
tomato	tomatoes

Certain plurals derive from their Greek or Latin roots.

crisis	crises
thesis	theses
datum	data
criterion	criteria

EXERCISE 1 » Forming Plurals

Change the following singular nouns to their correct plural form:

1. attorney _____
2. kiss _____
3. rodeo _____
4. crisis _____
5. foot _____
6. piccolo _____
7. bed _____
8. cargo _____
9. watch _____
10. buzz _____
11. analysis _____
12. canoe _____
13. patio _____
14. man _____
15. latch _____
16. basis _____
17. self _____
18. apology _____
19. zero _____
20. six _____
21. child _____
22. baby _____
23. goose _____
24. try _____
25. box _____

26. dress _____
27. paper _____
28. loss _____
29. chimney _____
30. miss _____
31. mix _____
32. knife _____
33. key _____
34. laugh _____
35. wish _____
36. duty _____
37. tool _____
38. roof _____
39. push _____
40. mouse _____
41. loaf _____
42. wall _____
43. bus _____
44. table _____
45. business _____
46. axe _____
47. belief _____
48. pass _____
49. donkey _____
50. penalty _____

Handwriting Versus Writing on the Computer and the Pitfalls of Spell Checkers

Because most of the writing we do can be put through a spell checker, the argument could be made that becoming a great speller isn't necessary. However, consider these points:

1. While many law enforcement agencies have laptops or tablets in their vehicles, the paper notebook is still standard protocol for note taking. The notes you take in your notebook will be used in court and are the property of the agency you work for. For the most part, the defence team will look at the computer-generated reports that constitute a case file. However, it is common for the notebook also to be included in the case file. Any discrepancies among reports and field notes—including spelling—will be picked up for possible use by the defence team.

2. Spell checkers do not catch every error. **Homophones** (see "Word Problems," below) and words that sound very similar to others can slip by spell checkers.

Examples:

There were too witnesses at the incident.
The driver claimed that unresponsive breaks caused him to hit the bus.
They are just going over there statement.

Word Problems

Troublesome words fall into four broad categories:

1. **Homographs** are words that have the same spelling, but have different meanings or uses.

2. **Homonyms** are words that have the same pronunciation, but have different spellings and often different meanings.

3. **Synonyms** are words with similar meanings.

4. **Antonyms** are words with opposite meanings.

Homophones are words that sound the same but have different meanings, such as *hour* and *our*.

Homographs are words that have the same spelling, but have different meanings or uses, such as *desert* (noun) and *desert* (verb).

Homonyms are words that have the same pronunciation, but have different spellings and often different meanings, such as *brake/break* and *mail/male*.

Synonyms are words with similar meanings.

Antonyms are words with opposite meanings.

Words Frequently Misused

The following list includes, in addition to words in the four troublesome word categories, a selection of words that are commonly misspelled, misused, or overused.

a, an   These words are *indefinite articles*, used with nouns. *A* is used with nouns that begin with a consonant sound. *An* is used with nouns that begin with a vowel sound.

accede, exceed   To *accede* to something is to go along with it. *To exceed* your limits is to go too far.

accept, except   To *accept* something is to receive it. *To except* something is to exclude it or leave it out. *Except* is also an adverb that means "excluding."

access, excess   *Access* is the way into something. *Excess* means "extra" or "too much."

ad, add   The word *ad* is an abbreviation of *advertisement*. It is best avoided in formal communications. *To add* is to combine or to take a total.

adapt, adept   To *adapt* is to change, either oneself or something else. *Adept* is an adjective meaning "skilled."

addition, edition   *Addition* is the process of adding, or the thing or person added. An *edition* is a version of something, usually a book.

advice, advise   *Advice* is a noun; it is the information that well-meaning people give you when they counsel or *advise* (verb) you.

affect, effect   To *affect* (verb) is to influence, or to put on an act. An *affect* (noun—psychologists' jargon word) is an emotion. *To effect* (verb) is to make something happen, and an *effect* (noun) is the result of what happens.

all ready, already   *All ready* means "to be prepared." *Already* means "previously."

all right, alright   Fundamentally, *all right* means "all correct." The expression also has a variety of colloquial meanings. It should not be spelled *alright*.

all together, altogether   *All together* means "as a group." *Altogether* means "entirely." *All together* is also a colloquial expression meaning "rational."

all ways, always   *All ways* means "in every aspect" or "in every direction." *Always* means "forever."

allot, alot, a lot   To *allot* something is to distribute or assign it. *Alot* is a common misspelling of *a lot*, which is an informal way of saying "a great deal" or "a large amount." A *lot* is also a piece of property.

allude, elude   To *allude* to something is to refer to it. *To elude* means "to escape."

allusion, illusion   An *allusion* is a reference to something. An *illusion* is an unreal picture or idea.

aloud, allowed   *Aloud* means "audible, not silent or whispered." *Allowed* means "permitted" or, in some cases, "admitted" or "confessed."

altar, alter   An *altar* (noun) is a raised ceremonial area, usually in a church or other place of worship. *To alter* (verb) something is to change it.

alternate, alternative   An *alternate* (noun) is a substitute, or a person or thing that replaces someone or something else. The verb *to alternate* means "to take turns"; as an adjective, *alternate* means "secondary." *Alternative* means "another option."

although   As a conjunction, *although* is synonymous and interchangeable with *though*. *Though* is also used as an adverb. *Tho* and *altho* are not acceptable spellings. *Although* means "in spite of the fact that." For example, "She is happy although she has no money."

among, between   *Among* means "surrounded by." It refers to a position in the midst of several or more. *Between* means "separating," and refers to the situation, or position, of being bounded by two people or things.

amount, number   The *amount* is the quantity, the sum total. It is not the same as *number*, which is the total of all the units.

annual, annul   *Annual* is an adverb meaning "yearly." *To annul* (verb) means "to cancel."

anyway, any way   *Anyway* is a colloquial form of "in any event" or "in any case." *Any way* means "any means" or "any path."

appraise, apprise   To *appraise* is to evaluate. *To apprise* is to let someone know something, to inform.

are, our, hour   *Are* is a present tense of the verb *to be*. *Our* means "belonging to us." An *hour* is a time unit of 60 minutes.

as yet   *As yet* often functions as a wordy synonym for *yet*.

assistance, assistants   *Assistance* means "help" or "aid." *Assistants* are those people or things who give help or aid.

attendance, attendants   Your *attendance* means "your presence." *Attendants* are those people who give assistance.

Words Frequently Misused (continued)

between See *among*.

born, borne *Born* means "given birth to" or "created." *To be borne* is to be carried.

brake, break *To brake* (verb) means "to put a stop to something"; the *brake* (noun) is the device on a car or piece of equipment that makes it stop. *To break* something is to make it come apart or shatter.

canvas, canvass A *canvas* is a heavy piece of cloth used to cover things, camp under, or paint on. *To canvass* (verb) means "to solicit," as in the case of opinions or money.

capital, capitol As an adjective, *capital* means "important" or "chief." As a noun, it commonly means "the city in a province, territory, or country that is the centre of government." *Capitol* refers to the building where a legislature meets.

cease, seize *To cease* is to stop. *To seize* is to take hold of or to capture. Note the spelling of *seize*, which violates the "*i* before *e*" rule.

cite, sight, site *To cite* means "to refer to" or "to award." *To sight* is to see; a *sight* (noun) is what is seen. *To site* is to locate; a *site* (noun) is a location.

close, clothes *Close* is a homograph; pronounced one way, and used as an adverb, it means "near" or "in the vicinity." Pronounced another way, and used as a verb, it means "to shut." *Clothes* are the garments you wear.

complement, compliment *To complement* is to add something that completes or enhances, and a *complement* (noun) is a supply of something. *To compliment* means "to praise," and a *compliment* (noun) is a piece of praise.

comprise, consist of, constitute *To comprise* means "to contain." It is used informally to mean *consist of*, which means "made up of." *To constitute* means "to compose" or "to form" or "to create." The phrase *is comprised of* is always grammatically incorrect; use *is composed of* instead.

conscience, conscious Your *conscience* is your inner moral feeling. *Conscious of* means "aware of."

continual, continuous *Continual* means "occurring constantly, again and again." *Continuous* means "happening without interruption."

could of, should of, would of These word combinations are ungrammatical. *Could*, *should*, and *would* combine with the verb *have*: could have, should have, would have.

council, counsel, consul A *council* is a group of advisers, or *councillors*. *Counsel* means "advice," something a *counsellor* would give. A *consul* is a country's representative, whose office is a *consulate*. In a legal environment, *counsellor* is rarely used. The *counsel* is an outside adviser who is a lawyer.

credible, creditable, credulous Something that is *credible* is something that can be believed. *Creditable* means "praiseworthy." *Credulous* means "easily deceived."

decent, descent, dissent *Decent* means "morally proper" or "adequate." *Descent* (noun) is the act or process of descending, while *dissent* means "disagreement."

desert, dessert A *desert* (noun) is a dry wasteland, while *to desert* (verb), pronounced differently, means "to leave without permission." *Dessert* is what is served after the main course of a meal.

device, devise A *device* is "an instrument" or "a means of achieving an end." *To devise* (verb) means "to plan" or "to put together."

discreet, discrete *Discreet* means "tactful" or "inclined to keep things to yourself." *Discrete* means "separate and distinct."

dual, duel *Dual* (adjective) means "consisting of two parts." A *duel* is a single-combat fight between two people.

elicit, illicit *To elicit* something is to extract it or draw it out from some source, as when you ask for information. *Illicit* means "illegal."

elude See *allude*.

emigrate, immigrate To leave a country permanently and live in another country is *to emigrate*; to enter a country and live there permanently is *to immigrate*.

eminent, imminent *Eminent* means "well known" or "famous." *Imminent* means "on the point of arriving."

employ, use *To employ* is to use something or someone in a specified way, usually with the sense of paying someone a wage in return for services.

Words Frequently Misused (continued)

exceed See *accede*.

except See *accept*.

expand, expend To *expand* is to increase in size. *To expend* is to use up or to spend.

farther, further Both *farther* and *further* can indicate physical distance, but *further* is preferable when you mean "also," "to a greater extent," or "in addition to."

feel Avoid the overworked expression *I feel* when you want to render an opinion. Instead use *I believe* or *I think*.

fewer, less *Fewer* means "a smaller number," while *less* refers to quantity and means "a smaller amount."

firstly An overused adverb, replaceable by *first*.

forth, fourth To go *forth* is to go onward. To finish *fourth* is to arrive after three others.

four, for *Four* is a number; *for* is a conjunction, a connecting word.

great, grate *Great* means "large" or "renowned." A *grate* is a framework of bars, usually criss-crossed pieces of metal or wood.

if, whether Both words are conjunctions. Use *if* in a conditional situation ("She will work if I pay her"); use *whether* when you are dealing with alternatives ("She will work whether or not I pay her," or "I don't know whether she will work").

illicit See *elicit*.

illusion See *allusion*.

imply, infer To *imply* means "to insinuate," "to suggest something without saying it." *To infer* means "to draw a conclusion."

incidence, incidents *Incidence* means "rate of occurrence" ("There was a high incidence of theft"). *Incidents* are events, occurrences.

irony, sarcasm *Irony* involves saying one thing but meaning something else, usually the opposite of what is said, and doing so in a subtle manner so that the real meaning may not be clear. *Sarcasm* is a form of heavy, often bitter irony that leaves no question that the real meaning is opposite to what is being said.

irregardless, regardless There is no word *irregardless*. Use *regardless* to mean "despite everything," "in any event," or "heedless."

its, it's *Its* is the possessive form of *it*. *It's* is a contraction for *it is* or *it has*.

knew, new *Knew* is the past tense of *know*. *New* means "not old."

know, no To *know* is to understand. *No* expresses negation or refusal.

last, latest, previous The *last* comes after all the others; the *latest* is the most recent in a series; the *previous* one is the one that went before in time or order.

later, latter *Later* means "afterwards." The *latter* is the second of two items.

lay, lie To *lay* means "to put," and always takes an object. For example, "Lay the book down." *To lie* means "to recline," and never takes an object. For example, "Lie down if you are tired." *To lie* is also a verb meaning "to tell an untruth."

liable, likely, libel, slander *Liable* means "legally responsible" or "likely to do something" (usually something undesirable). It is used informally in the sense of *likely*, meaning "probable." A *libel* is a false written statement, damaging to someone's reputation. A *slander* is a false statement, spoken rather than written, that is damaging to someone's reputation. *Libel* and *slander* are not opposites.

like, as *Like* and *as* are often used interchangeably as connectors ("He is the same as I am"; "He is like me"). *As* can be used as a conjunction or a preposition ("It is as dark as night") while *like* should be used only as a preposition ("She is like her mother"). *To like* is also a verb meaning "to feel affection for."

loose, lose *Loose* means "not tight." *Lose* is an antonym of win, and also means "to misplace."

maybe, may be *Maybe* is an adverb, synonymous with "perhaps." *May be* is a conjugation of the verb *to be*, expressing possibility.

new See *knew*.

no See *know*.

number See *amount*.

off of *Off* alone does the job; it doesn't need the *of* ("He jumped off the bike").

pain, pane A *pain* is something that hurts; a *pane* is a panel, usually of glass.

Words Frequently Misused (concluded)

past, passed *Past* can be a noun, an adverb, or an adjective ("She lives in the past"; "She ran past the tree"; "She thought of her past loves"). *Passed* is the past tense of the verb *to pass*, meaning "to go by" or "to move beyond."

patience, patients *Patience* means "forbearance" or "endurance." *Patients* are people under medical care.

peace, piece *Peace* is an antonym of war. A *piece* of something is a part of it.

personal, personnel, personally *Personal* indicates something owned by or affecting a person; something private. Employees are collectively known as *personnel*. The word *personally* is overused as a qualifying word, as in "Personally, I think he was wrong."

plane, plain A *plane* is a flat surface, a flying machine, or a tool for smoothing wooden surfaces. *Plain* means "unattractive" or "unadorned," as well as "a large expanse of usually flat land."

presence, presents *Presence* means "being in a place" or "attendance." *Presents* are gifts.

principal, principle *Principal* indicates "most important" or "first." *Principles* are implied rules or ethics.

quiet, quite *Quiet* means "not noisy," "silent," "unassuming." *Quite* means "entirely" or "to a considerable degree."

raise, rise *To raise* means "to make something move up" or "to grow," and always takes an object. For example, "I raise the flag." *To rise* means "to stand up" or "to move upward," and never takes an object. For example, "I rise in the morning."

regardless See *irregardless*.

right, rite, write, wright *Right* means "the opposite of left" or "a privilege." A *rite* is a ceremony, usually religious. *To write* is to form words on a page. A *wright* is a craftsperson who makes a specified thing ("wheelwright," "playwright").

role, roll A *role* is a part played by an actor. A *roll* is, among various other things, a list or a bakery product. *To roll* as a verb means "to turn over."

sarcasm See *irony*.

set, sit *To set* means "to put something in position," and always takes an object. For example, "Set the book over there." *To sit* means "to take a sitting position," and never takes an object. For example, "Sit in the chair."

should of See *could of*.

sight, site See *cite*.

so Don't use this word as a lone intensive: "She was *so* lucky." Use *very* instead.

stationary, stationery *Stationary* means "not moving." *Stationery* refers to the materials used for writing and typing; office supplies.

than, then *Than* is used in comparisons ("bigger than"). *Then* is used in time sequences ("now and then").

their, there, they're *Their* means "belonging to them." *There* is a place. *They're* is a contraction of *they are*.

though See *although*.

threw, throw, through, thorough *Threw* is the past tense of the verb *to throw*. *Through* is an adverb expressing passage into and out of something, and an adjective meaning "finished." *Thorough* is an adjective that means "exacting," "done with care," "leaving no room for doubt."

to, too, two *To* is, among other things, a preposition indicating a direction or destination. *Too* means "excessively" or "also." *Two* is a number.

weak, week *Weak* means "not strong." A *week* is seven days.

weather, whether The atmospheric condition is what we call the *weather*. We use *whether* to indicate a choice between, or a question involving, alternatives. ("He didn't know whether to buy the blue one or the grey one.") See also *if*.

who's, whose *Who's* is a contraction of *who is*. *Whose* is the possessive form of "who" and can function either as an adjective ("Whose coat is that?") or as a pronoun ("Whose is that?").

would of See *could of*.

write See *right*.

your, you're *Your* is an adjective, the possessive form of *you*, meaning "owned by you." *You're* is a contraction of *you are*.

EXERCISE 2 » Choosing the Correct Word

Correct the following passage by identifying and changing the misused words:

When going for an interview, your wise too exercise patients. Be prepared. Find out about the personal of the company, than any other peace of information your likely to need if your asked about the company. Find out whose in charge. Be through in your answers. Your more liable to be considered if you no the amount of employees. Perhaps the boss is an imminent person in the community. Go further in your analysis of questions than expected; the less number of things you know about the company, the less likely youll feel grate about the interview. Irregardless, its important that you do your best and ask for assistants if you can't answer a question. Sight any awards you know the company has received, and complement the company for its successes. Appear credulous to your interviewers, present yourself as a descent person, use whatever devises you need to make your points, and don't forget—wear proper close.

EXERCISE 3 » Selecting the Right Word

Choose the correct word in each of the following sentences:

1. Counsel for the defendant has (acceded, exceeded) to the Crown attorney's request for additional information.

2. The judge prefers witness statements not to (accede, exceed) two pages.

3. The court documents will be delivered this afternoon. Please (accept, except) them on my behalf.

4. Everything is in the file (accept, except) the list of witnesses.

5. The divorce settlement awarded custody of the children to the wife, but the husband has (access, excess) to them on weekends.

6. If he drinks to (access, excess), however, he will lose this privilege.

7. Sometimes it seems that more television time is devoted to (ads, adds) than to programs.

8. The figures in this bill are wrong. Please (ad, add) them up again.

9. Correctional personnel must (adapt, adept) their communication styles to meet the needs of specific situations.

10. You need to be (adapt, adept) at comforting victims of crime.

11. Is this new task an (addition, edition) to my regular duties?

12. Please order the latest (edition, addition) of the *Globe and Mail Stylebook*.

13. The client is going to seek the (advice, advise) of counsel in this matter.

14. I strongly (advice, advise) you not to be late for your court hearing, as this judge is known to be impatient.

15. The new insurance regulations will (affect, effect) your premium for next year.

16. At the examination for discovery, the defendant displayed a confused (affect, effect).

17. The new manager is (affecting, effecting) many changes in procedure.

18. Poor communications skills will have a negative (affect, effect) on your career in law enforcement.

19. Mrs. Smith's will (allots, a lots, alots) various sums of money to all her beneficiaries.

20. We don't have (allot, alot, a lot) of time to prepare the case for court.

21. We expect (allot, a lot) of donations to the holiday fund.

22. We are (all ready, already) for the meeting (all ready, already).

23. I have (all ready, already) finished my report on the shoplifting suspect.

24. The documents are (all together, altogether) on my desk.

25. I'm not (all together, altogether) sure that this is true.

26. We agree in (all ways, always) that matter.

27. I will (all ways, always) remember my first job.

28. Rehearse your presentation (aloud, allowed) to determine how it sounds.

29. Driving without a licence is not (aloud, allowed) by law.

30. The judge (alluded, eluded) to the defendant's previous offences when she sentenced him.

31. They won't be able to (allude, elude) justice for long.

32. The speaker made constant (allusion, illusion) to the news of the day.

33. I was under the (allusion, illusion) that this would be an easy job, but I was wrong.

34. Too often, principles are sacrificed on the (altar, alter) of profit.

35. The witness wants to (altar, alter) her statement.

36. Each director appoints an (alternate, alternative) in case he or she cannot attend a meeting.

37. The classes (alternate, alternative) between Mondays and Wednesdays.

38. I took the (alternate, alternative) route because of construction on the highway.

39. The evidence left the jury no (alternate, alternative) but to convict.

40. (Though, Although) Joan writes excellent research reports, it's not her favourite part of the job.

41. The security firm had to choose (between, among) three excellent candidates for the investigator's position.

42. Just (between, among) the two of us, I'm looking for a new job.

43. A huge (amount, number) of accidents take place on this corner every year.

44. The large (amount, number) of snow that fell overnight made it difficult to drive to work this morning.

45. The association holds its (annual, annul) conference in June.

46. I'm afraid you don't have grounds to (annual, annul) the contract.

47. (Lie, Lay) the petition on his desk.

48. (Rise, Raise) the table a bit to put this book under the broken leg.

49. I don't have much chance of winning the race, but I'll enter it (anyway, any way).

50. I want you to be successful, and I will help you in (anyway, any way) I can.

51. You need to have your property (appraised, apprised) early in the process of selling it.

52. As a police officer, you should keep your superiors (appraised, apprised) of any information you receive about criminal activity.

53. We (are, our, hour) expecting to arrive at (are, our, hour) destination in an (are, our, hour).

54. We requested (assistance, assistants) from the RCMP in the investigation.

55. Arthur is such a busy lawyer that he needs not one but two (assistance, assistants).

56. Your (attendance, attendants) at the meeting is essential.

57. The bride and her (attendance, attendants) looked radiant.

58. Please complete the application form by inserting the year you were (born, borne).

59. My belief in his innocence was (born, borne) out by the evidence presented.

60. This candy is hard enough to (break, brake) my teeth.

61. The accident happened when the car's (breaks, brakes) failed.

62. The team worked six hours without a (break, brake).

63. The new tents are much lighter than the old (canvas, canvass) ones.

64. I will (canvas, canvass) the staff to see what they think about taking up a collection for the victim.

65. The (Capitol, capital) is one of the main attractions in Washington, the (capitol, capital) of the United States.

66. The court ordered the company to (cease, seize) violating its competitor's copyright.

67. His assets were (ceased, seized) when he declared bankruptcy.

68. The lawyer (cited, sighted, sited) several precedents in her argument for the defence.

69. For the exhausted marathon runners, the finishing line was a welcome (cite, sight, site).

70. We have chosen an excellent (cite, sight, site) for our new cottage.

71. The course in English grammar (complements, compliments) the writing program I took last year.

72. The accused was represented in court by a formidable (complement, compliment) of seven lawyers.

73. The client (complemented, complimented) David on the fine job he did on the file.

74. The new firm (comprises, constitutes) 50 lawyers.

75. The thief showed no signs of a guilty (conscience, conscious).

76. Rebecca was very (conscience, conscious) of the importance of her job.

77. I can't rely on an assistant who (continually, continuously) arrives late for work.

78. Our softball team held the league championship (continually, continuously) for ten years.

79. The new town (council, counsel, consul) has vowed to clean up the streets.

80. This is a complex legal matter on which we must seek the advice of (council, counsel, consul).

81. If you should find yourself in trouble in a foreign country, seek help from the Canadian (council, counsel, consul) there.

82. He presented a great deal of evidence, very little of which was (credible, credulous).

83. He is so (credible, credulous) that he believes what he sees on television commercials.

84. Although he lost the race, he gave a (decent, descent, dissent) effort.

85. We are beginning our (decent, descent, dissent) into Toronto's Pearson International Airport.

86. Freedom of speech can result in loud expressions of (decent, descent, dissent).

87. Much of the land that is now (dessert, desert) was covered in water millions of years ago.

88. They say rats always (dessert, desert) a sinking ship.

89. Since I am on a diet, I won't have (dessert, desert).

90. A restraining order is a legal (device, devise) to keep offenders away from their victims.

91. Ms. Wilson (deviced, devised) a brilliant defence strategy.

92. The nature of their work demands that social workers be very (discrete, discreet).

93. A Crown brief can be a complex document with many (discrete, discreet) elements.

94. Since he has (dual, duel) citizenship, my father carries two passports.

95. Fortunately, arguments are no longer settled by a (dual, duel) at dawn.

96. Detectives need good interviewing skills in order to (illicit, elicit) needed information from clients.

97. The police discovered an (illicit, elicit) gambling operation in the basement of the old building.

98. Canada owes much of its development to the work of (emigrants, immigrants).

99. I left my home and (emigrated, immigrated) to Canada.

100. Everyone was pleased when an (eminent, imminent) judge agreed to take the case.

Canadian Spelling

There are many words that are spelled differently in Canada than they are in the United States. Be sure you become familiar with these words, and pay close attention to using the Canadian spelling. Here are some examples:

Canadian Spelling	American Spelling
calibre	caliber
centre	center
colour	color
defence (counsel)	defense (counsel)
licence (noun)	license (noun)
manoeuvre	maneuver
neighbour	neighbor

It might be a good idea to have a list for Canadian/American spelling differences in your spelling journal.

EXERCISE 4 » Expanding Your Legal Vocabulary

Every profession has additional words that are used frequently by persons working in or with that profession. You must not only be able to spell these workplace words but also know their meanings. Carefully go through this list. Add words you cannot spell or define to your spelling journal, and be sure to include definitions for the words you do not know.

1. abeyance
2. abrasion
3. abscond
4. accelerate
5. accessible
6. accessory
7. accomplice
8. accused
9. acquit
10. acquittal
11. action *in personam*
12. action *in rem*
13. ad hoc
14. adjourn
15. adjudicate
16. admissible
17. admissible evidence
18. affidavit
19. affirmative
20. aggravate
21. aggravated
22. alcohol
23. alleged
24. altercation
25. amendment
26. analyze
27. anonymous
28. appeal
29. apprehend
30. arbitration
31. arraign
32. assailant
33. assault
34. attorney
35. bailiff
36. boulevard
37. boycott
38. brief
39. calibre
40. cartridge
41. case law
42. *caveat emptor*
43. circumstantial
44. citation
45. civil
46. civilian
47. codicil
48. collision
49. complainant
50. concurrent
51. condemn
52. confession
53. confiscate
54. conspicuous
55. continuance
56. contributory negligence
57. corroborate
58. credibility
59. culpable
60. defeasance
61. defendant
62. delinquent
63. deposition
64. detention
65. deterrent
66. disperse
67. disposition
68. embezzle
69. enforceable
70. evasive
71. evidence
72. exhibit
73. exploitive
74. extenuating
75. fabricate
76. federal
77. felon
78. fugitive
79. grievance
80. grievous
81. *habeas corpus*
82. habitual
83. homicide
84. incarcerate
85. incorrigible
86. indictable
87. injunction
88. inquest
89. interrogate
90. judicial
91. jurisdiction
92. juvenile
93. laceration
94. lenient
95. liable
96. litigant
97. loitering
98. malicious
99. mandatory
100. *mens rea*
101. mitigating
102. municipal
103. negligence
104. nuisance
105. occurrence
106. ordinance
107. pedestrian
108. penitentiary
109. perpetrator
110. pertinent
111. plaintiff
112. preamble
113. precedent
114. preliminary
115. *prima facie*
116. proceeding
117. provocation
118. recidivist
119. recognizance
120. refute
121. *Regina*
122. reprieve
123. repudiate
124. *res gestae*
125. resuscitate
126. retainer
127. solicitor
128. specimen
129. statute
130. statutory
131. subpoena
132. subrogation
133. summons
134. supplementary
135. surveillance
136. tactical
137. tangential
138. testimony
139. tort
140. trajectory
141. trauma
142. truancy
143. velocity
144. verdict
145. vicious
146. vigilance
147. waive
148. waiver
149. warrant
150. zealous

200 Frequently Misspelled Words

Here are more words that typically give people trouble. As with the earlier lists, go through this one to determine which words you should add to your spelling journal.

1. absence	32. bookkeeper	63. development	94. imitation
2. accessible	33. boundary	64. digestible	95. immensely
3. accidentally	34. cafeteria	65. dining	96. inaccuracy
4. accommodate	35. calendar	66. disappeared	97. incidentally
5. accumulate	36. candidate	67. disease	98. independence
6. accurately	37. captain	68. division	99. inevitable
7. achieve	38. carrying	69. earnestly	100. influential
8. acquainted	39. catalogue	70. eighth	101. insistence
9. acquisition	40. certain	71. electricity	102. intelligence
10. address	41. characteristic	72. embarrassed	103. interfere
11. advantageous	42. chocolate	73. emphasize	104. interrupt
12. agreeable	43. choice	74. essential	105. invitation
13. allegiance	44. column	75. exaggerate	106. laboratory
14. almost	45. compelling	76. excitement	107. lightning
15. already	46. competent	77. exercise	108. literature
16. amateur	47. competition	78. exhausted	109. loneliness
17. amount	48. compulsory	79. extraordinary	110. maintenance
18. apparatus	49. concentration	80. facilities	111. mathematics
19. appetite	50. concern	81. familiar	112. mechanically
20. approach	51. confident	82. formula	113. merely
21. appropriate	52. conquer	83. generally	114. miniature
22. argument	53. conscientious	84. grammar	115. mischievous
23. associate	54. continually	85. gymnasium	116. mysterious
24. athlete	55. controlled	86. harass	117. negligence
25. athletic	56. courteous	87. height	118. niece
26. attendance	57. dealt	88. hindrance	119. ninety
27. aviator	58. deceive	89. humorous	120. noticeable
28. awkward	59. deficiency	90. hygiene	121. obedience
29. bachelor	60. definition	91. illegible	122. occasionally
30. beneficial	61. dependent	92. illiterate	123. occurrence
31. biscuit	62. desperate	93. imagination	124. o'clock

200 Frequently Misspelled Words (concluded)

125. omelette	**144.** prejudice	**163.** repetition	**182.** strength
126. omitted	**145.** preparation	**164.** reservoir	**183.** succeed
127. original	**146.** presence	**165.** respectability	**184.** successfully
128. parallel	**147.** privilege	**166.** restaurant	**185.** surround
129. paralyze	**148.** probability	**167.** rhyme	**186.** technical
130. pastime	**149.** procedure	**168.** rhythm	**187.** tenant
131. perform	**150.** professional	**169.** sacrifice	**188.** tendency
132. permissible	**151.** professor	**170.** sandwich	**189.** truly
133. perseverance	**152.** prominent	**171.** scarcely	**190.** twelfth
134. persistent	**153.** pronunciation	**172.** scissors	**191.** unaccustomed
135. perspiration	**154.** pursuing	**173.** seize	**192.** unanimous
136. persuade	**155.** recipe	**174.** sentence	**193.** unusual
137. physically	**156.** recognize	**175.** separate	**194.** vacuum
138. physician	**157.** recollect	**176.** sergeant	**195.** valuable
139. picnicking	**158.** recommend	**177.** serviceable	**196.** varied
140. politics	**159.** referred	**178.** severely	**197.** vegetable
141. possession	**160.** rehearsal	**179.** shining	**198.** villain
142. practically	**161.** relieve	**180.** siege	**199.** weird
143. predicament	**162.** religious	**181.** specimen	**200.** wholly

CHAPTER SUMMARY

The English language is complicated. While spelling rules apply to many words, there are certain words that, especially in their verb tenses and plural forms, do not follow these rules, and such words must be learned individually. Knowing how to spell is important, but you should also understand the meanings of words; it is of little value to be able to spell a word without knowing its meaning.

It is critical for law enforcement professionals to take great care with their writing, and perfect spelling is one element of excellent writing. Take the time to improve your spelling skills by

- keeping a spelling journal
- setting aside time to study the spelling of words you have trouble with
- using a spell checker wisely—always double-check your writing yourself after running it through a spell checker
- reading more to expand your vocabulary and become familiar with word spellings.

Law enforcement professionals can make themselves more effective by learning the vocabulary that applies to the legal profession.

KEY TERMS

antonyms, 48
homographs, 48
homonyms, 48
homophones, 48
preceded, 41
suffixes, 41
synonyms, 48

REVIEW AND REFLECTION QUESTIONS

1. What are specific ways you can improve your spelling?

_____

_____

_____

2. What are specific ways you can increase your vocabulary?

_____

_____

_____

3. What kind of speller have you been so far, and why do you think that is?

_____

_____

_____

4. Why is it critical to spell correctly in workplace writing?

_____

_____

_____

5. What are the benefits of having a strong, varied vocabulary?

_____

_____

_____

4 Writing Foundations and Grammar

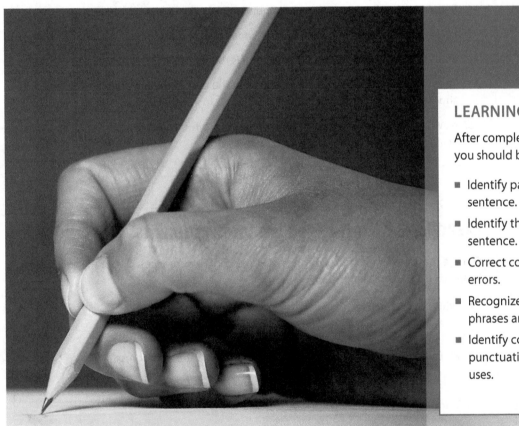

LEARNING OUTCOMES

After completing this chapter, you should be able to:

- Identify parts of speech in a sentence.
- Identify the purpose of a sentence.
- Correct common grammar errors.
- Recognize different kinds of phrases and clauses.
- Identify common punctuation marks and their uses.

Introduction

Correct grammar is important because it helps people understand each other in the communication process. Conversely, poor grammar can be a significant barrier to communication, especially when it leads to misunderstanding and misinterpretation.

To begin this chapter, complete the following pre-test to check your knowledge of grammar usage. Doing so will help you locate your areas of weakness.

Grammar Pre-Test

EXERCISE 1 » Finding Subjects and Verbs

Underline the subject with one line and the verb(s) with two lines in the following sentences:

1. People are retiring from law enforcement agencies at an alarming rate.

2. In Canada, many law enforcement positions are unfilled.

3. Many reasons are given, but the main one is that baby boomers are retiring.

4. There has not been much attention given in the past to the impending personnel shortage.

5. Now, law enforcement agencies must scramble to recruit new people without sacrificing standards.

EXERCISE 2 » Correcting Sentence Fragments

Change the following sentence fragments into complete sentences. One of the examples is already a complete sentence.

1. While on routine patrol.

_____

2. PC Dubois received a radio call about a break and enter in progress.

_____

3. Two suspects running from a house.

_____

4. At 198 Queen St.

_____

5. Were apprehended near the scene.

_____

EXERCISE 3 » Using Subordination and Coordination

Use subordination or coordination correctly to combine each of the following pairs of sentences. One of the sentences is already correct.

1. Upon arrival at King Street. The officer noticed a broken window.

    _____

    _____

2. A blue late-model Chevrolet was stopped for customs inspection; the driver was acting suspiciously.

    _____

    _____

3. The inmate population of the Workplace Detention Centre increased dramatically, it was thought to be a major problem.

    _____

    _____

4. Store security observed a woman hide a candy bar in her purse; and they moved in to arrest her.

    _____

    _____

5. Perimeter security patrol of an abandoned building is boring. And dangerous as well.

    _____

    _____

EXERCISE 4 » Recasting Run-On Sentences

Correct the following run-on sentences. One of the sentences is correct as it is.

1. I was asked to take photographs of striking workers I decided to do so.

   _____

   _____

2. Strong competition exists among private security companies they are each trying to build up their business.

   _____

   _____

3. A female hailed the cruiser when she was approached she refused to identify herself.

   _____

   _____

4. At the start of the shift it's important to note details of stolen cars they might be encountered while you're on patrol.

   _____

   _____

5. Information that may prove useful during your shift may be discovered by means of searches in specific cell blocks.

   _____

   _____

EXERCISE 5 » Using Commas

Correctly punctuate the following sentences with commas. One of the sentences is correct as it is.

1. White-collar criminals dishonest employees and Internet scam artists are surfacing in growing numbers.

2. Recent arrests especially among technology manufacturers have been making headlines.

3. Even owners of sports franchises have been charged.

4. Small fines short prison terms or absolute discharges have not been effective.

5. Corruption reduces public trust in business corporations affects the stock market and has an overall negative effect on the economy.

EXERCISE 6 » Using Other Punctuation Marks

Place punctuation marks (colons, semicolons, quotation marks) where they belong in the following sentences. One of the sentences is correct as it is.

1. He was advised to plead guilty the evidence was stacked against him.

2. The key term, say lawyers, is plea bargain.

3. The *Highway Traffic Act* concerns the following motorists, passengers, and pedestrians.

4. Private security agencies have three areas of concern personal protection, technological protection, and intellectual protection.

5. The motto of the Associated Protection Agency is "We protect your assets."

EXERCISE 7 » Ensuring Subject–Verb Agreement

Correct the errors in subject–verb agreement in the following sentences. One of the sentences is correct as it is.

1. The history of law enforcement go back thousands of years.

2. Some writers from ancient Rome has described a system of law enforcement in that city.

3. Laws were modified so that the people could understand them.

4. Each group of explorers who went to America were surprised at the codification of laws in certain cultures.

5. The Iroquois Confederacy were able to formalize rules of behaviour.

EXERCISE 8 » Establishing Parallel Structure

All but one of the following sentences lack parallel structure. Revise to create parallel structure.

1. In the past, officers were expected to be male, have big muscles, and tall.

_____

_____

2. Having women in front-line law enforcement positions offers many advantages, and to have them achieve senior positions is better yet.

_____

_____

3. With good planning and luck, retirement packages for law enforcement personnel can be quite lucrative.

_____

_____

4. Observing, waiting, and listening are in reality more common police activities than those depicted in the action-filled lives of police officers on television.

_____

_____

5. He was a good officer, a brave man, and he worked hard.

_____

_____

EXERCISE 9 » Editing Sentences for Errors

Each of the following sentences contains an error in grammar or punctuation. Revise each sentence so that it is complete and correct.

1. These sort of experiences are helpful when applying for promotion.

2. No one wants to spend all their time writing reports.

3. I haven't kept my memo book up to date however I know I'm going to need it for court.

4. The Breathalyzer technician plan to come during the next shift.

5. All of my partners is very friendly.

6. The *Criminal Code* is long complicated and important.

7. Guns are dangerous they can cause a lot of trouble.

8. The siren wailed and we covered our ears loudly.

9. The files were lost for three weeks before the assistant found it.

10. Is a great detective.

Grammar Essentials: Sentences

A sentence is a group of words that contains a complete thought. Every sentence must contain a subject and a verb.

Subject

The **subject** of a sentence is the word or group of words that the sentence is about or that the sentence concerns.

> **Fred is a corrections officer.**

The subject here is *Fred*. Fred is who the sentence is about. If you wrote *Is a corrections officer*, you wouldn't know that the sentence is about Fred. This type of subject is called a **simple subject**.

The simple subject may be a noun (Fred), a pronoun (he), or a word ending in *-ing*, also known as a *gerund* or *verbal noun*.

> **Reading is her favourite hobby.**

In the previous sentence, *reading* is what the sentence is about, or the focus of the sentence.

The subjects in the following sentences are italicized.

> *I* **am on the midnight shift.**
> *Driving* **is a chore.**
> **The** *tree* **fell in the storm.**
> **The** *store* **was robbed last night.**
> *She* **became a police officer.**
> *Bill* **is in jail.**

A subject can consist of more than one word, in which case it is called a **complete subject**. The complete subject contains the simple subject.

> **The man on the jury seems to be asleep.**

Here, *man* is the simple subject, and *the man on the jury* is the complete subject. The complete subject describes the simple subject by distinguishing the particular man from all other men in the courtroom. In the following sentences, the simple subject is italicized, and the complete subject appears in parentheses:

> **(***Pat* **and** *René***) are partners.**
> **(***Corrections officers* **and** *customs officials***) attended the seminar.**
> **(***Arresting criminals* **and** *testifying in a court***) are my favourite parts of my police work.**

Subject is the word or group of words that the sentence concerns.

Simple subject is a subject consisting of one word.

Complete subject is a subject consisting of more than one word.

In every case, remember that for a sentence to be complete, it must have a subject or subjects. Without a subject, a sentence is called a sentence fragment, which will be discussed later in this chapter.

EXERCISE 10 » Adding Complete Subjects

Add complete subjects to turn the following fragments into sentences:

1. is responsible for border security.

   _____

2. were my favourite courses at college.

   _____

3. teaches law enforcement courses at the college.

   _____

4. takes emergency calls from the public.

   _____

5. manages the marine unit.

   _____

   _____

Verb

The **verb** is the action word in a sentence. Every sentence must have a verb; otherwise, as in the case of a sentence without a subject, a sentence fragment occurs, which is a grammar error.

The verb in the following sentence is italicized:

> The attorney *impresses* the jury with her argument.

The subject of this sentence (*the attorney*) does something, or causes an action to take place (*impresses*). Therefore, *impresses* is the verb.

> Ming *operated* the radio.
> She *arrested* the offender.
> Jane *questioned* witnesses on the stand.
> The human resources officer *orients* the new recruits.

A **verb** is the action word of a sentence.

Tense refers to when the verb took place—in other words, its past, present, or future form.

The **tense** of a verb indicates when the action took place (past), is taking place (present), or will take place (future).

Past:	I *walked* to work every day.
Present:	I *walk* to work every day.
Future:	I *will walk* to work every day.

Many verbs in the English language are known as **regular verbs**; these can be changed from present to past tense by adding *-ed* to the present form of the verb. This is not true of **irregular verbs**, which are dealt with below.

Changing the present tense to the future tense usually involves adding a word such as *will* or *shall* to the verb:

I *will apply* to a small law firm.
She *shall obtain* her diploma.

There are some verbs that don't appear to be "action" words; the action isn't obvious. These verbs are called **linking verbs** because they link subjects to other parts of the sentence. They are as much verbs, however, as any action word. The most common linking verbs are various forms of the verb *to be*: *is, am, are, was,* and *were*.

The lawyer *is* efficient.
I *am* a private investigator.
They *are* guilty as charged.
The officers *were* on patrol.

These forms of the verb *to be* are irregular because they don't take the forms of most regular action verbs. For instance, instead of adding *-ed* to the present form of *to be* to form the past tense, use the following forms:

Present	Past
I *am*	I *was*
You *are*	You *were*
He, she, it *is*	He, she, it *was*
We, you, they *are*	We, you, they *were*

Regular verbs are verbs that can be changed from present to past tense by adding *-ed* to the present form of the word.

Irregular verbs are verbs that involve adding words to change the tense.

Linking verbs are words that don't appear to be action words; the action isn't obvious, including forms of the verb *to be*.

The various tenses of the irregular verb *to be* may combine with an *-ing* word, or present participle, to produce the progressive verb tense.

> **I** *am* **running.**
>
> **He** *was* **training.**
>
> **They** *will be* **exercising.**

These present participles, ending in *-ing*, form part of the complete verb; in the examples above, *am running*, *was training*, and *will be exercising* are complete verbs.

Another irregular verb is *to have*. Note that *to be* and *to have* are called **infinitives**. The infinitive is the "to" form of the word—the basic verb form, without inflections to show person, number, or tense.

Present	Past
I *have*	I *had*
You *have*	You *had*
He, she, it *has*	He, she, it *had*
We, you, they *have*	We, you, they *had*

Below is a list of some irregular verbs in their infinitive, present tense, and past tense forms.

Infinitive	Present	Past
to break	break	broke
to catch	catch	caught
to do	do	did
to drive	drive	drove
to eat	eat	ate
to give	give	gave
to go	go	went
to know	know	knew
to see	see	saw
to sit	sit	sat
to speak	speak	spoke
to take	take	took
to write	write	wrote

A final point to keep in mind is that there can be more than one verb in a sentence.

Infinitives are the basic verb form without inflections to show person, number, or tense, as in the case of *to have*.

EXERCISE 11 » Changing Verb Tense

Underline the complete verbs in the following passage. Then rewrite the passage, changing the verbs from the present to the past tense.

At 2330, I arrive at the residence of Fred Goldman, 211 Quiet St., to check on a possible break and enter. I check each window, being as quiet as I can, and find that nothing is broken. Then when I am walking through the front yard, I find that the front door is open. I am thinking that I should call for backup, but since the lights are on in the house, I suspect that it might be a false alarm. I enter the house and find Mr. Goldman sound asleep in front of the television. I wake him up, and he tells me that he often leaves the front door open.

_____

_____

_____

_____

_____

_____

_____

_____

_____

_____

_____

Subject–Verb Agreement

Subjects and verbs must agree in their person and their number. Follow the "rule of *s*." Put an *s* on the end of either the subject or the verb, but not both at once:

> **Cars speed.**
> **A car speeds.**

When trying to ensure that your subjects and verbs agree, take particular care in the following situations:

1. *Words intervening between simple subject and verb.*

> **One** of the pictures *shows* the wanted man.
> **The *suspect*** in the robberies *was* arrested yesterday.

2. *Subject following verb.*

> *Have* John and Solly started a new security firm?
>
> Around the corner *ride the cyclists*.

3. *Two or more singular subjects joined by* or *or* nor.

> John *and* Bill *work* in litigation. [Compound subject takes plural.]
>
> John *or* Bill *works* in litigation. [One of John or Bill, but not both, works there.]

4. *Collective noun (group word) subject.*

> The jury *is* ready with its verdict. [The entity is acting as a single unit.]
>
> The jury *were* not in agreement. [Individual actions within the whole entity are meant to be considered.]

5. *Nouns plural in form but singular in meaning.*

> The news *is* reporting that the bank was robbed.
>
> The West Indies *is* a group of islands.
>
> Politics *is* of no concern to the law.

6. *Periods of time, fractions, weights, amounts of money.*

> Three days *is* a long time to spend on a cross-examination.
>
> Three-quarters of the stash *was* seized.
>
> Fifty pounds of contraband *is* in that car.
>
> A hundred dollars *is* the fine for the bylaw infraction.

   If a fraction refers to a quantity ("three-quarters of the membership"), it is treated as singular; if it refers to a number, it is treated as plural ("three-quarters of the pencils").

7. *Relative pronouns.* These pronouns (*who, which, that*) agree with their antecedent (the word to which they refer or the word that they replace) in number.

> These are the *employees who are* always reliable. [The antecedent of *who* is *employees*.]
>
> Bill is one of the *employees who are* always reliable. [*Employees* is the antecedent of *who*, requiring the plural verb *are*.]
>
> George is the *only one* of the clerks *who is* on vacation. [*Only one* is the antecedent of *who*, requiring the singular verb *is*.]
>
> Lian is one of the *women who work* undercover. [*Women* is the antecedent of *who*.]

8. *Indefinite pronouns.* The following indefinite pronouns are always singular: *one, each, anybody, anyone, somebody, someone, everybody, everyone, nobody, no one, either,* and *neither.*

> One *is* not obliged to purchase a raffle ticket.
>
> Each of the students *has* an assignment.
>
> Anyone who *wants* to join may do so.
>
> Someone *is* following them.
>
> Everyone in the room *is* a suspect.
>
> No one *has* a salary increase.
>
> Either suspect *fits* the description.
>
> Neither Joe nor Dave *has* a girlfriend.

The following indefinite pronouns are always plural: *both, many, few,* and *several.*

> Both of the cars *were* blue.
>
> Many of the students *speak* French.
>
> A few of the officers *are* at the scene.
>
> Several of the people *were* victims of the scam.

The following indefinite pronouns are singular for quantity and plural for number: *all, any, most, none,* and *some.*

Quantity (singular)	Number (plural)
All of the parking lot *was* full.	All of the parking spots *were* taken.
Any time *is* good for me.	Any days *are* good for me.
Most of the audience *likes* the show.	Most of the people *like* the show.
None of the laundry *feels* dry.	None of the clothes *feel* dry.
Some of the food *was* spoiled.	Some of the eggs *were* spoiled.

9. *Compound subjects that do not agree in number.* In a compound subject, where one subject is singular and one is plural, make the verb agree with the *nearest* subject.

> Either the manager or the *assistants are* at the workshop.
>
> Either the assistants or the *manager is* at the workshop.

EXERCISE 12 » Revising: Subject–Verb Agreement and Pronouns

1. Correct the errors in subject–verb agreement and any pronoun errors in the following passage:

   I think that a person who drinks and drives should be shot because they get in their car and do a lot of damage. You may be at a bar all evening and think you are okay, but when the person gets in their car, look out! Often when we have been drinking, you lose your ability to make rational decisions, the biggest decision being whether we should get in our car or take a taxi home. Often this is a difficult decision for the person because, like most people, they have stayed at the bar until it is too late: all your money is gone, and a taxi is now out of the question. Maybe we should make this decision at the start of the evening when your head is still clear and one has money in their pocket. If a person does not have enough sense to do this, I would stop drinking altogether until you can learn to control yourself, for one's own safety and for the safety of those around us.

2. Complete the following sentences, using the correct present tense of the verb *to be*:

   a. Anyone _____ .

   b. Each _____ .

   c. Somebody _____ .

   d. Neither _____ .

   e. Either _____ .

   f. No one _____ .

   g. Something _____ .

   h. Much _____ .

   i. Everyone _____ .

Sentence Fragments

Since every complete sentence must have a subject, must have a verb, and must make a complete thought, any group of words without one of these three characteristics is a **sentence fragment**.

She reads a training manual.

This is a complete sentence: It has a subject (*she*) and a verb (*reads*), and it is a complete thought; it makes sense, and it's understandable. However, if the subject were left out, the remaining words would be

Reads a training manual.

A **sentence fragment** is a group of words that is not a complete thought, or a group of words missing either a subject or a verb.

This is a sentence fragment because the sentence now has no subject. Who reads a training manual? A subject is needed.

Examples of different kinds of sentence fragments are set out below.

> **Parked in the centre of town. [What or who parked in the centre of town?]**
>
> **My report on my sergeant's desk. [What about the report on the desk?]**
>
> **With only my jacket. [What happened with the jacket?]**
>
> **Waiting for the shipment. [Who was waiting?]**

Adding a subject and/or a verb to these fragments makes them into complete thoughts.

> **I parked in the centre of town.**
>
> **My report is on my sergeant's desk.**
>
> **With only my jacket, I fought off a swarm of bees.**
>
> **The mailroom clerk was waiting for the shipment.**

Any group of words that contains a subject and a verb is called a **clause**. A sentence is a clause in most cases, but not always. There are two types of clauses: independent and dependent.

An **independent clause** contains a subject, a verb, and a complete thought; therefore, independent clauses are also sentences.

> **He will answer for his crimes.**

A **dependent clause** contains a subject and a verb, but it does not express a complete thought. It is a fragment that needs something else to complete it.

> **Because he was caught.**

He is the subject, *was caught* is the verb, but the clause does not explain what happened because he was caught. Therefore, this group of words does not contain a complete thought and is a sentence fragment.

> **Because he was caught, he will answer for his crimes.**

A **clause** is any group of words that contains a subject and a verb.

An **independent clause** is a complete thought containing a subject and a verb; therefore, these clauses are complete sentences.

A **dependent clause** is a group of words containing a subject and a verb, but not a complete thought; therefore, it is not a complete sentence, and it needs something else to complete it.

As shown above, a dependent clause at the beginning of a sentence must be followed by a comma. If the dependent clause falls at the end of a sentence, the comma is not needed.

> **He will answer for his crimes because he was caught.**

Another type of sentence fragment to be considered is the "list" fragment.

> **Law enforcement professionals must be. Intelligent, resourceful, and cautious.**

Both of these fragments are dependent. The first fragment has a subject and a verb, but it needs the list ("intelligent, resourceful, and cautious") to complete its meaning. The list doesn't have a subject or a verb. The straightforward solution is to combine the two:

> **Law enforcement professionals must be intelligent, resourceful, and cautious.**

Two further examples of common sentence-fragment errors are set out below, along with their corrected forms.

> *Fragment*: **I like card games. Such as euchre, poker, and blackjack.**
> *Complete*: **I like card games, such as euchre, poker, and blackjack.**
> *Fragment*: **We went to court. Saw the judge, the bailiff, and the lawyer.**
> *Complete*: **We went to court, where we saw the judge, the bailiff, and the lawyer.**

Finally, be aware that commands, brief though they usually are, do not qualify as sentence fragments.

> **Stop!**

The subject *you* is implied here, so the sentence is complete.

Remember, too, that an *-ing* word, also known as a present participle (e.g., *running, shooting*), can never be the complete verb in a sentence.

> *Fragment*: **I running to keep in shape.**
> *Complete*: **I am running to keep in shape.**

EXERCISE 13 » Correcting Fragments

Form the following fragments into complete sentences:

1. I worked hard. So that I could get a promotion.

2. We went into law. Because we love helping people.

3. Tell me the truth. If you know it.

4. He was arrested; because he was drinking and driving.

5. I love facing danger. Wherever I find it.

6. You will find your shirt. In the drawer. Where you keep your socks.

7. Because the traffic was heavy.

8. If they get their act together.

9. While running for the bus.

10. .22 calibre, .32 calibre, .45 calibre.

Run-On Sentences

The **run-on sentence** is the opposite of the sentence fragment. While the fragment is part of a sentence, the run-on is two complete sentences or independent clauses that have been joined together in an inappropriate way.

> **I always stop here for doughnuts it is my favourite place.**

The sentence can be corrected in one of the following four ways:

1. You could use two sentences.

> **I always stop here for doughnuts. It is my favourite place.**

A **run-on sentence** is two complete sentences joined together in an inappropriate way.

2. You could use a conjunction.

> **I always stop here for doughnuts because it is my favourite place.**

3. You could use a semicolon.

> **I always stop here for doughnuts; it is my favourite place.**

4. You could use a dependent clause.

> **Since it is my favourite place, I always stop here for doughnuts.**

Keep in mind that an independent clause contains a complete thought, but only one complete thought. A run-on sentence expresses more than one thought with no division between the thoughts.

EXERCISE 14 » Correcting Run-ons

1. Correct the following run-on sentences:
   a. Just let me do the talking you'll get us a ticket if you don't keep quiet.

   _____

   b. The cabin was cold however it had a wood stove.

   _____

   c. A strong wind was blowing the boat from the yacht club nearly sank.

   _____

   d. Most people have 20/20 vision that is a requirement for a job here.

   _____

   e. Career opportunities are good for students in law enforcement some employers also demand volunteer experience.

   _____

   _____

2. Correct the run-on sentences in the following paragraph:

   Thank you for your attention to this matter if I can be of any assistance to you in collecting the necessary documents please contact me I will do what I can to expedite the process it is important that this be completed as soon as possible if any of the documents are missing your case could be dismissed you would still be liable for court costs.

   _____

   _____

   _____

   _____

Another type of run-on is the **comma splice**.

> **There is a leash law, no one obeys it.**

In this case, the comma is misplaced; two independent clauses can't be separated by a comma without a conjunction or linking word. A comma splice can be corrected in the same four ways as any other run-on.

1. You can use two sentences.

> **There is a leash law. No one obeys it.**

2. You can use a conjunction.

> **There is a leash law, but no one obeys it.**

3. You can use a semicolon.

> **There is a leash law; no one obeys it.**

4. You can use a dependent clause.

> **Although there is a leash law, no one obeys it.**

Modifiers

A modifier is a word or phrase that refers to, describes, or explains another word in a sentence. Modifiers must be placed as close as possible to the word or words they modify. There are two types of sentence errors involving modifiers: misplaced modifiers and dangling modifiers.

Misplaced Modifiers

Misplaced modifiers are modifiers that are placed within a sentence in such a way that it is unclear what word they apply to.

> **The audience cheered when we graduated from college excitedly.**

The modifier *excitedly* is misplaced here because it is unclear whether it modifies *graduated* or *cheered*.

Consider these other examples, in which the misplaced modifiers are italicized:

> **He protested at the noise of the siren wailing *angrily*.**
> **The police officer approached the hostile-looking dog *with a hockey glove on*.**
> **Our lawyer rated our chances of winning *without much enthusiasm*.**

In a **comma splice**, two independent clauses are joined together with a comma, but they are missing the essential conjunction or linking word. Commas do not join sentences.

Misplaced modifiers are modifying words placed within a sentence in such a way that it is unclear what word they are meant to modify.

To correct the sentences, place the modifiers closer to the words they modify.

> **He angrily protested at the noise of the siren wailing.**
>
> **With a hockey glove on, the police officer approached the hostile-looking dog.**
>
> **Without much enthusiasm, our lawyer rated our chances of winning.**

EXERCISE 15 » Correcting Misplaced Modifiers

Correct the misplaced modifiers in the following sentences:

1. The woman was stopped for speeding with the hat.

2. He made cookies for his friends with chocolate chips in them.

3. The lawyer being recruited vigorously believed it was time for a change.

4. The police chief led the parade in full dress uniform.

5. Customs officers intercepted the smugglers guarding the coast line.

6. The criminal laughed when she was almost convicted maliciously.

7. The man escaped before the fire spread barely.

8. We planned to start work early Christmas Eve a long time ago.

9. The defendant stood in the dock without any signs of cracking.

10. The suspect said he was at home with a bow tie.

Dangling Modifiers

The other form of modifier fault is the dangling modifier. A **dangling modifier** is one that doesn't logically modify anything in its sentence.

> **Crossing the border, my bags were searched.**
> **Expecting a lot of work, extra help was requested.**

In both of these cases, the modifier is dangling. In the first case, who was crossing the border? *My bags*? In the second sentence, *who* is expecting a lot of work? Correct the sentences as follows:

> **When I was crossing the border, my bags were searched.**
> **Expecting a lot of work, we requested extra help.**

To fix a dangling modifier, add a word to which the modifier refers, and put the modifier as close to that word as possible.

EXERCISE 16 » Correcting Dangling Modifiers

Correct the dangling modifiers in the following sentences:

1. Risking her life, the accident victims were rescued by the lifeguard.

2. Crossing the street, my hat blew away.

3. To pass the communications course, one essay every week is required.

4. Driving through the suburbs, several luxury vehicles were seen.

5. Jogging through the park, a dog bit me.

6. On receiving an offer of employment, tears filled his mother's eyes.

7. When learning the *Highway Traffic Act*, memorizing is often used.

8. Driving at night, his mind began to wander.

9. Being a qualified legal assistant, a framed certificate was proudly displayed.

10. While attending the theatre, the apartment was looted.

Dangling modifiers are modifying words that don't logically modify anything in their sentence.

Pronoun References

A pronoun is a word that replaces a noun. It may be used as the subject of a sentence (the word that indicates who or what performs an action). A pronoun may also be the object of a sentence (the word that indicates upon whom or what an action is performed).

Noun:	**Roy works in the traffic unit.**
Pronoun:	*He* **works in the traffic unit.**

Noun:	**Sylvie and Ruth conduct secondary vehicle inspections.**
Pronoun:	**Sylvie and Ruth conduct** *them.*

Pronouns may also be used as both the subject and the object of a single sentence.

Nouns:	**Joe writes his report.**
Pronouns:	*He* **writes** *it.*

Joe is the subject of the sentence, which is replaced with the pronoun *he*. The thing being written, *his report*, is the object of the sentence, which is replaced with the pronoun *it*.

When replacing a subject, use the following personal pronouns:

Singular	Plural
I	we
you	you
he, she, it	they

When replacing an object, use the following personal pronouns:

Singular	Plural
me	us
you	you
him, her, it	them

Note the use of both subjective and objective personal pronouns in the following examples:

Nouns:	**Rex ran away from the intruders.**
Pronouns:	*He* **ran away from** *them.*

Nouns:	**The police officer told Fred to move the van.**
Pronouns:	*She* **told** *him* **to move** *it.*

EXERCISE 17 » Using Pronouns

Underline the correct pronoun in parentheses in each of the following sentences:

1. We expect you and (they, them) at the meeting.

2. Wait for my partner and (I, me).

3. (He, Him) and Amad worked together.

4. The receptionist told you and (her, she) to stay here.

5. Everyone was at the party except (we, us).

6. You and (I, me) are both in line for promotion.

7. Professionals such as you and (he, him) should help younger employees.

8. Was it (she, her) that you saw?

9. I think that the shoplifter was (he, him).

10. It could have been (they, them) who won the race.

Pronouns and Case

The case (subjective, objective, or possessive) of a personal pronoun is determined by the function it serves in a sentence. Pronouns can be subjects or subject complements (subjective case); they can be direct objects, indirect objects, or objects of prepositions (objective case); or they can indicate ownership (possessive case).

Subjective pronouns	Objective pronouns	Possessive pronouns
I	me	my (mine)
you	you	your (yours)
he	him	his
she	her	her (hers)
it	it	its
who	whom	whose
we	us	our (ours)
they	them	their (theirs)

He (*subject*) **made the donation for me** (*object*).
With whom (*object*) **did I** (*subject*) **see you last night?**
Her (*possessive*) **litigation caseload is much heavier than his** (*possessive*).

A subject complement following a linking verb (*to be* [am, is, are, was, were, have been], *to act, to appear, to become, to feel, to grow, to seem, to look, to taste*) takes the subjective case; for example, "It was I who opened the file."

Ambiguous and Indefinite Pronoun References

It is important to eliminate ambiguity in pronoun references.

> **When Rebecca saw Jane, she was angry.**

Which woman was angry? To indicate that it was Rebecca and not Jane who was angry, the sentence can be recast as follows:

> **Rebecca was angry when she saw Jane.**

To indicate that Jane was the angry one, recast the sentence as follows:

> **When Rebecca saw her, Jane was angry.**

Use a pronoun to refer to a single noun, not a group of words.

> **He admitted that he defrauded the client. This was welcome news.**

Does *this* refer to the fact that he defrauded the client, or to his admission of the fact? Rewrite the sentence to remove this ambiguity:

> **He admitted that he defrauded the client. His admission was welcome news.**

Avoid the indefinite use of *it* and *they*.

> **They say that private security is the career of the future.**

Who is *they*? Rewrite the sentence to give *they* a face:

> **Economists say that private security is the career of the future.**

EXERCISE 18 » Removing Ambiguous and Indefinite Pronoun References

Correct the pronoun errors in the following sentences:

1. They did not see the Smiths arrive because they were having lunch.

   _____

2. I don't know what he said to him, but he was angry.

   _____

3. The girl's mother studied law, and she is going to be one when she grows up.

4. He began his career as a private investigator, which was terminated by his death.

5. In my first job, I learned to change a toner cartridge without getting it all over me.

6. I let my relatives help me with the new cars although they were rather dirty.

7. The assistant told her manager that whatever she did she could not please her.

8. They say that crime is decreasing in the city.

9. He fell while addressing the jury, which was embarrassing.

10. They have good traffic laws in Ontario.

Parallel Structure

Parallel structure involves joining similar structures together in a sentence.

> **writing, listening, speaking**

These -*ing* words all refer to forms of communication, and they are parallel in structure because they all end in -*ing*.

> **Svetlana is intelligent, witty, and charms people.**

This sentence does not use parallel structure. To obtain parallel structure, you must rewrite the sentence as follows:

> **Svetlana is intelligent, witty, and charming.**

Parallel structure should be used when phrases, clauses, or infinitives are connected by conjunctions:

Two phrases:	**up the hill and down the valley**
Two clauses:	**that he is a thief and that he is in jail**
Two infinitives:	**to go or to stay**

EXERCISE 19 » Using Parallel Structure

Correct the parallel structure faults in the following sentences:

1. The day shift or the night is fine by me.

2. I don't enjoy foot patrol when it is raining or it snows.

3. He had trained himself in juggling and to type.

4. I knew all the risks of crime and avoiding them.

5. He didn't know the bylaw or the *Criminal Code*.

6. The sergeant taught us memo books, writing reports, and how to do summaries.

7. Every law enforcement officer is taught the value of following orders and how to think independently.

8. The inspector is influential and a popular person.

9. He is not happy nor satisfied with his job.

10. My dream is to have a job with Corrections Canada, a family, and buy a house.

Correlatives

Correlative conjunctions are specific sets of words that require parallel structure when used together. Some common correlative conjunctions are the following:

> **either ... or**
> **neither ... nor**
> **not ... but**
> **not only ... but also**
> **both ... and**

These groups of words don't have to be used if there is no parallel structure involved in the sentence:

> **The job required *both* concentration *and* speed.**
> **I like both colours.**

IN THE FIELD

Detectives read a supplementary report written by patrol officer Sally White regarding a break and enter.

Supp Report:

We arrived at the citing of the break and enter in the office of the building where the many workers's had computers at there desks in a busy office downtown on Spruce street. Because the computers were knew and there was alots of boxes delivered to show that they were, this is why they were stolen.

The employee, Ronald Brown said that he saw a car drive away when he arrived at work speedily. The car hit him and there was damage at the front bumper.

He said the plate was "ABCD 123."

When fleeing the scene, he admitted that he struck him, this was good news.

The detectives discussed this case with one another and decided that they would charge the registered owner of ABCD 123 with break and enter, hit and run, and assault on Ronald Brown. When a photographic lineup was shown to Mr. Brown, he asked in surprise, "Why is my brother in these photos?"

The detectives were confused. One asked, "You did tell Officer White that the plate was ABCD 123, isn't that correct?"

"Yes," said Ronald Brown, "but that was the vehicle I was driving. I knew I had to report the damage to my brother's insurance company. Who was assaulted anyway?"

A detective replied, "We understood from the report that you were struck by the suspect."

"No," answered Mr. Brown, "my vehicle was struck by the suspect as he drove away. I was never assaulted."

Can you identify where some assumptions were made and how these assumptions could have caused confusion? What are some of the grammar issues present? How do you think the quality of your work may affect your reputation?

Grammar Essentials: Punctuation and Capitalization

Commas

As a rule of thumb, fewer commas are better than many. Don't use a comma if you're not sure you need one. However, there are certain rules for comma use that should be followed.

1. Use a comma to separate three or more items in a series.

   The warrant was signed, sealed, and delivered.

   Some people prefer not to use a comma before the word *and* in a series. The only firm rule here is to be consistent.

2. Use a comma between two independent clauses separated by the coordinate conjunctions *and*, *but*, *or*, *nor*, *yet*, and *so*, especially if the subject changes in the second clause.

   He was a kind man, and his life was an inspiration to many.

3. Use a comma after a long introductory element.

   After ten years with the company, Tom became president.

4. Do not use a comma if such an expression is put at the end of the sentence.

   Tom became president after ten years with the company.

5. Use commas to separate "interrupters" from the rest of the sentence. Interrupters are words or phrases that are not essential to the meaning of the sentence. Taking interrupters out of the sentence does not change the meaning of the sentence.

   I knew, *of course*, that I would be caught.

6. Use commas to surround material that is not essential to the sentence. The difference between this rule and the preceding one is that, in this case, the information surrounded by commas adds some substance to the meaning of the sentence.

   Police officers, although they have a reputation for eating a lot of doughnuts, are usually in good shape.

7. Use a comma to separate different parts of addresses and dates.

   198 Queen Street South, Hamilton, Ontario L8P 3S7
   November 10, 2002

8. Do not use commas unnecessarily in addresses and dates.

> 198 Queen Street South, Hamilton, ON L8P 3S7
> [A comma is not needed between the province and the postal code.]
> 10 November 2002

9. Do not use commas with the 24-hour clock or when dates are written as numerals.

> 1320 (1:20 p.m.)
> 44.05.31 (31 May 1944)

10. Use commas before or after a direct quotation.

> She said, "I'm here for the Written Communication Test."
> "I'm here for the Written Communication Test," she said.
> He answered, "You must be joking!"

EXERCISE 20 » Using Commas

Insert commas where necessary in the following sentences:

1. Her alibi of course was completely ridiculous.

2. By the way you have been promoted.

3. The elderly man coughed staggered and fell to the ground.

4. She smuggled drugs was caught as she left the plane and now has to pay for the crime.

5. The court date is set for August 8 2016.

6. I live at apartment 5 216 Bold Street Toronto Ontario.

7. Tomorrow July 31 is the anniversary of the day I was hired.

8. That's the best way I think to take creases out of your uniform.

9. I said "Your last statement isn't the truth."

10. You have to comply with the court order or you'll be arrested.

Apostrophes

The apostrophe shows possession. It is also used in contractions.

> *Possession:*   John's [belonging to John]
> *Contraction:* Didn't [did not]

Possessives

The possessive indicates ownership or affiliation. Most possessives can be written by adding an apostrophe and an *s* to a singular noun.

> *Possession:*   **Theo's whistle [Theo owns the whistle.]**
> *Affiliation:*   **Manny's club [Manny is a member of the club.]**

It often helps in determining possessives to rephrase a sentence using the word *of* to show possession.

> **The whistle of Theo**

When forming the possessive of plural nouns ending in *s*, add the apostrophe after the noun.

> **The cars' noise [More than one car is making noise.]**

Compare this to the singular possessive.

> **The car's noise [One car is making noise.]**

A review of various forms of the word *car* is provided below.

Word	Part of speech
car	singular noun
car's	possessive singular noun [belonging to one car]
cars	plural noun
cars'	possessive plural noun [belonging to more than one car]

The following rules will assist you in creating possessive nouns:

1. If a singular word ends in *s*, add *s* to the final letter.

> **My boss's office [There is one boss with one office.]**

2. Words that are already plural take an apostrophe followed by an *s*.

> **My children's toys**

3. Statements relating to time need apostrophes in certain situations.

> **I am eligible for a week's vacation [a vacation of one week].**
> **I am eligible for three weeks' vacation [a vacation of three weeks].**

4. Never use an apostrophe with the following pronouns:

my	your	yours	his
whose	their	theirs	her
its	our	ours	hers

Note that *it's* is a contraction meaning "it is" or "it has"; it does not show ownership or affiliation.

EXERCISE 21 » Using Apostrophes

Use apostrophes correctly in the following sentences:

1. Junes mother works for the Ministry of the Attorney General.

2. Those are the employees [plural] records we seized.

3. The clerks salaries were up for review.

4. The rooftops slant made it difficult to repair the tiles.

5. Is that Carloss desk?

6. We will be there in about a minutes time.

7. The ropes mark on the corpse was a clue.

8. Jeff Saunders daughters will be married next week.

9. The lawyers offices had to be cleaned.

10. Tobaccos high cost is leading to more smuggling.

11. Its against the law.

12. Theyre coming with their lawyers this afternoon.

13. Youre going to be promoted.

14. Whos going to pay for the damage?

15. Its Russs car that was involved in the accident.

16. Weve been working late every night.

17. Thats the sergeants problem.

18. Theyve got a chance to carry drugs across the border.

19. Youll never get hired with that attitude.

20. Whats the problem?

Contractions

Contractions are formed from a combination of two words. Both contractions and possessives use apostrophes, but contractions do not show ownership or affiliation. The contraction is formed by replacing a letter or group of letters with an apostrophe.

> *I am* becomes *I'm*.
> *You are* becomes *you're*.
> *It is* becomes *it's*.

Common contractions include the following:

I'm (I am)	they're (they are)
I'd (I had/I would)	they'd (they had/they would)
I'll (I will)	they'll (they will)
I've (I have)	we're (we are)
you're (you are)	we'd (we had/we would)
you'd (you had/you would)	we'll (we will)
you'll (you will)	who're (who are)
you've (you have)	who'd (who had/who would)
he's (he is/he has)	who'll (who will)
he'd (he had/he would)	it's (it is/it has)
he'll (he will)	it'd (it had/it would)
she's (she is/she has)	it'll (it will)
she'd (she had/she would)	let's (let us)
she'll (she will)	isn't (is not)
aren't (are not)	hadn't (had not)
wasn't (was not)	wouldn't (would not)
weren't (were not)	would've (would have)
don't (do not)	couldn't (could not)
doesn't (does not)	could've (could have)
didn't (did not)	shouldn't (should not)
hasn't (has not)	should've (should have)
haven't (have not)	

Periods

1. Use a period at the end of a sentence.

> **We had a quiet evening at home.**

2. Use a period after most abbreviations.

> **Mr. (Mister)**
> **Oct. (October)**

3. Note that certain organizations do not use periods in their abbreviated names.

> **RCMP (Royal Canadian Mounted Police)**
> **CSIS (Canadian Security Intelligence Service)**

4. Note that the names of most provinces have alternative abbreviations, some of which do not contain periods.

> **Ont. or ON (Ontario)**
> **Alta. or AB (Alberta)**

Question Marks

1. Use a question mark after a direct question.

> **She asked, "Are you writing the promotion examination?"**

2. Do not use a question mark in an indirect question.

> **She asked whether I was writing the promotion examination.**

Exclamation Points

Use an exclamation point after an emphatic statement or command.

> **Stop, or you'll go off the road!**

Quotation Marks

1. Use quotation marks to enclose the exact words of a speaker.

> **I said, "I'm going on vacation next week."**

2. Do not use quotation marks around an indirect quotation.

> **I said that I'm going on vacation next week.**

3. After quotation marks, use a capital letter unless the quotation is split.

> **"I'm going on vacation," I said, "next week."**

4. Use quotation marks to enclose the titles of short works. Short works include poems, essays, articles, short stories, songs, and radio or television programs. (Longer works, such as novels, are italicized.)

> **I read the pamphlet "Better Reports" before my test.**

Semicolons

1. Use a semicolon to indicate connection between two independent clauses. In the following example, the two independent clauses can be either separated by a period or, if you want to stress the connection between the two statements, joined with a semicolon:

> **I witnessed the accident. I will testify in court.**
> **I witnessed the accident; I will testify in court.**

2. Certain conjunctions need to be preceded by a semicolon and followed by a comma. These conjunctions are the following:

however	otherwise	nevertheless
moreover	therefore	nonetheless

> **I did not see the accident; however, I was asked to testify in court.**

3. Do not use a semicolon with the coordinate conjunctions *and, but, or, nor, yet,* and *so.* When these coordinate conjunctions separate two independent clauses, a comma is used in preference to a semicolon.

> **I witnessed the accident, but you will testify in court.**

Colons

1. Use a colon after an independent clause to introduce a list of particulars.

> **I have three favourite career choices: police officer, customs inspector, and legal assistant.**

2. The introductory clause may often conclude with the terms *the following* or *as follows.*

> **The thieves stole the following: a camera, a television, and a computer.**

Capital Letters

1. Capitalize the first word in a sentence.

> **Capitalize the first word in a sentence.**

2. Capitalize the first, last, and important words in a title.

> *Communications for Law Enforcement Professionals*

3. Capitalize the names of specific persons, places, languages, nations, and nationalities.

Mayor Huang	Hamilton	French	Canada	Canadian

4. Capitalize the names of days, months, and holidays. Do not capitalize the seasons.

Monday	November	Labour Day	summer

5. Capitalize the first word in a direct quotation.

> **I told her, "The prison is located in Kingston."**

6. Capitalize the word *I*.

> **I mean what I say.**

7. Capitalize the names of specific academic courses. Do not capitalize general words that refer to a type of course.

> **I am taking Communications I.**
> **I am taking a communications course.**

EXERCISE 22 » Applying the Rules: Grammar and Punctuation

Correct the errors in the following sentences:

1. Mrs Ames appeared to be ready to settle her lawsuit.

_____

2. If I had to do it over.

_____

3. Get away from me he yelled.

_____

4. I warned my sister to "drive slowly on icy roads."

5. Stop you're going to hit that pole.

6. The second chapter of this book is entitled effective listening.

7. I have read: a book, a poem, and a short story.

8. I lost the following from my wallet; my money, my identification, and my credit cards.

9. There's 200 students enrolled in the legal program.

10. Prof Brown is the director of the law clerk program at the college.

11. He failed the grammar, and the spelling part of the communications course.

12. The instructor said both him and I should pass the course.

13. When I suddenly heard a car door slam and the sound of many voices.

14. The hearing was supposed to begin at noon yet however the witness had not arrived.

15. She was employed by a woman who owned a van named Mary.

16. They're are the children who were called to the principals office.

17. That's the forth traffic ticket I've received.

18. Each of the constables owns their own house.

19. Neither the defendant nor the witness impress the judge.

20. I don't mind postponing the trial. Because that's my time for vacation.

Voice

Voice is the form of a verb that indicates whether the subject of a sentence is the instigator of the action or the receiver of the action. There are two voices: active and passive. A sentence is in the active voice when the subject of the sentence initiates the action.

> He *sued* his former employer.
>
> Our client *cannot sell* his property because of liens against it.

A sentence is in the passive voice when the subject receives the action. When an active verb is made passive, a form of the verb *to be* is used.

> He *was sued* by his former employer.
>
> Property with liens against it *cannot be sold*.

The active voice is more forceful and direct than the passive voice, and should be used in most writing when possible. However, when it is the action itself that is important, and the person initiating the action is less important (or indefinite or even unknown), or when you wish to emphasize the receiver of the action rather than the person initiating the action, use the passive voice.

See Chapter 5 for more on active voice and passive voice.

Voice is the form of the verb that indicates whether the subject of a sentence is the instigator of the action or the receiver of the action. There are two voices: active and passive.

CHAPTER SUMMARY

Studying grammar will help you understand that there are different ways of expressing yourself. While there may be more than one correct method of writing, grammar rules must be followed. Correct grammar helps you to write with clarity and to eliminate potential misunderstandings and ambiguities.

KEY TERMS

clause, 78

comma splice, 82

complete subject, 70

dangling modifiers, 84

dependent clause, 78

independent clause, 78

infinitives, 73

irregular verbs, 72

linking verbs, 72

misplaced modifiers, 82

regular verbs, 72

run-on sentence, 80

sentence fragment, 77

simple subject, 70

subject, 70

tense, 71

verb, 71

voice, 100

REVIEW AND REFLECTION QUESTIONS

1. Why is correct grammar important in law enforcement?

2. What is the purpose of a sentence?

3. What must each statement contain to qualify as a complete sentence?

4. Explain the difference between a sentence fragment and a run-on sentence.

5. Parallel structure involves joining similar structures together in a sentence. Explain why this grammar skill is effective. How might you apply it to paragraphs and larger pieces of writing such as essays and reports?

5 Polishing Your Writing

LEARNING OUTCOMES

After completing this chapter, you should be able to:

- Edit your writing to remove cliché and slang.

- Know when it is appropriate to use jargon and when it is necessary to use alternative vocabulary.

- Recognize bias and subjectivity in your work and be able to rephrase to write objectively.

- Know the difference between writing in the first and third person.

- Use the active voice for clarity and detail.

Introduction

In addition to always using correct grammar and spelling, you will need to consider other elements in your writing as a law enforcement professional. To master the skill of writing excellent reports, you must learn to 1) edit your writing for any wording or phrasing that deviates from fact and 2) clearly include all detail necessary to tell the complete story of your actions, your observations, and the accounts told to you by witnesses, victims, and suspects.

There is no room in legal reports for creativity, speculation, opinion, or bias. This means you must be careful to use factual language devoid of slang or cliché. You must limit your use of jargon, and explain its use where necessary. Report writers must also consider whether a report is required to be written in the first person (I saw the suspect run north) or in the third person (This report writer saw the suspect run north). Both points of view are used by law enforcement agencies for different circumstances. One last topic discussed in this chapter about polishing your writing is the use of the active voice and its role in providing clarity and detail.

While the number of elements you must be aware of in order to write excellent reports may seem daunting, report writing is seen by most writers to be an easier style to master than creative writing or research writing because the writer does not need to invent or embellish. Unlike what you may have experienced as a student writer, there is no "word length" you need to reach. Instead, your job as a report writer is to be concise, be precise, and use plain, clear language.

Clichés and Slang

Clichés and slang can make language colourful, creative, and interesting to read. It can also make language seem dated and tired. Clichés and slang are also sometimes not understood. It is common, for example, for EAL (English as an additional language) learners to take a course on idioms and clichés because mastery of a language at the native speaker level is the ultimate goal. Slang is, by nature, generational, regional, or even local. For example, you can no doubt think of some slang words you use that your older relatives would not understand. (And maybe you don't want them to!)

Clichés

Clichés are phrases that are well known and are so frequently used they can become meaningless:

> **sick as a dog**
> **home free**
> **right as rain**
> **wrong side of the bed**
> **like water off a duck's back**

There are also some tired phrases that we insert into our writing without even realizing it:

this day and age	**the fact of the matter is**	**turn a blind eye**
come what may	**fight fire with fire**	**rule of thumb**
it goes without saying	**by and large**	

The expression "rule of thumb" is said to have originated from an early English law that stated a man was allowed to beat his wife as long as the weapon he used was no wider than his thumb. Although there is no proof that this was ever written in English law, the phrase has become linked with violence against women, and you should pay special attention to avoid using it.

What would a person just learning English make of this paragraph?

> **Why don't you wake up and smell the roses? Your boyfriend dumped you like a hot potato. You're better off without that low-life snake.**

Now consider the impact of clichés on a report:

> **The suspect fled like the wind. I was in the weeds and had no clue as to how to find her. I struck out on that pursuit.**

Would you be comfortable realizing you wrote that in a report?

Clichés can easily slip into your writing, so you'll need to be vigilant to avoid them.

EXERCISE 1 » Using Clichés

1. Write a paragraph describing your typical morning routine. Use as many clichés as you can to make your paragraph as boring, meaningless, and poorly written as possible. Take turns reading your paragraphs out to the class.

   For inspiration, consider this paragraph that describes a trip to a concert:

   > It was raining cats and dogs, but we decided to hit the town anyway. The band we wanted to see was probably going to be a one-hit wonder, but time will tell, I guess. My best friend wore the same shirt as me, but instead of letting off steam, I turned a blind eye. At the door, we found out the tickets were $60.00. I'm not made of money, but I bit the bullet and paid. The band was dull as dishwater. Easy come, easy go. But then my friends left without me, leaving me high and dry. What a write-off of a night.

2. In pairs, look up the history or origin of the following clichés:

read the riot act	white elephant	the writing on the wall
the third degree	time will tell	bite the bullet
high and dry	a diamond in the rough	

Slang

Slang is an important element of our ever-evolving and expanding language. Slang words are either words that are invented by someone and then picked up and used by others, or they are existing words to which someone gives a new meaning, and again, this new meaning is picked up and used by others. If a slang word is used often enough, by a large enough audience, and over a long enough time, it will gain official status as a word and be put into the dictionary. William Shakespeare invented many words that started out as slang and then became mainstream words (e.g., gloomy, lonely, rant). Here are three mainstream words that started out as early computer slang: Internet, email, and blog.

But just as some slang words become part of our **lexicon**, other slangs words fade away, having been used for only a short time by a small group of people. As well, slang can seem dated (cool, groovy, shindig). To keep your writing clear and original, avoid using slang unless you are quoting someone. For example, read this report excerpt:

> I chased the perp into the back alley, and then he stopped, turned, and threw an empty bottle at me. Not cool. He was acting squirrelly and yelling a lot. He was also pacing and making odd hand gestures. I think he was tripping on some far-out meds. He pulled out his cell and yelled, "I'm calling for backup! You better leave now, pig!" I wasn't worried about his posse. He then tried to throw a tire at me and missed completely. LOL. I was able to cuff him and then haul him downtown.

The events of this chase are clearly described, but it's hard to take the writer seriously as a professional. Here's a rewrite of the same excerpt with the slang removed:

> I chased the suspect through the back alley. He stopped, turned, and threw a bottle at me. He was fidgeting, yelling, and making odd hand gestures as he paced back and forth. His erratic behaviour suggested that he may have been under the influence of a narcotic. He then took out his cellphone and began texting. He then yelled, "I'm calling for backup! You better leave now, pig!" He then picked up a tire and threw it at me. The tire missed me. I was then able to handcuff the man and transport him to St. Patrick Station.

While slang allows us to speak and write with creativity, you can see why using slang in a report would not be effective.

EXERCISE 2 » Thinking About Slang

1. In groups of four, collaborate on a list of slang words you know. After ten minutes, get together with another group of four to compare lists. Were there words known to one group and not the other?

2. Get back together as a class and share lists, focusing on words that are not familiar to the whole class. What kinds of communication breakdowns could occur if these words were used in reports?

Lexicon is the body of vocabulary used by a person or group.

Jargon

Jargon is workplace terminology that is particular to a specific profession or organization. Jargon can be constructed from **acronyms** or by inventing phrases to suit the purpose of the job. Workplace jargon evolves naturally when new products are invented, new systems are put in place, or new policies are designed. Some organizations, such as the military, tend to rely heavily on jargon for communication.

Jargon allows for more efficient workplace communication. Short forms that everyone understands can make messages brief and get information across quickly. They can also allow for a level of discretion or security sometimes needed by an organization. Think of the 10-codes used by bylaw, border control, airport security, and police services. These codes allow for quick communication and also keep information limited to only those who need to know it. This is often critical for officer and civilian safety. Other organizations such as hospitals also use a form of codes to tell staff about dangerous situations they do not want the public to know about. For example, an announcement over the hospital's speakers might say, "Paging Mr. Green to Five West." This could be the hospital's code (jargon) for alerting security that there is a dangerous individual on Five West.

But using workplace jargon for communication to individuals outside your workplace will likely confuse—or worse, annoy—your intended audience. This, of course, means that your message will not have the intended effect.

Imagine this report excerpt being read in court to a civilian jury:

> At approximately 2215 hrs on Wednesday, July 20, 2016, I was on duty at YOW and was patrolling S-2, level 1. I responded to a 10-86 in progress at N-3, level 2. I called in a 10-17 and was able to apprehend a WM, early 20s, who had two bottles of Johnny Walker Red Label scotch stuffed into his pants.

Note that it is customary for officers to use 10-codes, the 24-hour clock, and some common short forms in their notebooks, because these are all necessary for clarity and efficiency at calls. When officers then transcribe their notebook notes into the various reports required for case records, they will change jargon to plain writing where they can.

This message would be clear to any airport security personnel, and also many court officers. But the jury would be confused, and since it is these people who need to know the story of the crime, your report should be written for a civilian audience, as in the following example:

> At approximately 10:15 in the evening on Wednesday, July 20, 2016, I was on duty at Macdonald-Cartier International Airport. I was patrolling on south corridor number two, level one. I responded to a call of a theft in progress. I called in to say I was on route to the scene—north corridor number three, on the second level. I apprehended a white male in his early 20s who had two bottles of Johnny Walker Red Label scotch stuffed into his pants.

An **acronym** is a word invented by putting together the first letters of several words. Sometimes vowels are added to make the acronym easy to pronounce. AWOL (absent without leave), VSA (vital signs absent), and LOL (laugh out loud) are examples of jargon created from using the first letters of words in a phrase.

EXERCISE 3 » Editing for Jargon

1. Think about the jargon used where you work or at your previous jobs. Write a list of the jargon and the meanings of the terms. Compare your list with a partner and discuss the jargon you each came up with.

_____

_____

_____

2. With the same partner, write a list of jargon that is used at your college or university. Get together with the class and create a list on the board of all of the school jargon the group came up with.

_____

_____

_____

3. Use your phone, tablet, or laptop to find the meanings of the following jargon. The terms below come from politics, the restaurant business, the medical profession, sports, retail, and technology.

BTW	POTUS	big league
CPU	hard copy	link sales
MVP	blitz	cookies
ICU	in the weeds	

Subjectivity and Objectivity

When you think or write about something or someone *subjectively*, you include emotions, opinions, and attitudes. Conversely, thinking or writing *objectively* involves leaving out all emotions, opinions, and attitudes. Compare the two following pieces of writing:

> **Subjective statement: The tiny, rundown bachelor apartment was littered with old newspapers. There was a heap of broken small appliances in one corner of the living room. The dilapidated kitchen table and stained countertops were piled with rotting food containers, and the sink was filled with greasy water, filthy dishes, and more rotting food. The saggy sofa bed was unmade, and the dirty bedding was stained with blood and possibly other fluids.**
>
> **Objective statement: The bachelor apartment contained several piles of newspapers lining both sides of the hallway, and 20 to 30 small appliances were piled in one corner of the living room. The kitchen table and counters contained take-out food containers and food scraps, and the kitchen sink was filled with dirty dishes and food scraps. The sofa bed was unmade, and there were red stains on the pillow and blanket.**

The subjective statement creates a vivid image in our minds, and it's easy to feel the disgust of the writer. The objective statement may still evoke the same picture, and it's hard not to be appalled by the scene depicted. However, the writer has been careful to record only observed, factual information and avoid descriptive adjectives and value-laden language.

It is challenging to write completely objectively. The English language is colourful, and throughout your elementary and high school years, you have been taught to make good use of adjectives and vivid description when you write for scholastic purposes. Law enforcement writing requires ignoring your creative side and channeling your inner robot.

To write objectively, you will have to train yourself to avoid

- using words with strong connotations (as discussed in Chapter 1, The Importance of Communications in Law Enforcement)
- showing a positive or negative attitude or bias
- drawing conclusions or sharing theories.

Connotative Language

As discussed in Chapter 1, many words have connotations associated with them. Describing someone as slender seems complimentary, while describing someone as skinny seems uncomplimentary. Yet they both have the same denotative meaning. Cop and police officer mean the same thing. Which would you rather be called? Read these word pairings and circle the word that seems more positive to you:

> petite / short
>
> childish / childlike
>
> cheap / thrifty
>
> discrete / close-mouthed
>
> spontaneous / impetuous

Discuss your choices with a partner. Did you come up with the same choices? Discuss the impact of using any of the ten words in a report. How could you rephrase each pairing to give objective information? For example, you could simply avoid short and petite and give the height of the person. What could you write for the remaining four pairings?

Avoiding Bias

Having a positive or negative bias toward the people and situations you will be involved with as a law enforcement officer will be unavoidable. You bring your values, attitudes, and beliefs with you wherever you go. That's expected and accepted. However, those values, attitudes, and beliefs have no place in your interactions or reports. Your job is to stay neutral.

Consider this statement:

> **The complainant told me he had scattered the ashes of his dead cat in the park because it was apparently some important ritual in his animal-worshipping cult or society.**

The bias in the above statement is subtle, but it's there in the way that the writer used "apparently," "some," and "cult or society."

Where is the bias in these statements?

> The filthy and hungover teenage runaway couldn't even recall where he had been the night before.
>
> The female witness was so hysterical, it was hard for me to understand her ranting.
>
> The suspect actually claimed he was at home watching TV on the night of the murder!
>
> I was able to reunite the cute and intelligent young girl with her worried parents, who were both doctors.

Fact Versus Inference

One common mistake that new officers tend to make involves drawing conclusions without realizing they are doing so. This happens when they confuse fact with **inference**.

For example, this statement may seem factual to you:

> The man we picked up for questioning was drunk.

However, this is actually an inference. You looked at the man's behaviour and concluded he was drunk. There is nothing in your statement that supports your conclusion.

Here is a factual statement:

> The man we picked up for questioning was slurring his words, smelled strongly of alcohol, and could not walk in a straight line.

You will be instructed (firmly, and many times!) that it is not your job as an officer to draw conclusions. That is the job of judges and juries. Your job is to simply state the facts as you observed them. Remember that the defence counsel is always on the lookout for ways to discredit officers' testimony as a way to get their clients released. If in your notes you conclude a suspect was drunk, and it later turns out he was suffering from a condition that mimics behaviours displayed by someone who is drunk, your reliability will be questioned. And perhaps a guilty person will go free.

(You may be thinking that the first statement would be preferable, as it is more concise than the second. Sometimes it will be necessary to sacrifice brevity to ensure all facts are presented.)

Making inferences is an important part of law enforcement work, as it can lead investigators to uncover new evidence and allow for cases to be solved. However, in report writing, it is necessary to include only observed, concrete facts and allow the reader to make the inferences.

Inference is a conclusion drawn by making assumptions.

EXERCISE 4 » Editing for Subjectivity

1. For each of the neutral words below, write one synonym that has a positive connotation and one synonym that has a negative connotation. The first one is completed for you as an example. If you get stuck, consult a thesaurus to find synonyms.

Neutral	Positive	Negative
house	home	hovel
child		
car		
senior		
crowd		
suspect		

2. Choose a music genre you feel strongly about (love it or hate it). Write one brief paragraph describing the genre as though you were asked to provide a neutral, informative entry for a wiki on music genres.

    Then write a second paragraph describing the genre in a way that clearly shows your bias.

3. Rewrite the following statements so that they become factual and avoid inferences. The first one is completed for you as an example.

    a. The homeowner was very angry.

    The homeowner was red in the face and yelling threats at her neighbour. She paced back and forth.

    b. The passenger at the customs security desk was acting suspiciously and clearly had something to hide.

    c. When I arrested the suspected shoplifter, she was definitely under the influence of a narcotic.

    d. An axe had been used to gain entrance through the back door of the convenience store.

    e. From my viewpoint in the courtroom, I could see that the witness was afraid to testify.

    f. I spoke to the youth and knew he was lying about his involvement in the armed robbery.

Supplementary Report of Constable Bias

I attended 15 North Street for a call to the home of an unstable mental patient who falsely believed that his boss was at his home looking in the window. It was obvious to me that there was nobody there. This mental person clearly makes up stuff so that he can justify planning to hurt his boss. I arrested the man and brought him to the hospital so they can decide what to do with him.

A videotape review captured the interaction:

Officers arrive and engage in a conversation with Cliff in calm voices.

Police: Hi Cliff, my name is Samantha and this is my partner, Shaun. We work with the Sudbury Police and we are here to try to help you.

Cliff: Oh, it's not good! I need them to go away! Not good at all!

Police: OK, it sounds to me like you are afraid of something. You are safe. We are not going to harm you and we are not going to let anyone else harm you either. Can you help us understand what it is that is upsetting you?

Cliff: Can't you see him? He is there at my window looking in and holding a hammer. Can't you hear the voices? I need to get to work and stop my boss before he gets back there and hurts everyone.

Police: OK, I understand you are hearing voices that are upsetting you. Are you hearing voices other than mine? What are they telling you?

Cliff: That I need to stop my boss, and the only way is to start a fire in his office. Can't you hear them? They are saying this is the only way to make it stop and help my work friends or he will hurt them too.

Police: OK, I need you to focus on my voice for right now and not listen to the other voices. OK?

Cliff: I will try but they are always there.

Police: The voices are always there? That must be very frustrating for you. Well, your dad is here with us, and we would all like you to help us get these voices to stop more permanently. Would you like that?

Cliff: Yes.

Police: OK, our first step is to go see Dr. Houghman. We can explain to him what the voices are saying, and he can help us work through it together. Would you like to do that?

Cliff: Yes, please help me.

Supplementary Report of Constable Unbias

A concerned family member, Robert, called 911 to get help for his adult son, Cliff, who has been diagnosed with schizophrenia. Robert advised that Cliff has been off of his medication for several days, causing the return of his delusions and auditory hallucinations.

I attended 15 North Street and spoke with a male who appeared to be experiencing a mental health crisis. I observed a male by the name of Cliff responding to voices of a person who was not present. While speaking with Cliff, he made several comments consistent with someone experiencing delusions and hallucinations. He stated that he could see his boss looking into his window and that his boss wanted to hurt him and his co-workers. I checked the window and there was nobody else present in the home or area. Cliff explained that he was hearing voices as well and that he believed the voices were warning him that the only way to stop his boss from hurting his co-workers was to set fire to his office. Cliff was apprehended under the *Mental Health Act* as he posed a danger to himself and others. He was brought to hospital for a psychiatric assessment.

Being Precise and Concise

The most important goal when writing in law enforcement is to tell the correct, exact, and complete story. **Precise** details are necessary to give a narrative that does not require interpretation or questions. Being precise also helps your writing be **concise**. Getting to the point quickly will allow your readers (judges, lawyers, complainants, media, and so on) to understand the particulars of the call, incident, or crime you are reporting on. Being concise also requires that you choose vocabulary that is simple and pared down.

Being Precise

Consider the difference between the following two statements:

> **The complainant was a civil servant who lived in the east end of Hamilton.**
>
> **Complainant Sarah Patrick, an accountant for Health Canada, lived on Kenilworth Avenue, Hamilton.**

The second statement is precise: It includes three important details, and has fewer words than the vague first statement.

Keep in mind that the notes you take are for record keeping. Your notes will often not be used in court for months or years after you took them. If you leave out important details, the odds are slim that you will be able to recall the missing details, or even the actual call.

Being Concise

Read this report excerpt:

> **Pursuant to the collection of pertinent assorted items of a contraband nature, namely two handguns, two kilos of white powder, and a large knife, the blade of which appeared to be covered in a red substance that I postulated was, indeed, blood, I vacated the first floor of the felonious dwelling and proceeded, with appropriate caution and vigilance, to ascend to the second level in order to ascertain that the premises above were indeed clear of suspicious persons and further items of a contraband nature. Having completed a thorough investigation, I expediently regained the ground floor and exited the felonious dwelling with aforementioned articles of contraband.**

What went through your head as you were reading this excerpt? (Maybe you thought, "Get to the point!" or "Stop hurting my brain with the fancy language!" or "This writer really thinks a lot of herself!")

Sometimes in an effort to write well, we fall into the trap of using elevated language and padding our writing with unnecessary words. This could be a habit learned in high school (as mentioned in the introduction to this chapter), when all writing tasks seemed to come with a minimum word count. The temptation was to write 700 great words for a 1,000-word essay, and then throw in 300 words of nonsense to achieve the word count.

Being **precise** means using as specific language as you can to effectively describe something.

Being **concise** means using as few words as possible to effectively describe something.

Here's a better version of that excerpt:

> **After I collected the contraband—two handguns, two kilos of white powder, and a large knife with a red substance on the blade—I went to the second level of the house to confirm there were no suspects or more contraband up there. The second floor was clear. I left the premises with the contraband articles.**

Keep in mind that your supervisors will be reading all of your notes and reports. They read volumes of reports daily to look for trends, assign casework, and plan special projects. They can either become impressed by concise factual reports and single individuals out for more challenging assignments, or they can be frustrated by poorly written reports and keep bad writers in low-level positions. No supervisor wants suspects avoiding conviction due to faulty paperwork.

EXERCISE 5 » Being Precise and Concise

1. Change the words or phrases in the left-hand column into more precise writing (you may need to invent details) or more concise writing (you may need to omit words). The first phrase is done for you, as an example.

red in colour	*red*
this day and age	
dialogue with the individual	
very tall	
sedan	
small in size	
subsequent to	
due to the fact	
in my personal opinion	
ascertain the location	
end result	
square in shape	

navigate the vehicle	
at the present time	
formulate a course of action	

2. Read the following request and then rewrite it, being as precise and concise as possible. Try to pare down the original to between 30 and 40 words.

    As a consequence of an ill-advised and spontaneously undertaken outing to a nearby aqua park, I inadvertently subjected my left scapula to an injury-promoting action when I attempted to navigate an aqua slide made for humans of small stature. As a result of my contact with said structure, my left scapula was pulled out of the socket in which it normally resides. As such, it is my opinion that I cannot, at the present time, operate my service vehicle. I respectfully request an assignment to a non-active position until such time as my scapula has regained its former capabilities. My medical professional has estimated that this return to full capacity should take place in approximately 14 days, or two weeks.

_____

_____

_____

_____

_____

Points of View: First Person, Second Person, and Third Person

There are three points of view you can write from:

1. First person: I, we, us, me
2. Second person: you, your, yours
3. Third person: he/she, they, them, her/him, hers/his

Choosing the appropriate point of view to write from depends upon the situation.

Points of View and Their Uses

Using the first person gives a clear picture of who did what, and *most* Canadian law enforcement services, including security, police, border patrol, and bylaw require officers to complete notebook entries and reports using the first person. However, there are some law enforcement services that require officers to complete all of their writing in the third person (e.g., "This officer then questioned the victim" or "This writer then left the scene to report to headquarters"). It's important for you to know the differences in the three points of view, but you will be informed of your service's standard once you are hired on.

The following table summarizes the three main points of view and how they're used.

Perspective	Uses	Examples
First person: Writing from your own point of view (I, me)	Reporting information Recording first-hand experience	I correctly identified the suspect from the lineup. I gave the complainant my business card. At the station, the victim gave me his complete statement.
Second person: Writing by addressing the reader (you)	Giving instructions Writing persuasively	To get to the police station, you need to take the Queensway east to Elgin Street. You must wear a bike helmet that is fastened correctly. You will benefit from hiring two police officers as security for your event.
Third person: Writing that describes thoughts, observations, or actions from an outsider's perspective (they, her)	Recounting an event or information told to you by another News writing Fiction writing	The witness then described her attacker as very tall and completely bald. The passengers were taken to hospital where they were treated for their injuries. He claimed that the contraband was not his.

Crown briefs are written in the third person. (The Crown brief is the case summary sent to the Crown attorney's office when the police are ready to present a completed case for trial.) These summaries are the result of complex investigations involving many officers (often generated by more than one service) and spanning months and perhaps years of many individual interviews, actions, and investigations. It would be impossible to use *I* or *we* in the Crown brief narrative. For other law enforcement agencies, culminating reports would also be written in the third person for the same reason. Crown briefs and culminating reports would be accompanied by all of the supporting reports and other documents that would have been written throughout the investigation. These, usually written in the first person, will identify individual officers and investigators.

EXERCISE 6 » Changing Points of View

1. Rewrite the following paragraph into the first person point of view.

   Officer Dylan Johnston was able to interview the witness about the accident. He gave the witness his card in case the witness could remember anything else she wanted to tell Officer Johnston regarding the incident. He then approached the detained suspect to question her. The suspect did not cooperate with Officer Johnston and refused to talk. Officer Johnston then read the suspect her rights and arrested her. He then transported the suspect to the police station.

2. Rewrite the following paragraph into the second person point of view.

   When considering safety in the home, one should research alarm systems to determine the correct one to suit one's budget and security needs. One should also consider investing in a good outdoor lighting system that one can easily set up and maintain. As well, people should put interior lights on timers, so it looks as though they are home when they are out. They could also consider buying a dog.

3. Rewrite the following paragraph into the third person point of view.

We completed surveillance of the pub and concluded we needed two undercover officers for the operation. I was detailed to begin work as a part-time bartender, and my colleague Sarah Campbell would become a regular customer. We estimated that it would take us four to six weeks to confirm the bar was serving underage clients from the university on a regular basis.

Active Voice and Passive Voice

The terms *active voice* and *passive voice* can be misleading because neither is associated with action or passivity. Rather, writing in the active voice requires putting the actor (or doer) into the sentence. Writing in the passive voice requires leaving the actor (doer) out of the sentence.

Consider the following examples:

> **Active voice: I was able to complete the paperwork and submit it to my sergeant by the deadline.**
>
> **Passive voice: The paperwork was completed and submitted by the deadline.**

Both the active and passive voices have their uses. For the most part, we write in the active voice, and this is particularly true of law enforcement writing, where it is critical to give all information possible.

Passive writing is mostly used in the scientific community in the preparation of lab reports and journals of scientific findings. In science, all actions must be strictly monitored and clinical procedures must follow rigorous protocols. A stronger measure of objectivity—and a smaller margin for error—can be suggested by eliminating any evidence of individual human action. Consider this lab report excerpt:

> **The beaker of isotopes was then tested for foreign substances. The beaker was determined to be uncontaminated. It was determined that the experiment could continue as planned.**

The reader does not know who tested the beaker or who determined the experiment could continue. This may seem odd to you if you haven't worked in a lab, yet this style of passive writing is required for scientists.

But this is the opposite of what is required for law enforcement writing. Law enforcement involves human interaction—lots of it. At every stage of reporting, you will be required to be clear about who did what to whom. For example, the following would be unacceptable to write in an airport security report:

> **The suspicious briefcase was examined. It was determined that it contained neither contraband nor explosives.**

What if the investigator did a shoddy job, and the case did contain contraband in the lining, which hadn't been checked? What if the investigator missed a hollowed-out cavity, which turned out to be hiding a small explosive device that detonated and injured two people? We would want to talk to the investigator, and we would need her name in order to do that.

To change a passive sentence into an active sentence, you simply need to make sure you have an actor (doer) for any action in the sentence.

Passive: The results of the Glock ballistics testing were then compared against the results of the Sig-Sauer ballistics testing.

Active: I compared the results of the Glock ballistics testing against the results of the Sig-Sauer ballistics testing.

Passive: The coffee shop was under surveillance from September 20 to October 4. During that time, three deliveries from the suspect white van were observed.

Active: Officer Ahmed surveilled the coffee shop from September 20 to October 4. During that time, Officer Ahmed observed three deliveries from the suspect white van.

There is one more step for creating active sentences: Remove *was* or *were* from your writing and put the actor (doer) at the beginning of the sentence. For example, you can change this passive sentence:

The abandoned puppies were removed to a safe location.

Into an active sentence:

The abandoned puppies were removed to a safe location by Officer Wilson.

But a better and more efficient active sentence would be:

Officer Wilson removed the abandoned puppies to a safe location.

EXERCISE 7 » Writing in the Active Voice

Change the following sentences so they are written in the active voice. You will need to add pronouns and names.

1. The visiting officers were briefed at roll call.

   _____

2. The fire victims were asked for their statements.

   _____

3. After the suspect was detained in the bookstore, he was asked to give his statement.

   _____

4. Upon their arrival at the multi-vehicle collision, firefighters were directed to the location of a Ford pickup truck, which contained a trapped and unconscious driver.

   _____

5. After investigation, it was determined that it was safe for the homeowner to enter his house to retrieve his phone and car keys.

   _____

6. A restraint was performed on the hallucinating and violent individual.

7. The sergeant was asked to turn in his badge and gun pending an internal investigation into his actions.

8. There were many bystanders adding confusion to the scene, so they were asked to disperse.

9. At the border, the driver of the tour bus was ordered to pull over so that the passports of the passengers could be checked.

10. The homeowners were cautioned that they were breaking the noise bylaw and could be fined if the noise continued.

EXERCISE 8 » Putting It All Together

Rewrite the following report excerpts so that they are objective and contain no slang, clichés, or jargon. Edit for extraneous information to ensure that the excerpt is precise and concise, and make sure the active voice and first person are used. Note: Your improved versions of each of these excerpts should be at least one-third shorter than the originals.

1. At approximately 0230 hrs on Friday, November 4, this officer booked it to a 10-32 at Gage Park. I was really flying. When this officer got to the scene, it was a zoo. A white chick was yelling at a homeless guy who was lying on the ground. Two old ladies were also yelling at the dude. I pulled the woman over to the side and asked her what was going down. Turns out the guy wasn't homeless, he just looked it. According to the chick, he had stolen her purse. She chased after him and jumped on him. He went down and screamed that she had broken his ankle. The old grannies said they saw the whole thing, and it was just like the girl said. The dude was questioned. He refused to give his handle and had no ID on him. When I sat him up, I saw a cell and a wallet under him. The ID in the wallet confirmed that the woman was the owner. The dude told me he was minding his own business when he saw that the lady had dropped her purse. He then told me, "This is what you get for being a good Samaritan. I was trying to return the blasted thing when she attacked me!" The bad guy was then arrested, read the riot act, and taken to Northeast Division Station for processing.

2. On Saturday, February 13, at the Cornwall Canadian/American border crossing, I asked the owner of an old beater to pull over for a search. A BOLO had come in just 20 minutes earlier for a gold 2001 Chevy Montana with Florida plates, suspected of transporting an illegal handgun into Canada. The guy gave me the finger as he pulled into the search area. Charming. Buddy slowly got out of the car and glared at me. As if that would help. I took the guy into the office to be watched while I inspected the van. I performed a thorough search of the back and it was clean. No joy there. The driver's side front seat was searched and a handgun was found under the seat. Jackpot! I radioed my find to the office and requested back up and the dog. May as well be thorough. No other contraband was found.

_____

_____

_____

3. On Thursday, August 11, I was checking for expired parking meters on the north side of Front Street West. I was minding my own business when an angry woman grabbed my arm and yelled, "Hey, my meter just expired now. I'm here on time. I timed it exactly. You cannot ticket me. Take this back!" She shoved a ticket in my face and nearly gave me a paper cut. It was for a white 2013 Beemer sedan I had just papered. I told the crazy lady she had better calm down. I told her my name and badge number were on the ticket if she wanted to waste the court's time and fight the ticket. But I knew my ticket was righteous. I proceeded to ignore the civilian and moved up the street. The nutjob then proceeded to spit on my car and run back to her land yacht. She peeled out going east on Front Street. I radioed dispatch to call the car in to the cops.

_____

_____

_____

4. On Sunday, June 26, I was on duty at the Glenhurst Transit Station. At approximately 1500 hrs, I was approached by two street bums. The female, who seemed to have no teeth, claimed her bag had been stolen by a small hairy alien. Seriously. The male character backed her up, and said their Presto passes had been in the bag and they no longer had a way to get home. I felt sorry for the two of them, so I did a quick search of the station. No hairy aliens. The five passengers waiting for a northbound bus were questioned to see if any had seen the theft. None had seen anything. Two other people, a nicely dressed couple in their 40s waiting for a southbound bus, were also questioned. The woman told me she did hear a shout coming from the far end of the southbound platform, but when she looked that way, she did not see anyone. The male said he had seen and heard nothing unusual. I went back to the homeless folks. They looked so hopeful. I gave each of them a day pass and told them to hold on to the passes carefully. The old girl actually hugged me.

_____

_____

_____

CHAPTER SUMMARY

After completing five chapters of this text, it may seem to you by now that there is an overwhelming number of elements you must be mindful of when writing for the law enforcement profession. While it is true that law enforcement writing must meet a very high standard, with practice you will soon develop your own excellent report-writing style. As well, recruits in all law enforcement professions have mentors assigned to them. You can be sure that your mentors will regularly review your notes and reports and give you guidance as needed.

These tips will help you develop strong report-writing habits even before you begin your law enforcement career:

1. Consider regularly writing reports about events, incidents, and arguments you witness or are involved in. After taking notes, put the notes away for a few days. Then pull out the notes and examine them. Do they contain any errors in spelling and grammar? Are they free of slang, jargon, and clichés? Are they objective, precise, and concise? If not, what errors do you tend to make? (It would be a good idea to destroy these practice notes after you've reviewed them.)

2. Regularly read Canadian law enforcement periodicals such as *Blue Line*, *Let's Talk*, or the *Canadian Journal of Police and Security Services*. These periodicals often include sections reporting on cases or ongoing investigations. If you can afford it, subscribe to one or two. You can also check out your school and municipal libraries for copies.

3. Be conscientious in your completion of the writing exercises in this text. Do extra work by finishing even the exercises not assigned to you by your instructor.

4. Ask any law enforcement professionals you know about their report-writing styles and any tips they might have for you. In some cases, it may be possible for you to see examples of the reports they've written.

KEY TERMS

acronym, 107
concise, 113
inference, 110
lexicon, 106
precise, 113

REVIEW AND REFLECTION QUESTIONS

1. How do slang, clichés, and jargon undermine the message in a piece of writing?

_____

_____

2. How does bias affect a report?

_____

_____

3. If a poorly written report is handed in to a superior, what could it say about the writer?

_____

_____

4. What are the benefits to you of becoming an excellent report writer?

_____

_____

5. Reflect on your current writing style. Identify one or two errors discussed in this chapter that you identified most with.

_____

_____

6 Emails, Memoranda, and Letters

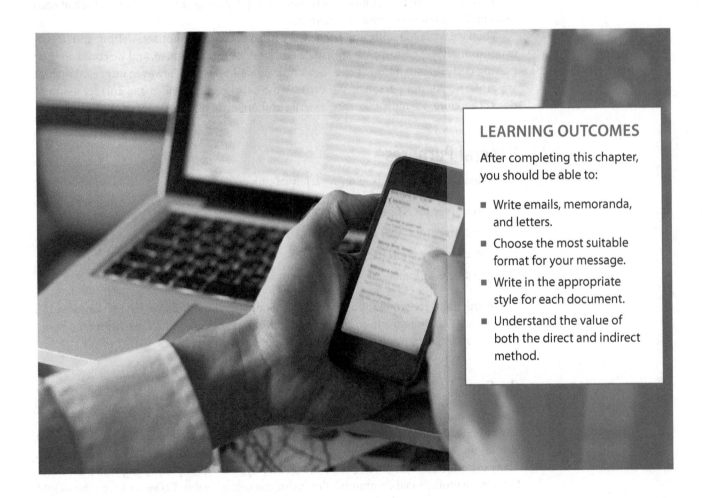

Introduction

There are three types of documents used for general correspondence in a professional setting: emails, memoranda, and letters. Although they share important general principles, each has a different purpose, format, and style.

Today, most professional written communication is exchanged electronically using email. In many ways it has replaced the traditional **memo** and letter. Traditionally, the memorandum (*memo* for short) is an informal written statement, usually brief, that is used for communicating within an organization and that may be consulted in the future or used as a memory aid. The letter is used for correspondence sent outside the organization. Letters give a sense of formality to your message. Email allows you to choose between these formats and styles when you deliver your message electronically.

Although we all write and receive emails and letters, the focus of this chapter is not on how you write them for family, friends, and acquaintances, or on the more specific cover letter you may write to accompany a resumé. The purpose of this chapter is to look at each as it applies to law enforcement situations.

When we write to family and friends, we focus on quick responses, writing and organizing our messages casually. We anticipate quick responses from them, and we count on their making correct assumptions since they know us well. At work, however, our relationships are professional, not personal. We can't assume that readers will make correct assumptions. Therefore, we must take care to write and organize our messages carefully.

General Purposes

These documents can be used for a variety of purposes:

- to convey messages to large groups
- to convey messages to individuals
- to convey complicated information
- to create a permanent record

Regardless of its original purpose, your document should always be written with the expectation that it may be used later as a source of information. Much like the memo book, it can be an important record of past events and circumstances.

On Social Media

Law enforcement agencies reach out to the public using various social media strategies. The website of your local police force will likely contain an embedded Twitter account, a blog composed by the chief, and other innovative strategies for general communication. Many experiments with social media are underway in an attempt to engage the public and to improve professional communication using the digital realm. However, given the weight of the written word in the legal system, social media is generally used only by specifically designated officers sending approved messages. If you are a good communicator, you may aim at taking on these responsibilities once you're hired. Learn to compose clear, concise, and accurate messages using the traditional forms of writing.

A **memo**, short for *memorandum*, is an informal written statement, usually brief and used for communicating within an organization. Today, the memo format is used when sending email. Also note that the memo format is now used for short informal reports containing headings, tables, and more.

Emails

Specific Purposes

You can use email to

- send messages within an organization
- send messages outside an organization
- send memos or letters
- send attached files such as formal letters, reports, and other electronic files.

Email is a fast and convenient method of delivering documents. It's easy to create copies of your messages for others and to attach other files to your messages. It also provides a permanent record of statements, reports, and agreements because electronic documents are always recoverable. This fact means that email is often used to ensure accountability—it's easy to check the history and details of email exchanges. Furthermore, email is discoverable in the case of a lawsuit. Your messages may be entered into court as evidence.

For these reasons, avoid the temptation to "dash off" a quick email you may later regret. Remember, once you send your message, you can't retrieve it. For example, you want to avoid "firing off" replies written in an emotional state. Such messages can ruin relationships.

One advantage of email systems is that they generally contain a "Drafts" folder for incomplete messages. Use this to your advantage. Save email messages you write in the "Drafts" folder for a second look before you send them; this way, you can consider your message and minimize unexpected consequences. Separate the writing stage from the sending stage for important messages.

Is That Email Necessary?

Before you compose your message, consider whether it is really needed, or whether your information might be transmitted just as effectively by a personal interview or a telephone call. We must consider that busy people tend to get flooded with electronic messages today. Furthermore, keep in mind that email creates a permanent record that may not be called for.

Format

The basic email format is reproduced on the following page.

Style

There are some important style points to consider when sending email correspondence.

Headings

- *To:* This section contains the receiver's email address.
- *Cc: Cc* stands for *carbon copy*. This section contains the email addresses of secondary recipients—others you wish to copy on the message. These addresses are visible to everyone receiving the message.

Send	Save as Draft	Add Attachments	Delete

To:	
Cc:	
Bcc:	
Subject:	
Attachments:	

Salutation

Body

Closing

- *Bcc:* Bcc stands for *blind carbon copy*. This section contains the email addresses of other recipients whose email addresses are invisible to everyone receiving the message. Generally, this function is used for batch messages and offers privacy protection.
- *Subject:* The subject line does not have to be a complete sentence. You'll see in the discussion of formats later in this chapter that the subject line for the **direct order** refers specifically to your topic, but the subject line for the **indirect order** is more general in nature. For instance, in the case of a direct order that concerns the time and place of a staff holiday party, your subject line might be as follows:

Subject: **C Division holiday party**

However, you might use the indirect order to request payroll deductions for a charitable cause. Your subject line might be as follows:

Subject: **United Way campaign**

- *Attachments:* This section displays any files attached to the message. For formal messages, attach a letter to the email, and use a simple memo in the body to request

---

A **direct order** is a writing structure used to convey positive or neutral messages to the reader, such as good news or a request for information.

An **indirect order** is a writing structure used to convey unwelcome news that will likely be met with resistance or negativity. It is also appropriate in cases where you expect a lack of interest. The indirect order is a "bad news approach."

that the reader open the **attachment**. Review "Letters," later in this chapter, for further details.

Salutation

Because the *To:* and *From:* fields of an email can't contain title and rank, include this information at the beginning of your message. This approach is especially important when writing to your superiors. For example, you can begin your message with "Staff Sgt. Smith," and continue with your message.

Body

Write using complete sentences and organized paragraphs. Choose the direct order approach for routine or good news messages, and the indirect order approach for bad news or persuasive messages. Review "Direct and Indirect Order," later in this chapter, for details.

Closing

End your email message by typing your title, name, and division or branch at the bottom of the message. Most email software packages offer a simple way to create an electronic signature that automatically inserts this **closing** material into your message.

Replying

This function enters the email address of the sender, and it generally repeats the subject line of the original message. You may choose to change the subject line if you decide your message varies significantly from the original conversation.

A Word of Warning

When replying to an email message, be careful that you choose the correct button; using the Reply All button will send your message to all the addresses inserted into the original email—including addresses in the *Cc:* section. Use the Reply button if you want to send your response only to the address in the *To:* section of the original message. It is common for people to mistake these two functions, which often leads to unintended consequences. Unless you want everyone to read your reply, be careful to check the address sections of your message.

Carefully consider the implications of sending your email before hitting the Send button. It's particularly easy to "fire off" a quick response you may later regret, especially when you have received a hostile message or unwelcome news.

Context and Clarity

To avoid confusion when replying to a message, quote the original document to provide context. For example, rather than simply typing "Yes" in response to a question, include the original message or line to which you are responding, and respond using a complete sentence so that your meaning is clear:

An **attachment** is a document sent with your written communication. Indicate the number of attachments in your email or letter.

In the **closing** of email and memos, type your title, name, and division; in letters, use a complimentary close such as "Yours truly" or "Sincerely."

> Did you find someone to help you with the report, or would you like to meet to discuss the specifics?
>
> Yes, I met Officer Davies and completed the report. I don't think a meeting is necessary. I'll put the report on your desk tomorrow.

Formatting and Attaching Documents

Because people use a variety of software platforms to receive electronic messages, it is best to keep formatting simple. Format your message so that the person with the simplest email setup will have no problems understanding your message.

The same idea applies to attachments. Make sure the receiver can open your attachment. Use well-accepted formats and avoid sending attachments saved in cutting-edge versions of programs unless you know in advance that the receiver can read the attachment.

Memoranda

Specific Purposes

You can use the memo format to

- announce meetings
- discuss meeting agendas
- describe organizational policies or changes in policies
- announce changes to external policies, such as amendments to the *Criminal Code*
- announce changes in organizational structure
- announce social functions
- convey any other information that employees need to know.

Format

The basic memo format is as follows:

Letterhead

Memorandum

To: _____

From: _____

Date: _____

Subject: _____

_____

Body

_____

Initials or signature

Style

Memos can be either formal or informal, depending on their intended use. But a single set of guidelines applies to all cases.

Headings

It is customary and courteous to include the title of the person to whom a memo is addressed as well as your own title or rank. This rule applies regardless of whether the person you're addressing is of higher or lower rank than yourself.

To:	**Staff Sgt. G. DiFlorio, C Division**
From:	**Cst. H. Sheckley, 0372, C Division**

or

To:	**Traffic Branch, C Division**
From:	**Staff Sgt. G. DiFlorio, C Division**

Note that there is no salutation ("Dear Staff Sgt. DiFlorio").

Subject Line

The subject line indicates the content of the message, as discussed above (see "Emails").

Closing

For print memos, initial or sign your memo after you proofread it, for the following reasons:

- It personalizes the memo and indicates to the reader that you care about the topic.
- It signifies to the reader that you are responsible for its contents and for any errors it may contain.
- It verifies to the reader that the memo was sent with your authorization.

Note that there is no complimentary closing (e.g., "Yours truly," "Sincerely,") in a memo.

Letters

Specific Purposes

Email is making the traditional print letter less common; these days, you are more likely to find letters attached to email rather than delivered in hardcopy. However, in law enforcement, letters remain an important form of communication. They are written to convey information, to deal with complaints, and to request information. Letters convey a sense of formality and importance. Your letters are more likely to be answered completely and promptly if you follow commonly accepted practices for letter writing and adopt the philosophy of the "Three Cs": Be *clear*, *concise*, and *courteous*.

Format

The basic business letter format is reproduced in outline form in the box below.

Letterhead
Date
Receiver's name and address
Salutation
Body
Complimentary closing

Today, letters are usually written in the full block style using open punctuation (see Figure 6.1). Variations of style do exist. You will see the traditional style with closed punctuation (Figure 6.2), and a modified block style with open punctuation (Figure 6.3).

Style

As you are writing letters, there are a few matters of style that should be taken into consideration.

Headings

Avoid abbreviations such as "St." for "Street," not only in your headings but also in other parts of your letter (with the exception of titles such as "Dr." for "Doctor" in your salutation). Abbreviations indicate informality on your part, or a desire to get through the letter quickly. Be sure to include your postal code in the return address (if you are not using letterhead) so that a return letter can be addressed correctly.

Salutation

You can use the receiver's given name or one of a number of courtesy titles (Ms., Miss, Mrs., and Mr.) in the **salutation**. Much will depend on how the person wishes to be addressed. For instance, if you receive a letter signed "Mrs. Edna Jones," send a reply to "Mrs. Edna Jones." Otherwise, "Ms." is now the standard courtesy title for women. When addressing both men and women, it may be easier to use the person's full name (e.g., "Dear Edna Jones") along with the person's business title and department, if you know it, in the inside address. Avoid "Dear Sir or Madam" or "Ladies and Gentlemen."

Closing

Use a neutral closing in your letter, such as "Yours truly" or "Sincerely," and note that the first letter of the second word is not capitalized.

A **salutation** is a greeting at the beginning of your communication. Use the receiver's given name and title, unless it is impossible to do so, such as in the automatic fields in email software.

FIGURE 6.1   Full Block Style with Open Punctuation

MITCHELL'S BAY POLICE SERVICE
1237 Chieu Street
Mitchell's Bay, Ontario N0P 1V0

16 November 2017

Dr. Geraldine Kehnon
22 Cherry Lane
Mitchell's Bay, Ontario N0P 1V0

Dear Dr. Geraldine Kehnon

XXX XXXXXXXXXXXXX XXXXX XXXXXXXXXXX XXXXXX XXXXX XXXXX
XXXXXXXXXXXX.

XXX XXXXXXXXXXXXX XXXXX XXXXXXXXXXX XXXXXX XXXXX XXXXX
XXXXXXXXXXXX. XXX XXXXXXXXXXXXX XXXXX XXXXXXXXXXX XXXXXXX
XXXXX XXXXX XXXXXXXXXXXX.

XXX XXXXXXXXXXXXX XXXXX XXXXXXXXXXX XXXXXX XXXXX XXXXX
XXXXXXXXXXXX.

XXX XXXXXXXXXXXXX XXXXX XXXXXXXXXXX XXXXXX XXXXX XXXXX
XXXXXXXXXXXX.

Sincerely

Cst. J. Allison
Community Relations

Note: No punctuation is used with the date, receiver, salutation, and complimentary closing. Use punctuation within the text and at the ends of sentences. Do not indent paragraphs.

FIGURE 6.2 Traditional Style with Closed Punctuation

MITCHELL'S BAY POLICE SERVICE
1237 Chieu Street
Mitchell's Bay, Ontario N0P 1V0

November 16, 2017

Dr. Geraldine Kehnon
22 Cherry Lane
Mitchell's Bay, Ontario N0P 1V0

Dear Dr. Geraldine Kehnon,

    XXX XXXXXXXXXXXXXX XXXXX XXXXXXXXXXX XXXXXXX XXXXXX XXXXX XXXXXXXXXXXXX.

    XXX XXXXXXXXXXXXXX XXXXX XXXXXXXXXXX XXXXXXX XXXXXX XXXXX XXXXXXXXXXXXX. XXX XXXXXXXXXXXXXX XXXXX XXXXXXXXXXX XXXXXXX XXXXXX XXXXX XXXXXXXXXXXX.

    XXX XXXXXXXXXXXXXX XXXXX XXXXXXXXXXX XXXXXXX XXXXXX XXXXX XXXXXXXXXXXXX.

    XXX XXXXXXXXXXXXXX XXXXX XXXXXXXXXXX XXXXXXX XXXXXX XXXXX XXXXXXXXXXXXX.

Sincerely,

Cst. J. Allison
Community Relations

Note: Use punctuation between items within a line (the date, for example) and within the body of the letter. End the salutation and the complimentary closing with a comma, and indent paragraphs.

FIGURE 6.3 Modified Block Style with Modified Open Punctuation

MITCHELL'S BAY POLICE SERVICE
1237 Chieu Street
Mitchell's Bay, Ontario N0P 1V0

November 16, 2017

Dr. Geraldine Kehnon
22 Cherry Lane
Mitchell's Bay, Ontario N0P 1V0

Dear Dr. Geraldine Kehnon:

XXX XXXXXXXXXXXXXX XXXXXX XXXXXXXXXXXX XXXXXXX XXXXXX XXXXX
XXXXXXXXXXXXX.

XXX XXXXXXXXXXXXXX XXXXXX XXXXXXXXXXXX XXXXXXX XXXXXX XXXXX
XXXXXXXXXXXXX. XXX XXXXXXXXXXXXXX XXXXXX XXXXXXXXXXXX XXXXXXX
XXXXXX XXXXX XXXXXXXXXXXX.

XXX XXXXXXXXXXXXXX XXXXXX XXXXXXXXXXXX XXXXXXX XXXXXX XXXXX
XXXXXXXXXXXXX.

XXX XXXXXXXXXXXXXX XXXXXX XXXXXXXXXXXX XXXXXXX XXXXXX XXXXX
XXXXXXXXXXXXX.

Sincerely,

Cst. J. Allison
Community Relations

Note: Use punctuation between items (such as city and province) within a line and within the body of the letter. End the salutation with a colon, and end the complimentary closing with a comma. Do not indent paragraphs.

General Principles for Correspondence

Regardless of what type of communication you choose to use, keep in mind the importance of the following elements.

Content

Organize your material. You should limit your messages to one topic. If the information in your message is accurate, complete, and free from confusing or irrelevant detail, the recipient will respond more quickly. If you have two topics to discuss, send two documents.

Tone

Adopt a courteous, businesslike tone, even if you are writing an informal memo. The overall impression created by your document is important. A courteous tone will elicit a much quicker response than will a threatening or sarcastic tone.

Readability

The ease and speed with which your reader can grasp the main points and supporting details of your message will often determine how the message is handled. Check carefully for errors; spelling and grammar mistakes are unacceptable.

Spell Checks

Most email and word processing systems include a spell-checking program. This review function is useful for pointing out potential errors. The review feature allows you to choose from suggestions for each potential error. However, avoid automatic correction because this process often introduces mistakes. Computers can't grasp the context of law enforcement, and must be trained to recognize specialized language such as acronyms. If you use the spell-check feature, always read over your work yourself to catch errors that the spell checker itself may have created.

Writing Strategies

The "You" Approach

Point out the advantages for the reader(s) in doing what is requested, or make it clear why the information in the written communication is important to those being addressed. Consider your reader's point of view. Don't tell the reader what he or she can do for you; tell readers what you can do for them.

Direct and Indirect Order

Depending on your purpose, your email, memo, or letter will take one of two forms: direct order or indirect order.

Direct Order

The direct order memo (see Figure 6.4 for an example) is a short, three-section memo that conveys good news or a neutral message to a group, and usually requests information. You expect a positive, or at least a neutral, response to your message. The format for this type of memo is as follows:

- *Section 1*: State the news, the reason for the request, or the information you are conveying.
- *Section 2*: Explain the reasons for your position in section 1, in list form if possible.
- *Section 3*: Write a goodwill closing paragraph, providing any details necessary, requesting additional information, or requesting action.

Indirect Order

The indirect order memo (see Figure 6.5 for an example) is a longer, four-section memo that is primarily used to convey unwelcome news that will likely be met with resistance or negativity. It is also appropriate in cases where you expect a lack of interest in your message. This type of memo takes the "bad news approach."

FIGURE 6.4   Direct Order Memo

MITCHELL'S BAY POLICE SERVICE

Memorandum

To: Officers of C Division

From: Staff Sgt. G. DiFlorio, C Division

Date: 18 November 2017

Subject: Holiday schedule 2017

The holiday schedule for 2017 is being prepared. All officers are requested to submit their holiday requests by 1 December 2017.

Submitting your requests on time

1. increases the chances we will be able to provide you with the days off you requested
2. allows us to inform you promptly should we not be able to provide you with any of the days off you requested.

Send your requests to DiFlorio@copmail.ca. Your cooperation is greatly appreciated.

—GD

FIGURE 6.5   Indirect Order Memo

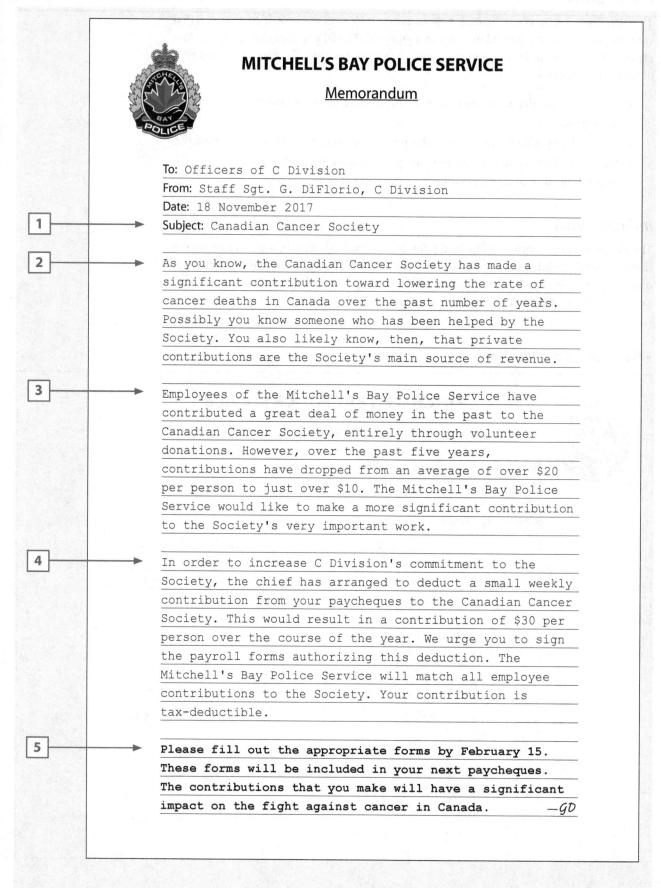

MITCHELL'S BAY POLICE SERVICE

Memorandum

To: Officers of C Division
From: Staff Sgt. G. DiFlorio, C Division
Date: 18 November 2017

1 → **Subject:** Canadian Cancer Society

2 → As you know, the Canadian Cancer Society has made a significant contribution toward lowering the rate of cancer deaths in Canada over the past number of years. Possibly you know someone who has been helped by the Society. You also likely know, then, that private contributions are the Society's main source of revenue.

3 → Employees of the Mitchell's Bay Police Service have contributed a great deal of money in the past to the Canadian Cancer Society, entirely through volunteer donations. However, over the past five years, contributions have dropped from an average of over $20 per person to just over $10. The Mitchell's Bay Police Service would like to make a more significant contribution to the Society's very important work.

4 → In order to increase C Division's commitment to the Society, the chief has arranged to deduct a small weekly contribution from your paycheques to the Canadian Cancer Society. This would result in a contribution of $30 per person over the course of the year. We urge you to sign the payroll forms authorizing this deduction. The Mitchell's Bay Police Service will match all employee contributions to the Society. Your contribution is tax-deductible.

5 → **Please fill out the appropriate forms by February 15. These forms will be included in your next paycheques. The contributions that you make will have a significant impact on the fight against cancer in Canada.** —GD

Unlike the direct order memo, the indirect order memo states the point of the memo in the third section. Also, the subject line is of a more general nature because a more specific indicator of the memo's contents might cause readers to discard it unread. The format for this type of memo is as follows:

- *Section 1*: Write a goodwill opening, which may introduce the general subject of your memo, but doesn't yet specify a request, refusal, or complaint.
- *Section 2*: Give detailed reasons for the message to follow, but don't yet convey it. You may imply it.
- *Section 3*: State your request, refusal, or complaint, showing (if possible) how your message is for the benefit of the reader.
- *Section 4*: Write a goodwill closing, where you offer alternatives to what you have suggested, or politely request that some action be taken.

Note that the sections may consist of more than one paragraph.

Consider the following features of the indirect order memo shown in Figure 6.5:

1. There is no mention made of payroll deductions or contributions in the subject line. There is merely a general reference to the Canadian Cancer Society (CCS).

2. The first section of the memo talks about the good works of the CCS and, by reminding readers that the CCS relies on voluntary contributions, hints that a request is coming.

3. The second section gives detailed reasons for the request that follows in section 3. It discusses the fact that contributions from the police service have fallen off (possibly a bit of guilt is being applied here), reviews the service's history of generosity, and indicates that it's time to be generous again.

4. The third section contains the request. The emphasis here is on the following facts:
   a. The amount requested is small.
   b. Management will handle all the administrative work.
   c. The police service will match contributions.
   d. The contributions are tax-deductible.

5. The fourth section contains a final goodwill gesture and makes the following points:
   a. The deadline is far enough away that employees will have time to give the matter some thought.
   b. Forms will be provided, making it easy for employees to respond.
   c. The significance of the contribution is appreciated.

Staff Sergeant DiFlorio could have included other things in this memo in order to persuade employees to contribute to the Canadian Cancer Society, such as the fact that the CCS may offer a free "quit smoking" campaign. He might have used a specific case study to show how the CCS has helped a particular individual. He might even have created a contest making all those who contribute eligible for a free trip. These would all be effective methods of overcoming resistance to the measures outlined in the memo.

Note that reports can also be written in memo or letter form.

Examples of the direct and indirect order letter are set out in Figures 6.6 and 6.7.

FIGURE 6.6 Direct Order Letter

MITCHELL'S BAY POLICE SERVICE
1237 Chieu Street
Mitchell's Bay, Ontario N0P 1V0

16 November 2017

Mori and Associates
Barristers and Solicitors
886 Lorente Avenue
Hamilton, Ontario L7P 3R5

Dear Harold Mori:

Re: Your file # 33465

I am responding to your request for information, our file 02-011.

Thank you for your payment of our fee for this information, which was received today. Your receipt and the records you requested are enclosed.

If you have any questions, please contact this office at 905-555-2652.

Sincerely,

PC D. Wedmark
Freedom of Information Branch

FIGURE 6.7   Indirect Order Letter

MITCHELL'S BAY POLICE SERVICE
1237 Chieu Street
Mitchell's Bay, Ontario N0P 1V0

16 November 2017

Mori and Associates
Barristers and Solicitors
886 Lorente Avenue
Hamilton, Ontario L7P 3R5

Dear Harold Mori:

Re: Your file # 33465

Thank you for your request for information regarding our file 02-011.

The *Freedom of Information Act* allows law enforcement agencies to release certain information to the public that will not materially harm the person or organization named in the information. Law enforcement agencies are unable to release information that will affect the prosecution of an ongoing criminal investigation, specifically if the person making the request has no direct link with either the Crown or the defence in a criminal matter, or is not a lawyer representing either the Crown or the accused.

Since your client cannot show a relationship to the matter under consideration, I must deny your request for information.

I am returning your payment for this service. Please contact me at 905-555-2652 if I can provide you with additional information.

Sincerely,

PC D. Wedmark
Freedom of Information Branch

EXERCISE 1 » Writing Emails and Memoranda

1. You are a constable with your local police service. During your time off, you volunteer as president of a club that provides recreational activities to disadvantaged children. You have decided to hold a fundraiser, and you would like your chief of police to be a guest speaker. The fundraiser will be held on February 1 next year, and numerous local athletes have already agreed to be speakers. The theme of the fundraiser is "Don't do time with crime." Write a memo to the chief, asking him or her to be a speaker. You will have to fill in some of the details, such as the location of the event, the time, and any other information that you feel might help convince the chief to participate.

2. As a first-year probationary inspector with your local customs service, you are the employee with the least seniority. Vacation schedules for next year have already been set, and you find that you're working the evening shift next New Year's Eve. However, family members from Newfoundland, including your mother, whom you haven't seen in five years, have decided to visit you for the holidays and plan to spend New Year's Eve at your home. Write a memo to your superior asking for the time off.

3. Assume that you are the personnel director of Deltex Security. Write an email to all employees, inviting them to a retirement party in honour of Antonia Morris. Antonia has worked for the company for 23 years, initially as a security officer, and now as the director of the company's mobile security units. The party will be held at the Holiday Inn on the 15th of next month. A cash bar will open at 7 p.m., followed by dinner at 7:30. Tickets cost $30 each, part of which will go toward a retirement gift for Antonia.

EXERCISE 2 » Writing Letters

1. You are applying for a job. Write a letter to your local police service, the Canada Border Services Agency, Corrections Canada, or a local private security firm to request application information. Obtain addresses from the Internet.

2. Write a letter to your local police service requesting permission for you and your class to view the service's facilities. Be sure to give the reason for your request, the number of people involved, the name of your instructor, and suggested dates for the visit.

3. Write a letter to your local police service complaining about cars speeding in front of your house and asking that a radar trap be placed there.

4. You have applied for a position both with the Canada Border Services Agency and with Corrections Canada, and you have been accepted by both agencies. Write an indirect order letter to one of the agencies, stating that you have decided not to accept its offer of employment. Write a direct order letter to the other agency that is offering you employment, accepting the offer.

CHAPTER SUMMARY

Emails, memoranda, and letters share important general principles, but each has a different purpose, format, and style. Email is the standard today, yet there is still a place for the traditional memo and letter. The memo format is appropriate for internal and informal communication whereas the letter format is appropriate for formal communication outside the workplace. The body of your message will appear either in the direct order or indirect order format, depending on your purpose. Be aware of accepted etiquette for correspondence. Whether conveying information to large groups or simply conveying information to an individual, keep in mind that professional correspondence differs from personal correspondence.

KEY TERMS

attachment, 127
closing, 127
direct order, 126
indirect order, 126
memo, 124
salutation, 130

REVIEW AND REFLECTION QUESTIONS

1. How is professional email different from personal email? What are the consequences of confusing these two approaches?

2. Today, special officers are designated to communicate using social media. Why? If all officers used it to communicate with the general public, what problems might it create for law enforcement? What problems might this create for the individual officer?

3. Are you aware of exciting innovations in digital communication within the law enforcement field? What opportunities do you see? What problems do you think these might bring?

7 Research Skills

LEARNING OUTCOMES

After completing this chapter, you should be able to:

- Use appropriate sources for your research papers.
- Take thorough research notes.
- Summarize effectively.
- Avoid plagiarism by using in-text citations and reference lists.

Introduction

While most of the writing you will do in your law enforcement career will be report-based, there will still be occasions where research is necessary, as in the following examples:

- You may be directed by your commanding officer to research crime trends or new enforcement methodologies for the purpose of creating a specialty unit that serves as an elder abuse task force.
- You may be tasked with developing a community outreach program on a topic such as bicycle safety in which you will use statistics and other information you research.
- You may be asked by your supervisor to put together a report on smuggling trends at North American borders for a training exercise for your colleagues.
- You may attend a provincial or national security conference and be asked to give a detailed report and presentation to your organization to share what you learned.

And of course, while you are a student at your current school and at future post-secondary institutions, you will write research papers and give researched presentations on a variety of topics.

Preparing ethical, good-quality research papers and presentations requires commitment to using appropriate sources and documenting those sources accurately. As well, you'll need to learn the skills of summarizing research material, as it is preferable to use direct quotes sparingly. And lastly, you will need to write in-text citations for all borrowed material and, at the end of your paper, include a reference list that credits all of your sources.

Using Appropriate and Credible Sources

Most people immediately turn to the Internet when they have to do research. The Internet is an excellent source for up-to-date and comprehensive information on just about any topic. The Internet is also an excellent source for erroneous and misleading information on just about any topic. So how do you weed out the poor sources from the excellent sources?

- Look at the ending of the web address. Is it .com, .ca, .edu, .gov, or .org? Addresses with .com are commercial websites. This means they could be hosted by anyone with an interest in the subject—from an informed, objective party (e.g., blogs) to someone with a vested interest in sharing their point of view (e.g., product advertisements). Use sources from .com addresses with caution and an awareness of possible subjectivity. Sources with an .edu ending are educational sources, and sources with .gov are U.S. government sources. (For government of Canada sources, look for the .gc.ca ending.) Both can be counted on to have up-to-date information that is well researched and well written. Be aware that bias can slip in to any piece of writing. Bias does not render a source useless: You just need to know it is there.
- Find the author(s) and dates posted of the sources you are considering using. Is there an author? Does the author list **credentials**? Has the site been updated? Does the source make reference to additional sources, and are these listed?

Credentials are qualifications that demonstrate a person has the appropriate background on a topic to give an opinion or argument about the topic with some authority.

- Before resorting to a general search engine such as Google, consult your school's library: This is the most efficient and foolproof method of finding excellent sources on your topic. One of the many roles that librarians and library technicians perform at your library is to put together databases of the resources that might be useful for students in the programs offered by your school. These databases are listed by subject matter, and each database contains hundreds of sources—print and electronic—that have been vetted by experts. Google and other search engines are so comprehensive they offer hundreds of thousands of sources per topic, which is daunting. Why weed through that when you can simply visit your library— online or in person? Try it; you'll make a librarian very happy—and find some excellent resources.

EXERCISE 1   »   Comparing Sources

1. Use Google to look up sources about Tasers. Find two sources that have opposing views about their safety and effectiveness. Who are the authors of each source? Does the bias make sense once you take note of the authors?

2. Choose a topic you are interested in or think you might need to learn about for one of your courses. Visit your school library's online site and investigate the databases for the topic. List three sources you think look promising for possible use in future assignments.

Note Taking

After you've identified as many relevant and appropriate sources as you can for your research paper, it's time to take notes. For each source, as you come across what looks like useful information, jot down—on an index card or in a notebook specifically designated for this task—information such as call numbers of books, titles, chapters, page references, names of journals, tables of contents, Internet addresses—in short, the names and locations of potentially useful material. This is the first step.

Next, go over your sources to collect facts. If you have accurately listed your sources the first time around, it won't be a problem retrieving them. Extract specific information, jotting down ideas, direct quotations, links to other sources, and any information that is relevant to your topic. You might want to summarize or write a **précis** of a newspaper article, journal article, or Internet article. Never lose track of your sources, because you must acknowledge them in your research paper. Failure to attribute the source of your material constitutes plagiarism.

For example, if you are writing a paper on police use of force, you might use an index card to take notes similar to the example in the box below. (A notebook is a good writing tool, but for papers, you might consider using large index cards. The benefit is that you can easily shuffle each card around as you decide on the format of your paper. You can also easily remove a card if you later decide it does not belong in your paper.)

A **précis** is similar to a summary. In a précis, you condense the original text significantly, while capturing its main points in a concise, precise way.

Side A of Index Card

Edward J. Hedican. "The Ipperwash Inquiry and the Tragic Death of Dudley George." *The Canadian Journal of Native Studies*, vol. XXVIII, no. 1, 2008, pages 159-174.

- "at approximately 9 p.m. the Ontario Provincial Police closed the roads leading to the park"
- see p. 164
- in campus library

Side B of Index Card

Article summary (see "Writing a Summary," below)

Put quotation marks around any material you've taken directly from the source. Later, when you're writing your paper, you'll know whether you've used the source directly or paraphrased or summarized it.

Once you have completed your notes, you're ready to begin writing an outline for your paper. The outline will help you determine which sources go where, and if you have enough information for each area.

Writing a Summary

Law enforcement officers frequently need to **summarize** material. Witness statements need to be reduced to essentials; the most important information from memo books must be selected and included in reports—the need for summaries is constant. A summary allows the reader to know the contents of an original piece of writing without having to read it in its entirety. In a profession where paperwork can be overwhelming and decisions often need to be made quickly, effective summaries are critical.

The summary writing you will do in your academic career will build your skills for the field.

The summary, which can also be called an abstract or a synopsis, teaches you three skills: to read carefully, to select wisely, and to write concisely. In the context of law enforcement, summarizing can help you not only with witness statements and reports but also when you need to take effective notes, to listen, or to describe an incident in the fewest possible words while conveying the maximum amount of information.

The purpose of the summary, then, is to condense a piece of writing into your own words. The summary gives the reader the main ideas from the original, so that he or she doesn't need to consult the primary source. Remember, a summary is written in *your own words*.

To condense an original piece of writing into a summary written in your own words, follow these guidelines:

1. *Read the document carefully several times (do not take notes at this point).* As you read, be sure you understand the thesis and recognize any bias in the original.

2. *Underline the main ideas.* Eliminate anything that is not essential to the meaning of the original.

Summarizing is capturing the main points of something larger in a briefer, concise way.

3. *Count the words in the original.* The summary should be about one-third or one-quarter the length of the original. It may consist of one sentence, one paragraph, or several paragraphs, depending on the length of the original. Do not use point form.

4. *Without looking at the original, write a draft summary.* Be sure that the essential points and intent of the original appear in the summary passage. As you write, keep in mind the following:

   a. Change direct speech to indirect speech.

   b. Write in the third person, if possible.

   c. Do not make critical comments or add information.

   d. Do not lift passages verbatim.

   e. Keep the proportions of the original in the summary. (That is, if an original has three main ideas, and the first idea takes up half of the document, that idea should also take up approximately half of your summary.)

   f. Identify and eliminate minor supporting details.

   g. Eliminate wordy expressions. For example, change *as a result of* to *because* and *in the end* to *finally.*

   h. Identify and eliminate unimportant modifiers such as *extremely*, *huge*, and *friendly.*

5. *Look again at the original.* Check that you

   a. haven't quoted from the original

   b. have covered all the main points

   c. have excluded all non-essential material

   d. haven't included your personal point of view.

6. *Edit your summary for spelling and grammar.*

EXERCISE 2 » Removing Wordy Expressions

Find single words to replace the following phrases:

1. conduct a discussion of _____

2. perform an analysis of _____

3. create a reduction in _____

4. make a discovery of _____

5. engage in the preparation of _____

6. give consideration to _____

7. make an assumption of _____

8. is of the opinion that _____

9. on account of the fact that _____

10. carry out an investigation of _____

Changing Direct Speech to Indirect Speech

Direct speech is the word-for-word (verbatim) reporting of what someone says.

> **As he was being escorted into the courtroom, the suspect shouted, "I'm innocent!"**

When you record direct speech, you put quotation marks around the person's exact words.

The general procedures for changing direct speech to indirect speech are set out below.

1. *Direct words become an indirect statement, question, or command.* Quotation marks are eliminated.

> *Direct*:   **"I finished writing the incident report yesterday," she said.**
> *Indirect*: **She said she had finished writing the incident report yesterday.**
>
> *Direct*:   **"Are you attending the use-of-force seminar?" he asked me.**
> *Indirect*: **He asked me if I was attending the use-of-force seminar.**

2. *Pronouns usually change from first to third person.* For example, *I* and *we* change to *he*, *she*, or *they*.

> *Direct*:   **The protesters could be heard chanting, "We want fair wages for fair work!"**
> *Indirect*: **The protesters could be heard chanting that they wanted fair wages for fair work.**

3. *Verbs in the present tense usually change to some form of the past tense.*

> *Direct*:   **"I won't speak until my lawyer gets here," the suspect told me.**
> *Indirect*: **The suspect told me she wouldn't speak until her lawyer got there.**

EXERCISE 3 »   Changing Direct Speech into Indirect Speech

Change the following into indirect speech:

1. "I refuse to testify against my fellow gang member!" shouted the defendant.

   _____

2. She then told the court the following: "I was hit from behind by what felt like a fist."

   _____

3. The entire platoon was surprised at roll call by the sergeant, who said, "There is to be absolutely no more overtime for the foreseeable future."

   _____

4. "Why not write the report now?" I asked.

   _____

5. The witness stated, "I saw the little boy kick the circus clown in the shin."

   _____

Counting Words

Your summary should contain one-third or one-quarter the number of words contained in the original. Count the words in the original, and then count the words in the completed summary. When counting words, observe the following rules:

1. Articles (*a*, *an*, *the*) count as one word.

2. Abbreviations count as one word.

3. Numbers count as one word.

4. Dates (23 October 2016) count as three words.

5. Compound words (e.g., *first-rate*) count as one word.

6. Words separated by a slash (e.g., *either/or*) count as one word.

7. Times (e.g., 7:10, 1430) count as one word.

Sample Summaries

Compare the following passage with the summarized version below it:

> We wish to acknowledge receipt of your letter of 22 September. We regret to inform you that we cannot fulfill your request at this point in time to bring a group of students to tour the city jail because the cell blocks are undergoing renovation. Within the next three months, we expect renovations to be complete and we will again allow civilians to visit the facility.
>
> We do not usually book appointments for tours this far in advance, but under the circumstances, if you are still interested in a tour when renovations are complete, we would be happy to book an appointment with you immediately. I enclose a brochure concerning the city's law enforcement agencies with pertinent telephone numbers.
>
> We hope that this arrangement will meet with your satisfaction.

▼

> Concerning your 22 September letter, we cannot meet your request since the cells are undergoing renovation and will not be ready for three months. We will, however, book an appointment for a student tour when renovations are complete. A brochure is enclosed for your information.

The following passage contains 160 words, the summary version below it has 54 words:

> Community outreach officers are able to offer support to many community members. They can visit seniors' homes to talk about financial fraud awareness and personal safety. They can play sports with youth in community centres and provide role models for youth with troubled family lives. Officers also spend time talking with small business owners, who share their concerns about loitering, shoplifting, and vandalism, among other petty crimes. Community officers also assist school resource officers in elementary schools and high schools to give workshops on such topics as street smarts, bicycle safety, and drug and alcohol awareness. The presence of their police cars helps calm traffic and provides greater safety to pedestrians. Often they can stop trouble before it really starts, and they are a good source of information for specialty task forces and prevention initiatives. Overall, the value of community police officers cannot be overstated. They give people in a community a chance to be heard and to feel safe.

▼

> Community police offices help seniors, youth, and business owners by spending time with them and talking to them about their concerns. Outreach officers can also add to community traffic safety. They help other law enforcement officers with initiatives in the community. Community officers are valuable: They listen and give people a sense of security.

EXERCISE 4 » Practising Summary Writing

1. Summarize each of the following paragraphs into no more than two sentences.

   a. Gossip is a message that is not factual. It is not acceptable to consider gossip as fact. There may be several reasons for gossip: mischief, misunderstanding, boredom, or inattention by the person who is passing on the gossip. On the other hand, gossip may be offered as fact because people are in a rush, are busy, or simply don't get the message straight.

   b. It seems as if busy people attract business. There is always more to do for the busy person and more responsibility to accept. It is important that a law clerk keep active and busy when not on the job. The more a person becomes involved with things outside of work, the more that person learns. At the same time, one should not neglect other important things in life such as family and friends.

   c. Every law enforcement officer is faced with problems that need solving. He or she can take the easy way out by reporting each and every problem to the supervisor and then simply following instructions. A better idea, however, is to take some initiative and attempt to solve a problem before it has to be taken to a supervisor.

2. Refer to the two articles you found about Tasers and summarize each article.

Writing a Paraphrase

The paraphrase and the summary are often thought to be the same. Both are summaries, but with a difference: the main point of the summary is to condense the basic concepts of a longer passage into a specific number of words. The summary is true to the meaning and tone of the original, but significantly reduced. A paraphrase translates a written passage or discussion into simpler terms; it entails a more radical "rephrasing" or rewording of the original. It does not have to be true to the tone or mood of the original, and *it need not be reduced in length*, but it should offer the reader or listener a clearer understanding of the original.

A paraphrase, then, is:

- The rewriting of original material in your own words, not necessarily reduced in length.
- Not merely a restatement of the original's main points; it is an attempt to establish understanding of them.
- An attempt to interpret the original message so as to determine its intended meaning.

Methods of Paraphrasing

There are a number of steps to follow when paraphrasing a written passage:

1. Reread the original passage until you understand its full meaning.
2. Set the original aside, and write your paraphrase on a note card.
3. Write a key word or phrase at the top of your note card to indicate the subject of your paraphrase.
4. Check your paraphrase against the original passage to make sure that your version expresses all of the essential information of the original.
5. Indicate, with quotation marks, any material you have borrowed directly from the original.
6. Record the source of your material.

Consider and compare the following examples of summary and paraphrase:

ORIGINAL: Students frequently overuse direct quotation in taking notes, and as a result they overuse quotations in their final paper. Probably only about 10 percent of your final manuscript should appear as directly quoted matter. Therefore, you should attempt to limit the amount of exact copying of source materials while taking notes. **(51 words)**

▼

PARAPHRASE: In research papers, students often quote excessively, failing to keep quoted material down to a desirable level. Since the problem usually originates during note taking, it is essential to minimize the material quoted directly. **(34 words)**

▼

SUMMARY: Students should take only a few direct quotations from sources to help minimize the amount of quoted material in a research paper. **(22 words)**

Source: Lester, J.D. (1976). *Writing Research Papers: A Complete Guide* (pp. 46-47). Glenview, IL: Scott, Foresman.

EXERCISE 5 » Paraphrasing

1. Working in groups of three, select a legal topic, and ask the members of your group their opinion on that topic. Paraphrase what the other people have said in an attempt to reach understanding.
2. Paraphrase the newspaper article "Police Fume at Security Firms."

Police Fume at Security Firms

Business improvement associations want to see more police walking the beat, but the police say they don't have the time. So private security guards are hired to do it.

Homeowners want more attention paid to speeders and people who run stop signs in their neighbourhoods, but police say traffic violations aren't a priority. So city council asks the province for permission to use red-light cameras at intersections in residential areas.

It's becoming more common for individuals and groups, unable to get the police to do what they'd like, to find other ways to get those services.

While the debate among Canadians rages over the benefits and dangers of two-tiered health care, a kind of two-tiered policing has become a reality.

"There's no turning back on this, it's a question of ensuring it works well," said Nathalie Des Rosiers, president of the Law Commission of Canada, about what she calls the "blending" of security and police . ...

Police and their supporters say citizens are in danger from the dramatic expansion of the largely unregulated "rent-a-cop" industry, which is taking over many traditional police roles. This is happening, the police union says, because politicians underfund the police.

Security guards, often paid little more than minimum wage and with no special powers, now do a wide range of jobs from prisoner transport to fraud investigations to patrolling streets and arresting drug dealers . ...

Security firms argue they are providing services citizens want and police don't or can't do—and for a better price . ...

Whether public money spent to keep citizens safe could be more effectively spent by divvying up jobs between the police (doing the dangerous difficult jobs) and private security (taking care of low-level tasks) is something that should be examined, the law commission's Des Rosiers says.

"There's no doubt the citizen would prefer to see a full-fledged police officer come to his or her door, but they want them to come within a reasonable time," Des Rosiers said. "And the dilemma is do they want to spend all the dollars needed to have that or do they want to have health care (as well)."

Source: Gillespie, K. (2003, October 19). Police fume at security firms. *Sunday Star* (Toronto), p. A6.

Avoiding Plagiarism

Writing good summaries and keeping track of material you want to quote directly are the first steps in conducting ethical research. The next steps involve using in-text **citations** and reference lists.

The terms *in-text citation* and *reference list* come from the APA (American Psychological Association) style of referencing. APA style is used for research work written or presented in the social sciences (e.g., sociology, psychology, criminology, and social work). There are a few other referencing styles, including the MLA (Modern Language Association), used for the humanities (e.g., anthropology, linguistics, and classics); the *Chicago Manual of Style*, also used for the humanities but used primarily for advanced scholarly study; and the IEEE (Institute of Electrical and Electronics Engineers), used for engineering research.

A **citation** is a reference to an original source.

You will use APA style for the most part, but you may also be asked to use MLA. Following the upcoming discussion of APA guidelines for in-text citations and reference lists, this section concludes with guidelines for MLA parenthetical references and works-cited lists.

In-Text Citations in APA Style

Anything taken from another source must be cited—that is, you must acknowledge in the body of your research paper that the material you are using is not your own. This applies to written work (e.g., facts, ideas, concepts, opinion), images (e.g., photos, charts, graphs), and all creative work (e.g., song lyrics, poems, formulas, computer code). The examples in parentheses in the preceding sentence are comprehensive but not exhaustive; always acknowledge the work of someone else, no matter what form it takes.

It is important to understand that even if you put information from a source into your own words (summarize or paraphrase), you must identify the original source.

The in-text citation directly follows information you use from a source:

> **It is estimated that most new immigrants to Canada are most concerned with finding others from their country of origin, followed by learning "the basics of banking and shopping in the new country" (Macquistan, 2015).**

Frequently Asked Questions

There are three troublesome areas students struggle with when incorporating research into their work:

1. **Where do I put in-text citations in a paragraph where there are many facts from one source? Can I use just one citation at the end of the paragraph?**

   It's best to put a citation after each fact, but this can look cumbersome in a paragraph:

   > In 2014, 3,200 apartments in Edmonton "were found to be without smoke detectors" (Fry, 2014). There were 17 fatalities "in a two-month span (Fry, 2014). Tenants requested that housing authorities "get off their backsides and do something about the issue" (Fry, 2014).

   You can fix this by inserting more of your own writing into the paragraph:

   > In 2014, 820 apartments in Edmonton "were found to be without smoke detectors," and there were 17 fatalities "in a two-month span" (Fry, 2014). This is certainly an unnecessary tragedy, and it's no surprise that tenants requested that housing authorities "get off their backsides and do something about the issue" (Fry, 2014).

   Alternatively, you can use fewer facts from the original. You can also leave it as it is; you may get a comment about style from an instructor, but the format of writing a citation after each fact is technically correct.

2. **What is considered common knowledge?**

   Information that is common knowledge does not need an in-text citation or an entry on your reference list. For example, most Canadians know that Sir John A. Macdonald was our first prime minister. This is common knowledge. However, if asked who our fourth prime minister was, many would not know the answer. If you think something is common knowledge but are unsure, find a source for the information and cite it to be sure you are covered.

3. What do I do if I have comprehensive knowledge of a topic I'm writing about? Do I have to cite myself or resort to finding a source I can cite for facts I already know?

You've heard stories—or perhaps you've experienced it yourself—about people being accused of plagiarizing because they did not cite information that seemed to come from an outside source, when in fact, the person did have that knowledge and was not using an outside source. We all have our areas of expertise, after all. To avoid this situation, simply state your expertise up front:

> The International Scale of River Difficulty uses six categories to grade difficulty of passage for whitewater rafters. Very strong currents and rapids accompanied by narrow passages require split-second decisions for Class 4 whitewater. In my 15 years of rafting experience, I've ridden all six levels, but my favourite is Level 4, where I am challenged but do not feel out of control.

The following are guidelines for recording text citations in APA style:

1. When you use a quotation, or summarize or paraphrase an idea in the body of your assignment, the identification of your source must include the surname(s) of the author(s), and year of publication. This can be done in a number of ways.

> **According to Edson (2006), private security agencies …**
>
> **Charters and Dean (2005) found that private security agencies …**
>
> **A recent study (Saunders & Dean, 2006) found that private security agencies …**
>
> **The basis for this assumption is provided by a study of private security agencies (Peters, Aikens, Abell, & Ford, 2003).**

2. When a work has two authors, cite both and separate them with an **ampersand** (&). (Use the word "and" to connect authors' names when used in your own text, but use an ampersand in the parenthetical citation.) When a work has three, four, or five authors, cite all authors and insert a comma following each name and an ampersand before the final name. When a work has six or more authors, use the last name of only the first author followed by the term *et al.* ("and others").

> **In 2004, Sherman et al. conducted a study of private security agencies [six or more authors].**

3. If you use the author's exact words, you must put the words of the quotation in quotation marks, and you must include the author's name and the year of publication as well as the specific page number(s) on which the quoted words appear. Use *p.* (e.g., "p. 308") to indicate one page and *pp.* (e.g., "pp. 307–308") to indicate multiple pages.

> **A study by Saunders and Dean (2006) concluded that "private security agencies offer significant future career opportunities" (p. 76).**

An **ampersand** is a typographical symbol meaning "and." It looks like this: &.

4. Quotations of fewer than 40 words become part of the text, as in the previous example.

5. Quotations of 40 words or more are indented in a freestanding block. Quotation marks are not used. Start this block quotation on a new line, indented five spaces from the left margin. The reference source follows the last line of the quotation as part of the block, and is placed outside the final period in the quotation.

> **Klein (2005) notes that summer students working as border guards during peak periods of summer travel present certain problems:**
>
> > **Students are often not properly trained to handle the rush that accompanies long lines of cars at border crossings, and tend to overlook important procedures in order to keep things moving. With many experienced supervisors on vacation, assistance and advice aren't always readily available. (pp. 107–108)**

6. There must be an exact correlation between the text citations and the entries in the reference list, with two exceptions. Personal communications (e.g., conversations, memos, emails, interviews) and references to classical works, such as the Bible, are referenced in the body of the text, but not in the reference list. For personal communications, you should provide the name of the source (initials and surname) and the date of the communication:

> **In a telephone conversation with the author, on March 15, 2006, J. Sherrif, head of the Brant Intensive Care Unit, reported that there have been no occurrences of patients with gunshot wounds at Joseph Brant Hospital in Burlington.**

Reference Lists in APA Style

The reference list resides at the end of your paper, and it is a listing of the sources you used to write your paper. The complete reference list entry for a citation earlier in this chapter would look like this:

> **Fournier-Ruggles, L. (2016). *Canadian immigration and refugee law for legal professionals*, 3rd ed. Toronto: Emond.**

A reference list is

- composed of a list of resources you have specifically referred to in the body of your assignment
- arranged alphabetically by the last name of the first author (or editor), or by the title (ignoring the articles *a*, *an*, or *the*) in cases where there is no author
- placed on a separate page, entitled "References," at the end of the assignment.

The basic rules for preparing a reference list are as follows:

- Double-space within and between entries.
- Begin each entry at the left margin. If an entry runs more than one line, indent subsequent lines five spaces.
- In titles of books and articles, capitalize only the first word, the first word after a colon, and proper nouns. All nouns in a journal name are capitalized.

- Italicize titles of books and periodical names (e.g., journals, magazines, newsletters), as well as the volume number of periodicals cited.
- When a journal is paged consecutively from the first issue in a year to the last, give only the page of the article (that is, do not include the issue number). When each issue within a year starts paging from page 1, give the issue number as well.
- When there are more than six authors, record the first six followed by *et al.* This applies to books, magazines, and journals.
- In general, treat electronic sources as you would print sources, adding any necessary additional information that will help others locate the source.

  In many cases, the additional information will consist of either a URL or a digital object identifier (DOI). A DOI is a character string assigned by a publisher that provides a persistent link to an article's location online. DOIs are used mainly in scholarly or scientific materials. Record the DOI if one has been assigned by the publisher; record the URL if no DOI has been assigned. In general, provide the home page URL for periodicals, books, and reports, and the full URL for works that are difficult to find from the publisher's home page. Do not include a retrieval date unless you think the source material may change over time—as in the case of a Wikipedia article. (For a detailed discussion of APA electronic reference style, see the *Publication Manual of the American Psychological Association*, Sixth Edition, published in 2009.)

Following are some examples of entries in a reference list:

1. Journal/magazine article

   Palk, G. R. M., Davey, J. D., & Freeman, J. E. (2010). The impact of a lockout policy on levels of alcohol-related incidents in and around licensed premises. *Police Practice and Research, 11*(1), 5–15. doi:10.1080/15614260802586392.

2. Book (two authors)

   Rosnick, J.S., & McAleer, D. (2016). *Communications and report writing for law enforcement professionals* (4th ed.). Toronto: Emond.

3. Edited book

   Green, L. C., & Dickason, O. P. (Eds.). (1989). *The law of nations and the new world.* Edmonton: University of Alberta Press.

4. Article in a magazine

   Hayes, M. (2002, August/September). A clean case for security. *Canadian Security*, S4–S6.

5. Article in a journal

   Ouimet, M. (2002). Explaining the American and Canadian crime "drop" in the 1990s. *Canadian Journal of Criminology, 44*(1), 33–47.

6. Article in a newspaper

   Tyler, T. (2002, November 1). Talks blow dust off Criminal Code. *Toronto Star*, p. A3.

7. DVD

   Barry Greenwald Inc., National Film Board of Canada. (Producer). (1998). *High risk offender* [DVD]. Available from http://onf-nfb.gc.ca/.

8. Government publication (print)

Canada, Statistics Canada. (2006). *Market research handbook* (Catalogue No. 63-224-XPB). Ottawa: Statistics Canada.

9. Article on the Web

National Crime Prevention Council. (2010, March 16). *Anti-bullying programs are working.* Retrieved from http://www.ncpc.org/.

Citing Sources in MLA Style

If you are following MLA style, you must also acknowledge your sources in two places: in the body of the paper with parenthetical references (equivalent to APA in-text citations) and at the end of your paper with a works-cited list (equivalent to an APA reference list).

Following are some guidelines for recording parenthetical references in MLA style:

- Choose the appropriate format: page number (if the author's name is mentioned in your own introductory words); author and page number (if no mention of the author is made in your own text); or author, abbreviated title, and page number (if your paper cites elsewhere another work by the same author).
- Omit punctuation between author and page number.
- Omit the page number if a source lacks page numbers, as many Internet sources do.
- Don't use the word *page* or the abbreviations *p.* or *pp.*

Let's say, for example, your topic is criminal responsibility, and you have paraphrased a paragraph from page 4 of the book *Murder: "Whatdunit"* by J.H.H. Gaute and Robin Odell. Your parenthetical reference would look like this:

> **Criminal responsibility must include both action and intent. In common law, there must be both a guilty act and a guilty intent. Every crime, therefore, has two parts (Gaute and Odell 4).**

And your entry in your works-cited list would look like this:

> **Gaute, J.H.H., and Robin Odell. *Murder: "Whatdunit."* London: Chambers, 1982.**

Following are some examples of the different parenthetical references required for different modes of citation:

- Facts or ideas are rephrased in your own words and the author's name is not mentioned.

> **When investigating a murder, detectives must look for both the criminal act and the intent (Gaute and Odell 4).**

- Facts are quoted directly from the source and the author's name is not mentioned:

> **Under the common law, "simply committing an act does not of itself constitute guilt unless there is guilty intent" (Gaute and Odell 4).**

- Facts or ideas are expressed in your own words and you mention the author's name or the title of the work in your own text. Since you have already identified the source, you include only the page number in the parenthetical reference.

> Gaute and Odell state that *actus reus* and *mens rea* have to be present in order for criminal responsibility to exist (4).

The references in the three examples given above point the reader to the publishing information on the Gaute and Odell book that is listed in the works-cited list at the end of your assignment.

Formatting Quotations

Quotations of four lines or less are enclosed in quotation marks and incorporated in your own text.

> Gaute and Odell define criminal responsibility as "*actus reus*, which in murder is the physical act of killing a person, and *mens rea*, which is the guilty mind or intent" (4).

Quotations of more than four lines are indented in a freestanding block. Do not use quotation marks around the block. Begin the block on a new line indented 10 spaces from the left margin. The parenthetical reference follows the last line of the quotation as part of the block and is placed outside the final period.

> Criminal responsibility is defined by the terms *actus reus*, which in murder is the physical act of killing a person, and *mens rea*, which is the guilty mind or intent. It is held in common law that simply committing an act does not of itself constitute guilt unless there is guilty intent. Thus every crime has two parts—*actus reus* and *mens rea*. (Gaute and Odell 4)

Guidelines for Preparing a Works-Cited List

A works-cited list

- contains complete publication information for all the sources you cited in the body of your assignment
- is placed at the end of your assignment on a separate page entitled "Works Cited."

The basic rules for preparing a works-cited list are as follows:

- Double-space within and between entries.
- Begin each entry at the left margin. If the entry runs more than one line, indent subsequent lines half an inch or five spaces.
- Invert author names (last name first). If a work has more than one author, invert the name of the first author only.
- Arrange the list alphabetically by the first word in each entry (usually the last name of the author).

- If no author is given for a work, begin the entry with the title of the work. If the title has *a*, *an*, or *the* as the first word, alphabetize the title on the basis of the second word.

- Capitalize each significant word in all titles (that is, do not capitalize articles, prepositions, or conjunctions).

- Italicize the titles of books, magazines, journals, newspapers, film or video recordings, and websites.

- Use quotations marks around the titles of articles in magazines, journals, and newspapers. Also use quotation marks around the titles of short stories, essays, poems, and chapters from a larger work. Finally, use quotation marks around the titles of emails as given in the subject line.

- For works on a website, italicize the titles if the works are independent—that is, not part of a larger work. If the works are part of a larger work, use quotation marks instead.

- Include the medium of publication—print, Web, DVD, email, etc.

- For sources accessed electronically, give the date you accessed the source on the website.

Following are some examples of entries in a works-cited list:

1. Book with one author

   Bjorkquist, Bruce. *Police Ethics: Principles and Practice*. Toronto: Emond Montgomery, 2013. Print.

2. Book with more than three authors

   Shusta, Robert M., et al. *Multicultural Law Enforcement: Strategies for Peacekeeping in a Diverse Society*. Upper Saddle River, NJ: Prentice Hall, 2005. Print.

3. Edited book

   Green, L.C., and Dickason, Olive P. eds. *The Law of Nations and the New World*. Edmonton: U of Alberta, 1989. Print.

4. Government publication (print)

   Canada. Statistics Canada. *Market Research Handbook*. Cat. No. 63-224-XPB. 2006 ed. Ottawa: Statistics Canada, 2006. Print.

5. Government publication (Internet)

   Canada. Department of Justice Canada. "The Aboriginal Justice Strategy." *Department of Justice Canada*, n.d. Web. 15 Apr. 2010.

6. Article in a magazine

   Hayes, Michael. "A Clean Case for Security." *Canadian Security* Aug.–Sept. 2002: S4–S6. Print.

7. Article in a newspaper

   Dunphy, Bill. "Finger-Pointing Begins as Toronto Police Close Ranks." *Hamilton Spectator* 22 Jan. 2004: A12. Print.

8. Interview that you conducted

> Wu, Cst. Peter. Personal interview. 15 Mar. 2006.

9. Website

> *Canadian Security Intelligence Service*. Canadian Security Intelligence Service. Web.
> 16 Apr. 2010.

Additional Resources for Using APA and MLA

The brief referencing samples in this text are included to give you the basic idea of what citations and reference lists look like. However, there are many top-quality online resources you can access for help. No one is expected to memorize the rules for formatting citations and reference lists, so most post-secondary institutions have online referencing guides. Visit your school's library site to see what help is there. One outstanding source is Purdue University's OWL (Online Writing Lab) site. Purdue was one of the first universities to create a comprehensive site for research help. It is constantly monitored and updated. The address is owl.english.purdue.edu. The University of Calgary has online referencing help for citing the *Criminal Code* and other legal texts at http://libguides.ucalgary.ca/mcgillguide.

You can also make use of online citation programs. To use these, you simply plug in the information (address, author, date, etc.), and the program formats your citation and reference entry for you. Use these programs with caution; not all are of high quality, and it is not uncommon for there to be discrepancies in the results provided.

EXERCISE 6 » **Writing Research Papers**

1. Look in your school library for newspaper or magazine articles that contain opposing points of view on the same topic. For example, there have been many articles supporting the *Youth Criminal Justice Act* and just as many stating that the Act lets young offenders off too easily. There are many such articles in the media about a wide range of legal topics. Choose articles that are at least 300 words long.

2. Write a five-paragraph essay comparing and contrasting two articles that take opposing points of view on the same issue. Use this format:

   > Paragraph 1: Introduce your topic and state the theses put forward by the opposing authors.

   > Paragraphs 2 and 3: Summarize the contents of these two articles (one paragraph per article). Remember to use in-text citations.

   > Paragraph 4: Point out the bias in each article and use a direct quote from each to illustrate the bias. Remember to use an in-text citation for each quote.

   > Paragraph 5: Finally, conclude your essay by explaining which article was more effective and why. Be sure to include a properly formatted reference list.

3. Write an essay on a law enforcement topic about which you feel strongly. Research the topic to gather whatever facts you need. Point out your bias and the reasons for your bias. Remember that it's your opinion that counts, but you must back up your opinion with facts.

4. Conduct an employment search. Research employment opportunities available with each of the following:

   a. your local police service

   b. a police service outside your locality, a provincial police service, or the RCMP

   c. Corrections Canada

   d. Canada Border Services Agency

   e. a local private security firm

   Compile your findings in a research paper, quoting all relevant sources. You may write an essay covering all the law enforcement services mentioned above, or you may write a paper covering one of the services in greater depth, depending on your career interest.

CHAPTER SUMMARY

The research essay is the basic form of writing task in colleges and universities. To produce a well-constructed and ethical paper, you must employ three solid strategies:

1. Find up-to-date and accurate sources.
2. Use sources effectively in your work.
3. Acknowledge the work of others.

The strong research writing skills you perfect in college or university will be useful in your law enforcement career. It is not uncommon for new staff to be tasked with background work such as fact gathering. This allows seasoned officers to conduct investigations and be supported in their investigative work. Testing new recruits with research tasks also allows supervisors to see who is ethical, thorough, hard-working, and a strong writer. All of these qualities are necessary for assignment to special projects and for promotion within the law enforcement profession.

KEY TERMS

ampersand, 155
citation, 153
credentials, 144
précis, 145
summarizing, 146

REVIEW AND REFLECTION QUESTIONS

1. Why is it important to vet your online sources carefully?

_____

_____

2. What are the roles of the in-text citation and the reference list?

_____

_____

3. How could plagiarism affect your school and workplace careers?

_____

_____

4. If you are asked to write a research report or researched presentation in the workplace, how might you go about doing efficient and effective research?

_____

_____

5. When might you be asked to do research in your law enforcement career?

_____

_____

8 Essay Writing

LEARNING OUTCOMES

After completing this chapter, you should be able to:

- Consider your audience and your reason for writing.
- Construct a paragraph containing a topic and a thesis.
- Understand how different types of paragraphs are written.
- Write an essay using an effective introduction, support paragraphs, and a conclusion.
- Use transitional words and phrases between parts of your essay.

Introduction

Why do you write? People have many purposes in writing, but whatever their particular purpose may be, writers who hope to communicate their ideas must transmit them in a form that their readers will recognize and accept.

Purpose

In college, you most likely write because your instructor has given you an assignment. The purpose of these assignments is to teach you how to process information, how to be accurate, and how to convey a message in understandable prose and in the proper written form.

These components are essential to any type of law enforcement writing you may do. You likely won't have to write an "academic" essay while on the job as a law enforcement officer; however, you'll most certainly have to write an essay as part of applying for a law enforcement career. If you plan to pursue your education beyond the college level, perhaps in a university criminology program, knowledge of essay-writing skills will be essential:

> While the essay is required in any number of courses—law enforcement, business studies, office administration, technology, social sciences, journalism, broadcasting, and the like—its purpose goes beyond fulfilling the requirements of a post-secondary-level education. Writing essays also helps prepare students for careers by providing the skills necessary to write corporate reports, evaluations, summaries, research papers, letters, memos, and job applications. Although the structures of various forms of writing may vary, the essay is still the basic form of writing. Spelling, grammar, and logic, essential to the composition of an effective essay, remain paramount in all forms of writing, as does the ability to express yourself clearly. In short, the skills you develop when you learn how to write an essay are transferable in countless ways. (Lipschutz, G., Roberts, J., Scarry, J., & Scarry, S. (2013). *The Canadian Writer's Workplace* (7th ed., p. 188). Toronto: Nelson. ©2013 Nelson Education Ltd. Reproduced by permission. www.cengage.com/permissions.)

In general, a writer seeks to *inform*, to *explain*, to *persuade*, or to *put something on record*, and to do so as efficiently as possible. To determine which of these aims applies to your writing, ask yourself, "What do I want to happen as the result of my writing?"

Audience

It is important to analyze your audience before beginning any writing assignment. Ask the following questions:

1. Who will be reading this?
2. What does the reader want to hear?
3. What do I want to tell the reader?
4. How can I best arrange and present the message?

In the case of a college assignment, the answers to some of these questions are obvious. Good grades depend on identifying and fulfilling the instructor's expectations. Many of these expectations are identified in this book. This is what the instructor expects, and your grade for that assignment will depend on your ability to follow those guidelines.

Of course, the world of law enforcement brings a different audience. Different people will approach your written work differently, with diverse agendas. Consider the following, for example:

- Your sergeant will want to see that your writing is clear, concise, factual, and complete.
- The defence lawyer will examine your written work carefully, with an eye to catch any mistakes in spelling, grammar, or facts, which may bring your report into question and aid the defence.
- The Crown attorney will want to use your written work as a basis for prosecution, and will be looking to see that facts are not omitted, that opinion and hearsay aren't treated as facts, that spelling and grammar errors don't occur, and that you haven't been sloppy.
- The insurance company will examine your material with a view to determining fault and deciding on a possible settlement.

Your written words must be so effective that every person reading them will be able to visualize the situation as you saw it. The only way to learn how to write is to write. Writing begins with a letter, then a word, then a sentence, then a paragraph. From there, it evolves to the essay, the report, or another longer format. Figure 8.1 shows the structure of an essay.

Paragraph

A paragraph is composed of a number of sentences. Each paragraph contains one main idea, either as part of a longer piece of writing, such as an essay or a report, or as an independent unit. There is no prescribed length for a paragraph. But the paragraph must be long enough to fully express your main idea or your purpose for writing. Generally, paragraphs are from 5 to 12 sentences in length.

You express the paragraph's main idea in a **topic sentence** (see Figure 8.2). Every other sentence in the paragraph supports, describes, or explains the main point you are expressing in the topic sentence.

Most paragraphs begin with the topic sentence, although it does not have to appear at the beginning. Examine the following paragraph:

> **Growing up near a police station had a profound influence on my life. Every day I'd watch the police cruisers leave the station. I'd wonder where they were going and what adventures awaited them. I'd hear the sirens in the middle of the night and jump out of bed to watch the flashing lights disappear down the street. I'd watch people entering the police station and wonder what problems they had. I grew up considering myself part of the daily routine.**

The topic sentence in this paragraph is the first sentence. The main idea is that the writer grew up near a police station and was greatly influenced by what he or she saw. Every other sentence supports this main idea: the references to the cruisers, the sirens, the people, all contribute to the notion that proximity to the station had a profound influence on the writer's life.

A **topic sentence** includes two things: a *topic* and a *controlling idea*.

FIGURE 8.1   The Structure of an Essay

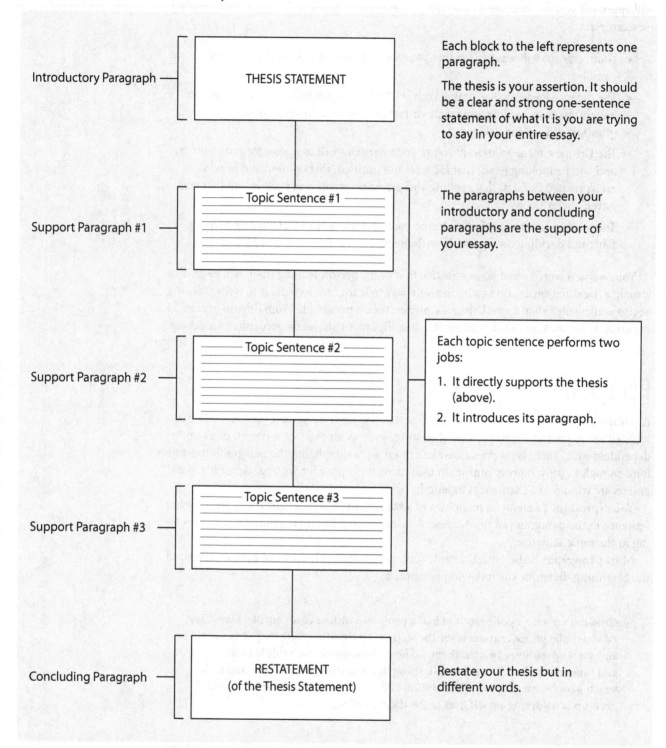

Introductory Paragraph — **THESIS STATEMENT**

Each block to the left represents one paragraph.

The thesis is your assertion. It should be a clear and strong one-sentence statement of what it is you are trying to say in your entire essay.

Support Paragraph #1 — Topic Sentence #1

The paragraphs between your introductory and concluding paragraphs are the support of your essay.

Support Paragraph #2 — Topic Sentence #2

Each topic sentence performs two jobs:

1. It directly supports the thesis (above).
2. It introduces its paragraph.

Support Paragraph #3 — Topic Sentence #3

Concluding Paragraph — **RESTATEMENT** (of the Thesis Statement)

Restate your thesis but in different words.

Source: Adapted from Lipschutz, Scarry, & Scarry (2013), p. 189. ©2013 Nelson Education Ltd. Reproduced by permission. www.cengage.com/permissions.

FIGURE 8.2   Paragraphs and Topic Sentences

Two Paragraph Types

TOPIC SENTENCE
REGULAR (5–7 sentences including the topic sentence)

TOPIC SENTENCE
EXTENDED   (8–12 sentences including the topic sentence)

Regular or Extended Paragraphs

A **regular paragraph** has 5 to 7 sentences. An **extended paragraph** (8 to 12 sentences) is longer because it has more supporting detail. The supporting detail of a paragraph is made up of sentences that directly support the topic sentence. These supporting sentences may be specific examples of the topic sentence, or they may be parts of an explanation.

Sample Paragraph

One of the areas in which having choice can be extremely valuable is that of friends. Like leaving home to seek greater knowledge of yourself, picking your own friends from a greater number of people can aid in your journey to seek self-knowledge. After all, if you go out with the same group of small-town friends all the time, not because you necessarily like them all that much but because they're the only ones available, this can prove quite limiting when it comes to your growth as an individual. The big city, on the other hand, offers an endless number of opportunities to meet people of like interests. You're much more likely to cultivate relationships with people who help you to grow.

Topic Sentence

A **topic sentence** includes two things: a *topic* and a *controlling idea*. The controlling idea is the attitude of the writer of the paragraph toward the topic identified in the topic sentence. A paragraph contains *one single idea*—that which is introduced in your topic sentence. The topic sentence does not always appear first in a paragraph, but until you are well practised, place the topic sentence first.

Transitions

Transitional words or phrases are used to organize the paragraph better and to make the paragraph flow more smoothly.

Stands on Its Own

Any paragraph, even if it is part of a longer work such as an essay, should be able to stand on its own, much like a sequel to a movie.

Paragraph Indication

There are only two ways **to indicate a new paragraph**:

1. **Indent** the first line of the paragraph (see sample paragraph above), or
2. **Skip a line** before starting the next paragraph. If you are already double-spacing your work, skip two lines, instead of one, before starting the next paragraph.

You will see later in this chapter that every essay has a topic (what is being written about) and a **thesis statement** (the writer's point of view on the topic). Like the essay itself, each paragraph has a topic and a thesis, in this case called a **controlling idea**. The controlling idea expresses the writer's point of view on the paragraph's topic. Consider the following topic sentence:

> **Working as a customs officer for the summer was both rewarding and frustrating.**

Here the author is writing about his or her summer job as a customs officer (the topic). It was at once rewarding and frustrating (the controlling idea, describing how the author experienced the job). The remainder of the paragraph should provide details about how the job was both rewarding and frustrating.

A topic sentence can have a wide variety of controlling ideas, depending on the writer. A summer job as a customs officer could have been rewarding yet frustrating for one writer and exciting, or boring, or challenging for other writers.

Once you have chosen your topic and have written a topic sentence reflecting your controlling idea, it is necessary to substantiate your topic sentence with *supporting details*. These are the sentences that support the main idea through detail and example. The previous example, "Growing up near a police station," illustrated how supporting details work within a paragraph. The writer of that paragraph used examples to demonstrate the main idea of influence.

Examples are specific illustrations or evidence that support the controlling idea. They must be clear and specific. The following paragraph lacks specific examples; it uses no specific information, and, in the end, it is clear that the paragraph as a whole does not support the topic sentence and controlling idea. The topic sentence is set out in italics:

> *Police officers are lazy.* **All they do is sit around and eat doughnuts all day, or they drive around ignoring everyone. Sometimes I see them writing in a little book, but they're likely making up their grocery list. And you can never find a cop when you want one. Just the other day, I called the police station to report my bike missing. It took forever for the officer to arrive to take the report. Boy, was I angry. It's a good thing I remembered I left it at my friend's house.**

A **thesis statement** is a complete sentence expressing the writer's point of view on a topic.
The **controlling idea** is the attitude of the writer of the paragraph toward the topic identified in the topic sentence.

EXERCISE 1 » **Writing Topic Sentences**

For each of the topics below, write a possible topic sentence with a controlling idea. Look at the examples before proceeding.

Sample topic: Canada's justice system

Possible topic sentence: Canada's justice system is among the fairest in the world.

Sample topic: Hand-held electronic devices

Possible topic sentence: Banning cellphone use while driving will reduce road accidents.

Sample topic: Restorative justice

Possible topic sentence: Restorative justice is a new method of dealing with offenders.

1. *Topic*: Choosing a career in law enforcement

   Topic sentence:

   _____

   _____

   _____

2. *Topic*: The *Criminal Code*

   Topic sentence:

   _____

   _____

   _____

3. *Topic*: Two years as an auxiliary police officer

   Topic sentence:

   _____

   _____

   _____

4. *Topic*: The Law and Security/Police Foundations program

   Topic sentence:

   _____

   _____

   _____

5. *Topic*: Young offenders

   Topic sentence:

   _____

   _____

   _____

EXERCISE 2 » Using Specific Examples

Rewrite the paragraph about the laziness of police officers. Compose a topic sentence and give specific examples to support your controlling idea. You can adopt the existing point of view, take an opposing point of view, or develop an entirely new controlling idea. Whatever point of view you take, be sure to use specific examples.

Types of Paragraphs

There are five main **strategies** for writing paragraphs: *narration* (tells a story), *description* (describes something using the senses), *exposition* (explains how something is done), *comparison/contrast* (points out similarities and differences between two or more subjects), and *cause and effect* (describes the result of something taking place). Following are topic sentences for each strategy and suggestions of ways in which to develop them.

Narration

When I transferred into the Police Sciences course, I knew that I had found my career. [*Then tell the story of how you came to choose the Police Sciences course.*]

Description

The line of cars waiting to clear customs inspection was long. [*Then describe the length, the line, and the attitudes of drivers.*]

Exposition

Loading and unloading a handgun is a simple process if you know what you're doing. [*Then give a step-by-step account of the process, being careful not to leave out anything important.*]

Comparison/contrast

American prison guards are trained differently from Canadian prison guards. [*Then point out similarities and differences.*]

Cause and effect

An ineffective parole system leads to increased crime on the streets. [*Then give specific examples of increased crime on the streets and how it is caused by an ineffective parole system.*]

Strategy is the method of presenting your point of view throughout the essay.

EXERCISE 3 » Writing Different Kinds of Topic Sentences

Write a topic sentence and controlling idea for the following topics, using the strategy in parentheses following the topic. An example is provided.

Example: Locker room (description):

The locker room was a picture of chaos.

1. My first week at college (narration):

_____

_____

_____

2. Prison guards (description):

_____

_____

_____

3. How to write a resumé (exposition):

_____

_____

_____

4. Police chiefs of Toronto and Vancouver (comparison/contrast):

_____

_____

_____

5. Illegal handguns (cause and effect):

_____

_____

_____

Write a whole paragraph based on one of the topic sentences you have written above.

Essay

The essay is the basic form of writing in many academic programs, and an essay is often required for the successful completion of law enforcement testing.

The essay helps prepare you for other forms of writing: the report, the summary, the job application, the letter, and the memo. Spelling, grammar, clarity, and proper structure are all essential parts of the essay.

An essay is a form of writing that contains a number of paragraphs. Writing one may also involve research, citations, and documentation to show the origin of facts used in the essay. An essay can be written on any topic, but whatever the topic, the essay always consists of a number of paragraphs in which you consider a topic much more thoroughly than you could in a single paragraph.

The essay may be *narrative* (it tells a story), *descriptive* (it describes something), *expository* (it explains something), or *persuasive* (it tries to convince the reader of the writer's point of view).

All essays must have an introduction, a body, and a conclusion. The introduction and conclusion are usually one paragraph each, although they may be longer.

The purpose of the *introduction* is to explain your essay to the reader and to capture his or her attention. This paragraph contains a topic sentence (what the essay is about) and a thesis statement (your point of view), which can be combined into one sentence. The opening paragraph "introduces" your essay.

The *body* of the essay is made up of the paragraphs between the introduction and the conclusion, and it provides the evidence to support your thesis. The body of the essay usually consists of at least three paragraphs that are connected by transitions.

The *conclusion*, usually one paragraph in length, summarizes the proofs that you have supplied in support of your thesis.

Getting Started

What to write about? Usually this isn't a problem: Your instructor will ask for a 2,000-word essay on the topic of the death penalty, or a job application will ask for a brief essay about "why you want to work for Corrections Canada." In some situations, the choice of topic is left up to you. The remainder of this chapter will tell you how to write the essay, but before beginning to write, you must choose a topic or develop some ideas about an assigned topic, and decide how to express these ideas.

One of the best ways to collect ideas is through *brainstorming*. Brainstorming is simple. It can best be accomplished in groups of four or more people, but the number of people involved isn't as important as the number of ideas you generate. The steps in brainstorming are as follows:

1. Come up with as many ideas as you can and write them down.
2. Don't initially criticize any idea. You can weed out poor ideas later.
3. Develop alternatives. If any ideas generate objections, work on varying the ideas rather than simply discarding them.
4. As you come up with ideas, discuss them. Your discussion will generate other ideas.
5. Make sure that everyone in the group completely understands the ideas generated.
6. Put your list of ideas aside for a while. Think about them occasionally, at your convenience. This back-burner approach will often generate further ideas.

Select your best ideas, use them as possible topics or thesis statements, and begin to prepare an outline.

EXERCISE 4 » Brainstorming

Assume that you must submit a report on one of the following topics:

- maintaining discipline in your Justice Studies class
- causes of car accidents
- problems with drugs
- ethical behaviour for law enforcement officers
- changes to the *Highway Traffic Act*

In groups of no fewer than four people, take ten minutes to brainstorm the topics. Have someone record the ideas you come up with, and be prepared to present them to the class.

Outline

An outline is the logical starting point in the writing process. An outline can be considered as a sketch, a plan, a focus, a framework, or a method of organization. It gives you an opportunity to organize your ideas into a plan or a pattern. It provides a framework for your facts, your main ideas, and your supporting points. Begin by developing a thesis statement that expresses your essay's overall message to the reader. You can organize your research, ideas, and facts around this thesis statement.

Thesis Statement

The thesis statement expresses the essay's main idea. It usually conveys the writer's position on the topic and is especially important in persuasive and expository essays. The thesis statement is a single, complete sentence that can be found anywhere in the introductory paragraph, but it is usually found at the beginning or end. It tells the reader what will be explained, described, proven, or answered in the essay, and it clearly states what position the writer is taking.

It is not enough to write "The crisis in our correctional system" as a thesis statement. This is a topic, or possibly a title, but the words do not meet the requirements of a thesis statement, which must

- be a complete sentence
- express the writer's point of view.

A thesis statement might take the following form:

> **The correctional system is facing a shortage of trained personnel, a situation that can be remedied only if more funding is allocated for training.**

Other sentences in the introductory paragraph should support this thesis statement with details, as in the following example:

> **Corrections Canada is facing a crisis. While the number of inmates in Canada's prisons is rising, the number of guards and administrators in the system is declining.** [*The writer may wish to quote the source of this fact here or give actual figures later in the essay.*] **The correctional system is facing a shortage of trained personnel, a situation that can be remedied only if more funding is allocated for training.**

In order to write an effective thesis statement, the writer should consider the following advice:

1. *Make sure the scope of the topic is not too broad.* For example, Canadian security is too large a topic for an essay. You may either limit or qualify the topic:

> *Limited topic*: **The number of security officers on Parliament Hill should be increased. [Topic limited to Parliament Hill only, not other issues relating to security.]**
>
> *Qualified topic*: **Surveillance has increased on Parliament Hill since 22 October 2014. [Topic suggests a function of security officers, and the discussion will be limited to that one function.]**

2. *Use a controlling idea.* State a personal point of view that you feel you can support with evidence.

> **There has been a dramatic, but necessary, increase in surveillance on Parliament Hill since 22 October 2014.**

3. *Indicate the strategy to be used in the essay.* While you may have facts to support the idea that surveillance has increased and is necessary, you need a method of presenting this point of view and evidence. Your strategy may be implied, though not stated, in your thesis statement or elsewhere in your introductory paragraph. Strategies include the following:

> *Comparison/contrast*: **A description of surveillance before and after 22 October 2014.**
>
> *Cause and effect*: **An analysis of what caused increased surveillance and what effect it has had.**
>
> *Advantages/disadvantages*: **An analysis of how increased surveillance has both helped and harmed Canadians' sense of freedom to visit Parliament Hill.**
>
> *Reasons*: **A statement of reasons why surveillance on Parliament Hill must increase.**
>
> *Persuasion*: **An argument that even those visitors inconvenienced by these changes must agree that surveillance was too lax in the past.**

EXERCISE 5 » Writing a Thesis Statement

Develop a thesis statement for each of the following topics:

- Prevalence of crime in Canada

_____

_____

_____

- Drinking and driving

_____

_____

_____

- Capital punishment

_____

_____

_____

- Conjugal visits for prisoners

_____

_____

_____

- Fraud against senior citizens

_____

_____

_____

_____

Organizing the Essay

Now that you have your thesis statement, you can go ahead and organize your research, your facts, and your arguments, keeping in mind that the thesis statement forms the focus of your organization. There are many ways of organizing the essay into a coherent unit. Some possibilities are as follows:

1. _Logical pattern._ Organize whatever notes, ideas, or research you have into what you consider to be a logical pattern. You might pick out major ideas and put them in sequence, then arrange information supporting these ideas.

2. _Generalities to specifics._ Organize your material so that it moves from general to specific facts.

3. _Order of importance._ Organize your material according to the importance of the various facts or ideas you may be using.

4. *Chronology.* Organize your material chronologically.

5. *Strategy.* Organize your material in relation to comparison/contrast, cause and effect, or any of the other strategies discussed thus far.

The nature and content of your essay will determine the best organization. For example, a narrative essay lends itself well to a chronological format. An outline based on your strategy selection will give the essay the beginnings of an organized look. You may notice areas that need more research or supporting facts, and you will see how the various parts fit together.

You may wish to organize your outline according to one of the two patterns set out below.

Introductory paragraph		Introductory paragraph
	or	
1. First major point 2. Supporting material		1. Major heading a. Minor heading
3. Second major point 4. Supporting material		2. Major heading b. Minor heading
5. Third major point 6. Supporting material		3. Major heading c. Minor heading
Conclusion		Conclusion

Writing the Introduction

Once the outline has been organized, you can begin writing the introductory paragraph. You have now decided on a topic and thesis statement along with a writing strategy. In the introductory paragraph, the topic and thesis are stated. A pattern for the essay must be developed, something that will attract the reader's interest while allowing you to implement your strategy.

There are various ways to write an introductory paragraph:

1. Select a general subject that can be narrowed down to a specific topic.

> **The need for prison reform seems to be generally recognized these days, and the one problem that needs immediate attention is that of overcrowding in prisons. With hundreds of inmates crowded into prisons built for half that number, and with prison cells filled beyond their intended capacity, small problems become large problems very quickly.**

2. Begin with an anecdote. A short, possibly amusing, personal story can lead into your topic.

> **I was arrested once. When I was in my final year of university, a couple of friends insisted that we go out for a few drinks. A few led to a few more, and we ended up in the drunk tank overnight. After what I saw that night, I resolved never to do anything that would get me sent to jail again. I also resolved to do what I could to help people who can't afford legal assistance. I met a few of those people that night.**

3. Give a definition.

> **Restorative justice is an approach to justice that has healing as its focus.**

4. Make a statement that is sure to attract attention.

> **Retired Saskatoon police officer Ernie Louttit, who patrolled the city's streets for nearly 30 years, said having a body camera would have been useful during his long career. He said the cameras would have cleared up any ambiguity about what an officer was doing while out on patrol. "I think the body cameras would have saved literally millions and millions in court costs because people could see what police are seeing," Louttit said (Hamilton, 2014).**

5. Be contrarian: start by echoing a widely held point of view, then take the opposite view.

> **Prisons can only rehabilitate their inmates if they are free from crime and can be places for reflection and retraining. Unfortunately, Canada's prisons are crime-ridden, dirty, degrading, and dangerous. They act more as a school for crime than a place of rehabilitation. In fact, a recent federal government study showed that incarceration was associated with a slight increase in recidivism (Morton, 2009).**

6. Start with a quotation.

> **"Prison is not the place to grow old." Prison used to be for young people, but in the past two decades, the number of offenders over 50 years of age in Canada's prisons shot up dramatically, and continues to grow (Sheppard, 2001).**

7. Start your essay with a description.

> **Imagine you are in your car at a border crossing, inching ahead with what seem to be hundreds of other cars waiting to be inspected. It's hot, your motor is over-heating, and cars in the other lanes always seem to be moving faster than yours. You don't care about possible terrorists entering the country. You've had a long drive, you're irritable, and all you want to do is answer the question, "Anything to declare?" and be on your way.**

8. Ask a question.

> **Are private security companies more effective than official law enforcement agencies? While the teaching and tools of private security have become more technical, the overall mission has remained the same for the past 300 years—the protection of assets, be they human, material, or technological. To complete this mission, private security personnel can do things that would be considered illegal if carried out by law enforcement agencies (Ingerman, 2001).**

Body of Essay or Support Paragraphs

The number of paragraphs in an essay depends on the number of points you need to make. It's not a question of how long an essay is supposed to be, but of how many words, sentences, paragraphs, or pages are needed to make the point defined by your thesis.

There is going to be an introduction and a conclusion—that's two paragraphs. The body of the essay will contain the number of paragraphs required to support the thesis of the essay. While there is no formula for length or quantity of paragraphs or words, the development of your essay will involve at least three other paragraphs (and likely more) to support your thesis.

EXERCISE 6 » Organizing Topics Within the Essay

You've been assigned an essay project entitled "Causes of motor vehicle accidents." Listed below are some of the topics you can use for this essay. Using as many topics as you consider relevant, organize them logically under headings that you create.

- acts of God
- aggression
- alcohol and drugs
- anger
- back-seat drivers
- bare feet
- bumblebees in car
- cellphones
- confusing traffic signs
- daydreaming
- distractions

- drivers' medical emergencies
- drivers under emotional strain
- drivers unfamiliar with car
- fog
- glare
- immature drivers
- impaired drivers
- lateness
- long hair
- mechanically unfit vehicles
- pedestrians

- poor driver skills
- poor eyesight and hearing
- poor mirrors
- poor seat adjustment
- poor tires and steering
- poorly lit roadways
- poorly marked highways
- potholes
- racing
- reckless driving
- road construction

- road hazards
- short drivers
- snow and ice
- student drivers
- suicide
- tall drivers
- other

Transitions

Transitions are words or phrases that connect thoughts within a sentence, between sentences, and between paragraphs. In other words, they form links between ideas. For example, in the sentence below, the words "instead of" are used to contrast two things within a sentence:

> **He spent his time investigating accidents instead of writing reports.**

Transitions are used to show the logical connection between ideas. The transitions are italicized in the following sentences:

> *Before* drawing your weapon, be sure you have cause.
> *Finally*, with all my reports typed and filed, my shift was finished.

In **transitions**, transitional words and phrases are used to organize the paragraph better and to make the paragraph flow more smoothly.

> I tried again to reach her by phone *but* I had no luck.
>
> The anonymous phone tip mentioned only a one-armed man; *nevertheless*, it was still a good lead to follow up.
>
> *To the left* of the prison stood a coffee shop.

Writing Strategies

Narration

Narration tells a story. The best way to tell a story is to start at the beginning and continue to the end; in other words, use chronological order. Tell what happened first, then what happened next, until you reach the end of the story.

Useful transitions for narrative essays include words that indicate the passage of time and the sequence of events, such as the following:

- after
- at once
- before
- first
- immediately
- next
- now
- suddenly
- then
- usually

Description

Description portrays something. The best way to describe something is to be concrete and appeal to the five senses. There are many adjectives and adverbs that can be used descriptively. While you can't appeal to every sense in describing a person, place, or thing, you can appeal to a number of them. A description of a handgun, for example, might engage all your senses. Before embarking on such a description, you might ask yourself the following questions:

Sight:	**What kind of handgun (revolver, automatic), and with what features?**
Sound:	**What sound does it make when fired, or when a cartridge is being loaded?**
Touch:	**Is it cold, plastic, smooth?**
Taste:	**Can you taste burnt powder on your tongue when the gun is fired?**
Smell:	**What about the smell of the oil used to preserve the weapon, or the smell of spent gunpowder?**

When describing something, start with a specific part of the item you wish to describe, then go in a specific direction: top to bottom, left to right, outside to inside. For example, in describing a person, your order might be as follows:

1. shape of head
2. hair colour
3. hair style
4. shape of ears
5. eye colour
6. shape of mouth

Exposition

Exposition tells how something is done. This type of essay is sometimes called the *process essay*. You use this mode for telling your reader how to complete a task (e.g., how to apply to the Ontario Provincial Police [OPP] for a job) or how an institution such as the Canada Border Services Agency (CBSA) was formed.

This type of essay requires that you include all the steps in the correct order. There is no use telling the reader the requisite steps for applying to the OPP if you omit some steps, such as obtaining a St. John Ambulance certificate or a driver's licence. Without these items, the applicant will certainly be rejected for employment.

There are a number of transitions helpful in writing the expository essay, including the following:

- after
- begin with
- finally
- finish with
- first
- next
- start with
- the first step
- the second step
- then

Persuasion

Persuasion involves an attempt to change a reader's viewpoint, or to convince a reader of your point of view. There are procedures to use when writing the persuasion essay:

1. *Define a clear thesis statement.*

   Canada must reform its prison system.

2. *Use examples.*
3. *Use authorities.* Quote others who support your point of view.

4. *Be aware of the opposition.* Because some readers will disagree with you, attempt to address potential disagreement in your essay. Don't ignore arguments. Deal with them.

5. *Point out the options.* Let your reader know the consequences of not accepting your point of view.

> **If Canada fails to reform its prison system, overcrowding in our prisons will only get worse.**

Comparison/Contrast

Comparison emphasizes similarities between things, while contrast emphasizes differences. Comparison and contrast essays can be organized according to either the *block method* or the *point-by-point method*. For example, consider the following:

> *Thesis*: **Applying for a job with Corrections Canada is similar to applying for other law enforcement positions, but there are also many differences in the process.**
>
> *Block method*: **Describe the entire process of applying for employment with Corrections Canada, then the entire process of applying to another law enforcement agency, so that the body of the essay is divided into two parts.**
>
> *Point-by-point method*: **Each paragraph in the body of the essay discusses Corrections Canada and another law enforcement agency in connection with a particular aspect of the application process. For example, begin with the requirements for both agencies in one paragraph, then the application process for both agencies in the next paragraph, then the interview process in another paragraph, and so on.**

Some useful transitions are set out below.

Comparison	Contrast
like	unlike
similarly	conversely
likewise	otherwise
also	but
on the one hand	on the other hand
generally	however
usually	instead
in keeping with	as opposed to

EXERCISE 7 » Developing an Outline

Using the contents of the following paragraph, develop an essay outline for each of the strategies discussed above (narration, description, exposition, persuasion, and comparison/contrast):

> **Customs officers are commonly seen as the opposition, threatening to confiscate that bottle of overproof rum you brought back from your Caribbean vacation. As they see it themselves, they are just enforcing rules made up by the government. Their chief targets are people who want to make exorbitant profits at the expense of their fellow citizens. But even the innocent feel intimidated. Confronted by a uniformed customs officer, most returning travellers feel guilty even if they don't have an undeclared jar of Uncle Sid's pickles hidden in their luggage.**

1. Tell a story about an incident at customs that involved you. (Use narration.)
2. Describe a search of your luggage and car at a border. (Use description.)
3. Describe the procedure for a secondary customs inspection. (Use exposition.)
4. Convince a customs officer that you have nothing to declare. (Use persuasion.)
5. Describe how the duties of a customs officer differ from those of another law enforcement officer. (Use comparison/contrast.)

Conclusion

Writing a good concluding paragraph is difficult. It is not enough to say, "In conclusion," and then repeat the thesis statement, as in the following example:

> *Thesis*: **Crime is on the increase in Canada because not enough criminals are stopped from entering the country.**
>
> *Inadequate conclusion*: **In conclusion, crime is on the increase in Canada because not enough criminals are stopped from entering the country.**

There are a number of methods you can use to write a successful conclusion:

1. *Rework and elaborate on the contents of your introductory paragraph.* Reword your thesis statement and the introduction's main idea.

> **Customs officers need more tools to do their job. They are restrained by a lack of technology, and their lack of public recognition compared with other law enforcement officers tends to minimize their effectiveness in the fight against crime. Much has been done, yet much remains to be done, to make our borders safe.**

2. *Summarize.* Repeat the main points of your essay.

> **Law and security programs are now found in every provincial community college, as well as in private training institutions. Coordinating these programs is**

essential if students are to graduate with acceptable minimum requirements acknowledged by all law enforcement agencies. Possibly the provincial government should step in.

3. *Offer solutions.* After making a number of points in the body of your essay, offer a solution to the problem you've presented, or make a prediction about what might happen if your advice isn't followed.

The need for private security has increased dramatically as law enforcement agencies become overwhelmed owing to rising crime rates and underfunding. However, formal training for private security officers has not improved with the demand for their services. The training should meet a minimum standard sanctioned by the government in cooperation with police, customs, and corrections agencies. In this way, private security could play a more important and more respected role in law enforcement.

4. *Tell a story that illustrates your thesis.*

Frederich Dumont, a convicted murderer, was on the streets of Saskatoon after having served less than two-thirds of his sentence. Two days later, he seriously injured a variety store owner in a failed robbery attempt and was arrested in the store. This is but one more brutal incident showing the need to reform the parole system.

EXERCISE 8 » Writing Conclusions

Return to Exercise 7 in which you developed outlines for each of the five writing strategies discussed in this chapter. Write a conclusion for each strategy based on the outline you developed.

The First Draft

As you have read in this chapter, writing happens in stages, and it's best to break up a large project into many steps and complete each step one at a time. Write your first draft knowing that you will return to it for revising, editing, and proofreading. In this way, you give yourself the freedom to express yourself as best as you can without the stress of trying to make it excellent the first time you sit down to write it. You will return to your sentences and paragraphs and improve them later.

Give yourself plenty of time over a few sittings to complete this stage, following your outline. Once you have a draft in front of you, you can question your work and consider what to add, delete, or rewrite. It's a more efficient process than expecting yourself to produce an excellent finished product from the start. Once your first draft is complete, use the Essay-Writing Checklist at the end of this chapter to help you revise and proofread your work.

Research Paper

The research paper and the essay are written in much the same way, except that with the research paper, you rely more heavily on facts from outside sources and use them in your paper. These facts must be documented—that is, you must list your sources in a bibliography, works-cited list, or reference list at the end of your paper, and cite them in the paper itself (as discussed in Chapter 7, Research Skills). In this way, you identify the sources of direct quotations and indirect quotations, as well as any ideas or other specific facts you have obtained from elsewhere.

Finding the Facts

The nature and sources of information you'll need for your writing project will vary with the situation. In most cases, the facts and information you need are readily available in your college or university library. All you have to do is find them.

But the research paper does not just involve finding great chunks of information from outside sources and inserting them into your research paper. Rather, you will try to match what you already know or suspect with facts established elsewhere. For example, if you have the opinion that the number of homicides has decreased in your city, you can search for sources that deal with the topic of homicides and look for information that confirms your belief. Sometimes, in the course of your research, you will discover an abundance of evidence that changes your belief—you may discover that the number of homicides has in fact risen in your city. In such cases, you may decide to change your thesis and take an opposite position. Local newspapers, magazine articles, visits to the police station, and other sources such as the Internet will provide you with the information you need. In another situation, you might want to investigate the job prospects with, say, the Calgary police force. You'll need to research different sources to find this information.

EXERCISE 9 » Writing Essays

1. Select a topic of local or national interest for law enforcement students and write a 500-word essay on it. Use an outline, an introductory paragraph, a closing paragraph, and supporting paragraphs. This essay should be an opinion-based one that does not contain research.

2. Turn the essay you have written into a research paper in which you include facts from outside sources to support your thesis. You should attempt to have at least three types of sources (e.g., a book, a newspaper, and a journal). Cite your sources in your text, and compile a bibliography, works-cited list, or reference list.

Essay-Writing Checklist
Format
- Have you provided enough background information for your reader to
  - recognize your thesis?
  - understand what follows?
  - want to read further?
- Do the ideas that you introduced in the beginning follow a continuous line of thought that moves from an introduction, to a discussion, to a conclusion?
- Have you used appropriate transitions?
- Is all of your discussion relevant to the topic and thesis?
- Are your time sequences logical and consistent?
- Does the last paragraph properly conclude the essay rather than simply restate information?

Grammar*
- Have you eliminated sentence fragments?
- Have you eliminated run-on sentences?
- Have you checked for parallel construction within sentences and between sentences?
- Have you checked for misplaced and dangling modifiers?
- Are the elements of each sentence clearly and logically related?
- Do subjects agree with verbs?
- Do pronouns agree with their antecedents and with each other in person and number?
- Is the relationship between nouns and pronouns clear?
- Are verb tenses consistent?

Style*
- Are the beginnings of your sentences varied? For example, do some start with the subject and some with an introductory phrase or clause?
- Have you mixed your sentence lengths effectively?
- Have you varied the structure of your sentences, making some simple, some compound, some complex, and some compound-complex?

* For further definitions of terms of grammar and style, see Chapter 4, Writing Foundations and Grammar.

Wording

- Have you used vocabulary suitable to your reader?
- Have you used active verbs wherever possible?
- Have you used appropriate adjectives and adverbs?
- Can you explain the reason for your choice of every word, and justify its location within the sentence?
- Have you used any words whose spelling or meaning you are not entirely sure about?
- Have you eliminated clichés, slang, jargon, idiomatic expressions, and acronyms that will be unclear to your reader?

Punctuation

- Have you used periods at the ends of sentences and after abbreviations?
- Are question marks used after interrogative sentences?
- Have you used exclamation marks very sparingly, only for very special emphasis?
- Have you used quotation marks for direct speech, direct quotations from sources, and titles of short works?
- Have you used—but not overused—commas to separate internal parts of your sentences and to clarify ambiguities?
- Are semicolons used to separate parts of a sentence that are grammatically distinct but logically related?

Spelling

- Have you checked the spelling of difficult words?
- Have you checked *ie* combinations, spelling changes caused by suffixes, and consonants that must be doubled?
- Have you used capital letters for titles, names, countries, and months of the year?
- Have you used apostrophes for possessive nouns, indefinite pronouns, and shortened forms of words?

Manuscript Form*

- Has your source material been documented correctly and cited?
- Have you used the correct form (MLA or APA) of documentation?
- Have you used the proper format conventions for the piece you are writing: essay, research paper, report?

* For further discussion about citing and documenting sources, see Chapter 7.

CHAPER SUMMARY

The essay is the basic form of writing task in colleges and universities, and to produce a well-constructed essay you must exercise organization, grammar, and spelling skills. Every essay is composed of a number of paragraphs: an introductory paragraph that contains a topic sentence and a thesis statement; supporting paragraphs; and a concluding paragraph. Transitions form a link between paragraphs and the main points of the essay. Research is properly documented.

KEY TERMS

controlling idea, 170
strategy, 172
thesis statement, 170
topic sentence, 167
transitions, 180

REVIEW AND REFLECTION QUESTIONS

1. The word *essay* comes from the French root word meaning "to try," and in English, it first meant "a trial." How is a writer of an essay like an attorney in a trial?

2. Based on the material in this chapter, discuss how writing the essay applies to other forms of writing, such as reports in policing, journals in the community justice field, or client reports in the investigative field.

3. Each paragraph requires a topic sentence. Usually, the topic sentence appears in the beginning of the paragraph. Why might you place the topic sentence in the middle of the paragraph? Why might you place it at the end?

4. This chapter introduced the technique of *brainstorming* to generate ideas for topics and subtopics. Discuss other techniques you have encountered. Do you have a favourite? Why does it work for you?

9 Speaking Effectively

LEARNING OUTCOMES

After completing this chapter, you should be able to:

- Speak effectively in front of an audience.
- Select a topic for an oral presentation.
- Organize an oral presentation.
- Understand the mechanics of oral presentations.
- Handle question-and-answer periods.
- Avoid nervousness and distracting gestures.
- Use audiovisual aids to enhance presentations.
- Understand non-verbal communication methods.
- Use influential language.
- Understand the SIR method of impromptu speaking.

Introduction

Effective speaking skills improve interpersonal communications and are an occupational necessity for all law enforcement officers. Whether you are interviewing witnesses, questioning people, or testifying in court, effective speaking skills will enhance your effectiveness as a law enforcement officer. One way to improve oral communication skills is to prepare and deliver an **oral presentation**. Many of the skills that you learn and refine by giving oral presentations can be used in all communications situations, personal as well as professional. You should also learn about **non-verbal communication skills** so that you can use them yourself and recognize their use by others.

Have you ever noticed that whenever certain people speak, no matter what they say, it hardly seems worth the effort to listen? Other people speak with such authority that whatever they say seems to be worth listening to. Speaking in such a way as to be heard, to be influential, and to command respect depends on three factors:

1. your words
2. your delivery and tone
3. your appearance

In other words, your message is made up of what you say, how you say it, and how you look when you say it. For a spoken message to be effective, all three must concur. Learning to prepare an oral presentation will help you develop skills that will be of permanent value in your professional and personal life.

Community Outreach

Today, law enforcement agencies place a great deal of importance on community outreach; speaking effectively informs people, creates trust, and improves the working atmosphere for everyone on your team. Look at a number of law enforcement websites and you will see that they devote many resources to these initiatives. Police, corrections, and security officers routinely meet the public in schools, libraries, and offices—in other words, wherever the need arises to keep the public informed and answer questions. Community outreach is an important part of modern law enforcement.

Academic Presentations

Speaking effectively for academic presentations is a skill that will serve you well as you progress through college into the workplace and any future educational opportunities. Whether it is a matter of completing a single day of in-service training or an entire course for upgrading purposes, you are likely to find yourself preparing presentations for academic purposes throughout your career.

An **oral presentation** is delivered through speech. Effective oral presentations have many purposes; in general, the purpose is to inform or persuade a group of listeners.

Non-verbal communication includes visual elements, vocal elements, and spatial elements.

Effective Oral Presentations

Purpose

An effective oral presentation can enable you to sway a group of people toward your point of view or merely to inform people about something that you think is important. You must ask yourself what you are trying to accomplish through any particular oral presentation. Initially, of course, you are attempting to obtain a good grade from your instructor. However, beyond this, you must decide whether you are trying to inform (through exposition), to persuade, or to tell a story (through narration). Decide on the subject of your presentation, and ask yourself what you expect from your **audience** after your presentation.

For example, you may want your audience to

- recognize the role of the customs officer
- realize that our jails are overcrowded
- understand the *Youth Criminal Justice Act*
- create a Community Watch program.

Whatever your purpose, select and develop a **topic** that suits your interests and those of your audience.

Selecting a Topic

You may be in a position to select a topic that is of particular interest to you, or you may be assigned a topic by your instructor. Selecting your own topic can become one of the most difficult parts of the oral presentation. It is not easy to come up with a topic that is both interesting and manageable in the time allotted for your presentation. If you have the freedom to select your own topic, there are a few guidelines that might be useful:

1. Draw on your own interests, experiences, and opinions.
2. Consider your audience.
3. Select a topic that is timely and of which your audience might already be aware.

A student who is interested in the legal field and is giving a presentation to a class of law enforcement students has a wide range of topics to draw from that meet the criteria outlined above. Look at websites for local newspapers for ideas: Stories relating to the field of law are usually well covered. If a topic is covered in the local newspaper, it is usually timely and of sufficient importance that most of your audience will be aware of it.

Your **audience** refers to the person or persons who watch your presentation. Your presentation is for the benefit of these participants; imagine their concerns when designing each aspect of the presentation.

The **topic** is the subject of your presentation and should be interesting and manageable. Find a way to approach the topic so that it is interesting to you and your audience.

EXERCISE 1 » Oral Presentation: Starting Research

Search the Web for local and national news and find between five and ten stories likely to interest people in the legal profession. List the titles of these articles and briefly summarize them. Be sure that each summary contains the article's thesis and main supporting points. For each article, determine the following:

1. Who is the intended audience for the article?
2. What do you know about the topic covered in the article?
3. Do you hold any strong opinions about the topic?
4. What more would you like to know about the topic?
5. How would you obtain additional information about the topic?

Narrowing the Topic

Once you have selected a topic, you don't just start writing your presentation. Now is the time to give even more thought to your topic and your presentation. Consider the following matters:

1. How much time is available for your presentation?
2. How many ideas can you cover in that time?
3. What are the most important parts of the topic, and how many of them can be covered in the given time?
4. Which ideas will be of most interest to your audience?

EXERCISE 2 » Oral Presentation: Gathering Information

Using the articles you have selected for Exercise 1, choose the one that you feel would be most interesting to an audience of law enforcement professionals. Assume that you have been assigned a five-minute oral presentation on the topic covered in this article. Within the time allotted to prepare your presentation, determine the following:

1. What is the purpose of your presentation (e.g., to inform, to teach, to entertain)?
2. What points to support your purpose can you cover within the allotted time? (Assume that the average speaker can deliver between 115 and 120 words per minute.)
3. What are some secondary issues you might want to cover? Are there issues related to the main topic that would help your audience understand your main point?
4. How much research on the topic will you need to do in order to make an effective presentation?
5. What is a thesis statement that effectively defines the purpose of your presentation?
6. What is an appropriate title for your presentation?

Conducting Research

Having decided on your topic, you must begin researching it, compiling as much information as you can within the time you have. Summarize any information you find, noting the main points found in your sources. Be sure to keep a full bibliographic record of each source so that you can find the source again if necessary. You may find it useful to record the following information:

1. a full citation of your source
2. a summary of the article's contents
3. the main points in the article
4. any direct quotations you'll be using
5. a paraphrased version of the ideas you'll be using
6. any additional references, indicated in your source, that might provide you with further information about your topic

Cite evidence accurately; avoid distorting data or taking it out of context. Credit your source for any information and ideas you've used, even when you have paraphrased the material. Eliminate unnecessary material or material that won't fit into your allotted time.

Preparing Your Presentation

An oral presentation must be prepared, and prepared well. In this way, it is like any of the written material discussed in this book. Whether speaking to a colleague, making a presentation to a superior, or delivering a classroom presentation, you must be prepared. Some things to remember when preparing your oral presentation are set out below.

1. *Prepare an outline.* Include a topic and thesis statement as you would for an essay or a paragraph. The topic is what you are speaking about; the thesis statement is your point of view, usually expressed at the beginning of your discussion.
2. *List your main points.*
3. *Revise your list.* Review your points, and omit those that are unnecessary.
4. *Arrange your remaining points in logical order.* Use the procedure you would use for writing an essay.
5. *Write your opening sentence.*
6. *Write your introduction and conclusion.*
7. *Prepare your final draft.* Do not write it out or memorize it. Put your topic, thesis, opening sentence, main points, and conclusion on cue cards. You should know your topic well enough that you need the cue cards only to jog your memory. If you have audiovisual material, you should indicate on the cue cards where the audiovisual material is to be used.

There are various strategies for beginning an oral presentation, and they are similar to those described in Chapter 8, Essay Writing. Some of the more common ones are as follows:

- Tell a story or an anecdote.

My only previous contact with the legal system occurred when I was finishing high school. I was arrested on my graduation night. A couple of friends insisted that we go out for a few drinks. No sooner had I sat down in the local pub and had a few sips of beer than an undercover police officer came up and asked me for identification. I was taken to the police station. After what I saw that night, I resolved to do what I could to help those who can't afford legal assistance. I saw a lot of unfortunate people that night.

- Read a quotation.

As I read in a recent newspaper report, "Judges in this country never cease to amaze me." I have the greatest respect for the Canadian judicial system and for the people who sit behind the bench. However, I want to tell you about some questionable, and humorous, decisions that have recently been reached in our courts.

- Use a gimmick.

I'm holding in this plastic bag a small amount of marijuana—no, it's not really marijuana, just some common grass clippings from my front lawn. Look at how small the amount of grass is in this bag. If it was marijuana, and I was caught, I'd be risking a jail term. Our marijuana possession laws have to change.

- Reveal an interesting fact.

The legal aid system in Ontario is in turmoil. Too few lawyers want to take legal aid cases because it is too expensive for them within the legal aid guidelines legislated by the province. At the same time, the number of people needing legal aid is exploding, and the system is not able to handle these people.

- Relate a new fact about the subject.

Recently, the Supreme Court of Canada ruled that police have the right to search cellphones without a warrant when making an arrest. Police, it said, have "extraordinary powers" to search and seize when making arrests, and cellphones are no different than purses or briefcases in these situations. Cellphones are essential to the illegal drug trade.

The conclusion of an oral presentation, like the introduction, may be approached in various ways, but try to ensure that you accomplish at least one of the following:

- Restate your main topic.

As I said at the beginning of this discussion, the legal aid system is in turmoil, and I have pointed out only a few examples to prove my point.

- Summarize your main points.

Law, justice, and security programs are now found in almost every provincial community college, as well as in private training institutions. The need to coordinate these programs becomes essential if students are to graduate with acceptable minimum requirements acknowledged by all law enforcement agencies. Possibly the provincial government should step in.

- End with whatever method you used to begin.

> **So, I guess the only thing I'll be holding in this little plastic bag is my grass clippings—at least until the law changes. I don't want to go to jail.**

- Leave the audience with a challenge.

> **As citizens of this country, we must stand up and speak out against this contemplated invasion of our privacy.**

- Set an example for the audience to follow.

> **Talk is cheap. Here's what I intend to do.**

EXERCISE 3 » Oral Presentation: Making an Outline

Prepare an outline that is appropriate for the topic you have selected. In point form, list the following:

1. topic
2. thesis
3. method of beginning (e.g., anecdote, interesting fact)
4. the main points you wish to cover

After creating this broad outline, list any subpoints you wish to cover.

Organizing Your Presentation

Many experts recommend a three-step method of organizing an oral presentation:

1. Tell the audience what you're going to say.
2. Say what you have to say.
3. Tell the audience what you've said.

These steps can be expanded into the "Six Ps" of public speaking:

1. *Preface.* What in your background qualifies you to speak on the chosen topic?
2. *Position.* What is your thesis—the position you take on the topic?
3. *Problem.* Define the problem and give some background to the topic, including relevant issues and any terminology that the audience might need to know.
4. *Possibilities.* Be sure to explore all sides of the issue, and be respectful toward points of view different from your own.
5. *Proposal.* Once you've explored an issue, suggest some possible solutions. Are all solutions workable?
6. *Postscript.* Restate the issue you've discussed, pointing out that you have proven something, solved a dilemma, or in some other way accomplished what you set out to do in your introduction.

A presentation that lasts from five to ten minutes can easily be organized along these lines.

EXERCISE 4 » Organizing an Oral Presentation

Using the principles of organizing an oral presentation, prepare an outline for one of the following topics, or a topic of your choice:

• Smokers' (or non-smokers') have rights too.

• Cats make better (or worse) pets than dogs.

• Students should have longer (or shorter) weekends.

• Conjugal visits should (or should not) be allowed in prisons.

Write a sentence for each of the Six Ps.

Building the Mechanics of Your Presentation

When the organizational part of your oral presentation is complete, you should begin working on the **mechanics** of it, including the following:

1. *Volume.* Speak to people at the back of the room. If they can hear you, everyone can hear you.

2. *Rate.* People speak at the rate of 115 to 120 words a minute. Practise this. Nervous speakers speak too quickly.

3. *Pause.* Pause between main ideas, and even slightly after sentences. This will give your audience time to consider what you've said.

4. *Stance.* Don't slouch; project confidence. If you use a lectern, stand behind it with your hands to either side of the lectern; don't lean on it for support. If you don't use a lectern, keep your hands out of your pockets, and do not jiggle your change. Use your hands to express yourself. If you can't think of anything else to do with your hands, leave them at your sides.

5. *Personality.* Be sincere, and smile. Show your audience that you care about the topic you're presenting.

Do's and Don'ts

1. Give your audience what it wants to hear; be relevant.

2. Know your audience.

3. Realize that humour can work for or against you.

4. Dress appropriately.

5. Don't read your presentation.

6. Don't exceed your time limit.

7. Use visual aids.

8. Rehearse.

9. Be aware of the level of your vocabulary.

Answering Questions

There are three common categories of questions that might be asked:

1. *Open.* Open questions ask for your opinion about something.

2. *Closed.* Closed questions require a specific "yes" or "no" answer.

3. *Clarification.* Questions seeking clarification invite you to expand on a point.

Here are some general guidelines for responding to questions:

1. *Listen and respond.* Listen to the entire question, and think before you answer. Be objective in your response.

2. *Restate and respond.* Restate the question to the person who asked it. This will give you time to think. Restating the question also ensures that you have understood it.

The term **mechanics** refers to the parts of a presentation that are not related to its content, such as volume, timing, and posture.

3. *Categorize and respond.* Be aware of the category of the question, and respond accordingly. Don't give an opinion if a factual answer is requested.

4. *Retain your point of view.* Don't change your point of view from the position you adopted in your presentation.

If you don't know the answer to a question, admit it. You can ask your audience for help, or refer the questioner to a source where the answer may be found, but don't try to fake an answer. This ruins the effectiveness of your presentation.

Overcoming Nervousness

Many people are nervous about speaking in front of an audience, but there are ways to overcome this anxiety:

1. *Observe others.* Watch other speakers and pick up on their strengths.

2. *Lower your blood pressure.* Run cold water over your wrists before you begin your presentation; this lowers your blood pressure.

3. *Try to relax.* Loosen tense muscles through stretching and self-massage.

4. *Move your body.* Relax by moving your body unhurriedly and deliberately when you present.

5. *Suck on a candy.* Suck on a small, hard candy before your presentation; this eliminates a dry mouth.

6. *Breathe.* Take deep, regular breaths.

EXERCISE 5 » Exploring Phobia

Fear of speaking in front of an audience is a common phobia. What is a phobia, and why do so many people have this particular phobia? Suggest some ways, apart from the techniques described above, that people might overcome their fear of public speaking.

Using Visual Aids

Visual aids, when used effectively, can enhance any presentation. There are a few things that must be kept in mind, however, when considering the use of visual aids.

1. *Use **visuals** to clarify or enhance.* Visual aids should be used judiciously. They should not be used excessively or without a specific reason.

2. *Keep visuals simple.* You don't want to give your audience so much information visually that they're too distracted to listen to your words.

3. *Make visuals large.* Visuals should be large and visible enough that all members of your audience can see them.

4. *Provide time to absorb the visuals.* After displaying a visual, give the audience a moment to absorb the information before you paraphrase it and incorporate it into your presentation.

5. *Practise using visuals.* Don't ignore your visuals when you practise your presentation. Be sure they go where they're supposed to go and work when they're supposed to work.

Visuals are aids meant to enhance a presentation, not to replace the speaker.

Visual aids help an audience to understand your presentation and to remember what you have said. It is important that you use appropriate visuals for your presentation. Each kind of visual has particular advantages.

1. *Presentation software.* Programs such as PowerPoint create professional results; offer sound, movement, colour; and can incorporate photos, videos, and hyperlinks to online material. These programs are widely available and easy to use. Generally, they offer templates to help you create and design your presentation, and allow you to print outlines and organize speaker's notes. When the visuals are complete, you can share your presentation by posting it online or by attaching it to email.

2. *Presentation slides.* Limit the amount of text you include on a slide. Use text to help the audience focus on key words or sentences. You will lose their attention if you ask them to read long lists or entire paragraphs. Your audience would rather listen to a dynamic speaker. Select a clear, large font, and make use of a lot of white space to keep things clear. Simplify your use of colour, movement, and sound. Avoid overkill if you want your audience to follow your presentation.

3. *Videos.* Videos can be effective if they are properly prepared in advance. It is very distracting to have to search for the right spot in a video during a presentation, or to find an alternative if the setup fails. It's always a good idea to test the equipment and your video before you present. If you are showing video by clicking hyperlinks to Internet sources, check that the link and the site are working. Another point to consider when you are linking to video is the host website's appearance. Some websites, such as YouTube, contain ads and other distracting material. It's best to avoid embarrassing delays, so you might consider embedding the video into a slideshow.

4. *Handouts.* Handouts are still common in presentations, and can be as effective as other visuals. The audience often likes these souvenirs, and they help retention, but you have to avoid having your audience focus on them rather than on what you are saying. Provide handouts *after* you've made your points. Today, it is common practice to share a copy of your computer presentation by providing a link and posting your work online, or by emailing your presentation as an attachment.

5. *Whiteboards.* Generally, whiteboards have replaced chalkboards in today's classrooms. They are an easy tool for recording spontaneous contributions from the audience and generating informal graphics. You can use a cellphone camera to keep a permanent record of the material and share it with your audience as a digital file.

6. *Flip charts.* Flip charts are becoming old-fashioned, but they are easy to prepare and use, are portable, and allow the speaker to create new visuals while the presentation is in progress.

7. *Overhead transparencies.* Overhead transparencies are less commonly used today, but they are easy to prepare and use, and they allow the speaker to maintain contact with the audience during the presentation.

Using Slides Effectively

The following example of a poor slide layout uses too much text:

> Jones makes three important points. The first point he makes is that prison populations are growing despite the fact that crime rates across Canada are falling. The second point Jones makes is that, overall, costs for maintaining the prison system are rising. These costs are growing at a time when conditions within prisons are becoming worse for inmates and officers. This is a result of stretching resources. Jones devotes a good portion of his book to analyzing the government of Canada's policies designed to increase prison sentences. If they are meant to prevent crime, they do not seem to be working.

The following example of a good slide layout uses limited text:

> Jones makes three important points:
>
> 1. Prison populations are growing.
> 2. Costs are rising.
> 3. The government of Canada wants to increase prison sentences (Jones, 2015).

EXERCISE 6 » Speaking Skills for Law Enforcement Students

1. As a class, discuss ways in which effective oral presentation skills are valuable in law enforcement. Be specific: What situations can law enforcement officers (police, customs, corrections, security) encounter where effective oral communication skills are valuable?

2. Select a topic found in a newspaper or magazine article that deals with a law enforcement matter, and prepare a brief oral presentation on that topic. Do your presentation one-on-one for another member of your class. Submit your topic, thesis, and conclusion to your instructor.

IN THE FIELD

A customs officer is called to testify in court regarding a drug seizure he made at the Canada/U.S. border.

Lawyer: Officer Loft, can you please tell the court why you decided to pull my client over for a secondary search? You had it in for him, didn't you?

Officer (glances at the judge, making eye contact, and begins in a clear and confident tone): Your Honour, I noticed a few behaviours that indicated to me this driver may have been nervous at my window. First, he repeatedly glanced back towards the trunk and licked his lips in what appeared to be a nervous way. He made no eye contact with me whatsoever and answered my questions in short form while changing his story several times. I am also aware that there is a hidden compartment in the type of van Mr. Saunders was driving, and I felt all of this together warranted a secondary search.

Lawyer: Isn't it true, Officer Loft, that my client could have been nervous because of the accusatory tone you used when speaking with him?

Officer: The tone I spoke to your client with was very calm and direct. I had no reason at that time to accuse him of anything.

Lawyer: You spoke with 20 vehicles before my client's and yet didn't pull any of them over for a secondary search—only my client. I suggest to you that it is because my client is of a different culture that you felt the need to stop him. In fact, you targeted him. You have heard of the term racial profiling, have you not?

Officer: With each of those vehicles, I examined all the facts and evidence before me. I noted the behavioural observations displayed by the drivers I spoke with. I made the decision to pull over your client because he demonstrated unusually nervous behaviour as I described earlier. In addition to this, I also smelled a faint odour of what I believed to be cannabis marijuana coming from within the vehicle. I also noticed that the area of the hidden compartment was bulging and had a patch repair job over it. The totality of the circumstances indicated a need to investigate this vehicle and driver further.

What do you notice about the answers Officer Loft provides? When Officer Loft is accused of wrongdoing, how does he handle it? Why is this effective?

Non-Verbal Communication

"Actions speak louder than words." This statement is certainly true in oral communication. Body language reveals a great deal about both the communicator and the person receiving the communication. Understanding non-verbal communication is essential for effective communication, for interpreting others' behaviour, and, in many cases, for discovering the truth.

Approximately 65 percent of our face-to-face communication is non-verbal; many of our messages are transmitted through facial expressions, gestures, eye movements, and tone of voice. Many speakers are unaware of the non-verbal dimensions of their communications, and therefore send unintended messages. Frequently glancing at the clock while someone is speaking, for example, is clearly sending the message that you're impatient or bored or that you consider the speaker's words to be unimportant.

Non-verbal communication can be divided into *visual* elements, *vocal* elements, and *spatial* elements.

Visual Elements

Eye Contact

People who fail to make or to maintain effective eye contact are not good communicators, since they are allowing others to take control of a situation or are indicating that they have something to hide, or are embarrassed, anxious, dishonest, or ashamed of something. A law enforcement officer should quickly take note of a resistance to eye contact in a person being questioned; it usually indicates that something is wrong or that something is being hidden.

Facial Expression

Your facial expression, which is the key to non-verbal communication, must match your message in order for you to be taken seriously. Scowling throughout your oral presentation will give the impression that you want to be anywhere else but in front of the class. And a sea of bored faces in a classroom sends an effective message to the teacher regardless of the verbal communication taking place.

Gestures and Posture

Using your hands during an oral presentation can be very effective. Generally speaking, your gestures and posture can contribute to your message. On the other hand, they can detract from it. Fidgeting, nervous hand movements, shuffling from foot to foot—all of these may signal that a speaker is nervous or insincere. Exaggerated gestures, such as excessive use of the hands, extreme body movements, or stabbing with the fingers to make a point, often indicate a lack of confidence on the speaker's part. If the "speaker" is someone being questioned in a law enforcement matter, the officer should look out for these signs of anxiousness or dissembling.

Body Orientation

The position in which a person places his or her body during a conversation or confrontation tells a great deal about that person's approach to the situation. If a person faces you head-on, with squared shoulders and feet and other indicators of aggression, a physical confrontation may follow. If this body attitude is taken within your personal distance, it demands the response, "Back off!" You might want to take a step or two backward, although such a retreat may suggest a lack of control on your part and may encourage the other person to follow you into your space.

Vocal Elements

Loudness

A loud voice can indicate that you have control over a situation, but it can also convey aggression toward the other party and provoke loudness and aggression in response.

"Please step out of the car," said in a firm, normal speaking voice asks for cooperation. A shouted command of "Step out of the car!" might indicate that you're expecting, indeed looking for, an aggressive response. The use of the word "please" indicates a desire for cooperation.

Rate

Rapid speaking indicates nervousness. There is also the fact that, if you speak quickly, the other person may not understand you. Combine rapid speaking with a loud voice and an aggressive tone and body language, and you have a potential confrontation.

Emphasis

A sentence can have different implications depending on whether and how you emphasize certain words. Consider how differing emphasis in the following sentences changes the meaning:

> "Step out of the car, please." [*Get out slowly.*]
>
> "Step *out* of the car, please." [*Get out before I drag you out.*]
>
> "Step out of the car, *please.*" [*This is the last time I'll tell you.*]

EXERCISE 7 » Practising Verbal and Non-Verbal Communication

Role-play in a number of different situations involving both verbal and non-verbal communication. Imagine that you are a law enforcement officer dealing with

- a 12-year-old shoplifter
- a striker on a picket line
- a tourist at the border returning to Canada
- an impaired driver
- a speeding motorist

Have someone in the class play the role of the person you're dealing with. Attempt to question the person, who should respond using different types of verbal and non-verbal communication. Afterward, discuss how you coped with the different communication styles.

Spatial Elements

Most people "need their own space"—that area surrounding a person that others aren't allowed to enter or are allowed to enter only under certain circumstances. Someone who "gets in your face" is aggressively asserting himself or herself. There are different types of space or distance.

1. *Personal distance.* Usually between 0.5 and 1.25 metres from one's body, this "arm's-length" distance is where we allow friends and acquaintances. It is not an intimate distance.

2. *Social distance.* Usually between 1.25 and 3.5 metres from one's body, this is the distance at which most of our social interactions occur.

3. *Public distance.* Usually 3.5 metres or more, this is the preferred distance for meetings, classroom teaching, and interviews.

Cultural differences are a factor in personal space preferences. Where North Americans usually prefer to communicate at arm's length, people from Asian cultures prefer a greater distance. On the other hand, some cultures from the Middle East or Latin America traditionally communicate at much closer quarters, in some cases toe to toe. When speaking to a client, try to establish a distance that is comfortable for both of you.

Impromptu Speaking: Say What You Mean, SIR

Your supervisor requests a report for an upcoming court hearing, but you don't have it ready yet. Don't give way to the stress of the moment and offer excuses in a hesitant or garbled manner. Instead, muster your resources, collect your thoughts, and offer an organized, cohesive response. This skill can be learned by following a simple formula whose initials form the acronym SIR. The letters stand for *statement*, *information*, *restatement*.

According to the SIR principle, you would answer your supervisor as follows:

1. *Statement*: "I can't complete the report you asked for because I'm still waiting for some information."

2. *Information*: (a) "The witness hasn't been cooperative." (b) "Information from one of the social service agencies involved has been late because of vacation schedules." (c) "I'm waiting for the detective involved in the case to clarify one of her statements."

3. *Restatement*: "Although I still expect to complete the report in time for the hearing, I wanted you to know why it's not ready yet."

The impression this message creates is of an organized, well-thought-out position. A closer look at the structure of the message reveals the following:

1. Your initial *statement* is your basic position. Take a moment to decide on this main point, then express it simply and clearly.

2. The *information* comes next. One of the key factors in this formula is providing three pieces of information. Human beings like things expressed in threes. So figure out a way to follow your initial statement with three pieces of information. You may have more than one sentence for each, but you should clearly enumerate the three points.

3. When you make your *restatement*, take the opportunity to add something. In our example, the supervisor is reassured that the report will be ready. This indicates that the situation is under control.

The ability to think on your feet and convey a message succinctly with little or no preparation is a highly regarded skill, and one worth cultivating for the sake of your career.

EXERCISE 8 » Impromptu Speaking

1. Use the SIR method to answer the following questions:

   a. Why were you late for work today?

   _____

   b. You didn't return my call. Were you ill?

   _____

   c. Where have you been? I've been trying to phone you all morning.

   _____

2. Work with a classmate to perfect the SIR technique. Throw questions at each other concerning a variety of topics, and work on coming up with appropriate answers, giving three pieces of information with every answer.

A Last Word About Oral Presentations: Don't Read

It is one thing to review a cue card for directions; it is fine to glance down and check a statistic; it is even acceptable to read out a quotation you've copied from your notes. However, it is not acceptable to read a report and pretend that it is an oral presentation. Without eye contact, gesture, and enthusiasm, without visuals and audience involvement, there is no oral presentation—only a reading. Watching someone read is a miserable experience. When someone stands up and reads a presentation, the audience becomes distracted and loses interest. In other words, *the presentation is a failure*. Do not read your report!

Don't read. Don't read.

One-on-One Communication

Law enforcement personnel often have to deal with difficult people who are severely stressed at finding themselves in a legal situation—in the unwanted position of accused, victim, or witness.

Dealing with a Difficult Person

In any confrontational or challenging situation, the most important thing you can do is be professional. Remember that you are dealing with an emotional person and that your best approach is to defuse the emotion and conduct the conversation on a practical level.

There are numerous ways of accomplishing this, many of which have been discussed in Chapter 2 under the heading "Nine Rules for Effective Listening." Keep the following in mind:

1. Adjust the behaviour. Emotional or difficult people react in a certain way for a reason: They may be angry or fearful; they may feel threatened; or they may feel that they have been accused unjustly. Instead of responding to the emotion, attempt to determine what is making the person react in a difficult or emotional manner, and then remove whatever is triggering that reaction. In other words, get to the root of the person's behaviour, and then use the principles of active listening to adjust it.

2. Be tolerant. Remember that the person's difficult behaviour is justified in his or her mind. Perhaps it has helped the person deal with problems in the past. Defensiveness or reticence in a victim, for example, may stem from long-standing mistrust of outsiders, and even though you're there to help, you are still seen as an outsider—someone who ultimately won't be affected by the victim's plight. You will get paid or keep your job regardless of what happens to the victim.

3. Reward non-defensive behaviour on a person's part by mirroring it when it occurs. Keep the pace of your conversation slow, do not exhibit negative non-verbal communication, listen carefully, and bring a calming manner to the situation.

4. Show that you are on the person's side and want to help by using phrases such as "I see what you mean," "I understand what you are saying," or "I think that I can help you." But don't make promises that you can't keep.

5. Give difficult people options and let them make decisions that will allow them to feel in control of their own lives. People often react negatively when they feel that their lives are entirely in the hands of a law enforcement professional.

6. Reassure the person with empathetic statements like, "After all you've been through, I can understand why you are angry."

7. Don't make the person feel anonymous by saying things like, "Every witness has to fill out these forms." It is embarrassing for a witness to be deprived of individuality this way.

8. If the person is abusive or non-responsive, look for any part of his or her conversation that is appropriate and constructive, and reward it with attention and gratitude. Be forgiving.

> *Victim:* **All you ever do is talk! I'm being threatened and all you can do is talk!**
>
> *Officer:* **I do talk a lot.**
>
> *Victim:* **If you were paying attention to what I've been saying, you might have some answers for me. That's why I'm talking to you!**
>
> *Officer:* **That may be true. I could be paying more attention.**
>
> *Victim:* **You're just like all of the other cops. You use me and use a lot of language that I don't understand, and I still have to face the consequences!**
>
> *Officer:* **So far there are no consequences. I talk a lot and ask questions because I'm trying to find the best way to help you.**

In *Impact: A Guide to Business Communication*, Margot Northey discusses ways to deal with aggressive behaviour:

> Sometimes emotions run high and, if left unchecked, they can create hostility. You can help by encouraging participants to stick to the facts, so that their comments don't become a personal attack. … Try to remain neutral rather than taking sides. … Create a constructive atmosphere where ideas are built up and developed (Northey, 1998).

In the end, you can maintain your professionalism with difficult people by simply maintaining good listening habits, responding when appropriate, and offering constructive advice.

Conferencing with Peers

Small conferences and workshops and discussions with your peers must be structured in much the same way as formal presentations. A presentation to your peers is more than a conversation, and the fact that you might be seated does not allow you to be offhand or casual. Your approach should be based on the following questions:

1. What is the purpose of your presentation?

2. Who is the audience, and how much do they know about your topic?

3. How much time will be allotted to your talk?

4. Will there be a question period?

5. Are other speakers involved?

After answering these questions, begin to prepare by

- brushing up on your topic
- planning a general outline
- gathering key facts and statistics
- preparing visual aids, diagrams, or handouts, if necessary

Following these suggestions and practising good speaking skills should allow you to make an effective presentation.

EXERCISE 9 » Presenting to Small Groups of Peers

Form the class into small groups and have the instructor assign topics to each member of each group. These topics will be related to either something taught in the course or something of which the participants have knowledge. Each class member will be responsible for making a presentation to his or her small group.

Applications of Speaking Techniques

Testifying in Court

Most law enforcement officers eventually must testify in court. In addition to applying the principles of effective oral presentations discussed above (and testifying in court is simply another type of oral presentation), remember to do the following:

1. Tell the truth.
2. Don't guess. If you don't know, say so.
3. Be sure you understand any questions put to you.
4. Take your time.
5. Give clear answers.
6. If you are estimating, say so.
7. Be courteous.
8. Avoid humour.

Remember, the purpose of testifying in court is to assist the court in getting at the truth. If your testimony is properly prepared, you will not have any problems.

EXERCISE 10 » The Debate

Having a debate involves making arguments for and against a particular statement or point of view. A debate is a contest in which different speakers take affirmative and negative sides of an issue. For this exercise, you will need to divide into even-numbered groups, and then settle on a topic for debate. You might consider the following questions: Should private security officers be given expanded police powers? Should restorative justice be instituted in Canada? Your debate might take the following format:

Resolved: That restorative justice be instituted in Canada	
Affirmative (Speaker 1):	**Opening statement**
Negative (Speaker 1):	**Opening statement**
Affirmative (Speaker 2):	**Expand on a specific point from the affirmative side's opening statement**
	Rebut points from the negative side's opening statement
Negative (Speaker 2):	**Expand on a specific point from the negative side's opening statement**
	Rebut points from the affirmative side's opening statement

When all members except one from each side have spoken in the manner outlined above, proceed to your closing statements:

Affirmative (Final speaker):	**Closing statement, or summary**
Negative (Final speaker):	**Closing statement, or summary**

In the debate, keep the following in mind:

1. When you prepare the debate, keep in mind that the opposing side will attempt to undermine your argument. Consider the opposition's point of view, and attempt to anticipate and counter any arguments that the opposition might make.
2. The strongest arguments for your position should appear in the opening statement.
3. Be persuasive; the opposition will be a hostile audience.
4. In your rebuttals, emphasize your opposition to the main points made by the opposing side.
5. Use the summary to repeat your side's main points, to repeat your rebuttals to the opposition's major points, and to re-emphasize your own side's strongest points.

Keep in mind that a code of conduct applies to debates. The following rules should be observed:

1. Stay with the subject in question.
2. Do not speak out of order.

3. Avoid personal attacks; deal with the issues.

4. Stand while speaking.

5. Address the chair or moderator rather than the other participants.

6. Limit your discussion or rebuttal to a maximum of three minutes.

The debate format outlined above might be done differently, depending on the nature of the topic and the time available. After the debate, the moderator or chair can decide which side won. Or the audience can decide through a show of hands or a secret ballot.

An Alternative Debate

Another way to organize a debate is for the teams to act as the jury coming to a verdict in the case presented in the "Facts for the Mock Trial" section of Exercise 11, below. Different speakers take affirmative and negative sides on the charge. Each side attempts to convince the other using arguments based on evidence from the text. At some point arranged by a moderator, open up the discussion so that participants are free to change their point of view. In the end, take a vote by a show of hands to decide the verdict.

EXERCISE 11 » The Mock Trial

Conducting a mock trial will help to improve the oral presentation skills of everyone involved, and it will give you a taste of courtroom behaviour. The focus is not, however, on courtroom protocol. What is important is the way participants conduct themselves and communicate the facts. The number of people involved will depend on the size of the class. At a minimum, students will play the following parts:

- a judge (the instructor might assume this role)
- a Crown attorney
- a defence lawyer
- a jury
- a complainant
- an accused

Staging the Mock Trial

The prosecution will present its case, and the defence will attempt to refute it. Then the judge (in a non-jury trial) or the jury will decide whether the accused is guilty. The trial procedure for a jury trial is as follows.

Opening Statements

1. The Crown attorney summarizes the prosecution's case.

2. The defence lawyer summarizes the defence's case.

Presentation of Evidence

1. The prosecution presents its case.

    a. The prosecution calls witnesses and questions them one by one.

    b. The defence can cross-examine each witness called by the prosecution.

   c. The prosecution can re-examine witnesses to clarify points.

   d. The prosecution rests its case.

2. The defence presents its case.

   a. The defence calls witnesses and questions them one by one.

   b. The prosecution can cross-examine each witness called by the defence.

   c. The defence can re-examine witnesses to clarify points.

   d. The defence rests its case.

Closing Statements

Each side points out the strengths of its case and the weaknesses of the case for the opposing side.

Deliberations by the Jury

The 12 members of the jury attempt to come to a unanimous decision; if they cannot reach a verdict, the case ends with a "hung jury," and a retrial is ordered.

However, the verdict is not important; what is important is how the participants conduct themselves and how the principles of effective oral presentations are applied.

The number of participants can be increased to include most members of the class. In addition to the roles listed above, the trial could include

- a bailiff (responsible for the conduct of the court)
- an assistant Crown attorney
- an assistant defence lawyer
- four witnesses (Blunt, Lynden, Caron, and Mayville; see the hypothetical situation that follows)
- a victim (Yaworsky)
- a police officer
- character witnesses (as many as required)
- expert witnesses (such as doctors and forensic experts)
- a stenographer

The following account involves a hypothetical hit-and-run incident. The accused has been arrested and brought to trial. It is the prosecution's job to convict the accused and the defence team's job to defend him. No critical evidence other than that contained in the scenario can be generated, although evidence can be expanded upon. For example, a twin brother can't miraculously appear at the trial and confess to the crime. However, certain things will need to be added. If you are going to call character witnesses, for example, these witnesses will have testimony not mentioned in the scenario, although it can't be contrary to the facts presented. For example, it is an established fact that the accused was the driver of the vehicle; therefore, you can't suddenly claim that he was having dinner with his mother when the crime occurred.

Decide among yourselves who is going to play each of the roles, and use class time to prepare the prosecution and defence and to conduct the trial. Regardless of the roles they are playing, class members can contribute to either the defence or the prosecution. The trial itself can take anywhere from one to six hours, depending on the depth of evidence presented.

If there are problems with points of law or objections from those assuming the roles of the lawyers, the judge can reserve his or her decision and consult with the instructor. The judge's decision on all matters is final and will not be subject to further objections or appeals. Remember, it is the effort put into the trial that is important, not the outcome.

Facts for the Mock Trial

You are a constable employed by the Brantford Police Service, Badge #372. On 21 August of this year, you are working the night shift in the downtown division, from 1900 until 0700 the following day. The weather is clear and the roads are dry. At 2125 on 21 August, you are dispatched by radio to 198 Queen St., Brantford, to respond to a hit-and-run accident. You arrive on the scene at 2130 and find a male sitting on the curb bleeding heavily from a cut on the forehead and suffering from a possible broken left arm. A female is administering first aid. An ambulance was dispatched to the scene at the same time you received the call, and it arrives at 2136. You speak with the victim briefly before he is transported to General Hospital, 1223 Festival St., by District Ambulance Services, at 2140. The victim's basic identity is as follows:

Victim:	**Charles Yaworsky**
Address:	**21 Bold St., Brantford, ON N4C 1T1**
DOB:	**30 May 1956**
SIN:	**471 832 136**
Telephone:	**519-555-1212**

After identifying himself, Yaworsky tells you that just before the accident he was walking southbound along the west side of Queen Street. He decided to cross the street to the east side near the intersection of Queen Street and King Street at approximately 2120. He was looking at a couple who appeared to be having an argument in a laundromat on the east side of King Street at the corner of Queen Street when he was sideswiped by a vehicle that didn't appear to have its headlights on. Yaworsky didn't see the vehicle, but he heard a loud blast of music just before he was hit. He doesn't remember anything else because he was rendered momentarily unconscious after being struck and thrown to the sidewalk.

You tell Yaworsky that you will be at the hospital as soon as you have gathered evidence and interviewed witnesses. By this time, a crowd of about 20 people has gathered at the scene. Two people come forward as witnesses. Following are the basic facts about one of them:

Witness:	**Mary Blunt**
Address:	**202 Queen St., Brantford, ON N8P 3S7**
DOB:	**16 July 1987**
SIN:	**411 756 027**
Telephone:	**519-555-2222**

Mary Blunt is a registered nurse. She was sitting in her living room watching television at approximately 2120 when she heard a loud thud and a scream. She ran out of her home to find a man lying on the sidewalk on the west side of the street in front of 198 Queen St. He was unconscious and bleeding from a cut on the forehead. His left arm looked as if it had been broken. Blunt called 911 on her cellphone. While she was tending to the victim's cut, he regained consciousness. He was groaning, but he didn't say anything. Blunt did not see the accident or speak to the victim or to anyone who saw the accident.

You call dispatch for an incident number (03-1350), write it on your business card, and give it to Blunt, asking her to call the police station if she thinks of anything else. Then you speak to the second witness, whose basic identity is as follows:

Witness:	**George Lynden**
Address:	**71 Duke St., Brantford, ON N7B 3W2**
DOB:	**15 September 1981**
SIN:	**400 351 058**
Telephone:	**519-555-3333**

George Lynden was walking his dog southbound on the east side of Queen Street sometime after 2100 on 21 August. He didn't know what time it was because he didn't have a watch. As Lynden was walking opposite Maggie's Bar and Grill at 130 Queen St., about two blocks north of King Street, he saw a man leave the bar. Lynden noticed him because the man was very unsteady on his feet. Lynden described the man as "middle-aged, wearing a green shirt and dark pants." Lynden didn't notice anything else about him. The description matches the clothing worn by the victim. As the man walked southbound on Queen Street, he fell several times and occasionally wandered onto the street from the sidewalk. As the man approached the intersection of Queen Street and King Street, he attempted to cross from the west side to the east side. Lynden is aware that there is a laundromat on the southeast corner of the intersection, but didn't hear any noise of an argument coming from there.

As the victim was nearing the centre of Queen Street, a vehicle going southbound approached at high speed. Lynden had the impression that the vehicle had no headlights on, although he was seeing it from behind. He did get a partial licence plate number. Like the victim, Lynden said that the vehicle's radio was playing very loudly. Lynden said that the right side of the vehicle, near the passenger door, hit the victim. The driver, whom Lynden didn't see, didn't apply the brakes and kept going after impact. Even though Queen Street is lit by streetlights on the east side, Lynden didn't get a good look at the vehicle because the accident happened so quickly. Lynden didn't assist Blunt, whom he saw running to help the victim, nor did he speak with her.

Lynden described the vehicle involved as a mid- to late-2000s model, possibly a Honda product, silver or grey, four-door, with an Ontario licence plate whose first two letters are "AJ." There was no visible damage to the car.

You give Lynden the incident number and ask him to call if he thinks of anything else.

You leave the scene at 2230, proceed to General Hospital, and interview Yaworsky. He is conscious and admits to having had "three or four" beers at Maggie's Bar and Grill in the hour or so he was there. He says he wasn't intoxicated. The attending physician reports that Yaworsky needed five stitches to close the gash on his head, that his left arm is bruised but not broken, and that he has other minor cuts and scrapes possibly caused by his being thrown to the sidewalk.

You leave the hospital at 2300 after broadcasting a description of the car allegedly involved in the incident, and resume general patrol. You also create a diagram (following page) of where the incident occurred based on the information you have obtained to this point in the investigation.

At 2320, you receive a call from dispatch directing you to see Maurice Small at 575 Oak St., who is complaining that his 18-year-old son took the family car without his permission. You arrive at 575 Oak St. at 2325 and interview Small. The basic facts about Small are as follows:

Complainant:	Maurice Small
Address:	575 Oak St., Brantford, ON N3T 5V2
DOB:	15 October 1968
SIN:	428 716 276
Telephone:	519-555-3022
Driver's Lic:	S6018-40715-81015 (ON) G
Employer:	Dade Enterprises, 22 Main St., Brantford, ON
	Telephone: 519-555-4177

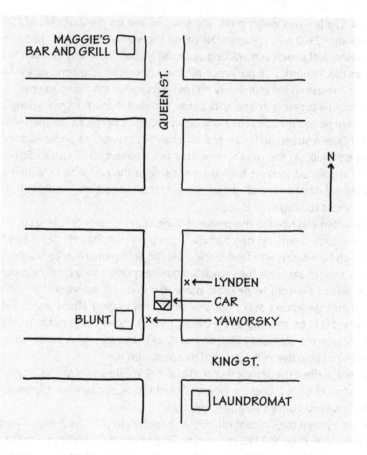

Small reports that earlier in the evening, his son Brent told him that he was going out with some friends. At approximately 2100, Small noticed that his car was missing from the driveway. The basic facts about this vehicle are as follows:

Vehicle:	Honda Civic DX-1
Year:	2007
Colour:	Silver
Plate:	AJXW 846 Ontario
Valtag:	1148131
VIN:	1G8LM5281RS293176
Insured by:	Boyson Insurance Brokers
Policy #:	NY93BC1176

Small didn't report the vehicle missing at the time because he suspected that his son, despite not having a driver's licence, might have taken it. This had happened before. His son hadn't arrived home by 2300, so Small decided to call the police, fearing that there had been an accident. Brent and his friends returned with the car at 2315, but Small decided not to report that the car was returned because he felt that his son needed to be taught a lesson. The son's identity is as follows:

Accused:	**Brent Maurice Small**
Address:	**575 Oak St., Brantford, ON N3T 5V2**
DOB:	**30 August 1998**
SIN:	**486 756 027**
Telephone:	**519-555-3022**
Employment Status:	**Unemployed**
Physical Description:	**Brown hair, hazel eyes, no facial hair, no glasses**
	No outstanding features
	Medium build, fair complexion
	Height—180 cm
	Weight—73 kg

You interview Brent Small on 22 August, beginning at 0012. Brent admits that he took his father's car and went joyriding with a couple of friends. They were driving on Queen Street at about 2130, when they noticed a police car parked in front of a house. Brent turned off the lights on his father's car and sped up, then turned on the lights again when he felt he was in the clear. He didn't want to get stopped without a licence. He says that the car's radio was quite loud.

When you tell him about the hit and run, Brent claims that he had nothing to do with it. He had noticed a man staggering along Queen Street, but the man was on the sidewalk. You examine the car and find a large scratch on the passenger door, but Small states that this could have happened previously. Small doesn't want to press charges against his son for taking the car. You arrest Brent at 0025, 22 August, for leaving the scene of an accident and for driving without a licence. You read him his rights. Brent Small is transported to the Downtown Division.

The two people who were in the car with Brent are as follows:

Passenger 1:	**Melissa Caron**
Address:	**923 Oak St., Brantford, ON N3T 4X6**
DOB:	**18 September 1998**
SIN:	**416 275 572**
Telephone:	**519-555-7777**
Passenger 2:	**Sandra Mayville**
Address:	**76 Harper St., Burford, ON N6L 9H6**
DOB:	**28 April 1995**
SIN:	**492 512 560**
Telephone:	**519-555-1256**

You interview Melissa Caron and she provides the following witness statement:

I was in the car with Brent Small last night. Sandra was staying at my place overnight, and Brent called and said that he had his father's car, and he'd stop by to pick us up. I guess he came around 9 o'clock, or maybe a bit after. We had the radio on kind of loud, and we drove around a bit. When we got on Queen Street, Brent turned out the lights on the car. I asked him what he was doing, because it was getting dark and I couldn't see very much, and he told me that he saw a police car parked by the curb, and he didn't want to be stopped because he didn't have a licence. I didn't know that he didn't have a licence, and I told him that he'd better take us home because I didn't want to get in trouble. My parents would kill me if they knew I was driving around with a guy without a licence. I guess I kind of freaked out, because I was upset and I was mad at Brent for not telling us. Brent was going pretty fast by this time, and he turned on the lights. I didn't see Brent hit anybody, but I wasn't really paying attention, because I was sitting in the front seat and I was yelling kind of loud at Brent and looking at him, so I wasn't watching the street. Brent took us home about 10 o'clock. I didn't hear anything more until you came to interview me.

You then interview Sandra Mayville and she provides the following witness statement:

My father says I should have a lawyer, but I didn't do anything, so I guess I'll talk to you. I spent the night at Melissa's house in Brantford. My parents said it was OK. She has this friend, Brent Small, who called to say he wanted to come over and take us for a ride. We weren't doing anything else, so she said it was OK. I don't know the town too well, but one time he was driving and all of a sudden turned off the head-lights. He said he didn't want the cops to see him because he didn't have a driver's licence, but it seems to me that turning off the lights was the quickest way for some-body to notice him. Brent and Melissa were having a big argument about Brent not having a licence, and the radio was real loud, so I just sat there and looked out the window. I can remember seeing somebody walking down the street. It looked like he was drunk—you know, staggering a lot and I even saw him fall down once, but Brent still didn't have the lights turned on in the car, so I couldn't see too good. I don't know if Brent hit somebody. I didn't see anything, but there was so much going on in the car that I wasn't paying much attention to what was going on outside.

Brent pleads not guilty to the charge of leaving the scene of an accident, and the case goes to trial.

EXERCISE 12 » Communicating Effectively to Make a Good Impression

After the class puts on the mock trial, try this scenario.

Imagine the Brent Small trial ended in a mistrial because of a hung jury. Two weeks ago, you were asked to evaluate your effectiveness in the trial, suggest ways you could improve in the upcoming retrial, and write a report. You've completed most of the report, but now you must finish the "Specifics" section.

Specifics

Obviously, the first impressions of witnesses, lawyers, and other parties in the courtroom are what start the credibility process. How individuals carry themselves, how they relate to those they question or answer, how they respond under pressure, whether they speak with confidence, their knowledge of the facts, their ability to get their ideas across clearly, the expression on their face, their general body language—all contribute to first impressions. And once that first impression is made, the individual's only challenge is to do nothing that will call into question the legitimacy of their word.

Analyze your impact on the trial and make suggestions about how you can improve your effectiveness in the upcoming retrial by completing the paragraphs below.

In the Small trial, I would evaluate my effectiveness as follows:

_____

_____

_____

_____

In the upcoming retrial, I can improve my effectiveness in the following ways:

_____

_____

_____

_____

CHAPTER SUMMARY

In order to communicate effectively, a law enforcement officer must understand and practise oral communication skills. One way to improve such skills is to prepare and present an oral presentation. Many of the skills you'll develop this way can later be applied to questioning people or to testifying in court. Non-verbal communication skills must also be mastered, both for improving the effectiveness of your own communications and for identifying the significance of non-verbal communication in others.

KEY TERMS

audience, 193
mechanics, 198
non-verbal communication, 192
oral presentation, 192
topic, 193
visuals, 199

Review and Reflection Questions

1. How can you show confidence when delivering your presentation?

_____

_____

_____

2. Why is it important to keep visual aids simple?

_____

_____

_____

3. What three things should you consider when selecting your topic?

_____

_____

_____

4. What approaches can you take to conclude effectively?

_____

_____

_____

5. What are the steps in the SIR method for impromptu speaking?

_____

_____

_____

PART II

Report Writing

10 Introduction to Report Writing

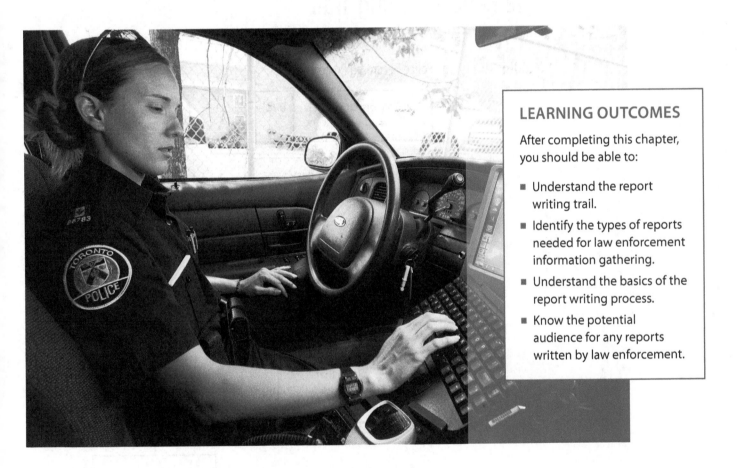

LEARNING OUTCOMES

After completing this chapter, you should be able to:

- Understand the report writing trail.

- Identify the types of reports needed for law enforcement information gathering.

- Understand the basics of the report writing process.

- Know the potential audience for any reports written by law enforcement.

Introduction

As law enforcement professionals, all interaction you have with the public—victims, witnesses, complainants, and suspects—must be recorded. The recording process is completed by writing notes in a variety of formats. This chapter explains the types of written recording you might do as an enforcement officer.

As well as considering the types of notes and reports you need to write, it is important to understand the wide range of audience you are writing for. Whether you work in policing, security, corrections, or bylaw, your reports will be read by a diverse population.

Each type of enforcement agency has its own specific protocol regarding the report writing trail, but this chapter outlines the basic process that all agencies will follow.

The Report Writing Trail

The chart in Figure 10.1 illustrates the recording process followed by police services.

FIGURE 10.1 The Police Recording Process

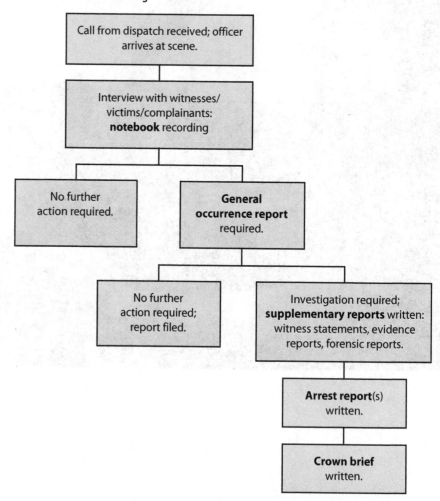

All law enforcement agencies follow a similar incident-recording process. For example, bylaw officers write notebook notes when called to a scene to investigate noise complaints or other infractions. These notes are used to write occurrence reports and witness statements. In cases where police investigation is required, bylaw personnel share the notebook entries and reports with the police service. Police investigators then begin their report writing process.

Border and airport security personnel also use notebooks and write occurrence reports and supplementary reports. They might share their reports with municipal police, provincial police, RCMP, or international law enforcement agencies.

As well, security guards use notebooks and write occurrence reports and supplementary reports. Again, in cases where police investigation is required, they will share their notes and reports as necessary.

Sample Scenarios

Scenario A

A bylaw officer receives a call to attend the home of a complainant who says his garbage cans have been vandalized. The officer interviews the homeowner, who tells her that when he came home from work, his garbage cans were lying in his driveway. He says when he left for work that morning, the cans were in their customary spot beside the garage. The officer writes the homeowner's complaint in her notebook and visits the neighbours on either side as well as the neighbour across the street. All three neighbours claim they saw and heard nothing regarding the garbage cans. The officer completes her notebook entry, but she does not write a report.

Scenario B

A security guard is dispatched to a college residence room. The student tells the guard that when he came back to his room from a morning class, his door was ajar, and his laptop, camera, and watch were missing. The guard questions the complainant and writes notes in his notebook. He then writes a general occurrence report (sometimes called an incident report). Police are called. The guard shares his notes and report with the police service, and the investigation is picked up by the police. The police write reports as their investigation requires. The guard might also conduct further investigation in residence and on campus and write supplementary reports.

Scenario C

A municipal police officer is dispatched to a domestic disturbance call at a suburban residence. The complainant tells the officer that he would like his son charged with assault. He tells the officer that his 25-year-old son came to the house looking for money. When the complainant refused to give his son money, the son punched him twice in the face. The officer observes blood and bruising on the man's face. The officer obtains the son's address and leaves to attend that address to question the son. No one is home at the son's address. The officer completes his notebook entries and writes a general occurrence report. The officer files the report and intends to visit the son's address the next day. Before going off shift, he is dispatched again to the complainant's house because a neighbour called 911 to report seeing the son's car in the complainant's driveway. The officer arrives at the scene and lets himself into the house after hearing someone inside yelling for help. The officer finds a man holding a bloody knife over the complainant, who is lying on the ground. The complainant has been stabbed in the left side of his torso. The officer arrests the man, who is in fact the complainant's son, and calls for an ambulance and a second car to transport the son to the police station. He then interviews the neighbour who called 911. The next day he interviews the complainant in hospital. Over the course of his investigation, the officer writes supplementary reports, an arrest report, and a Crown brief.

Types of Reports

In Figure 10.1 and the preceding scenarios, several types of reports are mentioned. Here is information about the roles and content of these reports.

Notebooks

Notebooks (also called duty books or memo books) are discussed in detail in Chapter 11, The Notebook. You should be aware of their importance as the first means of recording information for all law enforcement personnel.

General Occurrence Reports

General occurrence reports (also called incident reports or occurrence reports) are the first reports filed for any given occurrence or incident. They are the backbone of all investigations. They are written using the information that has been recorded in the notebook. General occurrence reports are described in more detail in Chapter 13, General Occurrence Reports.

Supplementary Reports

As an occurrence is investigated, officers gather evidence; interview witnesses, victims, complainants, and suspects; apply for warrants; describe crime scenes; and complete any other actions necessary to investigate and solve the crime. All of these actions are recorded in supplementary reports (also called investigation reports or investigative actions). Each supplementary report is carefully linked back to the original occurrence report by a case identification system. Every occurrence could have several supplementary reports appended to it. Supplementary reports are discussed in detail in Chapter 14, Supplementary Reports.

Arrest Reports

Once police arrest a suspect, a report must be written. Some services use specific arrest reports to write up arrests, and other services write up arrests in supplementary reports. There is one report per arrest. Arrest reports are described in more detail in Chapter 14, Supplementary Reports.

Crown Briefs

Once police have arrested a suspect, the Crown and defence must be made aware that the case is ready for the court. The Crown brief is the report that summarizes the crime and provides all of the evidence necessary for the Crown to proceed. Crown briefs are discussed in detail in Chapter 17, The Crown Brief.

Additional Reports

Law enforcement professionals complete a variety of additional reports on a regular basis. Many of these have to do with procedural matters within the agency or service, including the following:

- **briefing notes**
- **job shadow reports**
- **injury reports**
- **leave reports/absence reports**
- **equipment maintenance reports**
- **trend analysis reports**

The Report Writing Process

The process for writing reports varies from service to service, but the same basic protocols are followed by all law enforcement agencies. An officer (police, bylaw, security, border service, correctional) carries a notebook in which she records initial notes for any call or incident she is responding to. If further action is required, the officer writes a general occurrence or incident report at a computer in the office or in the service vehicle. Follow-up reports are then written as needed—either at the office or in the service vehicle. Depending upon the service or agency, as reports are filed they may be uploaded directly to a central database for immediate access by a variety of people: managers or staff sergeants; investigators; staff at the Crown Attorney's office; crime trends analysis personnel; and internal investigation personnel, to name a few.

Recent advancements in technology have led to the development of writing and recording software that could revolutionize the reporting process by providing a faster and more accurate way to record information, as discussed in the box "Police Reporting Enters the Digital Age," below.

Briefing notes are written for officers who are addressing the media or other interested parties. Subjects for briefing notes include details about ongoing investigations or successful arrests, police initiatives such as a new hiring or equipment purchase, or any other police-related news the public should know about.

New recruits and officers in line for promotion will often shadow mentors. They write **job shadow reports** detailing their experiences.

If an officer sustains an injury in the line of duty, an **injury report** must be filled out and filed with the human resources department and with insurance companies.

Officers requiring time off must complete paperwork, such as a **leave report** or an **absence report**, that will be submitted to superior officers and human resources.

In an **equipment maintenance report**, officers are responsible for notifying the garage of any vehicle maintenance needed. Likewise, officers would notify equipment maintenance personnel if other pieces of equipment, such as radios, computers, guns, vests, or helmets, require maintenance.

Trend analysis reports can be filled out by officers or by civilian personnel tasked with trends analysis. These reports are used to plan special operations, hire more officers, or start special investigative units, such an elder abuse unit.

Police Reporting Enters the Digital Age

By Brian Moorcroft, Centennial College

Source: SceneDoc.

Traditionally, police officers have recorded their observations, investigations, and reports using paper and pen, and more recently, personal computers based in patrol cars or at stations. However, this is often not the most efficient way to collect vital information.

Consider a typical assault investigation: A police officer is dispatched to the scene, where he or she begins recording information in a notebook. Notes could include personal observations, identification of those involved, and statements given by the victim or witnesses. The investigation is also likely to include photographs and video, recorded on stand-alone devices. Once all the information has been gathered, the officer must then return to the patrol car or the station in order to transfer it from the notebook to a police report, and videos and photos must be downloaded to a computer in the police station. These tasks may consume a great deal of an officer's valuable time.

In recent years, many police organizations in North America and elsewhere have begun replacing traditional tools with mobile, digital alternatives. SceneDoc, a Mississauga, Ontario–based company, has created a smartphone- and tablet-based software platform designed for police use. Using a device loaded with SceneDoc or a similar application, officers can gather all the necessary information at a crime scene, a motor vehicle collision, or another incident. They can take photos, shoot video, and even create sketches. There is also immediate online access to legislation and numerous departmental forms, reports, and procedures.

Information is instantly encrypted and uploaded to a secure, cloud-based server and stored permanently. Supervisors can view the recorded information almost instantaneously from any location with an Internet connection. The time saved can be significant:

SceneDoc suggests that its tools can help an officer to "clear the scene" up to 80 percent faster than when using previous methods.

The application also reduces the chance of introducing human error, which can occur when content is being transferred from one notebook, log, camera, or other device to another. For example, with these new digital tools, photo logs are automatically created, tagging each photograph with the date, time, and GPS location.

Once an investigation is completed, officers can compile a final report that includes logs of all documents, photos, and other information, and which notes any changes made to the original data, effectively documenting a chain of control for court and security purposes. Final reports can be printed or shared electronically as easily as sending an email.

While such tools can be valuable, it is important to note that technology cannot replace strong communication skills and investigative techniques; these applications may be helpful, but they cannot *think* for the officer. Strong communication skills are essential for completing accurate reports, no matter what format they appear in. And, as with any new technology or technique used by police officers, it remains to be seen what questions may arise in court concerning the use of these tools, and the admissibility of the evidence gathered with them.

Additional Information

To find out more about some of these emerging technologies, review the following websites:

- https://www.SceneDoc.com
- https://www.icrimefighter.com
- http://www.visionations.com

Discussion Questions

1. Can you foresee any potential problems that might arise with this shift in methods of information gathering and note taking by police officers?

2. What reasons might a defence lawyer give if he or she was to question the admissibility of evidence gathered using this sort of application? As a research project, try to find out the policy in your own jurisdiction about these tools.

Who Will Read Your Reports?

Your investigative writing will stand as a permanent record of events, observations, actions, and investigations. There are many people and groups that will have access to your reports.

Think about what the following audiences need from your reports. There is no question that excellent report writing is integral to solid enforcement work, and it is also integral to your reputation and career.

Supervisors

If you are assigned to regular patrol duties or front-line work, your supervisor (manager or staff sergeant, for example) will read your reports for a variety of reasons. She will want to be sure you are writing excellent reports and will recommend changes to sub-standard reports. She may also send you for training if your reports are consistently poor. For occurrences where investigation is required, your supervisor will assign cases to investigators, and they will read your reports. Your supervisor may also send your reports to crime trend analysts whose job it is to spot potential crime trends that need to be acted on.

Other Personnel at Your Service or Agency

If you respond to a call in which events, people, or evidence relate back to an ongoing investigation, all personnel involved in the original investigation will need to read your reports.

Other Enforcement Agencies

If any occurrences you write about involve multi-jurisdictional law enforcement agencies (e.g., RCMP, Canadian Border Services Agency, airport security, international agencies), those entities will need access to your reports.

People Involved in the Prosecution Process

Any reports you write that result in an arrest will be seen by Crown attorneys, defence lawyers, the defendant, judges, and many other people involved in the court process.

Insurance Companies

For any occurrences in which insurance damages are being claimed (e.g., personal injury, property damage), insurance personnel will read your reports.

Media

The media can be very helpful in spreading public awareness, and it is to the benefit of enforcement agencies to share information with the media as a means to help solve crime or alert the public to a danger. This means the media will have access to your reports when that is determined to be useful and appropriate by your supervisors and your agency's press office.

Following a Case

The following notebook entry and reports illustrate the police report writing trail and process for a case involving theft.

Background

On October 11, 2016, Officer Gail Barber was dispatched to the residence of a complainant who wanted to report the theft of his telescope from his back porch.

Notebook Entry

The following box contains Officer Barber's notes taken while attending the scene of the reported theft.

1620	Dispatched to 17 Wilkey Ave. regarding a theft
1630	Met with complainant Dr. Mitchell O'Brien
	DOB Oct. 23, 1970
	Dr. O'Brien reports that when he returned this afternoon from an
	outing at a nearby sports bar, he noticed that his telescope was
	missing from his back porch. He says he saw the telescope just prior to
	leaving the house. He remembers that the porch door was locked when
	he left. He arrived home approx. 1550. Dr. O'Brien led me to the back
	porch. I observed the back door ajar, but there was no damage.
	Dr. O'Brien led me to the back porch. I observed the back door ajar,
	but there was no sign of tampering on the lock or door handle.
	I asked O'Brien to describe the telescope.
	Coronado Solar Max II 60 Telescope
	serial #CSM2115617P112012
	approx. value $2,200.00
	I asked O'Brien if he had any idea who may have taken the telescope.
	He said he thought it could be his daughter's ex-boyfriend. The
	boyfriend knew where the spare key was kept. O'Brien also stated that
	the ex-boyfriend had a criminal record and had been very angry
	when O'Brien's daughter had broken up with him. O'Brien identified
	the ex-boyfriend as Samuel Markster. O'Brien does not know
	Markster's date of birth but stated Markster drove a red Mazda 3,
	licence ARLT 435.
	I asked O'Brien to describe his routine that day. O'Brien had been
	alone at home all weekend. His wife and daughter, who both live in
	the home, had been away on a trip.
	Wife - Dr. Marissa Treehorn
	DOB Aug. 2, 1971
	Daughter – Margo Treehorn
	DOB Nov. 19, 1995
	Dr. O'Brien stated he met with a group of friends every Sunday
	afternoon for beer.
	I asked Dr. O'Brien who knew of this routine. He stated that everyone
	who knew him would know, as the group had been getting together on

		Sundays for 15 years. He confirmed that Markster would know this, and
		he would also know that the house would be empty that afternoon.
		I left O'Brien my card and proceeded to canvass neighbours.
		No one was home at 15 Wilkey Ave. I left my card with a request to
		call me.
1705		*At 13 Wilkey, I spoke with Hamsa Abdul, DOB May 17, 1960, who*
		told me he had seen nothing suspicious but did recall a red Mazda
		driving down the street earlier that afternoon. It had been driving
		too quickly, which had annoyed Abdul.
1710		*I spoke with Mary-Ann Lerner, DOB Sept. 4, 1990, at 14 Wilkey Ave.*
		She confirmed the presence of the red Mazda on the street. She told
		me she saw it parked in the driveway of 17 Wilkey Ave. She said she
		thought nothing of it, as she has seen the car in that driveway
		numerous times. She knew the owner was the daughter's boyfriend.
		Lerner told me she saw the boyfriend exit the car and go around to
		the back of the house at approx. 1400 that afternoon.
		Lerner described the boyfriend as white, slender, about 6'2" with
		short dark hair.
1720		*I left the scene and ran the vehicle's licence plates through the database.*
		The database confirms the owner of the plate as
		Samuel Markster
		DOB April 8, 1990
		17-2660 Langton St., Ottawa
1740		*I returned to the station, wrote the occurrence report, and filed it.*

General Occurrence Report

The box on page 233 contains only the narrative portion of the general occurrence report written by Officer Barber, based on her notes taken at the scene. Note that the cover page of the report would list full names, addresses, dates of birth, descriptions of property, and other pertinent details.

Supplementary Reports

The case was assigned to Sergeant Doone, an investigating officer, and Barber's general occurrence report was sent to him. He wrote the supplementary reports on pages 234–236.

Note: Sergeant Doone would have taken notes in his notebook each time he conducted an investigative action for this case. Each of his six unsuccessful visits to Markster's residence would also have been recorded in his notes, but there would be no need to write reports for any of those unsuccessful visits.

Now that an arrest has been made, Sergeant Doone must write the summary sheet for the Crown brief that he will present to the Crown Attorney's office.

Summary

Summary

The charge of theft under $5,000.00 in this matter arises from an incident that occurred at 17 Wilkey Ave., Ottawa, ON, on October 9, 2016.

The person charged with theft under $5,000.00 is:

Samuel Markster, DOB April 8, 1990 of 17-2660 Langton St., Ottawa, ON

The circumstances of the offence are as follows:

On October 9, 2016, at approximately 2:00 p.m., Samuel MARKSTER drove his red Mazda 3, licence plate #ARLT 435, to 17 Wilkey Ave. for the purpose of letting himself into his ex-girlfriend's house by way of a spare key he knew of that was hidden on the premises. He parked in the driveway, exited his vehicle, and entered the house through the back porch. He intended to go through the house and retrieve letters he had written to his ex-girlfriend. He saw a telescope (Coronado Solar Max II 60 Telescope, serial #CSM2115617P112012) that he knew belonged to the homeowner, Dr. Mitchell O'BRIEN. The telescope is valued at $2,200.00. MARKSTER decided to steal the telescope and exited the premises with it. Two neighbours were able to confirm the presence of MARKSTER's car on Wilkey Avenue on the afternoon of October 9. Hamsa ABDUL of 13 Wilkey Ave., DOB May 17, 1960, confirmed he saw a red Mazda 3 drive quickly down the street mid-afternoon on October 9. Mary-Ann LERNER, DOB Sept. 4, 1990, at 14 Wilkey Ave., confirmed she saw MARKSTER's car in the driveway of 17 Wilkey Ave. that afternoon.

SGT DOONE went to MARKSTER's residence, 17-2660 Langton St., but no one was home. DOONE then visited Larry's Pawn Shop, 287 Wilbrod St., located four blocks east and one block south from MARKSTER's residence. DOONE spoke with shop owner Marilyn DEVRIES, DOB Jan. 22, 1962. DOONE inquired about the telescope in question, and DEVRIES brought DOONE to a case that held a telescope. DEVRIES removed the telescope from the display case for DOONE to examine. DOONE confirmed that the make, model, and serial number all matched the stolen telescope. DEVRIES volunteered to show DOONE surveillance footage from that day. DOONE identified MARKSTER on the surveillance from MARKSTER's picture on his licence. The surveillance footage showed MARKSTER entering Larry's Pawn Shop at 9:20 that morning, October 10, twenty minutes after the store opened. MARKSTER entered the shop with a large object under his right arm. He placed the object on the front counter. It was a telescope. The footage shows DEVRIES examining the telescope and then removing bills from the cash register. She handed the bills to MARKSTER, and he left the premises.

After repeated visits to MARKSTER's residence, on October 13, DOONE was successful finding MARKSTER at home. DOONE identified himself as a police officer and asked to be let in. MARKSTER let DOONE into his home and DOONE began to interview MARKSTER.

DOONE asked MARKSTER if he had visited 17 Wilkey Ave. on October 9 to steal a telescope. He denied doing so. DOONE asked MARKSTER his whereabouts on October 9. MARKSTER told DOONE he had been staying at a friend's house since October 8 for a video game marathon and that they hadn't left the house for four days.

DOONE then explained to MARKSTER that two witnesses had confirmed his car on Wilkey Avenue on the afternoon of October 9, when the telescope had been stolen. Further, Marilyn DEVRIES, DOB Jan. 22, 1962, owner of Larry's Pawn Shop, confirmed MARKSTER had sold the telescope in question to her on October 10.

MARKSTER then confessed to DOONE that he had visited 17 Wilkey Ave. on Sunday, October 9. He told DOONE he knew nobody would be home. He originally had planned to steal the love letters he had given his ex-girlfriend. He said he used the spare key to get into the house. On his way through the back porch, he saw the telescope. He then said this caused him to remember how much he hated Mitchell O'BRIEN, the owner of the telescope and father of his ex-girlfriend. At this point in the interview, MARKSTER became quite agitated. He stood up abruptly, began pacing and shouted, "That jerk of an old man made my Margo break up with me. He thought I wasn't good enough for them. I hate him! I should have smashed that telescope. He loved it more than he loved his family. I'm glad I took it."

DOONE then advised MARKSTER that he was being placed under arrest. DOONE charged MARKSTER with theft and asked him if he understood. He said, "Yes, I friggin' understand." DOONE handcuffed and then searched MARKSTER and took him to Westside Station where MARKSTER was turned over to the custody officer on duty.

Sample Reports for a Private Enforcement Agency

General Occurrence Report

Occurrence #: 607-15

Date of Occurrence: October 9, 2016

Reporting Officer: Gail Barber

Type of Occurrence: Theft

At 1620 on Sunday, October 9, 2016, I, Constable Gail Barber, was dispatched to 17 Wilkey Avenue to take a report of a theft. The roads were clear and dry, traffic was light, and I arrived on scene at 1630. I was met at the door by complainant Dr. Mitchell O'BRIEN.

I interviewed Dr. O'BRIEN, and this is what he told me.

After being out with some friends at a nearby sports bar, O'BRIEN returned home at approximately 1550 and prepared to do some reading on his screened back porch. As he entered the porch, he saw that his Coronado telescope was missing from its stand. He searched the property and the house and then called police.

I examined the door to the porch and noted that there were no signs of wear or tampering around the lock or door handle. I asked O'BRIEN if he had any thoughts about who may have taken the telescope. O'BRIEN said he thought his daughter's ex-boyfriend, Samuel MARKSTER, might have taken the telescope, as he knew where the spare key was kept and he was angry about his recent breakup with O'BRIEN's daughter. O'BRIEN told me MARKSTER drives a red Mazda 3, licence #ARLT 435.

I left O'BRIEN to canvass the neighbours. No one was home at 15 Wilkey Ave., but at 13 Wilkey Ave., I spoke with Hamsa ABDUL, who told me he saw a red Mazda 3 on the street that afternoon. He remembered it because it was driving too quickly. At 14 Wilkey Ave., I spoke with Mary-Ann Lerner. She told me she saw a red Mazda 3 parked at 17 Wilkey Ave. that afternoon. She said she thought nothing of it, as the car was often in that driveway. She believes it belongs to the daughter's boyfriend. She said she saw the boyfriend exit the car and go around to the back of the house at 1400 that afternoon.

I left the scene and ran the vehicle's licence plates through the database. The plates came back registered to a Samuel MARKSTER. Records showed that MARKSTER had two previous convictions for break and enter, several outstanding parking tickets, and a restraining order against him filed by Margo TREEHORN.

I returned to the station to write this report.

Supplementary Report

Re: Occurrence #: 607-15

Supplementary #: 1

Date of Occurrence: October 9, 2016

Date of Supplementary Report: October 10, 2016

Investigating Officer: Sergeant Wayne Doone

Further to the occurrence of the reported theft of a Coronado telescope from 17 Wilkey Ave. on October 9, 2016, I, Sergeant Wayne DOONE, went to 17-2660 Langton St. to question Samuel MARKSTER. MARKSTER was reported by the complainant, Mitchell O'BRIEN, as having access to the back porch where the telescope had been kept. O'BRIEN also stated that MARKSTER had been angry at his breakup with O'BRIEN's daughter and so might have a motive for the theft.

I arrived at 17-2660 Langton St. at 1000 and rang the doorbell. There was no answer, so I knocked loudly and announced myself as a police officer and requested MARKSTER open the door. No one came to the door. The driveway was empty, and there was no sign of a red Mazda 3 on the street. There was no garage at the premises.

I used my business card to write a request for MARKSTER to call me and left the card in the mailbox.

I left the premises to canvass a nearby pawn shop.

Supplementary Report

Re: Occurrence #: 607-15

Supplementary #: 2

Date of Occurrence: October 9, 2016

Date of Supplementary Report: October 10, 2016

Investigating Officer: Sergeant Wayne Doone

Further to the occurrence of the reported theft of a Coronado telescope from 17 Wilkey Ave. on October 9, 2016, I, Sergeant Wayne DOONE, went to Larry's Pawn Shop at 287 Wilbrod St. Larry's Pawn Shop is located four blocks east and one block south from 17-2660 Langton St., the address of a Samuel MARKSTER. MARKSTER is a possible suspect for the theft. Larry's Pawn Shop is the closest pawn shop to MARKSTER's residence.

I met with the owner of the pawn shop, Marilyn DEVRIES, DOB January 22, 1962, at 1045. I asked DEVRIES is she had bought a Coronado telescope recently. She said she had and led me to a glass display cabinet, which held a variety of cameras, binoculars, and one telescope. I asked Ms. DEVRIES to remove the telescope. She complied and put it on a counter.

I was able to confirm that the telescope was a Coronado Solar Max II 60 telescope, serial # CSM2115617P112012.

I asked DEVRIES if she could identify the person who brought the telescope in. She said she might be able to. I showed DEVRIES a photo lineup array containing MARKSTER's photo, which DEVRIES selected. She stated that she thought it was the right person but then volunteered to show me the morning footage from their surveillance camera.

I watched the footage and determined that at 0920 that morning, October 10, twenty minutes after the store opening, a man matching the photo of MARKSTER entered the pawn shop premises with a large object under his right arm. He placed the object on the front counter. It was a telescope. The footage shows DEVRIES examining the telescope and then removing bills from the cash register. She handed the bills to MARKSTER, and he left the premises.

I thanked DEVRIES and handed her my card and asked her to call if MARKSTER came back in. I left the premises to return to MARKSTER's address.

Supplementary Report

Re: Occurrence #: 607-15

Supplementary #: 3

Date of Occurrence: October 9, 2016

Date of Supplementary Report: October 13, 2016

Investigating Officer: Sergeant Wayne Doone

Further to the occurrence of the reported theft of a Coronado telescope from 17 Wilkey Ave. on October 9, 2016, I returned to the home of Samuel MARKSTER. I had visited the premises six times between my initial visit on October 10 and this visit with a 529(1) *Criminal Code* warrant to enter a dwelling-house. Each time, MARKSTER was not home.

I arrived at 0900 and knocked on the door. MARKSTER opened the door. I identified myself as Sergeant Wayne DOONE and asked MARKSTER if I could enter his house and ask him some questions. He agreed and let me in.

I asked MARKSTER if he had visited 17 Wilkey Ave. on October 9 to steal a telescope. He denied doing so. I asked him his whereabouts on October 9. MARKSTER told me he had been staying at a friend's house since October 8. He stated that he and the friend had had a video game marathon and they hadn't left the house for four days. I asked MARKSTER for the contact information for the friend. He gave it as

Derwitt Moss
19 Smythe Rd.

I then told MARKSTER that a witness confirmed MARKSTER had sold the telescope in question in a pawn shop on October 10.

MARKSTER then confessed that he had visited 17 Wilkey Ave. on Sunday, October 9. He told me he knew nobody would be home. He originally had planned to steal the love letters he had given his ex-girlfriend. He said he used the spare key to get into the house. On his way through the back porch, he saw the telescope. He then said this caused him to remember how much he hated Mitchell O'BRIEN. At this point in the interview, MARKSTER became quite agitated. He stood up abruptly, began pacing and shouted, "That jerk of an old man made my Margo break up with me. He thought I wasn't good enough for them. I hate him! I should have smashed that telescope. He loved it more than he loved his family. I'm glad I took it."

I put my hand on MARKSTER's shoulder, asked him to calm down, and advised MARKSTER that I was placing him under arrest. I told him I was charging him with theft and asked him if he understood. He said, "Yes, I friggin' understand." I searched MARKSTER and then handcuffed him and led him outside to my vehicle and placed him in the back seat. I secured his seatbelt and then took him to Westside Station where I turned him over to the custody officer on duty.

The following notebook entry and occurrence report illustrate the report writing trail for a security firm related to a shoplifting call at a mall.

1515	I, Samson Smit, was on duty patrolling the west wing of Wingate Mall, when I received a dispatch call to respond to a shoplifting at Sartorially Yours, a men's clothing store. I radioed I was on route and proceeded to the store in question. I met with salesperson Marty Coulas at 1517. Coulas told me that an older man, approx. 65, had left the store after trying on several suits, shirts, and ties. The man did not purchase anything. Coulas then told me that after the man had left, Coulas began to put the discarded clothing back on the racks. It was then that Coulas noticed three shirts and two ties were missing. Coulas recalled that the man had a large leather duffle bag with him. Coulas did not get the man's name but described him as just over 6' tall, bald, slim build with good posture, wearing black-framed eyeglasses. Coulas also stated that the man was polite and well-spoken. Coulas said the man had been heading toward the food court when he left the store.
1540	I left Coulas to canvass the mall.
	Marty Coulas
	DOB November 19, 1992
	519-555-1286
	56 Heron Ave.
	London, ON
	Has been employed at Sartorially Yours since September 2013.
1555	After canvassing the mall for 15 minutes, I spotted a man matching the description Coulas gave me.
	The man was sitting at a table in the food court. He was facing me but was not looking my way. As I moved closer, he looked up. He abruptly jumped up and ran out the southeast exit, which was across the corridor from his table at the food court. He left a brown leather duffle bag on the floor beside the table he had vacated. I pursued the man. When I exited the southeast door, I observed a #23 city bus travelling east hit the suspect as the bus was slowing down to stop at a designated bus stop.

		I ran over and saw that the suspect was lying beside the bus's front
		door. I instructed the driver not to open the door. I called 911 for an
		ambulance and police. I spoke with the man and got his name.
		Victor Tremblay
		The man then passed out.
		Paramedics arrived and began to treat Mr. Tremblay.
		Police arrived. I related the accident and shoplifting call details to
		officer Dayna Vasileva. She took over the scene. I entered the mall
		and retrieved the duffle bag, which I brought out to Vasileva.
	1635	*I returned to the office to write a report.*

Here is the occurrence report Smit wrote after the incident.

Occurrence Report

ACME Security Services

Occurrence Date: May 17, 2016

Occurrence Time: Approximately 1500 hrs

Occurrence Type: Shoplifting involving injury

Reporter: Samson Smit

Badge #319

Details of Occurrence:

I, Samson Smit, was on duty patrolling the west wing of Wingate Mall
when I received a dispatch call to respond to a shoplifting at
Sartorially Yours, a men's clothing store. I radioed I was on route and
proceeded to the store, which was located in the west wing on the north
side of the corridor. I met with salesperson Marty Coulas at 1517.
Coulas told me that an older man, approx. 65, had left the store after
trying on several suits, shirts, and ties. The man did not purchase
anything. Coulas then told me that after the man had left, Coulas began
to put the discarded clothing back on the racks. It was then that
Coulas noticed three shirts and two ties were missing. Coulas recalled
that the man had a large, leather duffle bag with him. Coulas did not
get the man's name but described him as just over 6 feet tall, bald,
slim build with good posture, and wearing black-framed eyeglasses.
Coulas also stated that the man was polite and well-spoken. Coulas said
he recalled the man had been heading toward the food court when he left
the store. I left Coulas to canvass the mall.

Marty Coulas

DOB November 19, 1992

519-555-1286

56 Heron Ave.

London, ON

Has been employed at Sartorially Yours since September 2013.

After canvassing the mall for 15 minutes, I spotted a man matching the description Coulas gave me.

The man was sitting at a table in the food court. He was facing me but was not looking my way. As I moved closer, he looked up. He abruptly jumped up and ran out the southeast exit, which was across the corridor from his table at the food court. He left a brown leather duffle bag on the floor beside the table he had vacated. I pursued the man. When I exited the southeast door, I observed city bus #23 that had been travelling east hit the suspect as the bus was slowing down to stop at a designated bus stop.

I ran over and saw that the suspect was lying beside the bus's front door. I instructed the driver not to open the door.

I called 911 for an ambulance and police. I spoke with the man and got his name.

Victor Tremblay

The man then passed out.

Paramedics arrived and began to treat Mr. Tremblay.

Police arrived. I related the accident and shoplifting call details to officer Dayna Vasileva. She took over the scene. I entered the mall and retrieved the duffle bag, which I brought out to Vasileva.

I returned to the office to write a report.

Security officer Smit would send a copy of his report, and his notes if required, to the police service. His report and notes would then become part of the report writing trail for the case.

CHAPTER SUMMARY

You can see that report writing is an integral part of every law enforcement career. Regardless of what types of reports law enforcement agencies or services use, the protocol is always the same: Take primary notes, write an initial report, and then write additional supplementary reports as needed.

Reports will be read by a variety of audiences within your agency or service, and they will also be read by many people in the justice system. Your reputation as an officer will in large part be determined by your report writing skills.

Chapter 12 discusses report writing conventions that must be adhered to in order to write reports that tell a complete, clear story and that will stand up in court.

KEY TERMS

briefing notes, 225
equipment maintenance reports, 225
injury reports, 225
job shadow reports, 225
leave reports/absence reports, 225
trend analysis reports, 225

Review and Reflection Questions

1. What is the typical report writing trail in law enforcement writing?

2. Who might read your reports?

3. What are some other non-crime or incident-related documents or reports that law enforcement personnel might write?

4. Why does it make sense to write separate supplementary reports for each new investigative action?

5. What can you do to prepare yourself to be an effective report writer once you are hired on?

11 The Notebook

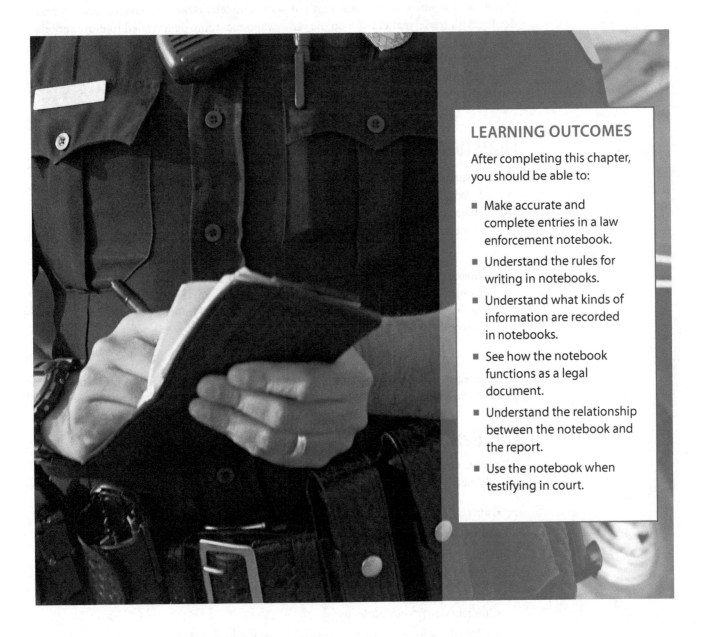

LEARNING OUTCOMES

After completing this chapter, you should be able to:

- Make accurate and complete entries in a law enforcement notebook.

- Understand the rules for writing in notebooks.

- Understand what kinds of information are recorded in notebooks.

- See how the notebook functions as a legal document.

- Understand the relationship between the notebook and the report.

- Use the notebook when testifying in court.

Introduction

A law enforcement officer's notebook, like a carpenter's hammer, is one of the most essential tools of the trade. Unaided, the conscious mind can recall only 10 to 30 percent of the impressions it has received during an event. However, with the help of notes taken during the event, the conscious mind can recall about 75 percent of the information received.

During any tour of duty, an officer will have reason to interrogate various persons and investigate different incidents. In most cases, reports are required. Since accuracy in reporting is essential, officers should maintain comprehensive notes, recording in chronological order and in detail all significant matters that come to their attention during their tour of duty.

Apart from containing information needed for reports, notebooks are a legally sanctioned means for officers to refresh their memories while giving evidence in court.

To some degree, an officer's ability, efficiency, and character are reflected in his or her notebook. The officer who consistently makes complete, clear, and concise notes when dealing with trivial matters will do the same when recording data related to more serious occurrences.

Prosecutions and other matters related to law enforcement are dependent, in large measure, on reports. Unless they are accurate, these reports are of little value—hence the need for notes that are legible, understandable, and meaningful.

Questioning to Obtain Information

The information recorded in an officer's notebook will be drawn from every useful quarter. In 1912, judges of the King's Bench Division in England prepared a set of rules for police officers investigating crimes. These rules constitute excellent guidelines for proper investigative procedure. Rule 1 is as follows:

> **When a police officer is endeavouring to discover the author of a crime, there is no objection to his putting questions in respect thereof, to any person or persons whether suspected or not, from whom he thinks useful information may be obtained.**

The effectiveness of this extensive questioning will depend on the law enforcement officer's verbal and non-verbal skills.

Effective Questioning

Effective notes depend on effective questioning. Effective queries will elicit clear answers and, ultimately, more information for the questioner. Ask questions of the speaker that

- increase your understanding
- help the speaker to relate his or her experiences
- build trust between you and the speaker

Don't ask questions that

- merely satisfy your curiosity
- allow the speaker to merely show off his or her knowledge

- criticize
- offer your opinions

There are two types of questions: **open-ended questions** and **closed-ended questions**. An open-ended question invites the speaker to say more about a topic; it does not impose limits on the answer. Open-ended questions tend to draw out and encourage the speaker to talk. Following are some examples of open-ended questions:

> **Can you tell me what happened?**
>
> **Could you say more about that?**
>
> **Can you help me understand what happened?**
>
> **What did you do next?**
>
> **What do you think was going on?**

Closed-ended questions invite "yes" or "no" answers. They tend to shut down communication and can make a speaker feel defensive. Some examples of this type of question follow:

> **Do you think you overreacted?**
>
> **Did you overhear the conversation?**
>
> **Did you see the accident?**

How to Ask Questions

The notebooks issued to police officers usually contain a section on how to ask questions. The following suggestions are based on some that appear in a notebook issued by Armour Dial Inc.:

1. *Don't use the "third degree."* Ask questions that help the other person think. Don't pry or degrade the other person in your role as questioner.

2. *Remember the "Five Ws and an H."* Questions that ask *who, what, where, when, why,* and *how* are the key to eliciting facts and information. "Who was with you at the time of the incident?" "What happened next?" "Where was the other car when you were approaching the intersection?" "When did you enter the United States?" "Why?" "How?"

3. *Ask questions that produce in-depth answers, not superficial ones.* Ask for evidence, explanations, or examples to discover the reasons or motivation behind actions.

4. *Ask "suppose" questions.* Introduce a new idea or bring up an overlooked point to break a deadlock. Preface your question with the phrase "Suppose we . . . ."

5. *If you are asked a question, avoid committing yourself to a position or opinion.* Try turning the question back on the questioner or referring it to another qualified person. You might say, for example, "Why do *you* think the accident occurred?" Or, "My sergeant will have to answer that question." Or, "That's a matter for the courts to decide."

Open-ended questions invite respondents to say more about a topic. There are no limits imposed on answers to open-ended questions. Open-ended questions tend to draw out respondents and encourage them to speak more.

Closed-ended questions invite "yes" or "no" answers. They tend to shut down communication and can make a speaker feel defensive.

6. *Ask questions that solicit agreement.* Offer likely answers in the form of questions. For example, "Don't you think that the car was on the wrong side of the road?" "You should have been aware of how much alcohol you could legally bring into Canada before you left, don't you think?"

EXERCISE 1 » Effective Questioning

Mary Blunt is a witness in an alleged hit-and-run accident. The basic information about Mary Blunt is as follows:

Witness:	**Mary Blunt**
Address:	**202 Queen St., Brantford, ON N8P 3S7**
DOB:	**16 July 1987**
SIN:	**411 756 027**
Telephone:	**519-555-2222**

Mary Blunt is a registered nurse. She was sitting in her living room watching the television at approximately 2120 when she heard a loud thud and a scream. She ran out of her home to find a man lying on the sidewalk on the west side of the street in front of 198 Queen St. He was unconscious and bleeding from a cut on the forehead. His left arm looked as if it had been broken. Blunt called 911 on her cellphone. While she was tending to the victim's cut, he regained consciousness. He was groaning, but he didn't say anything. Blunt did not see the accident or speak to the victim or to anyone who saw the accident.

Prepare a series of questions for Mary Blunt that will assist the investigating officer in obtaining information. Some sample questions follow, along with the rationale for asking them:

- "Can you describe your duties at the hospital where you work?" (To obtain Mary's qualifications and competence to give adequate first aid to the victim.)

- "You said that you heard a loud thud and a scream. Can you tell me what you mean by a 'thud'?" (To determine whether the thud was made by a car hitting the victim, from the victim falling, or from some other source.)

- "Would you tell me more about the victim's injuries?" (To determine whether the victim was injured from a fall or from contact with a vehicle.)

Note Taking

Keeping good notes is essential, so it is important to look at some strategies for effective note taking. In the first place, make sure that **irrelevant** material is not included in your notes. There *is* such a thing as taking too many notes. You want only facts. Any information that is not factual is irrelevant and cannot be used in a court of law. Material that is not factual includes rumour, **innuendo**, and second-hand information. The following, for example, would qualify as irrelevant inclusions in an officer's notes.

Irrelevant material is any information that is not factual and that cannot be used in court. Irrelevant material should not be included in your notebook.

Innuendo refers to comments that are suggestive about a person or situation but that are not necessarily factual. Innuendo is considered irrelevant material and should not be included in your notebook.

> All teenagers are disrespectful.
>
> I wasn't there, but I know he did it.
>
> That family has a bad reputation.
>
> I've heard about her, and I don't like her.
>
> The victim was having a cup of coffee before the robbery.
>
> Banks deserve to be robbed because their fees are outrageous.
>
> That's a horrible colour for a car.
>
> She must have done it; you know what those people are like.
>
> My friend told me that her friend is a smuggler.

Such statements should not go into your notebook.

EXERCISE 2 » Deleting Irrelevant Material

Eliminate the irrelevant material from the following statement:

I was walking down Oak Street approaching the intersection of Elm Street about 1:30 in the afternoon when I heard a loud crash. There were a lot of people just standing around looking at the scene of the accident. Don't these people have jobs? A blue Ford Fiesta was in the middle of the intersection facing north, while a silver Chevrolet Cruze had mounted the curb in front of 223 Oak St. A yellow Hummer was parked near the intersection. I've always wanted one of those. I know the drivers of the two cars: June Southern, who was driving the Ford, and Julie Ying, who was driving the Cruze. Julie's husband teaches at the college. Ying had a cut on her arm, while Southern looked like she had just come from a food fight. She told me she was eating her lunch while she was driving. I have to remember to call home after we leave here to see if I need to pick anything up for dinner. Ying told me that she couldn't find her cellphone. That's when the police arrived.

Tips on Note Taking

Following are some guidelines for taking effective notes:

1. Use common abbreviations for long or frequently used words, as long as they can be understood by anyone using your notes.

2. Stay alert and focused. Avoid distractions. For example, don't stop taking notes to give directions to a passerby while you are interviewing a witness.

3. Take careful notes on anything that is technical or complicated, even if you find it boring.

4. Ask questions about anything you don't understand.w

Tips on Taking Complete Notes

Following are some guidelines for taking complete notes:

1. *Record direct quotations accurately.* Recording a person's statement word-for-word, or **verbatim**, often provides important details. Record key sentences offered by

---

Verbatim describes a direct quotation—the record of someone's statement with word-for-word accuracy.

witnesses. These quotations will help an officer recall details in context and write precise and accurate witness reports. When you interview a suspect or an accused person, direct quotations may provide evidence or even prove that a person is guilty. Police officers will record the questions they ask or instructions they give to an accused person. This process demonstrates, for instance, that charges were read and understood by an accused. Direct quotations make excellent evidence and improve your **credibility** as a witness in court.

2. *Record observations accurately.* When you arrive on scene, describe the scene and note the locations of relevant items. Diagrams may be recorded in the notebook as a memory aid. Observe and record relevant conditions. For example, you might note that a traffic accident occurred during heavy rain. When you interview a person, pay attention to the speaker's tone of voice and body language. Many speakers give as many non-verbal clues as verbal clues about what they really think. These clues might indicate acknowledgement, agreement, or even confession to a crime. Your observations are important information.

3. *Record necessary information accurately.* The "Notebook Checklist" box at the end of this chapter indicates the amount of detail needed. For example, you need at least the following information about a witness:

- complete name with any nicknames
- date of birth
- address, including postal code
- home and business telephone numbers
- email address
- CPIC results (that is, the results from running the person's name through the Canadian Police Information Centre system, which will indicate whether he or she is wanted for something)

The points in the "Notebook Checklist" box would be followed to the letter in the case of an accused or a missing person.

IN THE FIELD

Arrest and Search Notebook Entry

Below are two notebook entries for the same incident. Compare the two entries. Observe the improvements in the second set of notes, outlined in the comments following the notes.

Notes missing helpful details:	
2300	10-7 300 North Street Mac's Milk re: Robbery
	—front door ajar
	—footprints in the snow
	—male running NB
	caught the male subject

Credibility refers to a quality of believability. As an officer, keeping an accurate and complete notebook improves your credibility as a witness in court.

	Arrested male	
	Sam STACHS DOB: 13 June 1996	
2306	*Advised him he was under arrest*	
	RTC were understood	
	Caution understood	
	Search was negative for weapons	
	note in jeans pocket	
	Give me all your cigarettes and cash and nobody gets hurt	
	backpack found cartons of Du Maurier light cigarettes,	
	$285 Cash	
2312	*Labelled items seized.*	
0100	*Desc. upon arrest: wm, 20 yrs, 5'10", long blond hair in a*	
	ponytail, goatee,	
	Wearing grey cargo pants, red backpack	

Notes containing helpful details:	
2300	*10-7 300 North Street Mac's Milk re: Robbery*
	–front door ajar
	–footprints in the snow leading behind the store
	–followed and observed a male matching the description
	running NB
2304	*caught up with the male subject – Central Street*
	Arrested male for robbery, advised him of same
	Provided a DL in the name of Sam STACHS DOB: 13 June 1996
	Escorted him to the cruiser
2306	*Advised "You are under arrest for robbery"*
	Read him his RTC from my dutybook
2307	*DYU?*
	A: "Yes."
	Wish to call a lawyer?
	A: "Ya, I think I better."
2308	*Read caution from dutybook*
	DYU?

	A: "Ya, ya, whatever."
	Can you tell me in your own words what this means?
	A: "Anything I say you are going to turn on me and use it in court against me. I get it OK?"
2309	I need to search you now. Do you have any weapons, needles, anything that could hurt me on you?
	A: "No."
2310	SIA found a handwritten note in left front jeans pocket
	Note said "Gimme all your cigarettes and cash and noboddy gets hurt"
2311	SIA opened the red Reebok backpack and found 17 cartons of Du Maurier Light light cigarettes, $285 cash
2312	Labelled items seized. Note labelled with property tag #1452001.
	Cigarettes with property tag #1452002.
	Cash under tag #1452002.
2315	Transitioned to writing supplementary police report
0100	LE
	Desc upon arrest: wm, 20 yrs, 5'10", long blond hair in a ponytail, goatee, wearing grey cargo pants, red backpack

Comments:

1. It is critical to get verbatim how the rights were given and the answers provided. This is why they are read directly from the dutybook rather than paraphrased. In a legal procedure, a judge is looking for the voluntariness and reliability of the statement, and exact words are often examined.

2. SIA means "search incidental to arrest." This would be explained in more detail in the supplementary report, which is essentially an elaboration of these notes. In the *Criminal Code*, refer to section 495 C.C. Annotations "Search incidental to arrest."

3. In the rights to counsel (RTC), there are two questions:
   a. Do you understand (DYU)?
   b. Do you wish to call a lawyer now?

   A common mistake in note taking is to provide only one answer: yes. The officer is then unable to testify whether this means, "yes, they understood" or "yes, they wished to call a lawyer."

4. The note is evidence, so spell it out the way it is written; whether the spelling is correct or not, copy it verbatim. It might be a pattern that will link the suspect to other crimes as well.

On Omissions

In *R v. Brown* (2014),[1] the judge compared omissions in an officer's notebook to inconsistencies in witness testimony and stated that these omissions must be considered on a case-by-case basis. The argument is frequently made in court that an omission in an officer's notebook indicates a failure in the process of collecting and sharing evidence; omissions raise the possibility of fabrication after the occurrence.

The true cost of omissions is a lack of necessary facts for writing complete reports. The notebook is primarily a memory aid, and the goal is to recall the various descriptions, observations, and knowledge of circumstances you obtained about an incident. This information justifies any actions an officer takes, such as searches and seizures. For example, an officer must prove that conditions are met for a specific offence to justify an arrest. This process is discussed in the following chapters and is known as *proving the facts-in-issue*.

Use of Notes in Court

When a law enforcement officer is testifying in court, the notebook becomes a valuable aid to his or her recollection of events. The following principles apply to the use of notes in court:

- Whether the court permits the officer to use the notes in court depends on when they were made. Permission may be denied if the notes were made a significant time after the event in question.

- When testifying, an officer should not read directly from notes unless quoting distances, measurements, or statements where details must be exact.

- The officer should thoroughly review his or her notes before testifying.

- There should be no discrepancy between information in the notebook and information in the report based on notes in the notebook.

- Notes may have to be physically presented in court. For example, a judge may order an officer's notes to be produced if a defence lawyer requests it, and these notes may be entered as an exhibit in the case.

- A witness who gave a statement to a law enforcement officer may refer to that statement while testifying, provided that the statement was recorded in the officer's notebook and that the witness has read the statement and signed it.

Diagrams in Notes

Clear, complete diagrams are an integral part of good notes, and they assist you and others in interpreting a situation. A good diagram can also help the investigating officer recall events at a later date and will help others to understand what the officer observed. Diagrams can be transferred from the notebook to the report, and there must be consistency between the notebook and report versions of the diagram. Don't make changes to the diagram at a later date.

Some elements that could be included in the diagram are

- directions (north, south, east, west)
- dimensions (the measurements from fixed objects at the scene of the incident)
- people's positioning (in relation to other objects or persons at the time of the incident)
- street names

---

1   *R v. Brown*, 2014 ONSC 1383, 304 CRR (2d) 29.

- positioning of vehicles (point of impact in a traffic accident, location of other vehicles involved)
- road markings
- intersection markings
- stationary objects relevant to the incident in question
- a legend describing symbols you use

You don't need to draw everything in the area, just those things relevant to the incident in question.

Use a black pen and a ruler to make diagrams, and use symbols that can be readily understood as representing, for example,

- an automobile
- a transport truck
- a stoplight
- a stop sign
- a crosswalk
- railway tracks
- a building with street number
- a hospital
- a church
- road markings (one-way street, two-lane street)
- intersections

There are variations you can use, but be consistent and clear (see Figure 11.1). You don't have to be an artist to draw an understandable diagram.

In Figure 11.2, you see a generic diagram of the following traffic accident: Cyril Jones was driving westbound along William Street and approached the intersection of Crabbe Lane, where he applied his brakes to stop at a red light. Because the roads were slippery, Jones slid into the intersection despite the brakes, where he struck a southbound car, driven by Lonny Smith, that had entered the intersection on a green light.

FIGURE 11.1   Common Symbols for Notebook Diagrams

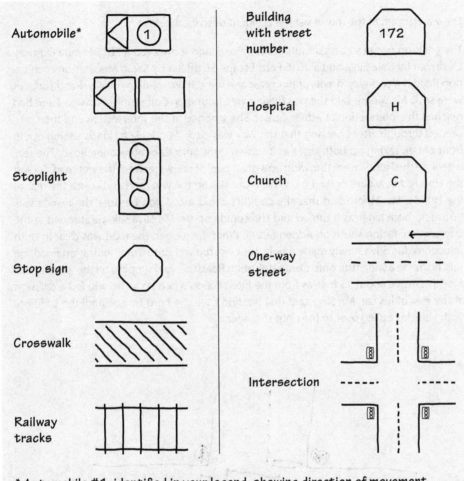

* Automobile #1, identified in your legend, showing direction of movement.

FIGURE 11.2   Diagram of a Traffic Accident

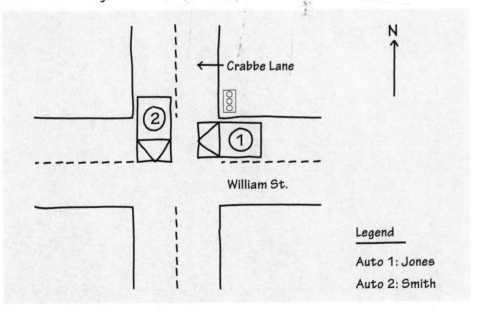

EXERCISE 3 » Diagramming a Motor Vehicle Accident

Draw a diagram of the motor vehicle accident described below:

The collision occurred on Communication Road, and it involved a 2015 Honda Odyssey EX driven by Dale Silva and a 2016 Ford Escape SE driven by Sarah Moore. Communication Road is a two-way street running east and west. It was raining heavily. Road surfaces were slick. Ms. Moore said she was driving westbound on Communication Road and had reached the intersection at Adrien Street. She stopped at this intersection and then proceeded through after checking that the way was clear. Suddenly a Honda swung out in front of her, taking up both lanes as it turned right onto Communication Road. The rear wheels of the Honda were throwing up a great deal of rainwater from the wet road. Seeing the Honda, Ms. Moore braked her vehicle but slid on the wet road and struck the rear of the Honda. Ms. Moore said that she couldn't avoid a collision because the Honda was taking up both lanes as it turned and she couldn't pass. Mr. Silva said he stopped at the intersection, facing south on Adrien Street. When he judged the road was clear in both directions, Mr. Silva slowly made a right turn westbound onto Communication Road. He said he made a wide turn onto Communication Road to avoid slipping on the wet surface. Mr. Silva drove about 15 metres from the intersection when he heard and felt a collision at the rear of his car. Mr. Silva said that he didn't see the Ford Escape until the collision. Both vehicles pulled over to the right shoulder.

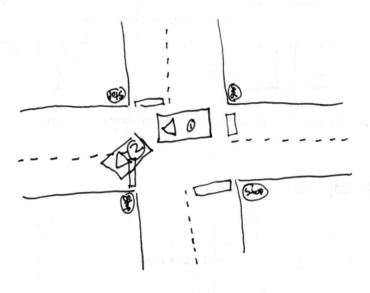

Guidelines for Notebook Entries

Following are guidelines for making entries in your notebook:

1. Begin with your rank, name, and badge number.

	PC Maria Gonzales #1298

- Use a black ballpoint pen for writing in the notebook.

2. Record the date on the next line.

	PC Maria Gonzales #1298
	Thursday 16/05/05

- Don't leave blank spaces between lines. If you do so accidentally, put a line through the blank space and initial it, as in the example below.

	PC Maria Gonzales #1298
	———————————————————— *MG*
	Thursday 16/05/05

- Be consistent in the manner in which the date is recorded. No particular format is required; however, on most forms, such as the incident report, the date is written as year/month/day. Fewer mistakes occur if the date format in the notebook is the same as the one used for reports.
- Don't tear any pages out of the notebook.
- Write on every page. If a page is missed, make a diagonal line through the page that was missed and initial the line. It is not necessary to cross out and initial every line on the page; one diagonal line for the entire page will do.

3. Record the weather and road conditions on the next two lines.

	PC Maria Gonzales #1298
	Thursday 16/05/05
	−2C, Overcast
	Roads dry MG

- If a spelling error or some other mistake is made, put a single line through the mistake and initial it.
- Don't use correction fluid or correction tape to cover up a mistake.
- Don't scribble over the mistake.
- No information of a personal nature is to be written in the notebook.
- If rough notes need to be made, make them on the back of the page, and clearly label them as rough notes.

4. Record the time you arrive for duty, the time of roll call, and any special circumstances, then record the time you go on duty (0800 in the example below).

	PC Maria Gonzales #1298
	Thursday 16/05/05
	−2, overcast
	Roads dry MG
0730	Arrive downtown division
0745	Roll call
	Assigned #3 patrol area, car 506, portable radio 3
	Partner: Don McAdams
	Special attention: 76 Lock St., ongoing vandalism
	Missing person: Tammy Kuhn
	128 Prosper St., North Bay, Ont.
	DOB 14 March 1956
	Last seen vicinity of King St. and Main St. bus station 1145, 11/29
	Contact regarding urgent family matter
	Stolen vehicles: 1. 2015 red Honda Civic ABFS 334 (ON)
	2. 2016 green Chrysler 300 766 NHT (ON)
0800	10-8 General patrol

- Record items such as lunch breaks, follow-ups from previous shifts, and warrants to be issued.

5. Begin to note events of the day, in chronological order. Wherever possible, write in complete sentences free from errors in spelling and grammar.

0810	Dispatched to 45 Elm St. regarding break and enter
0817	10-7 at 45 Elm St.
	Homeowner: Thuy Nguyen
	DOB 31 May 1964 10-60
	Ms. Nguyen reports that she and her husband were in Niagara Falls
	overnight and that they returned home about 0730 this morning.
	When Ms. Nguyen entered the house, she found that furniture
	had been overturned and drawers cleaned out. The back door of
	the house had been forced open. Ms. Nguyen states that she and
	her husband left the house sometime after 2000 last night, so the
	break-in must have occurred after that. She states that she didn't

	see anyone suspicious in the neighbourhood last night, but she says, "There have been a lot of kids hanging around the neighbourhood lately. It was probably one of them, after money for drugs. Why don't they get a job?" Ms. Nguyen does not have an alarm system on the house. I entered the house and found that the living room had been ransacked. Glass items and dishes were taken from the china cabinet and thrown onto the floor. Cushions were taken from the couch and chairs and cut open with a sharp object. Books and magazines were scattered across the floor. Ms. Nguyen says that nothing seems to be missing from the living room. The bedroom was also ransacked. A jewellery box was on the floor, and two diamond rings, valued at approximately $2,000 each, were missing. The mattress on the bed was overturned. Ms. Nguyen said that she usually keeps $300 in cash under the mattress for emergencies, and this was missing. Clothing from closets was strewn on the floor. Nothing else seemed to be missing. I checked the back door and found marks to indicate that the lock had been forced, likely with a crowbar or large screwdriver.
0840	*I radio Identification Branch and ask for an identification officer to attend. While waiting for ID, I question neighbours about any suspicious activity in the neighbourhood. No one reports anything suspicious.*
0910	*PC Joe Falls, identification officer, on scene* *Incident no. 16-335602*
0920	*10-8 from 45 Elm St. I inform dispatch that I will be parked in the Ryerson Public School parking lot on Robinson St. for paperwork on the break-in.*
1000	*Coffee break*
1020	*10-8 general patrol*
1033	*10-7 near 216 Progress St. for traffic violation* *Edward James Wall, DOB 16 November 1966 10-60* *37 Cumberland Dr., Hamilton, ON L9K 2C4* *905-555-5776* *2013 blue Toyota Matrix ACDH 990 (ON)* *Mr. Wall was stopped for failing to signal a left-hand turn from*

	Foss St. onto Turner St. Driver released with warning.
1040	10-8 general patrol
1110	Dispatched to Highway 403 westbound at Garner Rd. 10-50

6. Record the end of your shift.

1545	10-7 downtown division
1600	Off duty

- You must sign your notebook at the end of each shift. It is suggested that you indicate the end of a shift by drawing a line through the space following your signature at the bottom of the page.

EXERCISE 4 » Keeping a Notebook

1. Keep a notebook that records your daily activities in this course, beginning with your first class of the day. Note weather and road conditions, the time you start your first class, the topic for the class, any breaks, the end of class, and any assignments or homework you're given. Record the grades you receive for assignments or tests, announcements, seminars, workshops, and anything out of the ordinary that happens. Do this for every class. Your "shift" is over when your last class ends.

2. Make necessary corrections to the following notebook entries:

	Wednesday, 13 May
1630	Report for duty
1700	10-8
1735	Phone home to find out what my daughter wants for her birthday
1740	Pull over a red Chevrolet and writ a ticket to the driver for not wearing her seat belt
1800	Coffee break
1830	Resume general patrol
1845	Dispatched to 10-50 at Wilson St. Welcome St.

EXERCISE 5 » Organizing the Notebook

1. Organize the following notebook entry in logical order and enter it properly into your notebook.

> PC Maria Gonzales arrives at the downtown division at seven a.m. on Monday, September 26, of this year. At roll call, she learns that she will partner with Don McAdams in car 506 to patrol area number five. She makes a note about a stolen vehicle, a black Honda Civic with Ontario plate AJES 205. Roll call started at seven thirty a.m. and ended at seven forty-five. At eight o'clock Maria begins General Patrol. This morning, the roads are dry; the weather is dry, and the temperature is fifteen degrees Celsius. Dispatch sends them to 602 Alberta Street regarding a bicycle theft at eight thirty-two. They arrive at that address and are out of service at eight thirty-nine.

2. Continue the scenario. Start by reorganizing the list below in chronological order. Next, enter the information into your notebook.

___ Mr. Davies leaned the bicycle against the garage door and went back inside the house through the front door.

___ He returned to the house to retrieve the wallet.

___ 0915 10-8 from Alberta St.

___ Mr. Davies could not describe the driver of the truck.

___ He was inside looking for the wallet for about ten minutes.

___ Mr. Davies reports that he was riding the bicycle to work when he realized he had forgotten his wallet.

___ He described the bicycle as a Specialized Tarmac SL4 Expert Shimano Ultegra Di2, black men's racer, year 2014.

___ Mr. Davies said, "Come to think of it, a grey Ford pickup truck was passing by when I pulled into my driveway. Maybe it was him."

___ Incident no. 09-215336

___ Mr. Davies estimates the value of the bicycle at $3,000.00.

___ He came back outside to find his bicycle missing.

EXERCISE 6 » Accurate Note Taking

1. *Record descriptions accurately.* Bring to class photographs of persons, vehicles, valu-ables, and so on. Find a partner. One student holds a photograph and describes the person or object while the other student records the description into the notebook. The student recording the information should attempt to gain a precise description in his notes by asking clarifying questions and aiming for precise wording. After-wards, check your work for accuracy.

2. *Record facts, not judgments.* The following scenario contains many words that are actually judgments, not descriptions of facts:

   > I arrived on scene shortly after I was dispatched around 1410 to find Larry lying on the street near Queen and Main. Larry was injured. A kid assaulted him with a weapon. Apparently, he threatened him first, and when the victim didn't give him his wallet, he attacked him. I proceeded to investigate the situation and discovered two witnesses: a bartender on her break and a businessman walking by on the other side of the street. He looked like a gangster and headed down an alley.

   a. What questions would you ask about this paragraph in pursuit of accuracy? Record your questions and possible answers.

   b. When you are done, enter the information in your notebook. Follow the guide-lines, adding whatever descriptions or facts you can substitute for the abstract judgments in the passage.

Notebook Checklist

1. Upon beginning your shift, have you included the standard information? This would include

   a. your rank, name, and badge number
   b. the date (year/month/day)
   c. the weather conditions
   d. the road conditions
   e. the patrol area assigned
   f. your partner(s)
   g. matters requiring special attention (e.g., persons wanted, stolen cars, liquor checks)

2. Have you included all relevant times? These include

   a. time on duty
   b. time in service
   c. time out of service
   d. time you received a call or were dispatched
   e. time you arrived at the scene of an incident
   f. time the incident occurred
   g. time a statement was begun
   h. time a statement was finished
   i. time that other emergency personnel arrived
   j. time of arrest
   k. time a prisoner or suspect was transported
   l. time a search was begun
   m. time a search ended

   n. time a Breathalyzer demand was made
   o. time a Breathalyzer test was administered

3. Have you obtained all relevant information about persons connected with an incident? This information includes

   a. name (surname, first given name, second given name)
   b. nickname or alias
   c. race
   d. sex
   e. date of birth (day/month/year)
   f. marital status
   g. condition (e.g., sober, intoxicated, high on drugs, aggressive)
   h. home address
   i. home phone number
   j. occupation
   k. business address
   l. business telephone number
   m. social insurance number
   n. driver's licence number
   o. other identification
   p. relationship to victim or complainant

4. Have you obtained sufficient information regarding physical identification? This includes

    a. height (in centimetres)
    b. weight (in kilograms)
    c. hair (e.g., colour, moustache, beard, wig, bald, partly bald, short, long, straight, wavy, bushy, unkempt)
    d. eyes (e.g., colour, glasses, contacts)
    e. build (e.g., slender, medium, heavy)
    f. complexion (e.g., sallow, light, fair, ruddy, freckled, dark, swarthy, pock-marked)
    g. teeth (e.g., good, irregular, false, gold, stained, decayed, missing)
    h. physical condition (e.g., diseases, deformities)
    i. mental condition (e.g., suicidal, depressed, violent)
    j. scars
    k. marks
    l. tattoos (type, location)
    m. other outstanding features (e.g., disabled, juvenile)
    n. description of clothing

5. Have you obtained the necessary information about vehicles concerned with the incident? This includes

    a. type (e.g., automobile, truck, motorcycle, snowmobile, trailer)
    b. make (e.g., Pontiac, Jaguar)
    c. model (e.g., Sunbird, Newport, Corolla)
    d. style (e.g., convertible, station wagon, four-door)
    e. vehicle year
    f. colour
    g. licence number (with province or state of issue and year of issue)
    h. vehicle identification number
    i. Val-tag number
    j. special features (e.g., special equipment, damage)
    k. owner (with address, driver's licence number, and category/restrictions)
    l. insurance information (broker, insurance company, policy number)

6. Have you inquired about the value and storage status of the property (excluding guns) concerned in the incident? This includes property such as

    a. appliances
    b. bicycles and tricycles
    c. electronic equipment (e.g., radios, televisions, DVD players, cellphones)
    d. household articles
    e. jewellery
    f. machinery and tools
    g. musical instruments
    h. office machines
    i. personal accessories
    j. photographic equipment
    k. scientific devices
    l. sporting goods
    m. weapons

7. Have you inquired about the types of guns involved? The different types include

    a. air gun
    b. bolt action
    c. breech or muzzle loader
    d. flare or tear gas
    e. fully automatic
    f. multi-barrel
    g. pump action
    h. restricted
    i. revolver
    j. rifle
    k. semi-automatic
    l. shotgun
    m. single shot

8. Have you obtained relevant information about arrests in connection with the incident? This information would include

    a. charges
    b. dates and times of offences
    c. locations of offences
    d. dates and times of arrests
    e. locations of arrests
    f. arresting officers
    g. times of transport

9. Upon ending your shift, have you included

    a. the time
    b. your signature

An Expanded List of 10-Codes

Many law enforcement agencies have slightly different 10-codes from those found in the back of your notebook. Below is an expanded list of 10-codes:

10-1:	Transmitting poorly
10-2:	Transmitting well
10-3:	Stop transmitting
10-4:	Acknowledge/everything okay
10-5:	Relay message
10-6:	Busy
10-7:	Out of service
10-8:	In service
10-9:	Repeat
10-10:	Call home
10-16:	Pick up prisoner at
10-19:	Return to station
10-20:	What is your location?
10-21:	Call by telephone
10-22:	Talk car-to-car
10-23:	Permission to meet with another car
10-26:	Detaining suspect
10-28:	Vehicle registration information
10-29:	Checking for wanted
10-38:	Checking something
10-43:	Break
10-45:	Fatality
10-50:	Accident
10-51:	Need tow truck
10-52:	Need ambulance
10-60:	Suspect has no record
10-61:	Suspect has record, suspect not wanted
10-62:	Suspect possibly wanted
10-63:	Suspect wanted
10-64:	Proceed with caution
10-65:	Assist with 10-63
10-66:	Suspect under observation
10-67:	Suspect is parolee
10-68:	Suspect charged
10-78:	Officer needs assistance
10-90:	Alarm
10-92:	Prisoner in custody
10-93:	Set up roadblock
10-100:	Bomb threat

CHAPTER SUMMARY

The notebook is used to record information for future reference, and to refresh an officer's memory if an incident comes to trial. There are many rules covering the use of notebooks, and these rules must be followed. Most important, the notebook must be complete and free of errors. The most useful written statements are accurate records of people's spoken words.

KEY TERMS

closed-ended questions, 243
credibility, 246
innuendo, 244
irrelevant, 244
open-ended questions, 243
verbatim, 245

Review and Reflection Questions

1. Why do law enforcement officers keep notebooks?

2. What information about a witness should be recorded in your notebook?

3. What information is irrelevant and therefore should not be recorded in the notebook?

4. How, ideally, do you record a response from a suspect or accused?

5. When is it useful to create a diagram in your notebook? Provide some examples.

12 Report Writing

LEARNING OUTCOMES

After completing this chapter, you should be able to:

- Write reports from information recorded in a notebook.
- Understand the level of detail required in law enforcement reports.
- Eliminate errors from reports.
- Write reports that are complete and accurate.
- Establish the facts in issue.

Introduction

The writing skills you have learned from this book will be used to write reports. You will need to summarize as well as to write clearly and accurately, with excellent spelling and grammar. In short, you will need to use everything you've learned thus far to produce reports of the quality required by law enforcement agencies, courts, lawyers, and insurance companies.

It was pointed out in Chapter 8, Essay Writing, that writers seek to *inform*, to *explain*, to *persuade*, or to *put something on record*, and to do so as efficiently as possible. In writing for law enforcement, the last aim—to put something on record—is essential. Yet, to some degree, all four of these objectives apply to law enforcement writing. If you are writing a report about a traffic accident, for example, you might need the record for

- your supervisors
- the insurance companies
- the courts
- lawyers
- the person charged in the incident
- the victim
- anyone else who might need the information you gather

With such a diverse audience, you need to *inform* your readers about what happened, and *explain* the situation using the *who*, *what*, *where*, *when*, *why*, and *how* approach that is essential to all good reports. The information that you *put on the record* should clearly explain the background to the situation, the facts of the situation, and the outcome. Who are you trying to *persuade* in your report? There is an underlying element of persuasion involved in justifying the charge you may have laid against a motorist involved in an accident. You must "persuade" the motorist who was charged, your sergeant, and, if the matter comes to court, the judge, possibly a jury, and lawyers that your information is correct, that the situation is properly explained in your report, and that any fault you have assigned in connection with the incident is **substantiated** clearly and factually.

Recall the shoplifting report in Chapter 10, Introduction to Report Writing. The security guard's report must convince his supervisor and the police that he was justified in chasing the suspect out of the mall, especially given the fact that the suspect was consequently injured.

Parts of the Report

Reports are made up of two basic parts: the *summary page* and the *report narrative*. As with all informative writing, details of a report follow the sequence "Five Ws and an H":

- *Who?*
- *What?*
- *Where?*
- *When?*
- *Why?*
- *How?*

To **substantiate** something is to provide proof that what you claim to be true is real or correct. An alibi substantiates a suspect's claim that he was not at the scene of the crime when it occurred.

When writing a report, remember the elements of polished writing you learned in Chapter 5, Polishing Your Writing:

- Use professional language that avoids slang, jargon, and cliché.
- Avoid drawing conclusions by writing only observed actions and behaviours.
- Use the active voice and understand when to use first person versus third person.
- Use objective, non-biased vocabulary.

EXERCISE 1 » Identifying Parts of the Report

Mr. Melvin Gabriele stated that on Saturday, 2 April 2016, he was driving eastbound on Robinson Street in his 2007 silver Saturn Ion, licence AJXW 846, at a speed of approximately 55 km/h in the 50 km/h zone. At approximately 1529, a child's ball rolled in front of Mr. Gabriele's car, causing him to apply his brakes hard. As soon as Mr. Gabriele put on his brakes, he heard the screeching of tires behind his car. The rear of his car was then struck by a grey Mercury Sable, licence AYWN 202.

Ms. Kelly Mallory was the driver of the grey Mercury Sable. She stated that she was travelling eastbound on Robinson Street at approximately 50 km/h when she noticed Mr. Gabriele's brake lights come on. She stated that she immediately applied her brakes but failed to avoid a collision.

Mr. Gabriele identified himself by means of a valid Ontario driver's licence. His date of birth is 30 May 1985, and he lives at 314 Peach Lane in Paris, Ontario. Ms. Mallory identified herself verbally and stated that she lived at 444 Bales Rd., Kitchener, Ontario. Her date of birth is 22 April 1973.

The Saturn Ion has a bent rear bumper for an estimated damage of $700. The Mercury Sable received extensive damage to the front bumper and right headlight, for estimated damages of $2,000. Neither driver was hurt.

Who?	What?	Where?	When?
_____	_____	_____	_____
_____	_____	_____	_____
_____	_____	_____	_____
_____	_____	_____	_____
_____	_____	_____	_____
_____	_____	_____	_____

General Rules for Report Writing

The following are some general guidelines for writing reports:

1. *Start at the beginning, and describe events in chronological order.* This sequential format clarifies the **cause-and-effect** element of events and is essential to law enforcement reports. As well, it is important that you write out the events in the order in which *you* observed them and in the order of *your* actions.

   Imagine you were called to the scene of a disturbance at a convenience store. You begin talking to the owner, who tells you he was harassed by two youth who

---

Cause and effect describes the relationship between an action and the resulting event. If a defendant *causes* harm to a victim and she is caught, the *effect* is incarceration.

were demanding protection money from him. The owner tells you he demanded the youth leave. They complied but threatened they'd be back with reinforcements. You later find out from another officer that the youth were members of a youth gang called the West End Posse.

You wouldn't write

> **I was called to 89 Smythe Rd. to speak to a convenience store owner about a disturbance. Upon my arrival, I spoke with Mr. Hamish McIntyre, who told me that two members of the West End Posse had visited his store and demanded protection money.**

because at the time of the interview, you did not know the youths' gang affiliations. Instead you would write

> **I was called to 89 Smythe Rd. to speak to a convenience store owner about a disturbance. Upon my arrival, I spoke with Mr. Hamish McIntyre, who told me that two youth had visited his store and demanded protection money.**
>
> **I was later informed that the two youths were members of the West End Posse.**

A useful trick to remember to write in chronological order is to imagine you have a video camera on your shoulder as you write your report. Write out the events as they would appear on a camera recording.

2. *Write in the past tense.* The past tense reflects the fact that the report was written after the events being described.

3. *Use complete sentences, unless a list is called for.* In the following example, which involves a catalogue of features, the list format is appropriate.

> **The witness described the suspect as**
>
> - **approx. 185 cm tall**
> - **approx. 80 kg**
> - **having shoulder length brown hair**
> - **wearing a blue jacket and dark pants**

4. *Follow the rules of grammar and spelling.*

5. *When appropriate (threats uttered, claims made, details explained), quote exactly what was said, and put quotation marks around direct quotations.* You should write, for example, "The driver said, 'I didn't see the stop sign.'"

6. *Keep sentences under 20 words.*

Organization for Writing Reports

Organizing a report from your notebook is difficult. Once you have taken statements from several people, you'll have a number of different statements about the same incident. In the case of a traffic accident, for example, you will have statements from drivers, passengers, witnesses, and others, including emergency personnel. All of these must be grouped into a logical sequence, such as the Five Ws and an H sequence, and then organized chronologically.

Witness statements may be **contradictory** and contain **irrelevant** information. One driver involved in an accident may have seen things differently than another driver involved, especially if one of them is facing a charge under the *Highway Traffic Act*. To organize the information, use the following procedure:

1. Gather information.
2. Jot down topic headings in outline form (e.g., background, facts, outcomes).
3. Delete irrelevant information.
4. Group related topics.
5. Arrange topics chronologically.

EXERCISE 2 » Chronological Reporting

Arrange the following scenario written by a bylaw officer in chronological order.

I exited my vehicle and noted the front yard was littered with several empty alcohol bottles. The call to dispatch came at 0130. There was loud music coming from the residence, and several people were sitting on the front steps. The front door to the residence was open. I asked the people on the steps who the homeowner was. One of the men pointed inside. I then went inside and spoke with a Mr. Harvey Chin, who told me he was the homeowner. Dispatch said that there had been a noise complaint made by a neighbour. The neighbour said that there was a loud party in progress at 9 Willow Lane that had been going on since 1000 hrs. Mr. Chin told me they were celebrating his daughter's engagement. He told me he hadn't expected so many young people to attend the party and realized it had gotten out of hand. He promised to turn off the music and try to send everyone home. I arrived at 9 Willow Lane at 0215. Before I left, I reminded Mr. Chin of his responsibilities as host and told him to make sure that any of the party-goers who had been drinking had a safe way to get home.

Report Outline

It can be helpful to put information down in outline form before beginning to compose your report. Produce an outline by following the steps below:

1. Write an introductory sentence or paragraph that indicates in a general way the events that occurred. Indicate weather and road conditions if applicable. This section will become your summary.

2. List in point form—in the correct order—the information to be included:

   a. background (e.g., what led up to the event, what people and vehicles were involved)

   b. facts (e.g., what happened)

   c. conclusions (e.g., results of the events, such as damages, injuries, charges laid).

To **contradict** is to disagree with something said or claimed. A witness can be contradictory on the stand by telling the Crown attorney that what the suspect said about his actions was untrue.

For the purpose of writing reports or testifying in court, **irrelevant** information is information that is not connected, helpful, or useful to the investigation of the case.

Composing the Report

The best reports are derived from the spoken word (a good reason to keep accurate notebooks). A simple report appears in Figure 12.1, with an explanation of the sections, based on the report outline above, included in square brackets. Any law enforcement report follows this basic format.

FIGURE 12.1   A Simple Report

A two-vehicle accident at the corner of King Street and Queen Street resulted in severe damage to one vehicle and the hospitalization of the driver of the second vehicle. A charge of impaired driving was laid. It had been raining and the roads were slippery. [*Summary*: **This section provides a brief overview of the incident, and usually includes weather and road conditions.**]

On 12 March 2016, a 2009 Chevrolet Caprice was travelling westbound on Queen Street at 2150 approaching King Street. A 2007 Pontiac Vibe travelling southbound on King Street approached the intersection of King and Queen streets and stopped for a red light. [*Background*: **This section gives details of events leading up to the incident. It usually includes names of drivers, any additional information about the vehicles, measurements if necessary, and any other relevant information. Background information sets the scene. Usually written in the past tense, this section describes how the event began and answers the questions who, why, where, and when.**]

The light at the intersection turned green for southbound traffic. The driver of the Pontiac proceeded into the intersection with the green light. The westbound Chevrolet went through the red light and struck the Pontiac. [*Facts*: **This section tells what happened, and gives relevant details. Written in the past tense, this section answers the questions what and how.**]

The driver of the Pontiac sustained serious injuries and was transported to General Hospital by ambulance. The driver of the Chevrolet, who was not injured, smelled of alcohol and was unsteady on his feet. He was given a roadside Breathalyzer test and was subsequently arrested for impaired driving. Saadia Boffim was transported by Metro Emergency Services ambulance to General Hospital at 1115. Pedro Cidade witnessed the incident and gave a statement. Recommend additional checks at 257 Harbour St. for liquor violations. Case turned over to Cst. R. Smith of CIB. [*Conclusions*: **This section details the aftermath of the incident and describes anything that remains to be done. It can include information about medical attention given at the scene, about the time emergency services arrived and the time of the Breathalyzer test and results, about any statements given by persons involved, about names of witnesses, and so on.**]

EXERCISE 3 » Identifying Parts of the Report

Identify the summary, background, facts, and conclusions portions of the following scenario.

At 1110 on 20 September 2016, a single-vehicle accident occurred in the westbound lane of Highway 403 approaching Garner Road in Ancaster, Ontario. A half-ton "Hauler" truck overturned in the median between the eastbound and westbound lanes of Highway 403.

When you arrived at the scene at 1116, a number of containers from the truck were strewn around the median, although none were on the highway. Traffic had slowed in both directions, and a number of cars had stopped, with people attempting to assist a female who appeared to be the driver of the truck. She was sitting in the median near the overturned truck.

Fire and ambulance crews arrived simultaneously at 1123, and determined that the driver wasn't injured and that there were no fuel spills to be cleaned up. A tow truck arrived at 1127.

Based on her own words, a valid Ontario driver's licence, ownership papers for the truck, and an insurance card, the driver was identified as Muriel Wainman of Oakville, Ontario. The vehicle was a half-ton Chevrolet "Hauler" truck. Wainman stated that she was not injured. She was wearing her seat belt at the time of the accident. The weather was warm and dry, and the roads were clear.

Wainman stated that she was driving westbound on Highway 403 after picking up a dozen cartons of electrical supplies in Hamilton, to be delivered to Brantford, Ontario. She was driving in the right-hand lane of the highway at approximately 100 km/h, approaching the Garner Road exit, when a blue mid-sized car travelling in the passing lane suddenly swerved in front of her to exit at Garner Road. Anticipating a collision, Wainman turned the wheel hard to the left. The truck veered across the passing lane and onto the median, where it overturned, spilling some of the truck's contents onto the median.

No other vehicles were involved.

Wainman didn't get a description of the blue car or its licence number. She estimates the damage to the cartons at $1,500, and you estimate the damage to the truck at $4,000.

Cartons were placed back on the truck by representatives of Provincial Haulage, who were contacted by Wainman by cellphone. Wainman also called a tow truck. At 1142, Wainman's truck was towed by Towable Towing Co. to the Provincial Haulage offices in Oakville.

No charges were laid.

Summary	Background	Facts	Conclusions
_____	_____	_____	_____
_____	_____	_____	_____
_____	_____	_____	_____
_____	_____	_____	_____
_____	_____	_____	_____
_____	_____	_____	_____
_____	_____	_____	_____
_____	_____	_____	_____

Facts in Issue

Any report of an incident that could lead to a charge must include the facts in issue. The facts in issue are the components of an offence that the Crown must prove in order to get a conviction. In other words, they are the building blocks to or support structure for a conviction (see Figure 12.2). There are two types of facts in issue: *general* and *specific*. General facts include the *who*, *what*, *where*, *when*, *why*, and *how* of a situation. These facts are general because they apply to every offence. Specific facts relate to the statute that defines the offence. For example, in order to lay a charge of trespass by night, the *Criminal Code* requires that *all* of the following specific facts be present:

- The trespasser must be on the property without lawful excuse.
- The trespasser must loiter upon the property of another.
- The event must occur near a dwelling.
- The event must occur at night.

And in order to lay a charge of assault, the *Criminal Code* requires that the following facts be present:

- Physical force must be applied without consent.
- Physical force must be applied directly or indirectly.

Whether the assault qualifies as level 1, 2, or 3 depends on the nature of the injuries.

FIGURE 12.2   Facts in Issue

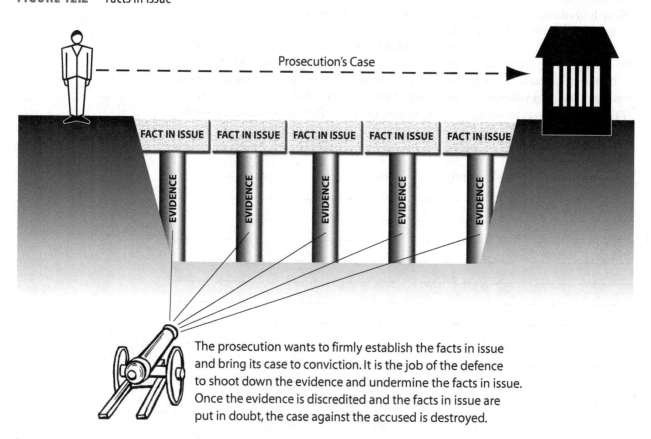

Source: Based on a sketch by John Grime, Public Safety and Security Branch, Mohawk College.

EXERCISE 4 » **Facts in Issue**

Are all of the necessary facts in issue present in the following scenario for a charge of trespass by night to be laid?

Sophia Robertson reports that she saw her neighbour, John Levine, walking around the Robertson residence at 2330, peering into the windows. Her husband was out of town on business, so Sophia called police, who questioned Levine at his residence. Levine admitted that he was on the Robertson property at the time stated, but said that he told Mr. Robertson that he'd keep an eye on the Robertson property while Robertson was away. Mr. Robertson had replied, "That's not a bad idea," although Mr. Robertson, according to his wife, assumed that Levine would merely watch the house, not actually go on the property.

Common Errors in Report Writing

Common errors in report writing include the following:

- omitting information, such as names and addresses of witnesses
- omitting details, such as information from the "Notebook Checklist" box in Chapter 11
- using poor grammar, which causes confusion regarding the meaning of sentences and details
- showing a lack of objectivity, which suggests a bias in recording information and favouritism shown to persons involved in an incident

From Notebook to Report

Not all notes from your notebook must be transferred onto a report, as sometimes the calls you attend will not require further action. (Refer to Figure 10.1 in the "The Report Writing Trail" section in Chapter 10.)

For example, if as a security guard you are sent to an office to unlock a door for an employee who forgot his keys at home, you'd write the call details in your notebook to account for your time. You would not write a report for this call. However, if the employee became verbally assaultive to you because he thought you had taken too long to get to his office, you would write a report detailing his treatment of you and describing any further action taken as a result.

Conversely, not all reports are written as a result of notebook notes.

For example, imagine you were walking into work on a snowy day, and you slipped on some ice hidden by snow and broke your ankle. You'd write an injury report but you would not write notes in your notebook.

EXERCISE 5 » Writing Reports from Notes

Write report narratives for each of the following scenarios. Some of the scenarios would have required you to transcribe notebook notes. For the purposes of this exercise, you are writing the reports directly from the details provided. Remember to write a *summary* statement that introduces the situation. Follow that with the *background* details, and the complete *facts* of the situation. *Conclude* your report with the aftermath of the event and a description of any follow-up actions needed.

1. You are a security guard at federal government building and are involved in the following event:

   November 30, 2016
   367 Federal Drive, main floor security desk

   You are working at the desk, and you have another security guard with you. A woman approaches the desk and tells you she has forgotten her building pass but must get to her office right away as she is late for a meeting.

   You tell the woman she must have someone vouch for her, and she needs her supervisor to come down to the desk. You tell her she will also have to leave some identification at the desk.

   She tells you her boss will be mad if she has to be called down, as the woman has forgotten her pass twice before in the last month.

   You tell her you must follow procedure and offer her the phone to call her supervisor.

   The woman then raises her voice and says, "You guards are like trained monkeys. You can't even think for yourselves. Just let me in, and I won't file a complaint against you."

   You repeat your earlier instructions and ask if she would like you to make the call.

   She pleads with you to let her in, claiming she might be fired if her boss finds out she lost her pass in the gym while working out last night. She offers to buy you coffee or lunch. She begins to cry and asks for a Kleenex. You slide a Kleenex box her way. She lunges and grabs your arm and begs you to reconsider.

   You firmly remove her hand from your arm and again offer to call her boss. As you move down the desk to reach for the phone, she picks up a stapler off the desk and throws it at you. It hits you in the nose, and you start bleeding.

   Your colleague rushes to your side. The woman ducks under the turnstile and runs for the elevator. Your colleague chases her while you call for additional help. The woman makes it onto the elevator.

   Three minutes later, your supervisor arrives and you tell her what has happened. Your supervisor asks for a description of the woman and then organizes a security search of the building, floor by floor. Your supervisor asks if you can remain on duty or if you feel you need to seek medical attention. You assure her you are fine to continue working as your nose has a cut on it, but it is not broken. Your supervisor tells you to remain at the desk and to write a report detailing the events.

   For your report, you must add missing details: a description of the woman, the location of elevators in relation to the security desk, which elevator the woman got on, and the names of your colleague and supervisor. You can also add some direct quotes that show what the woman says when she offers lunch and begs you to reconsider. Add any additional details you feel you need to write a complete report.

2. You are a police constable in a municipal police service and need to make a report about a problem with your service vehicle.

   Monday, February 1, 2016

   At roll call, you are assigned regular patrol duties and given service vehicle #282. You perform regular inspection of the vehicle and note that it seems to have a slightly scratched right front hubcap, but other than that, there is no damage to the vehicle. The interior of the vehicle is in good order.

   You are 35 minutes into your shift and are driving westbound on Wellington Street. As you start to brake for a red light, you feel your service vehicle pull to the right. You try to compensate by steering left, but as you also continue to apply the brakes, your service vehicle pulls even more to the right. You feel the right front wheel scrape along the curb.

   You are on route to a motor vehicle accident, so you continue on your way. You arrive at the scene and perform traffic re-routing duty until the vehicles involved in the accident are cleared away and the route is again open.

   You leave the scene and pull into a nearby Tim Hortons to inspect your vehicle. The right front hubcap is now very scratched and you observe a shallow four-inch dent in it. You radio in that you are out of service and head back to the station.

   On route back to the station, you spot a vehicle travelling well over the speed limit. It is travelling southbound on Greenbank Road. You radio in to say you are pursuing and follow the speeding vehicle. You engage lights and siren. After following the speeding vehicle for approximately two kilometres, the driver pulls over into a gas station. As you pull up behind the driver, your vehicle again pulls sharply to the right and you end up on a decorative flower bed.

You speak to the speeding driver, who tells you he had been listening to loud music and didn't hear your siren. He also says he pulled over as soon as he saw your lights in his rearview mirror. He has no excuse for his speeding. He does not refute that he was speeding and offers no excuse. He apologizes for speeding. You issue a ticket to the driver and send him on his way.

You speak with the gas station attendant and give her your card. You tell the attendant to have her supervisor call you in regards to the damaged flower bed. You also tell the attendant to tell her supervisor that the police service will pay for repairs. You then head to the station.

At the station, you take the car to the garage and ask the mechanics to look at the brakes. You then go into the station to write your report before returning to general patrol.

For your report, you must add missing details: times of events, name of gas station, name and particulars of the speeding driver, name of the gas station attendant, and any additional details you feel are needed to write a complete report.

3. You are a bylaw officer and sustain a badly sprained ankle as the result of a chase through a park.

Sunday, June 26, 2016
Riverfront Park, 1415

You are on duty and are assigned to patrol Riverfront Park. Your main responsibilities for the day include watching for parking infractions and making sure dog owners obey the dogs-on-leash bylaw.

You have just finished making a round of the three park parking lots and have decided to take lunch. You radio your status to dispatch and take a seat at a picnic table. Fifteen minutes into your break, you observe a woman with two large dogs in the nearby field. The dogs are not on leashes. You pack up your lunch, store your belongings in the car, and head out to intercept the woman.

When you are about 100 metres away from the woman, you observe a small girl go up to one of the dogs. You continue to approach and see the small girl reach her hand out to the dog. The dog starts to bark and runs away from the girl. By this time, you

are close to the woman and begin to explain the leash bylaw. At this time, you see the second dog rush at the small girl. It jumps on her, causing her to fall. The dog then grabs the girl's hat and runs away with it.

A man claiming to be the girl's father runs up and picks the girl up. He starts yelling at the dog owner. You tell the dog owner not to leave and turn to speak to the father and daughter. You determine that the girl is not hurt. The father demands that you charge the dog owner. You tell the man you will be giving her a ticket and give the man your card.

You speak to the woman, who seems to have no interest in apologizing or making amends for the dog's actions. You issue the woman a ticket and tell her she and her dogs must immediately leave the park. The woman calls to her dogs. The dog who had taken the small girl's hat is nowhere to be seen. You begin to walk in the direction the dog had run. After one minute of walking along a path, you find and pick up the hat. You then see the dog up ahead and begin to run toward it. You trip over a root and fall. Your left ankle is swollen, and you cannot walk on it. You call for assistance from another bylaw officer who is on duty in the west section of the park. After five minutes, your colleague arrives, splints your ankle, and helps you to her car, which she was able to bring to the edge of the path.

You go to the hospital where you are examined and sent home with a mild painkiller. Your colleague drives you to the office so that you can complete your report. Your colleague then returns to the park to see if the woman and her dogs have left.

For your report, you must add missing details: name and particulars of the dog owner, breeds of the dogs, name of your colleague, names of the girl and her father, particulars of the father, and any additional details you feel are needed to write a complete report.

4. You are a customs official at an airport and, on your way to starting your shift, you come upon a small boy who seems to be unattended.

Wednesday, November 16, 2016, 0910 hrs

You are walking through Terminal 3 on route to your shift at the international customs desk. You stop for a coffee and while in line you observe a young boy walking back and forth between the women's and men's washrooms. You think nothing of it, assuming the boy is waiting for a parent to emerge from a washroom.

After picking up your coffee, you continue on your way. As you pass the boy, you note that he is crying. You stop to ask the boy if he is OK. He just stares at you. You assure him you can help and point out that you are in uniform and that you are a worker at the airport. You tell him it is part of your job to make sure people in the airport are OK.

The boy tells you he is waiting for his mother, but she has been in the washroom for what seems like a very long time.

You get the child's name and call loudly into the washroom, asking if anyone in there had left a small boy waiting outside. You get no answer, so you tell the boy to stay where he is and enter the washroom. After a thorough search, you determine it is completely empty. You exit and talk to the boy. You ask him if he is sure his mother went into the washroom. He says yes. You ask him if he had left the area at any time. After some hesitation, the boy says he did walk across the hall to look at a cellphone display. He walked all around the display.

You realize he may have been hidden from view at some point, and the boy's mother may have thought the boy was missing when she exited the washroom. You radio to airport announcements and have them page the boy's mother and ask her to report back to the Terminal 3 washroom across from the cellphone shop. After approximately four minutes, a distraught woman comes rushing up, and the boy confirms her as his mother.

You speak to the mother, and she tells you she could not find the boy when she exited the washroom. She was at the help desk describing her son when your page came through. You are satisfied that the events unfolded as the boy and mother reported and that there is no cause for further investigation. You send the two on their way and go to the office to write a report.

For your report, you must add missing details: names and particulars of the mother and boy and any additional details you think are necessary to write a complete report.

5. You are a transit authority officer and have been called to a bus stop on Egan Street to give a lift to a bus driver whose bus has been impounded by police.

Friday, July 29, 2016, 0135 hrs
Corner of Egan and Dorchester Streets

When you arrive at the stop, you speak with a bus driver who is sitting on a bench beside the bus stop. A police officer was sitting with the driver. The officer had just finished interviewing the driver. The officer hands the driver her card and leaves.

You sit down beside the driver, and he tells you the following:

The driver had been assaulted by a young man when the driver came to the aid of a passenger who was being beaten by a male youth. The driver tells you he was driving westbound on Egan when he noted a disturbance near the back of the bus. There was yelling and the sound of punching, so he pulled over. He went to the back of the bus and on the way saw that a young man was leaning over a male passenger and was hitting the seated passenger repeatedly in the face. The male being attacked appeared to be unconscious, and there was a lot of blood on the victim.

The driver yelled at the assailant to stop. He did not. The driver then grabbed the attacker's arms in an attempt to stop him. The attacker was too strong for the driver, and the driver was flung to the ground. He suffered a broken nose and some cuts.

By this time, police had arrived. A passenger had called 911. Police arrested the attacker and took him off of the bus. Paramedics took the unconscious male passenger to the hospital. Police also had all passengers get off the bus.

The bus driver had called for a backup bus but did not want to get on the backup bus with the passengers. He called transit dispatch to request a ride home. The driver is clearly shaken, and you ask him if he wants to go to the hospital. He says he just wants to go home. You drive him home and report back to the office to write your report.

For your report, you must add missing details: the driver's name, the bus route number, the police officer's name and the police report incident number, the driver's home address, and any additional details you think are necessary to write a complete report.

6. You are a security guard at a stadium and find an abandoned wheelchair lying on its side outside a male washroom near the east gate entrance, level 2.

Thursday, October 6, 2016

You are doing rounds during a football game. You are detailed to level 2, and a fellow guard is also patrolling this level. She is patrolling counter-clockwise around the stadium, and you are patrolling clockwise.

On your third pass around the stadium, you notice a wheelchair lying on its side outside the men's washroom. You put it upright and carry on.

On your fourth and fifth pass, you note that the chair is still there. On your sixth pass, you enter the male washroom and ask the patrons in the washroom if the chair belongs to any of them. No one claims the chair.

You radio the central security deck to see if anyone had reported a lost wheelchair. The chair had not been reported as missing. On your seventh round, the chair is still there, but it is once again on its side. You right the chair again and carry on.

The game is now just about over, so you decide to do one last round and then stand by the chair to see if it is claimed. You stand by the chair as the fans stream out of the stands. You wait 20 minutes, but no one approaches the chair.

You decide to enter the stands. There you find an older man asleep on a seat in row FF, seat 10. You wake the man up. From the empty beer cups stacked in front of him and the smell of beer coming from him, you think he is intoxicated. You ask him if he is alright. He confirms he is fine. He says the beer and the warm sun put him to sleep. You tell him you will carry him out.

He looks alarmed and says, "Why the xxx would you do that? I'm a little fuzzy, but can still walk!" Sure enough, the man gets up and leaves.

You exit the stands and observe that the wheelchair is still there. Once again you call the main security desk, and once again no one has called in to report a missing wheelchair. You take the chair to the office and write a report.

For your report, you must add missing details: the name of the man you woke up, the name of your fellow guard, the times of your actions (e.g., calls to the desk, discussion with the sleeping patron), and any additional details necessary to write a complete report.

7. You are a special constable and have been asked by your supervisor to report on a training course you recently completed.

You took the course over three days: Monday, October 17, to Wednesday, October 19. You were in the classroom for 6.5 hours per day. The training took place at the local community college. The course, Introduction to Conflict Resolution, was a combination of theory and practice.

In the theory portion of the course, you were given a binder of course materials and listened to lectures supported by videos and PowerPoint presentations. You took many notes. You also had lectures from guest speakers from a municipal police service, a local security company, and an ethics officer from the city.

For the practical portion of the course, you completed many role-play exercises. These were graded, and you received a mark of 87/100 for that portion of the course. There was a final written exam for the course, and you received a grade of 85/100 on the exam.

You would like to take a few hours to share with your colleagues the highlights of the training you received. You got permission to do this from the course instructors, with the understanding that you could not certify your colleagues or officially grade them in any way. You were also told by the instructors that you could not give out the course materials.

As well, you would like to take part two of the course. This would give you the certification needed to become a conflict resolution instructor, Level 1, which would allow you to train your fellow officers. Part two is five days long and would cost $1,500.

For your report, you must add missing details: name and address of the community college, name of your instructor, when and where part two of the course will take place, and any additional details you feel are necessary to write a complete report.

CHAPTER SUMMARY

There will be countless occurrences or events for which you will write reports in your career as a law enforcement professional. As well as writing reports that directly concern the day-to-day business of responding to calls and conducting investigations, you will have occasion to write reports such as those you practised in Exercise 5.

If you can develop your own report-writing style that follows good report-writing guidelines, you will naturally and consistently write strong reports. Add to that a solid skill in editing your own reports for errors, and you will become known as an officer who can be counted on to write a clear, complete, concise, and professional narrative, no matter what the circumstances.

An added benefit to having a strong report-writing style is that you can always count on your ability to write well, even when tired, injured, or emotionally stressed—unfortunately, common circumstances for law enforcement professionals.

KEY TERMS

cause and effect, 265
contradictory, 267
irrelevant, 267
substantiate, 264

Review and Reflection Questions

1. What are the guidelines you should always keep in mind when writing reports?

2. What are some common errors you should avoid when writing reports?

3. Why is it important to be aware of the facts in issue when you write investigative reports?

4. How can using this chapter's guidelines help you in your day-to-day writing now, regardless of the task or occasion?

5. How can good report writing enhance and further your law enforcement career?

13 General Occurrence Reports

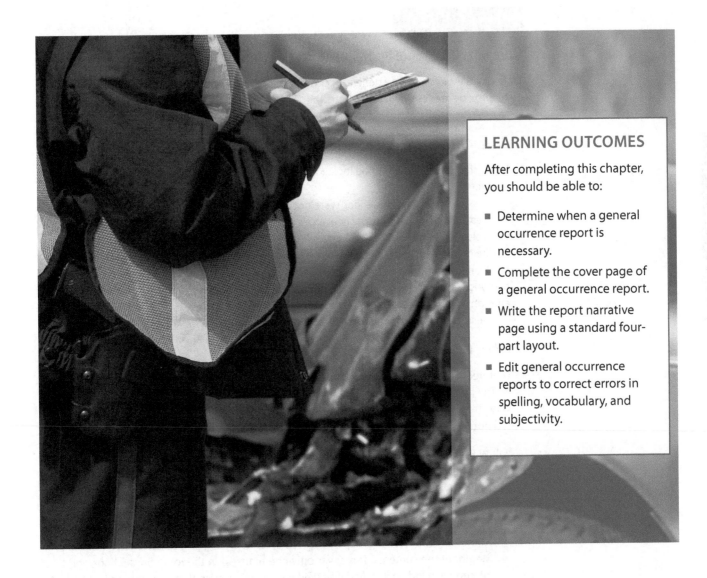

LEARNING OUTCOMES

After completing this chapter, you should be able to:

- Determine when a general occurrence report is necessary.
- Complete the cover page of a general occurrence report.
- Write the report narrative page using a standard four-part layout.
- Edit general occurrence reports to correct errors in spelling, vocabulary, and subjectivity.

Introduction

When an officer responds to a call regarding an incident, she will take notebook notes while she interviews the victim, witnesses, and anyone else involved. The officer then transcribes these notes into a general occurrence report. Not all calls require a general occurrence report. In Chapter 10, Introduction to Report Writing, Figure 10.1 illustrates the report writing trail and gives you a broad idea of when a general occurrence report would be required. There is also more information about when to use these reports in the next section of this chapter.

General occurrence reports consist of a *cover page*, which lists the informational details surrounding the incident or offence, such as dates, times, names, descriptions of suspects, and descriptions of property; and the *narrative page(s)*, where the narrative or story of the incident is recorded.

IN THE FIELD

General Occurrence for Failure to Provide Necessities

Two officers each wrote a general occurrence report detailing their observations at a failure to provide **necessities** call where the Children's Aid Society (CAS) requested police assistance.

Officer #1: Low in detail; high in judgment

I attended the rundown home located at 1 Shirley St. to check on the welfare of two CAS children.

It was obvious that these kids were not cared for by the parents. The parents drank a lot because we could see empty beer cases everywhere in the filthy kitchen that also hadn't been cleaned in months.

The children looked bored and lonely and were also very dirty. They will never learn to be clean living in a home like this. I wouldn't be surprised if they had lice in their hair and bed bugs too. The amount of money spent on alcohol that we could see would have been enough to have paid for a cleaner to come to the home.

These parents are unfit, and CAS should consider taking their kids away from them.

Officer #2: High in detail; low in judgment

I entered the home at the request of CAS to check on the welfare of two children.

The first thing that struck me was the overwhelming foul smell in the home. It smelled very strongly of urine.

I noted two areas in particular:

1. When I entered the kitchen I observed a blue bin full of food waste, pizza crusts, and maggots crawling on a mass of meat. There were cockroaches on the kitchen counter, which was piled high with dirty dishes. When I opened the fridge, I observed no food stored therein; however there were six cases of Brewers beer on the top shelf.

2. Next, I entered the children's bedroom and I saw two children, aged 3 and 5 years. They were both wearing diapers that appeared to be sagging and stretched from the weight of the contents. There was only one mattress in the room on the floor, and I placed my hand on it to find it soaked with a yellow stain that appeared to be urine. In the corner on the floor was a large pile of used disposable diapers. The smell in this

---

For legal purposes, **necessities** are those things needed to maintain life, such as food, water, shelter, and safety.

> room was so strong it made my eyes water. The two children were very quiet and had
> very little energy. I could see their bones through their skin.
>
> I called for an ambulance as I was very concerned for the health of these children.

When Is a General Occurrence Report Required?

For some calls officers respond to, no reports are required. The only recording of the call would be in the officer's notebook. Here are some examples of these types of calls:

- A homeowner has locked herself out of the home, and an officer on patrol sees her trying to break into the front door with a screwdriver. The officer talks to the woman, who is able to produce identification that shows her to be the homeowner. Her husband comes home and confirms that she lives there with him. There will be no investigation as a result of this call as there has been no criminal offence, so no report is required.

- An officer on patrol stops two young men who seem to be having a serious and escalating argument on the street. A group of young girls is playing nearby, and they clearly look worried about the yelling they are hearing. The officer talks to the men and discovers they are arguing about politics. He advises them to be mindful of their surroundings. They apologize and move off, talking quietly. Because the officer spent 15 minutes with the men, he would want to record his actions in his notebook, but no report would be necessary.

- An officer responds to a call where a homeowner had noted a suspicious smell coming from the house next door. The officer visits the person who called, and she tells the officer that she was supposed to feed the neighbour's cat while he was away. However, her husband had been in a serious car accident, and she had been at the hospital for five days. She forgot about the cat. She thinks the cat is dead but was too afraid to check on her own, so she called police. The officer visits the house with the neighbour, who lets them in with a key. The cat is dead. There would be no further investigation of this unfortunate incident.

Any time an officer responds to a call where an offence has been committed, or is believed to have been committed, she must write a general occurrence report. This type of call would include, for example, the following situations:

- traffic accident
- theft
- assault
- break and enter
- drug-related incidents
- public intoxication

The next reporting step after the general occurrence report is the **supplementary** or investigative actions reports, written over time as an investigation is conducted. For example, if an officer responds to a reported theft, a general occurrence report is written.

To supplement something is to add to it with further information or details; **supplementary** reports provide additional information.

Then, as the officer investigates further to find the suspect and arrest her, the officer writes subsequent reports detailing such investigative actions as interviews, searches, and arrests. These reports are discussed in later chapters.

In addition to these reports, you might also write

- **fraudulent** document reports
- homicide/sudden death reports
- vehicle reports
- missing person/escapee reports
- property reports

The structure and titles of police reports can vary somewhat from one law enforcement agency to another, but they all contain the same basic components, and they all need accurate detail recorded. The facts will come from your notebook. Keep in mind that *facts* consist of what you personally see or hear; anything else is *hearsay* (second-hand information, such as that offered by a witness) or *opinion* (conjecture, either yours or someone else's). For example, if you, as a police officer, see a break and enter in progress, your account of the break and enter is a *fact*. If a witness sees a break and enter, your report of the witness's account is *hearsay*. If a witness tells you that he thinks the kid down the street committed a crime because she looks like the type, the witness is offering you an *opinion*. Your account of the witness's opinion is *hearsay*.

Notice that all the information included in these reports (see, e.g., Figures 13.1 and 13.2) answers the questions posed by the Five Ws and an H: *who, what, where, when, why,* and *how*. If you don't have the information requested in the form, put a diagonal line through the box or line where the information should appear. Remember to sign the document.

As mentioned, the general occurrence report can be broken down into two parts: the cover page and the narrative.

The Cover Page

The cover page is the first document that appears in your package of documents. It records the details surrounding the offence or situation, and must be filled in completely. If certain information is not available, such as the hair colour of a suspect, a line must be put through the space supplied for that information, which indicates that the information is unavailable. Information for this report is taken from your notebook.

The Narrative

The **narrative** details the incident or situation, written by the responding officer from the officer's point of view. Usually, it is strictly factual, confined to information the officer actually witnessed. If it includes other types of information, such as testimony from a witness, this material must be clearly identified as such.

The narrative usually begins with a brief summary of the situation, including road and weather conditions if relevant. After the summary come sections containing information on the background and the facts, and then an outcome that indicates whether any charges are being laid, along with the reason for the charges.

To be **fraudulent** is to be dishonest, deceitful, or fake.

A **narrative** is a story or a telling of events or occurrences.

The narrative must contain the facts in issue, but these can be recorded more generally than they are on the cover page. For example, if a vehicle used by a suspect in a robbery is detailed on the cover page, the details need not be repeated here.

Sample General Occurrence Report

In Chapter 11, The Notebook, you learned how to make complete and accurate notes in your notebook. The notebook entries of PC Maria Gonzales were used as an example. Recall that Maria was dispatched to Highway 403 westbound at Garner Road at 1110. Assume that she was being called to the scene of a motor vehicle accident involving Muriel Wainman and that she made the following entries in her notebook.

	Thursday, 16/05/05
1110	*Dispatched to Highway 403 westbound at Garner Road*
	Fire and ambulance dispatched
1116	*10-7 Highway 403 and Garner Road Incident #16-9846*
	Truck overturned in median
	Female being assisted by passersby—no injuries
	Driver: Muriel Wainman
	12 Forest Lane
	Oakville, ON L9H 4S3 Phone 905-555-4121
	DOB 31 May 1974
	Ontario licence W6018-40716-40564
	10-60
	Vehicle: 2007 half-ton Chevrolet "Hauler" truck
	VIN 1H8ZH5282VZ2294022
	Valtag 2409127, Licence plate RH6103 Ontario 2009
	Registered to Provincial Haulage
	578 Crane St.
	Oakville, ON L8D 5A6 Phone 905-555-1793
	Insured by Market Insurance
	Policy LN84DD1061
1123	*Fire and ambulance on scene*
1125	*Interview with Wainman begins*
	Wainman states: "I'm not hurt, and I was wearing my seat belt. I
	was driving westbound along Highway 403 after picking up a dozen
	cartons of electrical supplies in Hamilton. I was delivering them to

	Brantford. I was driving in the right-hand lane of the highway at the
	speed limit. When I got close to the Garner Road exit, suddenly a
	blue mid-sized car swerved out of the passing lane in front of me to
	get off at Garner Road. I turned the steering wheel hard to the left
	because I thought we were going to crash. My truck skidded across the
	passing lane and onto the median. It rolled over, and cartons spilled
	onto the median. People stopped to help me get out of the truck. No
	other vehicles were involved. I phoned the police. I can't describe the
	blue car, and I didn't get the licence number. I think the damage to
	the cartons is about $1,500." I estimate the damage to the truck at
	$4,000. Wainman phoned for a tow truck from Towable Towing Co.
1127	Tow truck arrives on scene.
	Cartons placed back on truck by representatives of Provincial Haulage,
	who were contacted by Wainman by cellphone.
1142	Truck towed to the Provincial Haulage offices in Oakville.
	No charges laid.
1146	MTO contacted by dispatch for cleanup in the area.
1152	10-8

The sample cover page and narrative in Figures 13.1 and 13.2 are written from Maria's notebook information. The process for completing these forms is described below.

Sample Cover Page

There must be an entry made on every space of the cover page; leave nothing blank. If the information needed is not supplied, put a diagonal line through the space. Do not make any assumptions; don't add information you are not sure of.

As noted above, this incident is a continuation of Maria's notebook entries. Therefore, use "Downtown" for the division and "#3" for the patrol area (see Figure 13.1). The date of the incident is given (16/05/05), but the time of the incident is not given. The fact that the officer was dispatched at 1110 means that the incident occurred sometime before this time. The incident number is given (16-9846), the location of the incident is given (Highway 403 and Garner Road), the type of incident is known ("MVA" or "motor vehicle accident" or "10-50" or "hit and run"), and how the incident was committed can be derived from the complainant's statement (truck cut off by automobile).

- *Victim/complainant.* The victim or complainant is Muriel Wainman. The notebook entry states that she phoned in the accident, and we are told that she was the driver.
- *Reported by.* Wainman reported the accident. Rather than repeating all of the same information found in the previous section, write "Wainman" or "victim" or "SAME" in the area where the surname is required, and put a diagonal line through the rest of the section.

FIGURE 13.1   Sample Cover Page for a General Occurrence Report

MITCHELL'S BAY POLICE SERVICE
GENERAL OCCURRENCE REPORT

No. of supplementary reports   *1*

Division   *Downtown*   Patrol area   *#3*   Date/time of incident   *16/05/05*

Type of incident   *MVA*   Incident no.   *16-9846*

Location of incident   *Hwy 403 and Garner Rd.*

How incident committed   *Truck cut off by auto*

Victim/complainant

Surname   *Wainman*   Given (1)   *Muriel*   Given (2)

Address   *12 Forest Lane, Oakville, ON   L9H 4S3*

Sex   *F*   DOB (Y/M/D)   *74/05/31*   Marital status   Home phone   *905-555-4121*

Employer   *Provincial Haulage*   Business phone   *905-555-1793*

Reported by

Surname   *SAME*   Given (1)   Given (2)

Address

Sex   DOB (Y/M/D)   Relationship to victim   Home phone

Employer   Business phone

Vehicle used

Type   *auto*   Licence no.   Licence year   Province

Style   *mid-size*   Colour   *blue*   VIN

Owner surname   Given (1)   Given (2)

Outstanding features

Accused/suspect

Surname   Given (1)   Given (2)

Nicknames/alias

Address   Home phone

Sex   DOB (Y/M/D)   Height   Weight   Race

Hair colour   Moustache/beard/wig   Eye colour   Glasses

Build (slender/medium/heavy)   Complexion

Description of clothing

Victim/accused relationship

Physical/mental condition, marks, scars, tattoos, outstanding features

Employer   Business phone

Reporting officer

Rank/name/no.   *PC Maria Gonzales #1298*   Date/time report taken   *16/05/05*

Other officers attending

Case reassigned to

- *Vehicle used*. The vehicle used in this case is not Wainman's truck, but the other vehicle. This is the car that police will be looking for in relation to the accident. Not much is known about it—it's an automobile, it's mid-sized, and it's blue. Insert those three entries in their proper places on the incident report, and put a diagonal line through the other spaces, since the information required is not available.

- *Accused/suspect*. There is no accused or suspect, since Wainman didn't see the driver. One diagonal line through the entire section will suffice.

- *Reporting officer*. PC Maria Gonzales is the reporting officer. No other officers were involved in the preparation of this report, so put a diagonal line through the appropriate space.

Sample Narrative Page

Keep in mind four things:

1. All relevant information from the notebook must appear in the report, either on the cover page or in the narrative.

2. Information doesn't have to be repeated in the narrative if it's already on the cover page.

3. Each section of the narrative will be of a different length, depending on the amount of information provided. You can have more than one paragraph in each section.

4. The narrative usually contains four sections: summary, background, facts, and outcomes as discussed above.

First, fill out the information at the top of the narrative page(s) (see Figure 13.2). The report concerns Muriel Wainman, whose name is entered in full. Wainman is the victim (circle "victim"). Give her full address, including postal code. The type of incident is "MVA" or "motor vehicle accident" or "10-50" or "hit and run," and the incident number is 16-9846.

The first paragraph is a brief summary of the incident, and should contain brief information from the background, facts, and outcomes of the report. Weather conditions also appear in this paragraph, and in the Wainman case, these conditions are found in the first part of the notebook in Chapter 11.

The next section contains the background to the report, the information leading up to the accident. Everything that happened before the accident should be stated here. Also included in this section will be information about the driver that you don't have on the cover page.

The third section contains the facts—the information about the accident. In the Wainman case, all of the information for this section comes from her interview, and since Wainman was speaking in the first person, and the information she gave was transcribed into the notebook exactly as she stated it, the quotation marks should remain.

The final section contains the outcomes—what happened as a result of the accident, or what is to happen. Damages and injuries can also be found in this section, since both are the result of the accident (there are no injuries in the Wainman incident). Specifically, as a result of the accident, the following outcomes resulted:

1. Damage is estimated at $4,000.

2. Wainman phoned for a tow truck.

3. The tow truck arrived.

4. The cartons were placed back on the truck.

5. The truck was towed.

FIGURE 13.2   Sample Narrative Page for a General Occurrence Report

MITCHELL'S BAY POLICE SERVICE
NARRATIVE REPORT

Name   *Muriel Wainman*   (Victim)/accused

Address   *12 Forest Lane, Oakville, ON   L9H 4S3*

Type of incident   *MVA*   Incident no.   *16-9846*

A single vehicle accident occurred at the intersection of Highway 403 and Garner Rd. A truck was cut off by a car and the truck rolled over in the median. There were no injuries, but some property damage. Weather was warm and dry, roads clear.

I was dispatched to Hwy 403 westbound at Garner Rd. Fire and ambulance were also dispatched. I was on scene at 1116. I found that a truck had overturned in the median, and the female driver was being assisted by a passerby. There were no injuries. Fire and ambulance were on scene at 1123.

The driver of the truck, Muriel Wainman, identified herself with Ontario licence W6018-40716-40564. She is 10-60. She was driving a 2007 half-ton Chevrolet "Hauler" truck
  - *VIN   1H8ZH5282VZ2294022*
  - *Valtag   2409127*
  - *Licence plate RH6103 Ontario 2009*
  - *Registered to Provincial Haulage*
          578 Crane St.
          Oakville, ON   L8D 5A6
          905-555-1793
  - *Insured by Market Insurance*
          Policy   LN84DD1061

I began an interview with Wainman at 1125. She stated:
"I'm not hurt, and I was wearing my seat belt. I was driving westbound along Highway 403 after picking up a dozen cartons of electrical supplies in Hamilton. I was delivering them to Brantford. I was driving in the right-hand lane of the highway at the speed limit. When I got close to the Garner Rd. exit, suddenly a blue mid-sized car swerved out of the passing lane in front of me to get off at Garner Rd. I turned the steering wheel hard to the left because I thought we were going to crash. My truck skidded across the passing lane and onto the median. It rolled over, and cartons spilled onto the median. People stopped to help me get out of the truck. No other vehicles were involved. I phoned the police. I can't describe the blue car, and I didn't get the licence plate. I think the damage to the cartons is about $1,500."

Reporting officer

Rank/name/no.   *PC Maria Gonzales #1298*   Page no.   *1*

FIGURE 13.2   Concluded

MITCHELL'S BAY POLICE SERVICE   **STATEMENT CONTINUATION**

Name   *Wainman*   Page no.   *2*

Wainman phoned for a tow truck from Towable Towing Co., which arrived on scene at 1127. The cartons were placed back on the truck by representatives of Provincial Haulage, who were contacted by Wainman by cellphone.

At 1142, the truck was towed to the Provincial Haulage offices in Oakville, and at 1146 MTO was contacted by dispatch for cleanup in the area.

No charges were laid.

6. MTO was contacted.

7. No charges were laid (Wainman not responsible, the other driver not found).

8. The officer returned to patrol duty.

Reporting Information— Reviewing Key Concepts

In earlier chapters of this text, you learned about several key concepts you need to consider when writing as a law enforcement professional. You learned it is critical to review your work to ensure that you

- have not used slang, cliché, or jargon
- are writing objectively and leaving out your bias or opinions
- are spelling workplace words correctly
- are writing in the active voice
- know the difference between the first person point of view and the third person point of view

Before you practise writing general occurrence reports, refresh your knowledge of these key concepts by completing the following exercises. If necessary, refer to the first half of your text to further review the concepts.

EXERCISE 1 » Editing for Slang, Jargon, and Cliché

Edit the following report excerpts so they are free from slang, jargon, and cliché. You may have to research some of the terms in order to switch them for appropriate vocabulary.

> The perp then took off down the small side street. I took off after him on foot. After about a two-minute chase, he stopped and turned around with his hands in the air. I approached the low-life to arrest him. He had sleeve tats on both arms and a gang tat on his face.

> The victim had a righteous bruise on her left cheek, and her left eye was closed. She was known to us as a chronic junkie and is currently living on the streets. She is also the KA of one Riggles Menley, a mope we arrested last month.

After one hour of interviewing, the suspect said he needed to come clean. The suspect told me his buddy had been stealing crotch rockets from various dealerships in town and unloading them via the Internet. The perp then claimed he didn't really know his buddy's name or what he looked like. I felt the information was hinky, so I pushed the guy. He finally told me he was the one who did the heists.

As a result of an undercover op, on Tuesday, November 1, 2016, our SRO for the local high school reported that he caught two juvies trying to sell dope to some rug rats from the neighbouring elementary school. I was dispatched to the scene to assist in the arrests. It was quite a score for the team.

EXERCISE 2 » Editing for Bias and Subjectivity

Edit the following sentences so they are free from bias and subjectivity.

The low-life gang member refused to cooperate, so I arrested him for robbery.

_____

I was on route to a disturbance call in a lovely neighbourhood of large and beautiful homes.

_____

As I approached the bum, I could smell that he reeked of vomit and urine.

_____

The nice young man clearly and competently told me his side of the story.

_____

The lazy mother seemed uninterested in taking care of her children.

_____

EXERCISE 3 » Checking Your Spelling

Circle the correctly spelled word from the bold-faced word pairs in the following sentences. Try to pick the correct answers on your own without consulting a dictionary. This will give you a good idea of which words you need help with. You can add them to your spelling journal, if you have started one.

We have to determine **weather/whether** the suspect has had a criminal **passed/past**.

You will get a better story from the witness if you have more **patience/patients**.

Your **presense/presence** is required at the inquest.

There/Their were several police **chiefs/cheifs** at the **conference/conferance**.

The injuries were inflicted by a set of **sizzors/scissors**.

The **graffiti/grafitti** was likely done by **michevious/mischievous** students at the school.

If you study hard, you will **succeed/succede** at the WCT.

The car was **severly/severely** damaged by the collision.

It is **characteristic/charactoristic** of the media to be at motor **vechile/vehicle** accidents.

I must testify later today; **therefore/therefor**, I will be unavailable for lunch.

EXERCISE 4 » Writing in the Active Voice

Change the following sentences so they are written in the active voice. Remember that using the active voice involves putting the "doer" into the sentence.

Example:

> The victim was then escorted from the courtroom. (Who escorted the victim?)
>
> The bailiff then escorted the victim from the courtroom.

The suspect was then arrested on a charge of break and enter.

The police recruits were then shown how to load their revolvers.

The witness was brought to the interview room.

The uncooperative youth was restrained and led to the police vehicle.

The recruit was given a warning regarding her absenteeism.

EXERCISE 5 » Writing in the First or Third Person

Identify whether the first person or the third person is being used in the following report excerpt by writing an "f" or a "t" in the brackets.

> Officer Smith ( ) and I ( ) responded to a call of a possible domestic disturbance at 35 Ridgeway Ave. As I exited the police vehicle, I heard loud yelling coming from the residence. Officer Smith and I proceeded to the front door. He ( ) then knocked loudly on the door, which was opened by a white male, approximately 40 years old. The male ( ) was joined by a female. She ( ) was also white, approximately 30 years old. They ( ) both appeared to be holding bundles of papers. We ( ) each took one person into separate rooms to interview them ( ) individually. Neither of us ( ) was convinced our ( ) individual was giving the clear picture.

EXERCISE 6 » Putting It All Together

Imagine you are a staff sergeant who needs to review the following report written by one of your officers. Edit the report carefully to find and fix errors in the key concepts reviewed in Exercises 1–5.

On Tuesday, October 11, 2016, I was dispatched to the seen of a motor vehicle accident on Stanley Avenue between the intersections of Geneva Street and Prince Edward Avenue. The day was clear and cold. There was some ice on the roads. I was not told if their were injuries.

On my approach to the accident, I noted that traffic was being re-routed further up the street to detour around the accident. This officer continued to the scene and an officer let me threw to the sight. It was chaotic. There was a large amount of people standing around. A red, 2010 Toyota Rav-4 was resting on it's side up against a lightpost on the north side of Stanley Avenue between the intersections of Geneva Street and Prince Edward Avenue. An ambulance was parked at the intersection of Geneva Street and Stanley Avenue. Two paramedics were hanging out by the back of the ambulance. The lady paramedic was talking to a cute young women who was wrapped in a blanket. The woman had cuts and bruises on her face. I went over to interview the woman. As I got closer, I noted that the young woman was wearing a very short skirt, high heels and a low-cut top. She also had to much makeup on. She might be a cocktail waitress or even a dancer. I identified myself and asked the woman if she could tell me what happened. She identified herself as Charlene Harrington. She told me she had been driving home from work shortly before 12:00. She had worked the morning desk shift at Lidia's Motor Inn and was due back to work the evening shift at 7:00. As she passed the intersection of Geneva Street and Stanley Avenue, a car which she thinks came from Geneva Street, came speeding across the road and hit her car on the passenger side. The hit was hard enough to knock her car onto it's side. Harrington was not about to give me a description of the vechile in question. As Harrington was talking, I noted she was slurring her words. I asked her if she had been drinking that morning. She claimed she hadn't, saying, "No officer, I just feel a bit woozy." That seemed a bit bogus to me, but the paramedics seemed to buy it. They decided to take her to the hospital for treatment.

I asked Harrington if I could remove her insurance documents from her car. She said yes, and I did so. Everything was in order. Before the medics loded Harrington into the ambulance, left I gave her my card and told here I would be in touch.

By this time, four tow trucks had pulled up. I examined the Rav-4. I saw a large dent in the passenger door, and there was green paint in the dent. I gave one of the truck drivers the okey to take the car. He told me he was towing the car to Al's Car Lot. I wrote this down to pass along to Harrington. I was about to canvass the lookie-looks standing around for any intel they might have when a guy approached me, saying he had seen the accident. He identified himself as a Mr. Sabu, the owner of 365 Stanley Ave. He happened to be looking out his window when the accident occured. He was hard to understand. From another country, I guess. He said he saw a green four-door sedan hit the Rav-4. He thought the car was a Subaru. He thought the first three letters on the plate were ART. I left my card with Mr. Sabu and went to my vehicle to put a BOLO out for a green Subaru sedan, partial plate ART.

My search turned up two possible matches to the car in question. I will visit the owners of each of the too cars.

EXERCISE 7 » Practising Writing General Occurrence Reports

Write general occurrence reports for the following situations:

1. At 2230 on 12 June of this year, you were dispatched to Frank Rizzo's Bar at 125 Main St., Thorold, Ontario, to make a report on an assault.

   You are 10-7 at 125 Main St. at 2240.

   The owner of Frank Rizzo's Bar, Stephen Van Sickle, states that he was notified by bartender Irina Ossine, who called Van Sickle in his office at the back of the bar, that a fight had broken out on the dance floor. Irina had been informed by a bouncer, Peter Northwood, that the fight was in progress. Northwood and another bouncer, Ron Valentine, went to break up the fight. Ray Harewood, the victim, was dancing when he was pushed in the back by an unknown male. Harewood turned around on being pushed and was immediately struck in the face with a beer bottle, which did not break. He fell to the ground unconscious. Harewood regained consciousness several minutes later. A patron, Carlos Lopez, noticed a male running from the dance floor and exiting through a fire exit. Lopez chased the man and followed the suspect to his motorcycle. The suspect left the parking lot on a Harley-Davidson motorcycle.

   Stacy Cordiero, a friend of the victim, was standing beside the victim at the time of the assault. She corroborated Harewood's story. Earlier in the evening, the suspect had approached Cordiero and had made derogatory comments about her.

   Harewood had intervened, and Harewood and the suspect exchanged words. Harewood stated he had never seen the suspect before that evening.

   Harewood declined medical attention.

   You broadcast a description of the suspect and his vehicle. You are 10-8 at 2315 on routine patrol.

Witness:	Stacy Cordiero 10-61
DOB:	11 April 1975
Home address:	1566 Chrysler St., Thorold, ON
Phone:	905-555-1122

Witness:	Irina Ossine 10-60
DOB:	4 July 1979
Home address:	1569 Freeland Ave., Niagara Falls, ON
Phone:	905-555-6869

Witness:	Peter Northwood 10-61
DOB:	8 September 1961
Home address:	3 Queen St., Apt. 56, Thorold, ON
Phone:	905-555-7361

Witness:	Carlos Lopez 10-60
DOB:	24 January 1965
Home address:	29 Neo Rd., Thorold, ON
Phone:	905-555-8791

Witness:	Ron Valentine 10-60
DOB:	1 July 1977
Home address:	201 Oak St., Fonthill, ON
Phone:	905-555-5554

Victim:	Ray Harewood 10-67
DOB:	28 February 1978
Home address:	1073 Mallard Blvd., St. Catharines, ON
Phone:	905-555-9111

2. You were dispatched at 0215 on 25 June of this year to take a report about a hit-and-run accident.

You are 10-7 at 0223.

Catriona Hicks reports that she was driving northbound on Bay Street at approximately 0200 at the posted speed limit of 60 km/h. She proceeded through the intersection of Bay Street and Bloor Street on a green light. Hicks's car was then struck on the driver's side near the rear door by a car eastbound on Bloor Street. Hicks's car was spun around and ended up facing south on Bay Street. She could see that the car that hit her was speeding away eastbound on Bloor Street. Hicks managed to get out of the car and onto the sidewalk. A witness, Ashras Baddar, assisted her and called an ambulance through 911. Hicks complained of neck and back pain.

Baddar stated, "I saw the Ford Focus enter the intersection as I was waiting to cross Bay Street at the light. The Ford was struck by a red Pontiac Sunfire that entered the intersection against the light. I ran over to the Ford to assist the driver. I could see that the driver of the Pontiac was a white male with short dark hair and a large tattoo on his neck, on the left side. The licence number of the Pontiac was AMAX 133, Ontario plate. I called 911. I sat with the driver until the ambulance arrived. I heard the ambulance attendant say that Hicks had a concussion and possible neck injuries."

You tell Baddar to call the police if he has additional information. Your interview of Baddar began at 0245 and ended at 0257.

Victim:	Catriona Hicks 10-60
DOB:	12 July 1983
Home address:	214 Charles Ave., Kenora, ON
Phone:	705-555-1050
Valid driver's licence:	H4112-10728-35712 (ON)
Vehicle:	2000 silver Ford Focus, Ontario plate AJTZ 917, owned by Hicks
VIN:	2KFLA1545H831208
Insurer:	Albany Insurance
Broker:	Economical
Policy no.:	7024-Z-4G9

Witness:	Ashras Baddar 10-60
DOB:	1 December 1957
Home address:	455 Bay St., Suite 602, Kenora, ON
Phone:	807-555-8874

Suspect:	John McClure 10-60
DOB:	11 November 1980
Home address:	193 Young St., Kenora, ON
Phone:	None

Supply any information that might be needed to complete your report.

3. You are on duty at 2130 on 24 June of last year when you are dispatched to respond to a break-and-enter call at an abandoned warehouse at 4 Culver Rd., Pickering, Ontario. You are 10-7 at 2135. Since the warehouse is in an industrial part of the city, you request backup. PC Amy Zhang #2587 is 10-7 on scene at 2137. You enter the unlit building together.

After a thorough search of the building, you find nothing out of place, except that a door on the east side of the building is unlocked and open. Since there is a strong wind that night, it is possible that the wind blew open the door. PC Zhang returns to her patrol area, and you begin to write a brief report in your cruiser.

As you complete your report, you see a man come from around the corner of the building. He approaches your vehicle. He identifies himself as a security guard with Reliable Security Service, and he is wearing the appropriate uniform. He asks you if anything is wrong. You ask for his information:

> **Drew Simms 10-60**
> **76 Preston Ave., Pickering, ON L2A 5G6**
> **Cellphone 905-555-4069**
> **No home phone**
> **DOB 1 February 1986**
> **Employed with Reliable Security Service since 2010**

Simms tells you he has had a quiet shift with no incidents. He says he did not call in the break and enter. He tells you the east side door constantly blows open. He then tells you he had noted a strong smell of gasoline along the south wall of the building. He also noted a lighter and some rags there.

He goes on to tell you he overheard the owner of the building, Cameron Nolan, telling someone that he wished the building would just go up in flames, as he was having trouble renting it out and it was "bleeding him dry." Simms gives you Nolan's particulars:

Home address:	**1 Day Crescent, Pickering, ON L2A 5R5**
Home phone:	**905-555-7985**
Business phone:	**905-555-4127**

General Occurrence Report #05-01-2014

4. You are dispatched at 1832 on 24 February of this year to 8131 Book Lane, London, to take a report of a missing child, Leanne Burgess. You arrive at 1840 and interview the mother of the missing child, Lisa Burgess.

Mrs. Burgess (she prefers to be known as "Mrs.") states that her daughter left the house at approximately 3 p.m. today to go to the playground and see if any of her friends were there. The playground is on the next block, on Wave Street near Hagen Boulevard. Leanne was supposed to have been home at 4:30 p.m., and when she didn't arrive back by 5 p.m., Mrs. Burgess walked over to the playground to look for Leanne. She wasn't there, and one boy who was at the playground said that he hadn't seen anyone else at the playground. Mrs. Burgess says she hadn't seen the boy before today. Mrs. Burgess states that she phoned Leanne's friends, but none of them had seen her. She then phoned the police.

Mrs. Burgess tells you that she and her husband recently separated, and their relationship was not good. She hints that he might have had something to do with Leanne's disappearance, although she has no evidence to support this suspicion. Mrs. Burgess doesn't know where her husband is living, and doesn't have a telephone number for him. She tells you that his name is Roger Burgess, and that he was born 30 June 1975. The couple does not have a formal separation agreement, and Roger has been visiting his daughter regularly.

You interview neighbours, but no one is able to supply you with any additional information. You then drive to the playground, and find two boys there. You ask them if they know Leanne Burgess, and when both of them state that they go to school with Leanne, you ask them whether they had seen her earlier today at the playground. One of the boys, James Wardley, tells you that he had seen Leanne at that playground earlier, and that he had seen her leave with a man who James thought was her father. The man had been driving a brown car, and Leanne got into the car without resisting, indicating that she knew the man. You phone Mrs. Burgess, and she confirms that her husband drives a brown 2008 Ford Focus. You run the name through the police database. Information comes back confirming that the owner of the Focus is Roger Burgess.

You return to the Burgess residence at 1945 and enter the house to obtain a photo and description of Leanne Burgess when a brown Ford Focus pulls into the driveway. Mrs. Burgess runs to the window and yells, "That's him! That's my husband! And he's got Leanne with him! He's the one who kidnapped my daughter!"

Mr. Burgess enters the house with Leanne, who says, "Hi, Mommy. Daddy picked me up at the park and we went for a ride." She appears to be unhurt.

You interview Roger Burgess, who claims that he was driving past the playground on his way to the convenience store, saw Leanne, and stopped to take her with him. They drove around the city for a while because he wanted to spend some time with his daughter, and he lost track of time. When he realized how long they'd been gone, he hurried back to the house. He admits that he should at least have phoned Mrs. Burgess, but says that he didn't want to get into an argument, and besides, he never thought that she'd call the police.

Since there is no legal reason why Mr. Burgess could not take his daughter for a ride, no charges are laid. However, you remind Mr. Burgess that his inconsiderate attitude has cost a lot of your time that could have been useful elsewhere. You also tell him that you will submit a report on this incident. You are 10-8 at 2015.

Incident report #10-01-2010.

Complainant:	Lisa Burgess 10-60
DOB:	31 October 1976
Home address:	8131 Book Lane, London
Phone:	705-555-0099

Missing child:	Leanne Burgess 10-60
DOB:	25 October 2000
Home address:	8131 Book Lane, London (same as mother)
Phone:	705-555-0099 (same as mother)

Suspect:	Roger Burgess 10-60
DOB:	30 June 1975
Home address:	30 Fennel Ave., London
Phone:	705-555-1028
Vehicle:	2008 brown Ford Focus, Ontario licence BJDW 878
VIN:	1G8LM5281RS293176

Witness:	James Wardley 10-60
DOB:	23 July 1999
Home address:	21 Calibri Ave., London
Phone:	705-555-1234

CHAPTER SUMMARY

General occurrence reports tell, as much as is possible, the complete story of the events surrounding an incident or offence. On the cover page of a general occurrence report, the facts of the incident are recorded: names, dates, times; descriptions of persons involved; descriptions of property, vehicles, and any other objects involved; and charges laid. The narrative page of the general occurrence report is a summary of the officer's observations and actions; testimony from witnesses, victims, and suspects; and any other details needed to tell the complete story.

A well-written general occurrence report lays the groundwork for subsequent investigative actions and for all the supplementary reports that are written during the course of an investigation. The general occurrence report will form part of the package given to the Crown attorney's office once an arrest has been made.

KEY TERMS

fraudulent, 280
narrative, 280
necessities, 278
supplementary, 279

Review and Reflection Questions

1. What is the purpose of the general occurrence report?

2. What are some types of calls that an officer might respond to that wouldn't require a general occurrence report?

3. What types of information appear on the cover page of a general occurrence report?

4. What are the four parts of the narrative page of the general occurrence report?

5. What writing errors should you edit for when reviewing your general occurrence report?

14 Supplementary Reports

LEARNING OUTCOMES

After completing this chapter, you should be able to:

- Write supplementary reports from information recorded in a notebook.
- Understand how to link a supplementary report to an original.
- Write arrest reports that are complete and accurate.
- Record accurate information on the Statement from Accused.

Introduction

In the previous chapter you learned that general occurrence reports record the facts of an incident and that, generally, this incident cannot be closed immediately because further investigation is required. These further investigations are documented in **supplementary** reports. Each further investigative action must be reported and linked to the original general occurrence report. These reports add to the investigation of the initial occurrence; they are *added* to the original occurrence report. Supplementary reports track over time the facts of the investigation until the case is closed.

For example, an officer dispatched to investigate a reported theft may interview the complainant and record details of the scene, including information about stolen items. The officer would investigate, enter the information into the notebook, and write a general occurrence report; at this stage, the case remains open. If, however, the next day, the complainant finds other missing items and notifies police, the officer must return to interview the complainant and record further facts about the theft. The officer then writes a supplementary report to the initial general occurrence. As the officer investigates the incident, she writes reports for each stage of the investigation, including all interviews, searches, and **arrests**.

Bear in mind that this example simplifies the nature of the investigative procedure in many ways. Often, one officer will respond and write a general occurrence report, and another officer—working another shift that is hours, days, or weeks after the initial occurrence—will respond to a follow-up call. Typically, many officers are involved in a single case. The complications arising from these conditions require a high level of organization. You must record and transfer information accurately to preserve the integrity of the reporting process.

Supplementary Reports for Further Investigative Actions

Supplementary reports are like general occurrence reports; they consist of the following components:

1. The cover page
2. The narrative

Furthermore, these forms are identical to those used for the general occurrence report. The cover page holds the basic information of the situation, taken from the officer's notebook; the narrative tells the story of the situation, written by the officer from the officer's point of view, and limited, unless clearly noted otherwise, to information the officer actually witnessed.

However, there are important differences in the way you complete these two reports because they have different purposes. Since further investigative actions must be understood in the context of previous ones, supplementary reports must be linked. The relationship between reports must be identified both in the cover page and in the narrative. Let's examine how this is done.

A **supplementary** report is an additional report following an original incident and further reporting relevant information about the investigation.

Arrest means to take control of a person—that is, to take a person into custody.

Linking Reports

The first way to link files is to identify the original incident number. Today, files are easily uploaded and linked through computer systems; this procedure simplifies the process of linking and cross-indexing multiple reports relating to the initial occurrence. Officers can check the system to discover reports and access relevant information. Files are linked in various ways, sometimes using the name of the complainant or victim, but the conventional way to link supplementary reports to the general occurrence report is through the incident number given by dispatch to the original incident. This appears on the general occurrence report on the cover page. For example, here is the heading information on the cover page for the Wainman motor vehicle accident discussed in the previous chapter:

MITCHELL'S BAY POLICE SERVICE
GENERAL OCCURRENCE REPORT

No. of supplementary reports   _1_

Division *Downtown*	Patrol area *#3*	Date/time of incident *16/05/05*
Type of incident *MVA*	Incident no. *16-9846*	
Location of incident *Hwy 403 and Garner Rd.*		
How incident committed *Truck cut off by auto*		

The incident number assigned to this incident is 16-9846. If you review the heading portion of the narrative for this incident, you will notice this same incident number is recorded there, too:

MITCHELL'S BAY POLICE SERVICE
NARRATIVE REPORT

Name *Muriel Wainman*	(Victim)/accused
Address *12 Forest Lane, Oakville, ON L9H 4S3*	
Type of incident *MVA*	Incident no. *16-9846*
Rank/name/no. *PC Maria Gonzales #1298*	Page no. *1*

Supplementary reports use the incident number that is on the original occurrence report. This way, the officer indicates that the present report she is writing is connected to a previous incident. Thus, a chain of reports over time is established for a single case. Record this number on both the cover page and the heading information of the narrative portion of your supplementary report. Once again, this report might be a further interview, a search, or an arrest—these are just three possible investigative actions that might further supplement the original report. The incident number connects these reports.

The second way to indicate a report is supplementary to an original occurrence is to clearly and directly state this fact in the narrative. You can write this information into the first section of your narrative. In Chapter 12, Report Writing, you learned that narrative reports are organized into four sections: summary, background, facts, and outcomes. The narrative used to show the components of a simple report presented in Figure 12.1 began this way:

> A two-vehicle accident at the corner of King Street and Queen Street resulted in severe damage to one vehicle and the hospitalization of the driver of the second vehicle. A charge of impaired driving was laid. It had been raining and the roads were slippery. [**Summary: This section provides a brief overview of the incident, and usually includes weather and road conditions.**]

This example shows a typical introduction for a general occurrence report. In this example, there is no previous incident to consider. It is a new situation calling for an initial report. Now let's look at an example of how the summary section can be used to link a supplementary report to a general occurrence report.

Imagine a continuation of the break and enter reported by Ms. Thuy Nguyen in Chapter 11, The Notebook (see the "Guidelines for Notebook Entries" section). PC Maria Gonzales would have filed a general occurrence report using the details recorded in her notebook. Let's say that a call is made to police the next day from a witness, Katrina Wallender. She is calling to report more information about the incident.

Police respond to the call. In this case, the officer will go through the routine process of recording information into his notebook and then writing a report. On the cover page, the new information is recorded; however, the original incident number is used: #16-335602. The supplementary report narrative might begin this way:

> **On Friday, May 6, 2016, I was dispatched at 1030 to the residence of Katrina Wallender at 47 Elm St. to further investigate the break and enter at 45 Elm St., dated May 5, 2016, first reported by PC Maria Gonzales.**

The first sentence of the summary section clearly indicates the link between this report and the previous occurrence. The following words and phrases, along with their variations, are useful when you wish to indicate a link between reports:

- additional
- following
- further
- supplemental
- more

As noted in previous chapters, various templates are used in law enforcement for organizing reports, and you will follow the one provided by your supervisor. Nevertheless, you must develop your own reliable method for applying these templates. Use a clear and logical method for linking reports in the summary section of your report.

The background and facts sections report the new investigative action. Here the officer records the narrative of the present incident. In this case, the further investigative action is an interview with Katrina Wallender. The report might continue:

> I arrived at the Wallender residence at 1045. Ms. Wallender answered the door and stated that she wanted to report some details about the break and enter at her neighbour's house.
>
> Ms. Wallender reports that on the day of the incident, she noticed two men walk back and forth in front of her house many times while she watched from her bedroom window at approximately 1930 that night.
>
> She described the two men. One man she described as a white male, approximately 200 pounds, long black hair and beard, wearing a grey hoodie and jeans. The other man she described as a white male, approximately 175 pounds, with thin blonde hair, and wearing glasses, a black T-shirt, jeans, and red running shoes. She said she recognized this man from the neighbourhood, but did not know his name or address. She said, "I could identify him if I saw him again, no problem."
>
> Ms. Wallender agreed to come to the station this afternoon for a photo lineup.
>
> At 1115, I left the scene and resumed routine patrol.
>
> The investigation continues.

The outcome section of the supplementary report usually ends with an explanation of the investigation's progress; in the example above, the officer indicates that the investigation continues. See Figure 14.1 for a complete supplementary report based on the scenario above, and Figure 14.2 for a blank report you can photocopy and use for assignments. Whether a case remains open or closed is the decision of the lead investigator. One way to close an investigation is with an arrest. Let's look at how you would document an arrest after a series of supplementary reports.

Arrest Report

The arrest report, like the supplementary report, contains a cover page and a narrative. The cover page documents the information on the original general occurrence report that started the investigation. The narrative provides the context and details of the arrest. The general facts include the typical report questions providing context: the *who*, *what*, *when*, *where*, *why*, and *how* of the situation. For example, time, date, and location are three important general facts. The specific facts are the facts that relate to the conditions that define a specific offence. These facts establish the case against the accused, and all relevant facts of this kind should also be recorded accurately in the report.

Previously, we examined the charge of *trespass by night* and *assault*. If we examine the charge (252), *failure to stop at the scene of an accident*, the *Criminal Code of Canada* requires that the following specific facts be present:

- The accused must be the operator in charge of one of the vehicles.
- There must be an accident with a person, vehicle, or cattle.
- The accused must be aware of the accident.
- The accused must fail to stop, give his name and address, or offer assistance to anyone in need.
- The accused must flee to escape criminal or civil liability.

FIGURE 14.1   Sample Supplementary Report

MITCHELL'S BAY POLICE SERVICE
SUPPLEMENTARY REPORT

Name: *Thuy Nguyen*   (Victim)/accused

Address: *45 Elm St.*

Type of Incident: *Break and Enter*   Incident no. *16-335602*

I was dispatched at 1030 to the residence of Katrina Wallender at 47 Elm St. to further investigate the break and enter at 45 Elm St., dated May 5, 2016, first reported by PC Maria Gonzales.

Ms. Wallender lives beside the victim of the break and enter. She reported that on the day of the incident, she noticed two men walk back and forth in front of her house many times while she watched from her bedroom window at approximately 1930 the night of the incident.

She described the two men. One man she described as a white male, approximately 200 pounds, long black hair and beard, wearing a grey hoodie and jeans.

The other man she described as a white male, approximately 175 pounds, with thin blonde hair, and wearing glasses, a black T-shirt, jeans, and red running shoes. She said she recognized this man from the neighbourhood, but did not know his name or address. She said, "I could identify him if I saw him again, no problem."

Ms. Wallender was asked to come to the station this afternoon for a photo lineup, and she agreed.

At 1115, I left 47 Elm St. and resumed routine patrol.

The investigation continues.

Reporting Officer

Rank/name/no.   *PC Daljit Singh #2918*   Page no.   *1*

FIGURE 14.2   Blank Supplementary Report

MITCHELL'S BAY POLICE SERVICE
SUPPLEMENTARY REPORT

Name   Victim/accused

Address

Type of incident   Incident no.

Reporting officer

Rank/name/no.   Page no.

All conditions must be met in order to prove the charge and find the accused guilty. The officer writing the arrest report relates the specific facts to conditions of the charge. This proves the case against the accused and demonstrates that the accused was arrested with **reasonable grounds**.

An officer can arrest a person caught committing a criminal offence; the officer can also arrest a person if she believes a person has committed one. There are two main types of criminal offences. **Indictable** offences are serious offences such as homicide; **summary** offences are less serious crimes. Some offences are considered hybrid, meaning the offence might be treated as either type. The officer must have reasonable grounds for this arrest. Once an arrest is made, if the charge is a summary or hybrid offence, the police officer may release the person on an appearance notice or some form on which he promises to appear in court at a later date. Examples of summary offences include *trespass by night* and *harassing phone call*. In that case, the person may receive a summons in the mail. Alternatively, the officer will take the person into custody.

Documenting an Arrest

Police make an arrest when they take a person into custody. To make a lawful arrest, an officer will

- identify herself to the accused
- state that the person is under arrest
- state the reason for the arrest
- caution the person and inform him or her of the right to counsel
- show the person the **warrant** for the arrest if there is one

The accused must go with the officer if these conditions are met.

In the report, it is important that any actions taken by the officer are recorded accurately, including the above. This way, the report reflects the integrity of the arrest process and demonstrates that proper procedure was followed. In other words, the officer shows that he respected the rights of the person under arrest. The officer must be sure to record the following information:

- the accused person's name and information
- the date, time, and location of the arrest
- the time and method of the release, if released

Whether or not the person arrested is released without charge, once an arrest is made, the officer must write an arrest report.

Reasonable grounds are facts or circumstances that would lead a reasonable, objective person to believe an offence has occurred.

Indictable offences are serious crimes; examples of indictable offences include breaking and entering with intent (dwelling) (s. 348.1) and arson (s. 434).

A **summary** offence is a less serious crime; an officer might charge a person and release him or her using a promise to appear document.

A **warrant** is a court order giving authority to police to find and arrest a person; there are various kinds of warrants, including warrants to search, seize, enter, and arrest.

Warrants

Police often obtain judicial authorization for investigative actions. These actions include searches, seizures, entering a dwelling-house, and arrests. Your report should clearly state when you are acting on the basis of these legal orders. Use the summary section of your report to link your report to the original investigation, and indicate the precise warrant justifying your action.

Sample Arrest Report

Let's say that further investigative actions into the break and enter first reported by PC Maria Gonzales establish a number of facts: A witness sees two suspects, and is able to identify one of them through photographs provided by police; the suspect is known to police because he has previous charges and convictions; and one of the rings was recovered from a seller on a local online site, who claims he purchased it from the suspect, further identified by photograph. Each step in the investigation is filed in supplementary reports. Next, police arrest the suspect, and file the arrest report appearing in Figure 14.3.

In the sample arrest report in Figure 14.3, the investigation led to the arrest of one person, Wayne Roberts. We can imagine another arrest might come from this scenario. Since a witness noticed two men that night, let's say police interrogate Wayne Roberts about the other person. Mr. Roberts informs on his partner because he believes he was double-crossed; he confesses that their main purpose was credit-card fraud. He provides police with the name William Kats, DOB 1969/03/01, of 23 Willow St., Unit #1. Police check with Ms. Nguyen, and confirm she has since discovered she is missing a credit card she kept in a drawer overturned that night. Police prepare to search and arrest Roberts's partner in crime. This arrest exposes criminal activity of a much greater nature than the original occurrence. Examine the nearby In the Field box for a detailed search and arrest report.

IN THE FIELD

B&E Search Warrant Narrative

Reference Original Case #16-335602 Break and Enter at 45 Elm St.

On Thursday, June 2, 2016, police attended 23 Willow St., Unit #1, the residence of William Kats, DOB 1969/03/01. A search warrant had been signed by Her Honour Justice Jessie Warden to search for specific items taken in the break and enter at 45 Elm St., as well as evidence of credit card fraud. Present for the execution of the warrant were Cst. B. Smith (#123), Cst. C. Brown (#432), and myself, Cst. A. Lock, all of whom reviewed and signed the warrant.

We arrived at approximately 2009 hours and began knocking loudly several times followed by ringing of the doorbell, all the while announcing ourselves as "Police."

Within moments, the door was answered by a male I personally recognized to be suspect William Kats (DOB 1969/03/01).

Mr. Kats was advised that he was under arrest for break and enter and credit card fraud and was shown the warrant to search his premises for evidence of these offences. After reviewing the warrant, Kats stated, "OK, you got me." He was handcuffed and read his Rights to Counsel from my notebook to which he replied, "Yup I understand, I wanna call my lawyer Sam Smarts." He was then read the caution, to which he replied, "I know anything I say you'll use in court against me so I'm not saying anything else." He was searched incident to arrest and nothing was found on him. He was transported to the police station by Cst. V. Gillis (#897).

FIGURE 14.3 Sample Arrest Report

MITCHELL'S BAY POLICE SERVICE
ARREST REPORT

Name: *Wayne Roberts*   Victim/~~accused~~

Address: *51 Pine Street*

Type of Incident: Incident no. *16-335602*

Further to the original report of PC Maria Gonzales, on Wednesday, June 1, 2016, I arrived at 0700 at the residence of Wayne Roberts, 51 Pine St., apt. 908, with a warrant for his arrest.

Upon arrival, I met Mr. Roberts at the front door. I told Mr. Roberts he was under arrest for the break and enter. I informed him of his right to counsel and read him the Caution.

At 0715, Mr Roberts said, "I know my rights. I just called my lawyer. I ain't talking." When I asked him about his whereabouts on the evening of May 5 of this year, he stated, "I was at the movies." When I questioned him about the diamond ring he sold to Mr. Craig Kijbay, he said he received it as a gift from his grandmother, but he needed money to pay his credit card debt.

At 0730, I transported Mr. Roberts to Downtown Division.

Reporting Officer

Rank/name/no.   *PC Cindy Smith #432*

Page no.   *1*

Cst. B. Smith maintained control of the property ledger documenting and detailing items found during the search and their location where found.

Cst. C. Brown and I began to search the kitchen area and, at 2020 hrs, located a large stack of plastic Visa cards bound by elastic bands, which were located inside the top left drawer of the dining room cabinet. These cards ranging in number from 3021 to 3171. They were counted and totalled 150 Visa cards repeatedly bearing the name of "Thuy Nguyen." The cards were placed in a plastic property bag with tag #225 attached and turned over to Cst. B. Smith, who recorded it in the property ledger.

The search continued in the front bedroom, and at 2032 hrs, we located a black and silver card press with an impression plate bearing the imprint of "Thuy Nguyen." Also located was a jewellery box containing several gold rings and necklaces matching those described and listed in the warrant.

At approximately 2050 hrs, I searched the bathroom and seized five Visa cards from the garbage canister, which had what appeared to be errors on them. These were placed in a bag with property tag #226 attached. These cards were also turned over to Cst. B. Smith and recorded in the ledger.

At 2059 hrs, Cst. B. Smith located several documents containing personal identity data, including driver's licence #N234 9876 12 and birth certificate #5678 4321, both bearing the name "Thuy Nguyen." These were given property tag #227.

At 2114 hrs, Cst. C. Brown found several documents next to the Dell laptop computer, showing Internet searches titled "How to Duplicate a Credit Card" and "How to Make a Credit Card Seamless."

At 2127 hrs, the search ended. All officers exited and secured the premise together.

Investigation ongoing.

Statement from Accused

Once the statement from the accused is taken, it must be read back to him or her. The accused (that is, the person who is being charged with an offence) must then sign or at least initial the statement. (Figure 14.4 shows a sample Statement from Accused form.) If the accused refuses to do so, write "refused" in the appropriate space. As noted in Chapter 11, you must quote the accused's words directly, enclosing them in quotation marks. While you can't put words into the mouth of an accused, there are effective questioning techniques that can help you elicit information. (Review the section entitled "How to Ask Questions" in Chapter 11.) If you make a mistake, put a single line through the mistake and initial it. It is a good idea to have the accused initial the mistake as well.

FIGURE 14.4   Blank Statement from Accused

MITCHELL'S BAY POLICE SERVICE
STATEMENT FROM ACCUSED

Date _____ Time started _____ Time completed _____

Name _____

Address _____

Officer _____ Badge No. _____

You are charged with _____

_____

Do you wish to say anything in answer to the charge? _____

You are not obliged to say anything unless you wish to, but whatever you say may be given in evidence.

Q. Do you understand the charge? _____

A. _____ Signed _____

Q. Do you understand the caution I have read you? _____

A. _____ Signed _____

If you have spoken to any police officer or anyone with authority, or if any such person has spoken with you

in connection with this case, I want it clearly understood that I do not want that conversation to influence you

to make any statement.

Q. Do you understand that? _____

A. _____ Signed _____

Q. What, if anything, do you wish to say? _____

_____

_____

_____

_____

_____

_____

_____

_____

_____

_____

_____

_____

_____

_____

_____

_____

Signature _____ Witness _____

FIGURE 14.4 Concluded

MITCHELL'S BAY POLICE SERVICE   STATEMENT CONTINUATION

Name   Page no.

_____

_____

_____

_____

_____

_____

_____

_____

_____

_____

_____

_____

_____

_____

_____

_____

_____

_____

_____

_____

_____

_____

Signature   Witness

Exercises for Supplementary and Arrest Reports

To complete the following exercises, use the blank forms provided earlier in this chapter.

EXERCISE 1 » A. Continue the Investigation

Write a supplementary report based on the following information.

First, review the scenario outlined in the exercise in Chapter 13, Exercise 7 #1. Second, read the following continuation of the scenario before writing your report.

On June 15 of this year, three days after the assault occurring at Frank Rizzo's Bar, #16-3045, you were dispatched at 1500 to Phil's Diner, 89 Main St., Thorold, Ontario. Peter Northwood, one of the bouncers in the bar on the night of the assault, telephoned police to report that he was on his way to work when he saw the vehicle identified as belonging to the suspect. You are 10-7 at 89 Main St. at 1510. You inspect the parking area out front but find no motorcycle parked there. You enter the diner and interview the waitress on duty, Linda Griffiths. You ask her about the owner of the black Harley-Davidson motorcycle recently parked there. "Sure, he just left." She only knows his first name, Trevor. You ask her to describe this person, and she tells you, "He's a heavy guy, maybe 230 pounds, 6 feet, with short blond hair. He wears a black leather jacket with 'O'Doole Rules' on the back." Ms. Griffiths then tells you, "He's dating one of the other waitresses, Barbara Lucas. She's gone for the day." You speak to the owner of the bar, Mr. Fenton Ho, and he gives you Ms. Lucas's telephone number and address. The interview ends at 1530. You leave Phil's Diner at 1535 and resume routine patrol.

Name:	**Linda Griffiths 10-60**
DOB:	**26 May 1995**
Home address:	**87 Hudson Ave., Thorold, ON**
Telephone:	**905-555-4837**

Name:	**Fenton Ho 10-60**
DOB:	**21 June 1966**
Work address:	**Phil's Diner, 89 Main St., Thorold, ON**
Telephone:	**905-555-9860**

Name:	**Barbara Lucas 10-61**
DOB:	**12 November 1996**
Home address:	**271 Milton St., Thorold, ON**
Telephone:	**905-555-9321**

B. Continue the Investigation

Write a supplementary report based on the following information. Be sure to review the previous exercise to gather complete information for your report.

On June 16 of this year, you are dispatched at 1630 to interview Barbara Lucas. She meets you at the door. When you ask her about Trevor, she confirms that she is dating him, and that he drives a black Harley-Davidson motorcycle. You observe a photograph of her and a man that fits the description you obtained from Linda Griffiths, the waitress at Phil's Diner. You ask Ms. Lucas, "Is this your boyfriend?" She looks towards the ceiling and sighs. "Here we go again," she says. You ask her for Trevor's complete name and address, and she provides the information. Ms. Lucas tells you her boyfriend's name is Trevor Old, and that he lives at 341 Pike St., Thorold, Ontario. "I don't know where he is," she tells you, "I think he's out with the guys tonight." You ask her for his employer's address. She says, "Um, he works from home." You leave the scene at 1645 and proceed to Old's residence; you arrive at 1705. However, the driveway is empty and the lights are out. You ring the bell and no one answers. You leave Old's residence at 1715.

C. Investigation Leads to Arrest

Write an arrest report based on the following information. Be sure to review the previous exercises to gather complete information for your report.

On June 17 of this year, you arrive at Old's house, 341 Pike St., Thorold, Ontario, at 0900 and notice a black Harley-Davidson motorcycle parked in the driveway. The motorcycle is a black Harley-Davidson, Ontario plate, licence number 3M586. A man is on his back beside it. As you approach the man, you see he is a tall, heavy man with blonde hair wearing jeans and a leather jacket. He stands and says, "Hello." You ask him if his name is Trevor Old, and he says, "Yes. Why?" When you ask him about the incident at Frank Rizzo's bar, he admits he was there that night. He states, "That dude's lying, man. He came at me. It was self-defence. I just wanted to get away from that sh**. You can ask my mom; I never attacked nobody in my life." You inform him that he is under arrest for the assault at 0920. You read him his right to counsel and caution him of his rights, then transport him to downtown division.

D. Statement from Accused

Write the Statement of Accused for the scenario in part C in this exercise, using the blank form provided in Figure 14.4.

EXERCISE 2 » A. Write an Arrest Report

Write an arrest report for the search and seizure documented in the "In the Field" box in Chapter 11.

Review the "In the Field" box providing the officer's notes from the original incident. Using the information provided, write the arrest report. Include all the necessary details, and add any basic information you need to complete the report.

B. Write a Statement from Accused

Complete a Statement from Accused for part A of this exercise. Add whatever likely information you need to complete the statement, including the signature of the accused.

EXERCISE 3 » A. Write an Arrest Report

Review the hit-and-run scenario involving Catriona Hicks from Chapter 13, Exercise 7, #2.

The investigation leads to an arrest in the following scenario. Write an arrest report using the additional information provided below.

Investigating the hit-and-run scenario involving Catriona Hicks, you find information about the hit-and-run driver.

You check the licence of the Pontiac on CPIC. Information comes back that the owner of the Pontiac is John McClure. You proceed to McClure's address and arrive at 0330.

You see a red Pontiac Sunfire in the driveway with significant damage to the front panel on the passenger's side. You knock on the door, and it is answered by a man with a large tattoo on the left side of his neck. The man identifies himself as the owner of the Pontiac. You arrest him and read him his rights at 0340.

Suspect:	John McClure 10-60
DOB:	11 November 1980
Home address:	193 Young St., Kenora, ON
Telephone:	None

B. Write the Statement from Accused

Complete the statement for the McClure arrest described in part A of this exercise. Add whatever likely information you need to complete the statement, including the signature of the accused.

EXERCISE 4 » A. Continue the Investigation

Review the break and enter scenario outlined in Chapter 13, Exercise 7, #3. Write a supplementary report based on the following information.

You visit Cameron Nolan, owner of the abandoned warehouse on Culver Road. Nolan lets you into his home. You tell him about the break and enter call. He admits he made the call. He tells you two weeks ago he was talking with a friend about the warehouse. He told the friend he had wanted to sell the place but was having no luck. Nolan admits to you he had told the friend the place was bleeding him dry. Nolan goes on to tell you the friend offered to take care of the problem. Nolan says he thought the friend meant she would find a buyer for the place. He had no suspicion that the friend would attempt arson. He says, "I'm shocked, really shocked."

He gives you the friend's particulars:

Suspect:	**Sheena Barnaby 10-60**
DOB:	**11 November 1980**
Home address:	**2-461 Eastside Gardens, Pickering, ON L2A 2U2**
Telephone:	**905-555-1827**

Supply any additional information you think you might need to complete your report.

B. Investigation Leads to Arrest

Write an arrest report based on the following information.

The next day, you drive to the residence of Sheena Barnaby. She meets you at the door. When you ask her about her whereabouts the previous evening, she states that she was home alone. You ask her if she knows Mr. Nolan. She says, "I don't think so." You ask her if she made any calls from her cellphone the night of the incident. She glances back inside the door and says, "No, no. No calls." When you tell her that you visited Mr. Nolan the previous evening, her face turns red and she says, "I can't believe it. That guy sold me out already? Bring it on! I know things. You tell him that." You arrest Ms. Barnaby and read her rights to her.

Supply any additional information you think you might need to complete your report.

C. Complete the Statement from Accused

Complete a Statement from Accused for the Barnaby arrest described in part B of this exercise. Add whatever likely information you need to complete the statement, including the signature of the accused.

Niagara Regional Police Service Reports

The pages at the end of this chapter contain report blanks used by the Niagara Regional Police Service. These forms are reproduced with the permission of the Niagara Regional Police Service.

SUMMARY

The supplementary report is written much like the narrative for the original occurrence report. The report is organized by summary, background, facts, and outcomes. It answers the questions *who, what, where, when, why,* and *how*. However, the summary section must clearly link the narrative to the original report, and the outcomes must indicate the ongoing status of the investigation. The cover page must indicate the incident number of the original report. Similarly, the arrest report must reference the original; furthermore, the arrest report must document the officer's steps in making the arrest and record any statement made by the accused verbatim. A Statement from Accused must quote the accused directly, and should be signed by the accused. Supplementary reports continue the investigative action until the case is cleared.

KEY TERMS

arrest, 300
indictable, 306
reasonable grounds, 306
summary, 306
supplementary, 300
warrant, 306

Review and Reflection Questions

1. What are the similarities between a supplementary report and an original occurrence report?

2. In what ways does a supplementary report differ from an original occurrence report?

3. If an officer must react to a crime in progress and makes an arrest, what important information must the arrest report demonstrate?

4. Why is it important to record the verbatim response of the accused?

5. If the accused wishes to remain silent, what action should the officer take? Can an officer force an accused to reply?

NIAGARA REGIONAL POLICE SERVICE

General Incident ☐
Arrest Report ☐
Request for Summons ☐
Young Offender ☐

No. OF SUPPLEMENTARY REPORTS

DESCR. OF PROPERTIES / INJURIES (INC SER #) | VALUE | DAMAGED | RECOVERED

INJURIES: MAJOR ☐ MINOR ☐ NONE ☐

VICTIM SERVICES OFFERED? YES ☐ NO ☐

SPECIFY ON SUPPLEMENTARY: TYPE OF INJURIES SUSTAINED, TYPE OF FORC USED,
SUFFICIENT DETAILS FOR PLEA OF GUILTY, CO-ACCUSED, PREVIOUS ADDRESS OF ACCUSED, ETC.

FOR NARRATIVE COMPLETE SUPPLEMENTARY REPORT

DATE AND TIME OF ARREST | ARRESTING OFFICER | BADGE #

LOCATION OF ARREST | HAZARD ☐

CHARGES (IF WARRANT EXECUTED, STATE TYPE)

CHARGES

Y.O.A. - NOTICE TO PARENT SERVED? YES ☐ NO ☐

NOTIFICATIONS:
OTHERS: SPOUSE ☐ GUARDIAN ☐ OTHER - NAME ☐
PARENT ☐ NEXT OF KIN ☐

ADDRESS | HOME PHONE

ARRESTED FOR OTHER DEPT. (SPECIFY) | WHO NOTIFIED? | TIME

RELEASED TO (RANK / NAME / No.) | TIME HRS | YEAR MONTH DAY

FINGERPRINT DATE | FORM OF RELEASE | BAIL HEARING? YES ☐ NO ☐

BAIL AND RELEASE RECOMMENDATIONS | STATEMENT TAKEN YES ☐ NO ☐

CNI / CPIC QUERIED? RESULTS:

RELEASED BY OFFICER | BADGE # | NAME OF JUSTICE

DATE & TIME OF RELEASE | COURT LOCATION | COURT DATE AND TIME

HAZARD REMARKS (must be completed if any hazard is checked)

STATS CANADA CLEARED BY | INCIDENT CLASS | ADULTS | JUVENILES | INF.

CHARGE | OTHER | UNF | M | F | M | F

OFFICE ONLY | DATE ENTRY | DATE VERIF. | DATA RECEIVED | DATA CLEARED

DIVISION | PATROL AREA | INCIDENT CLASS | INCIDENT No.

YR MO DAY

TYPE OF INCIDENT | DATE AND TIME OF INCIDENT (OR TIME BETWEEN) | HAZARD ☐

LOCATION OF INCIDENT

HOW INCIDENT COMMITTED | MEANS (WEAPONS, TOOLS USED)

VICTIM / COMPLAINANT

SURNAME | GIVEN (1) | GIVEN (2) | RACE WHITE ☐ NON-WHITE ☐

ADDRESS | HOME PHONE

SEX | DOB - YR MO DAY | MAR. ST. | OCCUPATION | CONDITION SOBER ☐ HBD ☐ INTOX ☐ DRUGS ☐ | HAZARD ☐

PLACE OF EMPLOYMENT / EMPLOYER | BUSINESS PHONE EXT./LOCAL

REPORTED BY

SURNAME | GIVEN (1) | GIVEN (2) | GIVEN (3) | HAZARD ☐

ADDRESS | HOME PHONE

SEX | DOB - YR MO DAY | RELATIONSHIP TO VICTIM/COMPLAINANT | CONDITION SOBER ☐ HBD ☐ INTOX ☐ DRUGS ☐

PLACE OF EMPLOYMENT / EMPLOYER | BUSINESS PHONE EXT./LOCAL

VEHICLE USED

TYPE | LICENCE No. | LIC.YEAR | LIC PROV | VEH.YEAR | MAKE | MODEL

STYLE | COLOUR | VIN

OWNER | SURNAME | GIVEN (1) | ADDRESS
SAME ☐

OUTSTANDING FEATURES

ACCUSED / SUSPECT

SURNAME | GIVEN (1) | GIVEN (2) | NICKNAMES | ALIAS ☐ NEE ☐

ADDRESS | HOME PHONE

SEX | DOB - YR MO DAY | AGE | MAR. ST. | MHT (HT) | MASS (WT) | HAZARD ☐ | RACE WHITE ☐ NON-WHITE ☐

HAIR COLOUR | MOUSTACHE ☐ BEARD ☐ WIG ☐ | EYES COLOUR | CONTACT LENSES ☐ GLASSES ☐ | DESCRIPTION OF CLOTHING

BUILD: SLENDER ☐ MEDIUM ☐ HEAVY ☐

HAIR TYPE: BALD ☐ PART BALD ☐ SHORT ☐ LONG ☐ STRAIGHT ☐ CURLY / WAVY ☐ WELL DRESSED ☐ UNKEMPT ☐ BUSHY ☐

COMPLEXION: SALLOW ☐ LIGHT / FAIR ☐ RUDDY ☐ FRECKLED ☐ DARK / SWARTHY ☐ POCK-MARKED ☐

TEETH: GOOD ☐ IRREGULAR ☐ FALSE ☐ VISIBLE GOLD ☐ STAINED ☐ PROTRUD. UPPERS ☐ PROTRUD. LOWERS ☐ VISIBLE DECAY ☐ VISIBLE MISSING ☐

VICTIM / ACCUSED RELATIONSHIP? | DRIVERS LICENSE No. | PROV. | NRP No.

PHYSICAL / MENTAL CONDITION, MARKS, SCARS, TATTOOS, OUTSTANDING FEATURES | FPS No.

CNI CAUTIONS:
V: E ☐ A ☐ M ☐ S ☐ C ☐ | CONDITION SOBER ☐ INTOX ☐ HBD ☐ DRUGS ☐ | OCCUPATION

PLACE OF EMPLOYMENT / EMPLOYER / SCHOOL AND GRADE | BUSINESS PHONE (EXT./LOCAL)

REPORTING OFFICER (FULL NAME / RANK / No.) | DATE / TIME REPORT TAKEN | YEAR MONTH DAY TIME HRS

OTHER OFFICER(S) ATTENDING | IDENT OFFICER RESPONDING

REPORT CHECKED BY (FULL NAME / RANK / No.) | CASE REASSIGNED TO | BY | DATE

REPORT CHECKED BY (FULL NAME / RANK / No.) | INCIDENT STATUS (IF INVEST. COMPLETE CHECK SOLVED OR UNSOLVED) INIT. / DATE:
INVEST CONT'D ☐ INVEST COMP ☐ SOLVED ☐ UNSOLVED ☐

ALL SHADED AREAS MUST BE COMPLETED

-- ORIGINAL COPY --

Source: Niagara Regional Police Service.

NIAGARA REGIONAL POLICE SERVICE
Supplementary Report

CHECK APPROPRIATE BOX

ORIGINAL ☐ MISSING PERSON / ELOPEE ☐
ARREST ☐ FRAUDULENT DOCUMENT ☐
INCIDENT ☐ HOMICIDE / SUDDEN DEATH ☐
VEHICLE ☐ OTHER ☐

SURNAME: (OR NAME & TYPE OF BUSINESS):

DIVISION | PATROL AREA / ZONE | INCIDENT CLASS | INCIDENT NUMBER:

TYPE OF INCIDENT:

REFERENCE

POLICE INFORMATION:
VICTIM / COMPLAINANT ☐ ACCUSED ☐
(EXT./LOCAL)

DATE OF ORIGINAL REPORT

BUSINESS TELEPHONE | HOME TELEPHONE
(EXT./LOCAL)

ADDRESS:

HAZARD ☐

HAZARD REMARKS (MUST BE COMPLETED IF HAZARD CHECKED)

STATS CAN CLEARED BY	CHG.	OTHER	UNF.	INCIDENT CLASS	ADULTS M F	JUVENILE M F	INF.
OFFICE ONLY	DATA ENTRY	DATA VERIF.		DATE RECEIVED IN RECORDS	DATE CLEARED		

REPORTING OFFICER: (FULL NAME/RANK/No.)

DATE/TIME OF THIS REPORT | YR. | MO. | DAY | TIME

OTHER OFFICER(S) ATTENDING

I.D. OFFICER REPORTING

REPORT CHECKED BY (FULL NAME/RANK/No.)

CASE REASSIGNED TO | BY | DATE

REPORT CHECKED BY (FULL NAME/RANK/No.)

INCIDENT STATUS: (IF INVEST. COMP. CHECK SOLVED OR UNSOLVED):
INVEST. CONT. ☐ INVEST. COMP. ☐ SOLVED ☐ UNSOLVED ☐ INIT./DATE

ALL SHADED AREAS MUST BE COMPLETED

PAGE No.

-- ORIGINAL COPY --

1

Source: Niagara Regional Police Service.

15 Witness Statements

LEARNING OUTCOMES

After completing this chapter, you should be able to:

- Take witness statements that are complete and accurate.
- Understand the purpose of witness statements.
- Understand the process of taking witness statements.

Introduction

The purpose of witness statements is to help police document facts in issue. An officer reporting an incident writes a narrative to document words and actions he witnessed; in this sense, his report functions as the statement of what he might say should he appear in court to testify. Similarly, observations by civilians relevant to an incident help police establish facts in issue and justify actions and charges. Taking a statement of a **witness** demands a formal procedure ensuring the legal validity of the witness's observations; the officer makes sure he avoids influencing the statement. Furthermore, the written statement helps witnesses remember their observations if they must testify in court. Finally, a Statement of a Witness is an important part of the Crown brief; it informs the court of the evidence the witness will provide at trial.

A witness in the broadest sense is anyone with information relevant to an investigation. However, in the typical meaning of the word, a witness is someone with direct observations of an incident, implied in the term *eyewitness*. Direct observations are sense **perceptions**: Someone sees something happen, and tells police what they saw. However, observations are not limited to sight. A person may perceive important facts using any of the five senses, and might have heard, seen, smelled, tasted, or touched something important to the case. Relevant perceptions from a witness help police establish the facts in issue. For example, a witness might see the vehicle involved in a hit and run, hear the voice and words of a suspect committing an armed robbery, or smell the fumes of gasoline at the scene of an attempted arson. Police interview witnesses to help the witnesses recall these observations and to determine the relevance of their account; these interviews follow a formal procedure so that the statement's legitimacy is not called into question at trial.

Taking a Witness Statement

The Statement of a Witness form (a sample of which is shown in Figure 15.2, later in this chapter) can be used when interviewing witnesses. Ideally, a witness's statement will be a direct quotation. If the statement is not a direct quotation, be sure to indicate that. The information you obtain can initially be recorded in your notebook and transferred later, but it is preferable that the witness write their own detailed statement under your supervision. Whether you obtain the statement on this form or in your notebook, always read the statement back to the witness, ask whether the statement is correct, and have the witness sign the statement.

There are two types of witness statements:

1. An **exact statement** of the witness's words, recorded either on a form or in the notebook, and signed by the witness. Recording an account verbatim is the most credible method of taking a statement.

2. The **"will say"** witness statement. An officer unable to get a complete statement from a witness due to circumstances may write this type of statement. It is written in the officer's own words, and it occurs in cases where the witness is reliable and the facts are not disputable. For example, if a businessman witnesses a traffic accident but is

---

A **witness** is someone with direct observations of facts in issue. A witness perceives something relevant to an incident.

Perception is awareness through the senses: seeing, hearing, touching, smelling, or tasting. Through perception, we collect basic facts.

An **exact statement** is a verbatim account of the witness statement.

"Will say" is a phrase indicating that the witness will, in court, attest to the facts in the statement.

too busy to give a formal statement, he might simply tell the officer what he saw, then leave. The officer would then produce a "will say" witness statement. The "will say" indicates that the witness "will say" this statement if called upon in court.

If a Statement of a Witness form is used in your report, you do not need to write the witness statement in your narrative original or supplementary report. In the text of your narrative, you can summarize the main value of the witness statement and write

> **I recorded a Statement of a Witness; see attached.**

This makes it easier for you to focus on the narrative, and provides a separate document for the statement.

IN THE FIELD

Notebook Box Q&A

You are dispatched to a motor vehicle accident involving a possible impaired driver. You arrive to find another officer has arrested a female driver for Impaired Operation of a Motor Vehicle.

You speak to a witness who says, "Officer, she was all over the road. She is drunk."

You write these comments in your notebook verbatim. You then take an uninterrupted statement from this witness and he signs it.

Q. Can you tell me what happened starting from where you think it's important?

A. Well first of all, I was standing outside the Dairy Queen waiting to buy some ice cream when I saw this red truck swerving all over the road and sideswipe a blue van until it came to a stop in this lot where I was standing. I heard a loud bang and then screeching sounds; everybody turned to watch. Then the drunk woman exited the red truck and stumbled all over. She was shouting and swearing at everyone. She reeked like booze. Wow.

In an attempt to obtain more details without leading the witness, you question further:

Q. You mentioned you "saw this red truck swerving all over the road." Can you explain further?

A. Sure, the red truck had licence #ABCD 123 and it was a Ford explorer, an older model. It was in the middle lane and then swerved out into the fast lane very abruptly and tried to speed past the blue van but scraped the entire side of the van instead. The red truck then bounced off the blue van and back into the median and began to spin in circles, crossing two lanes of traffic and finally stopped in the parking lot of the Dairy Queen here.

Q. Describe what happened next.

A. The female driver got out of the vehicle and stumbled into traffic, so we tried to stop her.

Q. Where did she exit the vehicle?

A. Um, the driver's door, obviously.

Q. Explain what you mean when you say stumbled.

A. She was tilted to the right like she was falling, and her steps were heavy. She was waving her arms all around as if to balance herself but it wasn't working. She sounded drunk too when she was yelling and swearing at everyone. I approached her to keep her from getting hit.

Q. Tell me what happened when you approached her.

A. She had such a strong smell of alcohol. I could see it in her face. She was wasted.

Q. Explain what you mean by your last comment.

A. When she spoke, her mouth smelled of alcohol. Her eyes looked dazed and glassy like she was half asleep. I used to work in a bar and I know a drunk person when I see one. And she was VERY drunk.

Questioning a Witness

A complete statement depends on effective questioning. Ask questions of the witness that

- increase your understanding
- help the witness to relate his or her perceptions
- build trust between you and the speaker

Don't ask questions that

- lead the witness to a specific answer
- load the question with an accusation
- make the witness feel defensive

In Chapter 11, The Notebook, we learned that there are two types of questions: open-ended questions and closed-ended questions. When interviewing a witness, begin your questioning with open-ended questions that help the witness recall his or her experience, then move to closed-ended questions that help the witness focus on specific details.

An open-ended question invites the speaker to say more about a topic; it does not impose limits on the answer. Open-ended questions tend to draw the speaker out and encourage him or her to speak. Following are some examples of open-ended questions:

- Tell me, how did this event happen?
- What more can you say about that?
- How would you describe what you saw (heard, smelled, etc.)?
- What did the person do next?

Closed-ended questions invite "yes" or "no" answers. You can use this type of question to confirm or clarify important details. Some examples of this type of question follow.

- Did you overhear the conversation?
- Did you see the accident?
- Did you get a good look at the person's face?

Move between both types of questions to effectively interview a witness.

General Rules for Taking a Witness Statement

The following are some general guidelines for writing witness statements:

1. Maintain the sequence of events and the cause-and-effect element of events described by the witness.
2. Write in the past tense. The witness is describing events after they occurred; therefore, you should reflect this fact in your written record of their statement.
3. Use the wording provided by the witness. Verbatim responses reflect the actual account—in both form and content—that the witness told you.
4. Write in the first person for exact statements. Use "I" instead of "Mr. Jones" since you are not referring to the witness but representing the words of the witness. For example, "I looked out the window and noticed a man on my front lawn."

5. For "will say" statements, write in the third person. In this case, you are referring to a witness, indirectly giving his statement. Write, for example, "Mr. Jones will say that the vehicle drove over the lawn and continued down Main Street."

6. Avoid using parentheses (brackets) in witness statements. If the witness said it, it should appear on the same level of importance as everything else in the statement. For example, do not write, "I heard a loud thud and a scream (I thought it was my television) and I ran down the stairs to see the man lying in the street."

In the following sample, we read Dan Dibiacco's witness statement. Notice it is written in the first person, and he has organized it in a logical order, describing what he saw, heard, etc., before, during, and after the event; in other words, as we would normally narrate a story (see Figure 15.1).

FIGURE 15.1 Sample of a Witness Statement

I am 46 years old, DOB March 27, 1970. I live at 206 Mariah St., Hamilton, Ontario. I am employed as a teacher at Founder's Middle School. [*Summary*: **This section contains the information about the witness, including name, date of birth, address, etc.**]

My house is at the corner of Mariah and Long streets. Sometime before six in the evening of December 24, 2016, I was sitting in my living room watching television when I heard shouting from the street. I looked out my window and saw a car stopped at the intersection of Mariah and Long streets facing east. The door on the driver's side of the car was open and the motor was running. Two men were on the ground on my property. [*Background*: **Background sets the scene, and includes who, why, where, and when that led to the incident.**]

One man was punching another in the face. The man who was being punched was covered with blood on his face, and the other man kept punching him in the face. I could see both men reasonably well because there is a street light on the corner. After what I would say were 10 or 12 punches, the assailant stopped punching, got up off the ground, and said something to the man on the ground before walking away. He was walking southbound on Long Street. The man appeared to be in his mid-50s, was 150 to 160 pounds, medium build, and with salt and pepper hair. [*Facts*: **This section tells what happened—what the witness, saw, heard, etc. All relevant details relating to what the witness perceived are here. This section answers the questions what and how.**]

I went to the phone and called 911, then went outside to assist the man lying on the ground. He was nearly unconscious, and didn't say anything until the police and an ambulance arrived a short time later. Another man came from one of the side streets to assist. I identified the assailant verbally to the police. The victim was taken to hospital by ambulance and I gave a statement to police. [*Outcomes*: **This section describes the aftermath of the incident: details about medical attention, arrival of emergency vehicles or police, other witnesses, and so on.**]

On Procedure

After you interview a witness, record the witness statement. The Statement of a Witness does not contain a cover page; complete the header information, including name, date of birth, address, phone number, and so on. In addition, you should record the date, the time the interview started, and the time the interview was completed. Read the statement back to the witness, and ask the witness if the statement is correct. If it is correct, ask the witness to sign the statement to attest to its accuracy. If a **correction** needs to be made, cross out the error, correct the information, and have yourself and the witness sign it. Once this process is complete and accurate, you, as the reporting officer, should also sign the statement. See Figure 15.2 for a sample Statement of a Witness form that has been completed, and Figure 15.3 for a blank Statement of a Witness form.

Motor Vehicle Accident Statement

The motor vehicle accident statement (see Figure 15.4 for a sample blank form) is a shorter statement taken from those involved in a motor vehicle accident, including pedestrians and other witnesses. It is written in the same manner as other statements. Quote the participants directly if possible; use proper questioning techniques to acquire complete statements; use quotation marks around direct statements; use a single line to cross out errors, with yourself and the witness initialling errors; and have the witness sign the statement, attesting to its accuracy.

As of July 1, 2014, collision reports are to be submitted to the Ministry of Transportation of Ontario in electronic format. The use of an Ontario-standard Motor Vehicle Collision Report (see Figure 15.5) facilitates e-reporting.

A **correction** is a crossed-out error; both the witness and the officer should sign each correction.

FIGURE 15.2   Statement of a Witness

MITCHELL'S BAY POLICE SERVICE
STATEMENT OF A WITNESS

Page no. _____1_____

Name *Leonard Bloom*

Date of birth *June 6, 1968*

Address *60 Tower Rd., Wake, ON 3JM 4S4*

Phone no. *(519) 555-4904*

Business address *391 Ulysses Rd. Wake ON*

Occupation *Theatre Manager, River Run Cinemas*

Phone no. *(519) 555-9583*

Date *September 5, 2016*   Time started *2145*

Time completed *2215*

Officer taking statement *M. Gonzales #1298*

Leonard Bloom will say:

I am 48 years old. I manage the movie theatre in town, River Run Cinemas, and I've worked there for 15 years. I live around the corner at 60 Tower Rd. with my wife and two young children.

On September 5, at 5 p.m., I came to work as usual and opened the cinema for the early show at 6:30. Everything was going as usual. When the early show ended, I helped usher people out of the show, and helped ready the snack bar and the till for the late show. I do the same thing every night. Joyce Finnegan was handling the snack bar, and Stephen Young was handling the till. I didn't notice anything unusual as I went about these duties. At 8:30 p.m., I opened the doors for the second show. It was a small crowd, approximately 75 people.

At 8:55, just before we started the second show, I walked outside as I usually do. I noticed a woman getting out of her car, and I wondered if she was coming late to the show. It was dark by then, but the streetlights are strong near our theatre. No one else was nearby, except across the street at the Groan and Grovel pub where people were coming and going. I waited to see if the woman was going to the pub or coming to my theatre.

A man ran out from behind an SUV right towards the old woman. I saw him reach for her purse and heard her shout, "Oh no you don't!" The woman screamed and fell down. I ran toward them, and I could see the guy had her purse in his right hand. There was no way I could catch him.

I ran over to help the woman to her feet. She told me the man tried to grab her purse, but she kicked him, and he pushed her. She was wincing but she insisted on getting to her feet, so I helped her stand up.

The man ran across the street and north on Ulysses Road towards Beckett Park.

FIGURE 15.2   Concluded

MITCHELL'S BAY POLICE SERVICE	STATEMENT CONTINUATION

Name *Leonard Bloom*   Page no. *2*

At 9:15 p.m., I called police, and I helped Mrs. Barnacle into the theatre. I gave her a cup of tea, and she told me she wasn't hurt. She said she had all her cards and I.D. in the purse. He was a tall lean man, approximately 6'5", 200 pounds, and had a small backpack with a lot of ties and rings hanging off of it. He was wearing a light black jacket and jeans. I saw his face. He was a young man, approximately 25 years old.

End of statement.

Signature: *Leonard Bloom*   Witness: *PC Maria Gonzales, #1298*

FIGURE 15.3　Blank Statement of a Witness Form

MITCHELL'S BAY POLICE SERVICE
STATEMENT OF A WITNESS

Page no. _____

Name _____　Date of birth _____

Address _____　Phone no. _____

Business address _____

Occupation _____　Phone no. _____

Date _____ Time started _____ Time completed _____

Officer taking statement _____

_____
_____
_____
_____
_____
_____
_____
_____
_____
_____
_____
_____
_____
_____
_____
_____
_____
_____
_____
_____
_____
_____
_____
_____
_____
_____
_____
_____
_____
_____
_____

(Continued on the next page.)

FIGURE 15.3   Concluded

MITCHELL'S BAY POLICE SERVICE

STATEMENT CONTINUATION

Name _____

Page no. _____

FIGURE 15.4   Blank Motor Vehicle Accident Statement Form

MITCHELL'S BAY POLICE SERVICE
MOTOR VEHICLE ACCIDENT STATEMENT

No. of photos taken _____

Date _____   Time _____   Location _____

STATEMENTS

Driver 1

Name and address _____

Phone no. _____   Employer _____

Name of insurance agent _____

_____

_____

_____

_____

_____

_____

_____

_____

_____

_____

_____   Signed _____

Driver 2 (or pedestrian)

Name and address _____

Phone no. _____   Employer _____

Name of insurance agent _____

_____

_____

_____

_____

_____

_____

_____

_____

_____   Signed _____

FIGURE 15.5 Motor Vehicle Collision Report

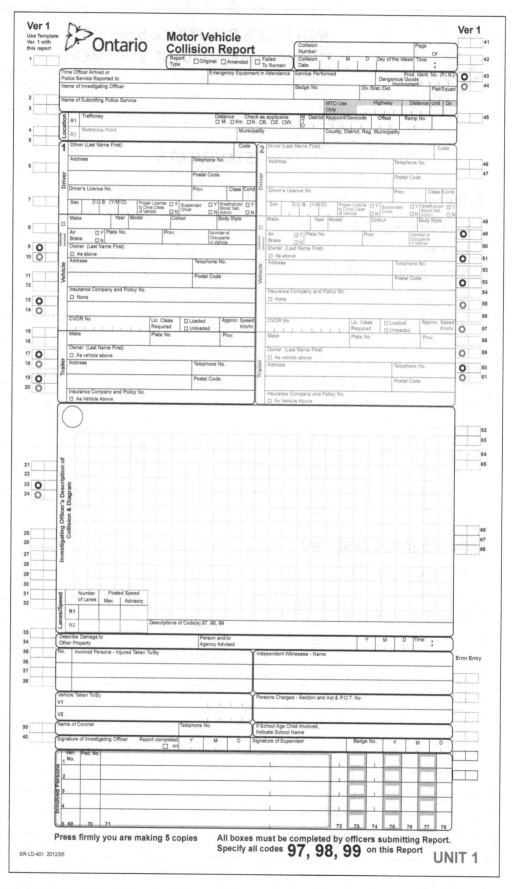

Source: © 2012 Queen's Printer for Ontario. https://www.apps.rus.mto.gov.on.ca/jtips/copyofaccidentreport.do?method=view&lang=EN.

Niagara Regional Police Service Reports

The following pages contain a blank report used by the Niagara Regional Police Service. These forms are reproduced with the permission of the Niagara Regional Police Service.

NIAGARA REGIONAL POLICE SERVICE

STATEMENT OF A WITNESS

NAME:	DATE OF BIRTH:
ADDRESS:	TELEPHONE NO.:
BUSINESS ADDRESS:	
OCCUPATION:	TELEPHONE NO.:
DATE:	TIME STARTED:	TIME COMPLETED:

OFFICER TAKING STATEMENT:

NIAGARA REGIONAL POLICE FORCE

STATEMENT CONTINUATION

NAME:	PAGE NO.

 An Accredited Agency

Form 105.98.05

EXERCISE 1 » Writing Witness Statements

1. Write a Statement of a Witness for Beth Williams, witness of an assault. Write her statement in the first person, and include any additional information you need to complete the exercise.

Witness:	**Beth Williams 10-60**
DOB:	**9 Feb 1995**
SIN:	**511 574 278**
Telephone:	**905-555-7876**

   Beth Williams is a receptionist at Ollie's Optical in Highview Mall. She was at the front desk answering phones when at approximately 1545 she heard shouting and banging. She ran out of the store to find a woman lying at the top of the stairs near the Top Lids store. She was dazed, and there was blood on her face and lips. Bruises were starting to form on her cheeks. Beth ran back into Ollie's Optical and called police from her desk. She returned to hold the woman's hand. The woman remained sitting on the floor. She said, "I know how to pick them." Williams didn't see the incident or see anyone flee from the woman.

   Add any additional information you need to complete the witness statement for Beth Williams.

2. Review the following scenario, first examined in Chapter 13, Exercise 7, #1. Using the additional information following the scenario, write a complete the witness statement for

Witness:	**Stacy Cordiero 10-61**
DOB:	**11 April 1975**
Home address:	**1566 Chrysler St., Thorold, ON**
Phone:	**905-555-1122**

   The scenario reads:

   At 2230 on 12 June of this year, you were dispatched to Frank Rizzo's Bar at 125 Main St., Thorold, Ontario, to make a report on an assault. You are 10-7 at 125 Main St. at 2240.

   The owner of Frank Rizzo's Bar, Stephen Van Sickle, states that he was notified by bartender Irina Ossine, who called Van Sickle in his office at the back of the bar, that a fight had broken out on the dance floor. Irina had been informed by a bouncer, Peter Northwood, that the fight was in progress. Northwood and another bouncer, Ron Valentine, went to break up the fight. Ray Harewood, the victim, was dancing when he was pushed in the back by an unknown male. Harewood turned around on being pushed and was immediately struck in the face with a beer bottle, which did not break. He fell to the ground unconscious. Harewood regained consciousness several minutes later. A patron, Carlos Lopez, noticed a male running from the dance floor and exiting through a fire exit. Lopez chased the man and followed the suspect to his motorcycle. The suspect left the parking lot on a Harley-Davidson motorcycle.

   Stacy Cordiero, a friend of the victim, was standing beside the victim at the time of the assault. She corroborated Harewood's story. Earlier in the evening, the suspect had approached Cordiero and had made derogatory comments about her. Harewood had intervened, and Harewood and the suspect exchanged words. Harewood stated he had never seen the suspect before that evening.

Harewood declined medical attention.

You broadcast a description of the suspect and his vehicle. You are 10-8 at 2315 on routine patrol.

Mrs. Cordiero provides further information about her activities that evening. These facts appear below in no particular order. Some details are irrelevant. Organize the facts, and write a first-person statement for this witness. Do not include the irrelevant details in the statement.

- She tells you that she and Ray Harewood arrived at Frank Rizzo's Bar at approximately 9:30 p.m.
- She described the suspect, giving you these details: heavy build, weight 102 kilograms; height 188 centimetres; very short blond hair on top of his head, long hair at back; Caucasian; black leather jacket, blue tapered jeans, brown cowboy boots, jacket had "O'Doole Rules" printed on back.
- She works as a florist at Nancy's Floral Boutique, 51 Kingsway St., Thorold, Ontario J51 L82, telephone 905-555-2121
- Tonight is Stacy's third date with Ray Harewood.
- The first sign of trouble came when the suspect had brushed against her and leered at her when she was on the dance floor with Ray.
- The next time, he spoke to her and made derogatory remarks.
- According to Stacy, he approached her on the dance floor and said, "You look like a whore in that dress. Come over here, hot little lady."
- She did not answer, and ignored him.
- Stacy is wearing a red dress, open at the back, mid-thigh in length.
- She screamed at the suspect when she saw what he had done.
- After the incident, she cried until Ray regained consciousness.
- He seemed okay once he woke up.
- She requested police find this man and put him behind bars where he belonged.
- She was drinking beer that evening, and consumed three or four before the incident occurred.

3. Write a Statement of a Witness for George Lynden, witness of a hit-and-run incident. Write his statement in the first person, and include any additional information you need to complete the exercise.

Witness:	**George Lynden 10-60**
Address:	**71 Duke St., Brantford, ON N7B 3W2**
DOB:	**15 September 1981**
SIN:	**400 351 058**
Telephone:	**519-555-3333**

George Lynden was walking his dog southbound on the east side of Queen Street sometime after 2100 on 21 August. He didn't know what time it was because he didn't have a watch. As Lynden was walking opposite Maggie's Bar and Grill at

130 Queen St., about two blocks north of King Street, he saw a man leave the bar. Lynden noticed him because the man was very unsteady on his feet. Lynden described the man as "middle-aged, wearing a green shirt and dark pants." Lynden didn't notice anything else about him. The description matches the clothing worn by the victim. As the man walked southbound on Queen Street, he fell several times and occasionally wandered onto the street from the sidewalk. As the man approached the intersection of Queen Street and King Street, he attempted to cross from the west side to the east side. Lynden is aware that there is a laundromat on the southeast corner of the intersection, but didn't hear any noise of an argument coming from there.

Lynden described the vehicle involved as a mid- to late-2000s model, possibly a Honda product, silver or grey, four-door, with an Ontario licence plate whose first two letters are "AJ." There was no visible damage to the car.

4. Complete the motor vehicle accident statement for the Catriona Hicks hit-and-run incident, from Chapter 13, Exercise 7, #2. Write the statement for Catriona Hicks in the first person; write a "will say" statement for the witness, Ashras Baddar.

You were dispatched at 0215 on 25 June of this year to take a report about a hit-and-run accident. You are 10-7 at 0223.

Catriona Hicks reports that she was driving northbound on Bay Street at approximately 0200 at the posted speed limit of 60 km/h. She proceeded through the intersection of Bay Street and Bloor Street on a green light. Hicks's car was then struck on the driver's side near the rear door by a car eastbound on Bloor Street. Hicks's car was spun around and ended up facing south on Bay Street. She could see that the car that hit her was speeding away eastbound on Bloor Street. Hicks managed to get out of the car and onto the sidewalk. A witness, Ashras Baddar, assisted her and called an ambulance through 911. Hicks complained of neck and back pain.

Baddar stated, "I saw the Ford Focus enter the intersection as I was waiting to cross Bay Street at the light. The Ford was struck by a red Pontiac Sunfire that entered the intersection against the light. I ran over to the Ford to assist the driver. I could see that the driver of the Pontiac was a white male with short dark hair and a large tattoo on his neck, on the left side. The licence number of the Pontiac was AMAX 133, Ontario plate. I called 911. I sat with the driver until the ambulance arrived. I heard the ambulance attendant say that Hicks had a concussion and possible neck injuries."

You tell Baddar to call the police if he has additional information. Your interview of Baddar began at 0245 and ended at 0257.

CHAPTER SUMMARY

A witness statement is a report of observations made by a person who perceived an incident. Ideally, this statement is recorded verbatim in either the notebook or on the Statement of a Witness form. There are two types of witness statement: the exact statement and the "will say" statement. Like other reports, the witness statement answers the questions *when*, *why*, and *how*. Witness statements help police document the facts in issue, and proper procedure should be followed to prove the objectivity of the statement. Finally, a Statement of a Witness becomes a component of the Crown brief; it informs the court of the evidence the witness will provide at trial.

KEY TERMS

correction, 324
exact statement, 320
perception, 320
"will say," 320
witness, 320

Review and Reflection Questions

1. What types of questions should you avoid when interviewing a witness?

2. Fundamentally, who makes a good witness?

3. When is it appropriate to take a "will say" statement?

4. After you take a witness statement, how do you make sure it is correct?

5. Why should you avoid using parentheses, or brackets, when writing a witness statement?

16 The Crown Brief

LEARNING OUTCOMES

After completing this chapter, you should be able to:

- Understand the purpose of the Crown brief and its place in the investigative process.

- Describe the sections of the Crown brief.

- Organize a Crown brief to include each of the necessary sections in the correct order.

- Write a clear and complete Crown brief summary page.

Introduction

The Crown brief is a package of documents—put together by police—that the prosecution uses to prove its case at trial against an accused person. Once a police investigation is complete, the primary investigating officer prepares the Crown brief and sends it to the Crown Attorney's office. This alerts the Crown Attorney's office that a case is ready for prosecution. The Crown Attorney's office is in charge of prosecuting cases under the *Criminal Code*.

Taken all together, the documents in the Crown brief package are structured in a specific manner and contain no unnecessary information. The Crown brief

- is prepared by the police officer primarily responsible for a case
- is passed on to the Crown Attorney to prepare the case against the accused
- is the police officer's primary method of presenting information and evidence against the accused
- is the prosecution's primary method of disclosing information against the accused to the defence
- is compiled and presented to the defence prior to the accused's first court appearance
- must be complete in every respect

The Crown brief must stand alone as a report that needs no clarification. It is often the case that the Crown attorney is presented with the brief mere hours (or with even less time) before the first appearance of the defendant. The attorneys must read quickly, take notes quickly, and be ready to present to the court quickly. You can see why it is critical that the brief is complete, clear, and correct.

As well, in larger police services, prosecution attorneys do not know individual police officers. This means that your sole means of establishing a professional persona with the Crown Attorney's office is through your writing skills. Conversely, poorly written Crown briefs that make the prosecution's job hard or impossible can impact your professional persona negatively.

Historically, the Crown brief would be delivered to the Crown attorney's office by courier. However, many police services now use an electronic system to upload reports. This system is shared with members of the prosecution, which allows for a faster and more efficient sharing of information.

Rules of Disclosure

All information given to the Crown must likewise be given to the accused.

As noted above, the accused must be given all material that has been compiled by the police and the Crown regarding the case against the accused. Refer to the *Public Prosecution Service of Canada Deskbook*, Section 2.5, for the complete statement of policy regarding rules of **disclosure**.

Disclosure is the act of sharing or revealing information.

Contents of the Crown Brief

The Crown brief usually contains the following documents, although some of the documents, such as the title page, may not be required by all police services:

- title page or cover page
- introduction
- **synopsis**
- witness list
- summary
- witness statements

These are the essential documents for the Crown brief. Other documents may be included as necessary, including

- officer's notes
- Statement from Accused
- exhibit list
- **indictment**
- appearance notice
- promise to appear
- criminal **subpoena**
- subpoena to a witness
- pre-sentence report
- victim impact statement
- consent from victim for release of medical records
- photos

Use whatever documents are necessary to ensure full disclosure. Incomplete disclosure could violate the Charter rights of the accused and seriously harm the prosecution's case. If additional information is obtained after the Crown brief is prepared, this information must be added to the documentation.

Writing the Crown Brief

Refer to the sample Crown briefs that follow (Figures 16.1 and 16.2) as you read what information should appear on each page of the Crown brief.

Title Page or Cover Page

On the title page (or cover page), you simply state *Regina* (or *Rex* if a king is on the British throne) v. (short form for "versus") defendant's name(s)—list all defendants on this page.

Note that there is no date or any other information on this page.

A **synopsis** is a shortened summary of a larger work.

An **indictment** is a criminal charge before the court.

A **subpoena** is a legal summons that orders a person to attend court as a witness or a party in a legal proceeding.

Introduction

This part of the Crown brief contains the following elements:

- OFFENCE: Include the name of the charge and the complete *Criminal Code* section(s).
- DATE: This is the date of the offence, not the date the brief was prepared or submitted.
- VICTIM: List all victims.
- ACCUSED: List the names, complete home addresses, and dates of birth of all persons accused.
- PLACE: This is the place where the offence occurred.
- OFFICER: This is the name of the senior investigator on the case. The names of many officers will appear in the supporting documents, but only the officer who is presenting the Crown brief is to be listed. There can be more than one senior investigating officer for a complicated case, and so more than one name can appear here.

Witness List/Synopsis

This is the complete list of every person the Crown attorney can expect to call to testify. Include each witness's complete name, home address, and work address, if available, so that the prosecution and defence attorneys can reach the witnesses regardless of the time of day or day of the week.

Beside each witness's name, write a brief synopsis that explains the witness's role in the case—what he or she saw or did.

Summary

This is the complete narrative of the case. The reader will be able to visualize the complete offence as it played out, up to and including the arrest of the accused. There are several things to keep in mind when writing the synopsis:

- Begin the narrative with an introductory sentence that sums up the offence, using the language of the *Criminal Code*.
- Follow the introductory sentence with the statement, "The person(s) charged with (name of offence) in this matter is (are):" and give the accused's name, date of birth, and home address.
- Follow that with the statement, "The circumstances of the offence are as follows:"

Now it is time to walk the prosecution team through the offence. The summary is written as though there is no doubt as to what happened. The police officers involved are confident that the crime occurred exactly as they have concluded and by the accused(s) they've arrested, based on their solid investigation and supported by witness testimony.

1. Start with the events before the offence to set the stage.
2. Next, describe the events of the offence itself, in detail.
3. Then describe the events after the offence—the investigation of the offence—ending the summary section with a well-detailed description of the accused's arrest, his/her charges, and where the accused was taken.

Additional Considerations

Crown briefs are written in the third person because, often, most of the actions regarding the investigation involve several officers. It would not make sense to use "I."

Use all capital letters for the last names of everyone named in the report. This allows readers to quickly identify individuals involved in the case.

Witness Statements

These are the statements you have gathered from the witnesses as your case progressed. Once the Crown knows who can be called as a witness, and what each witness will say, the Crown can begin to develop the structure of its prosecution. Complete information about witness statements can be found in Chapter 15.

Reviewing a Sample Crown Brief

The sample Crown brief shown in Figure 16.1 is concerned with the offence of assault causing bodily harm. Under the *Criminal Code* of Canada:

> **265.1(1) Assault—A person commits an assault when**
>
> **(a) without the consent of another person, he applies force intentionally to that other person, directly or indirectly;**
>
> **(b) he attempts or threatens, by an act or a gesture, to apply force to another person, if he has, or causes that other person to believe upon reasonable grounds that he has, present ability to effect his purpose; or**
>
> **(c) while openly wearing or carrying a weapon or imitation thereof, he accosts or impedes another person or begs.**
>
> **...**
>
> **267. Assault with a weapon or causing bodily harm—Everyone who, in committing an assault,**
>
> **(a) carries, uses or threatens to use a weapon or imitation thereof, or**
>
> **(b) causes bodily harm to the complainant**
>
> **is guilty of an indictable offence ...**

Assault causing bodily harm is usually considered a level 2 assault, which means that injuries to the complainant are more than transient or trifling.

FIGURE 16.1   Crown Brief One

Regina

v.

Eric Sanchez

(Continued on the next page.)

FIGURE 16.1   Continued

[Introduction]

OFFENCE: ASSAULT CAUSING BODILY HARM

SECTION 267, CRIMINAL CODE OF CANADA

DATE: 24 DECEMBER 2016

VICTIM: ROBERT JAMES PIDZERNY

ACCUSED: ERIC SANCHEZ

2010 Conrad St. North

HAMILTON, ON

(d.o.b. 08 December 1961)

PLACE: CITY OF HAMILTON

OFFICER: CST. GINO POLARI #372

(Continued on the next page.)

FIGURE 16.1   Continued

[Witness List]

```
        WITNESSES                  SYNOPSIS

(1)  DAN DIBIACCO          • witness from home

     206 Mariah St.        • saw partial incident and suspect

     Hamilton, ON

          or

     c/o Founders Middle School

     38 Robinson St.

     Hamilton, ON

(2)  RAN CAO               • witness driving past incident

     132 Dickens Ave.      • saw beginning of incident and
                             suspect
     Toronto, ON

          or

     c/o Graphics Video

     3 Drumm St.

     Toronto, ON
```

(Continued on the next page.)

FIGURE 16.1   Continued

[Summary]

The charge of assault causing bodily harm in this matter arises from an incident that occurred in front of 206 Mariah St., Hamilton, ON, on December 24, 2016.

The person charged with assault causing bodily harm in this matter is:

Eric Sanchez, d.o.b. 61.12.08 of 2010 Conrad St. N., Hamilton, ON

The circumstances of the offence are as follows:

On Christmas Eve 2016, Robert PIDZERNY was driving to church. He left the parking lot behind his house at 344 Long St., Hamilton, ON, and turned left onto Mariah St. at approximately 5:45 p.m., and stopped at the corner of Mariah St. and Long St. to allow traffic on Long St. to clear before making a right-hand turn onto Long St., which is a one-way street southbound. It was dark, roads were snow-covered, and mounds of plowed snow at the corner of Long St. obscured PIDZERNY'S view of traffic on Long St. While he was stopped waiting for traffic to clear, PIDZERNY heard two loud bangs at the left front of his vehicle. He was at this moment looking to the right to check for pedestrian traffic.

PIDZERNY saw a male kicking the left front quarter panel of his vehicle. The male began to scream incoherently. PIDZERNY decided to leave the vehicle to speak to the male, who PIDZERNY thought may have been involved in an accident and needing assistance. PIDZERNY opened the door

(Continued on the next page.)

FIGURE 16.1   Continued

Robert PIDZERNY Page 2

of his vehicle, and as he put his left foot on the ground, the male grabbed the door of the vehicle and slammed it on PIDZERNY'S right leg, which was still partially in the vehicle. PIDZERNY'S left foot slipped on the ice, and as he slipped, the male punched PIDZERNY in the face, breaking his glasses and opening two cuts around PIDZERNY'S left eye, caused by the lens of his glasses breaking.

As he fell, PIDZERNY was kicked in the face by the male. The male continued to scream incoherently. The male then jumped on top of PIDZERNY, who was on the ground, and continued to beat PIDZERNY about the face. PIDZERNY was essentially defenceless at the time since his eyes were covered with blood. His left eye was swelling and he had lost his glasses.

When PIDZERNY lapsed into a state of semi-consciousness, the beating ceased. The man got up and walked away, saying, "That will teach you to run over pedestrians."

The incident was witnessed in part by Dan DIBIACCO, 206 Mariah St., Hamilton, ON, and Ran CAO, 132 Dickens Ave., Toronto, ON. DIBIACCO heard noise on the street, and when he went to investigate, he saw the incident occurring near his house. He called 911. CAO was driving past the incident and saw PIDZERNY lying on the side of the street and a male walking away.

PIDZERNY, DIBIACCO, and CAO described the male as Caucasian, approximately 55 years of age, medium build, 170 cm in height, with grey hair and a green jacket. The male walked southbound along Long St. after the incident.

(Continued on the next page.)

FIGURE 16.1   Continued

Robert PIDZERNY   Page 3

PIDZERNY was transported by ambulance to Hamilton General Hospital, where he was reported to have been suffering from numerous facial cuts, most significantly a deep cut to the left of the left eye and a deep cut under the right eye. The left eye was swollen shut, and PIDZERNY had a broken left cheek bone under the left eye and a broken bone in the left eye socket. He also had cuts to his right leg from the vehicle door.

The area of the incident was searched. A male answering the assailant's description was seen walking southbound on Long St. near Rikley Dr. He was arrested at 6:12 p.m. on December 24, 2016. He was cautioned and informed of his right to counsel. He identified himself verbally as Eric SANCHEZ, 2010 Conrad St., Hamilton, ON, d.o.b. 61.12.08. He admitted to the arresting officer, Cst. Gino Polari #372, that he had been the assailant in the matter. SANCHEZ was transported to Central Division where he was held in custody pending a bail hearing.

(Continued on the next page.)

FIGURE 16.1   Continued

[Witness Statements]

Name: Dan Dibiacco   **Date of Birth**: 65.03.27

Address: 206 Mariah St., Hamilton, ON L5T 1M1

Telephone: (905) 555-1864

Business Address: 38 Robinson St., Hamilton, ON

Occupation: Teacher   **Telephone**: (905) 555-0000

Date: December 24, 2016   **Time Started**: 6:35 p.m.

                                   Time Completed: 6:45 p.m.

Officer Taking Statement: G. Polari #372

DAN DIBIACCO will say

I am 51 years old. I live at 206 Mariah St., Hamilton, ON.
I am employed as a teacher at Founder's Middle School.

My house is at the corner of Mariah and Long streets.
Sometime before six in the evening of December 24, 2016, I
was sitting in my living room watching television, when I
heard shouting from the street. I looked out my window and
saw a car stopped at the intersection of Mariah and Long
streets facing east. The door on the driver's side of the
car was open and the motor was running. Two men were on
the ground on my property. One man was punching another in
the face. The man who was being punched was covered with
blood on his face, and the other man kept punching him in
the face. I could see both men reasonably well because
there is a street light on the corner. After what I would
say were 10 or 12 punches, the assailant stopped punching,

(Continued on the next page.)

FIGURE 16.1   Continued

got up off the ground, and said something to the man on the ground before walking away. He was walking southbound on Long St. The man appeared to be in his mid-50s, was 150-160 lbs., medium build, and with salt and pepper hair. He was wearing a green jacket.

I went to the phone and called 911, then went outside to assist the man lying on the ground. He was nearly unconscious, and didn't say anything until the police and an ambulance arrived a short time later. Another man came from one of the side streets to assist. I identified the assailant verbally to the police. The victim was taken to hospital by ambulance and I gave a statement to police.

Signed Dan Dibiacco

24 December 2016

6:45 p.m.

(Continued on the next page.)

FIGURE 16.1 Continued

Name: Ran Cao   **Date of Birth:** 87.02.20

Address: 132 Dickens Ave., Toronto, ON M5T 1L3

Telephone: (416) 555-4171

Business Address: 3 Drumm St., Toronto, ON

Occupation: Video technician   **Telephone:** (416) 555-7196

Date: 16.12.24   **Time Started:** 6:25 p.m.

                                    Time Completed: 6:35 p.m.

Officer Taking Statement: G. Polari #372

<u>RAN CAO will say</u>

At approximately 5:50 p.m. on the evening of December 24, 2016, I was driving southbound on Long St., a one-way street. I came in from Toronto to spend Christmas with a friend in Hamilton. It was dark, but Long St. is well lit, and I could see the roadway clearly.

I noticed a commotion at the corner of Mariah St. A man was on the ground and another man was on top of him, punching him. I couldn't stop because I was in the left-hand lane, so I turned left onto Packard St. and went around the block. I parked at the corner of Mariah and Long streets and went across the road to see if I could help. By this time the man who was doing the punching had left the scene, but I could see him walking along Long St. I could see that he was middle aged, but he was slouching over, so I didn't see how tall he was. I did notice that he was wearing a lightweight green jacket, which didn't seem appropriate considering that it was quite cold. I think that I could identify the man if I saw him again.

(Concluded on the next page.)

FIGURE 16.1   Concluded

As I approached the man on the ground, another man ran from
one of the nearby houses and told me that he had called
the police and an ambulance. The man on the ground was
bleeding quite heavily from facial injuries, and was barely
conscious. We stayed with him until police and an ambulance
arrived a short time later.

Signed Ran Cao

24 December 2016

6:35 p.m.

EXERCISE 1 » Assessing the Crown Brief

Use Crown brief sample one (Figure 16.1) to answer the following questions:

1. Does the Pidzerny case meet the definition of assault causing bodily harm as defined by section 267 of the *Criminal Code*? What elements in this case meet the definition, or what more information would be needed in order to meet the definition?

2. Does the summary of the Pidzerny case list all of the necessary facts in issue required to secure a conviction in this case? What are the facts in issue in this case?

3. Does the summary follow the report-writing format—discussed in Chapter 12, Report Writing—of summary, background, facts, and outcomes? Define which details in the summary of the Pidzerny case fall into each of these categories.

4. Do the witness statements deal with the facts in issue of the case? For each witness statement, what are the facts in issue that are dealt with? Describe how each witness statement supports the facts in issue of the summary.

A Reminder about Chronological Order

In Chapter 12, you read about the importance of using chronological order in your report writing. When you are writing notebook entries, general occurrence reports, supplementary reports (or investigative actions), and arrest reports, you write in the order of your observations and your actions *as you* experienced them.

For the Crown brief, the summary page lays out the case using the chronology of the crime as it occurred, not the chronology of the investigation as it unfolded.

For example, in a notebook entry, Constable Swingles wrote this excerpt from a break and enter she was investigating:

> I examined the back door to the premises and noted that the door handle was dangling out of its hole, and the locking mechanism was dented and scratched. I observed large splinters of wood from the door frame on the ground. I then interviewed the convenience store owner, who told me the small hatchet he kept in the shed behind the store had been removed from the shed and that he had found the hatchet lying by the ice machine to the left of the door.

To maintain the proper chronology, Constable Swingles would not write

> I examined the back door to the premises and noted that the door handle had been broken by small hatchet. The locking mechanism was dented and scratched. I observed large splinters of wood that had been carved from the doorframe by a hatchet.

This is because at the time of her observations of the door, she did not know a hatchet had likely been used to break into the store.

The Crown brief summary lays out the crime as it happened; so here's what Constable Swingles would write for the summary:

> A hatchet belonging to the store owner had been used to break into the store. SWINGLES observed a dangling door handle and a dented and scratched door frame. There were large splinters of wood carved by the hatchet on the ground.

EXERCISE 2 » Writing the Crown Brief

1. Write three complete Crown briefs for the following three scenarios that first appeared in Chapter 13, General Occurrence Reports.

   a. The bar fight in Frank Rizzo's bar

   b. The hit-and-run accident involving Catriona Hicks

   c. The Culver Road break and enter

   For these three scenarios, you have already written general occurrence reports, supplementary reports, arrest reports, and witness statements. You are now ready to complete the cases and begin the prosecution process by writing the Crown briefs. Remember to include these parts:

   • title page or cover page

   • introduction

   • synopsis

   • witness list

   • summary

   • witness statements

   Consult the sample Crown briefs to help you with layout.

2. Look up fraud in the *Criminal Code*. List the facts in issue, and beside each, write the elements of the Van Buren fraud case that are needed to pursue a fraud case against Henderson (see Figure 16.2).

3. Choose a current criminal case that is being reported in your local newspaper. Using the information you can find about the case, and inventing any details you need to tell the investigative story, write a complete Crown brief.

FIGURE 16.2 Crown Brief Two

Regina

v.

Marie-Rose Henderson

(Continued on the next page.)

FIGURE 16.2   Continued

[Introduction]

OFFENCE: FRAUD

           SECTION 380, CRIMINAL CODE OF CANADA

DATE: MAY 2016 - SEPTEMBER 2016

VICTIM: ESTHER VAN BUREN

ACCUSED: MARIE-ROSE HENDERSON

           15-364 Scott St.

           OTTAWA, ON

           (d.o.b. 22 July 1988)

PLACE: CITY OF OTTAWA

OFFICER: CST. MARISSA LECLERC #593

(Continued on the next page.)

FIGURE 16.2   Continued

[Witness List]

```
        WITNESSES                    SYNOPSIS

(1)  MARK PETERS              • victim's son

     198 Victoria St.         • noticed bank balance discrepancies
                                in his mother's savings account
     Arnprior, ON

         or

     c/o Heritage Furniture Company

     57 Main St.

     Arnprior, ON

(2)  ROBERT MCKENZIE          • victim's neighbour

     57 Broadview Rd.         • spoke with victim about a charity
                                she had started giving to
     Ottawa, ON

         or                   • saw accused enter victim's
                                home twice
     c/o Loblaws

     487 Richmond Rd.

     Ottawa, ON
```

(Continued on the next page.)

FIGURE 16.2   Continued

[Summary]

The charge of fraud in this matter arises from a fraudulent charity scheme that took place between the months of May to September 2016.

The person charged with fraud in this matter is:

Marie-Rose Henderson, d.o.b. 88.07.22 of 15-364 Scott St., Ottawa, ON

The circumstances of the offence are as follows:

In mid-May 2016, Esther VAN BUREN was called upon at her home at 55 Broadview Rd., Ottawa, ON, by Marie-Rose HENDERSON, who was posing as a member of a fraudulent registered charity that HENDERSON told VAN BUREN supported education for girls in Somalia. HENDERSON asked VAN BUREN to be invited into VAN BUREN's home so HENDERSON could explain how the charity worked. VAN BUREN agreed and invited HENDERSON into her home. This initial visit lasted 20 minutes, during which HENDERSON explained that after a family visit to Somalia in 2010, the Henderson family had come home and set up a Canadian registered charity, the Henderson Family Education Fund. She showed VAN BUREN false documents that VAN BUREN believed to be authentic. HENDERSON asked VAN BUREN to sign up to make a monthly donation of $200.00. VAN BUREN said she did not have that kind of money but gave HENDERSON $20.00. HENDERSON left a card with her name and fictitious contact information with VAN BUREN.

(Continued on the next page.)

FIGURE 16.2   Continued

Esther VAN BUREN Page 2

HENDERSON also visited a neighbour of VAN BUREN's, a Robert MCKENZIE. HENDERSON tried to interest MCKENZIE in the fraudulent charity, but he declined to contribute.

Two weeks later, on May 28, 2016, HENDERSON again came to VAN BUREN's home. HENDERSON claimed that things were desperate in Somalia, and girls were being sold into prostitution because they weren't attending school. VAN BUREN was distraught at this news and immediately wrote a check for $200.00 to HENDERSON. HENDERSON thanked VAN BUREN. HENDERSON then asked VAN BUREN if she would be able to sponsor a Somalian girl monthly. HENDERSON explained to VAN BUREN that an automatic monthly donation could be easily set and convinced VAN BUREN to give HENDERSON her banking details. VAN BUREN gave HENDERSON her bank name, savings account number, and her password. VAN BUREN also gave HENDERSON her son's phone number and asked HENDERSON to call VAN BUREN's son to make sure the monthly donation was a good idea. HENDERSON falsely promised to do this.

HENDERSON's presence in the neighbourhood on this day was confirmed by Robert MCKENZIE, who recognized HENDERSON's car from her previous visit.

At the beginning of June 2016, HENDERSON noticed her savings account balance was not what she thought it was. She noted three $200.00 withdrawals that she could not remember making. She called her son, Mark PETERS, and asked him to look into the matter. PETERS was just leaving Canada for a five-week business trip and promised to look into the matter when he got back.

(Continued on the next page.)

FIGURE 16.2   Continued

Esther VAN BUREN   Page 3

On July 24, 2016, PETERS contacted Ottawa Police to say he believed his mother had been a victim of a charity scam.

CONSTABLE MARISSA LECLERC attended VAN BUREN's home on July 25 and interviewed VAN BUREN. VAN BUREN told LECLERC that she had been sponsoring a Somalian girl through the Henderson Family Education Fund, but she thought the bank information had been mixed up, as more money was being taken out of her account than what she had agreed to. VAN BUREN asked LECLERC to talk to VAN BUREN's son about the banking and gave LECLERC her son's contact information. VAN BUREN also gave LECLERC the business card of Marie-Rose HENDERSON.

LECLERC called the number on HENDERSON's card, but there was no service at that number. LECLERC's investigation into the Henderson Family Education Fund revealed that no such charity existed in Canada.

On July 28, 2016, LECLERC interviewed PETERS, who told LECLERC that he believed his mother had been the victim of a scam. His investigation into his mother's bank account revealed that a total of $4,500.00 had been withdrawn from her savings account between the dates of May 17, 2016, and July 19, 2016. The withdrawals appeared to be from the account holder, as the password for the account had been used for each withdrawal. PETERS told LECLERC he had the account closed and re-opened a new account for his mother.

(Continued on the next page.)

FIGURE 16.2 Continued

LECLERC interviewed VAN BUREN's neighbour, Robert MCKENZIE, who told LECLERC he had also been approached by HENDERSON, but he told her he was not interested in contributing to the charity. He recalled seeing HENDERSON's car at VAN BUREN's on May 28, 2016. He was coming home from shopping and had to drive partly on his lawn to get into his driveway, as the HENDERSON vehicle was partly blocking the way. He wrote down the make, model, and licence number but decided not to pursue the matter. He gave LECLERC the information.

LECLERC used the vehicle information to obtain HENDERSON's address and went to the location, 15-364 Scott St., Ottawa, ON. HENDERSON invited LECLERC in to her residence. LECLERC began to question HENDERSON about the charity and her involvement with VAN BUREN. HENDERSON then faked a coughing fit and said she was going into the kitchen to get water. After one minute, LECLERC entered the kitchen to find the kitchen door ajar. LECLERC ran out the door and was able to apprehend HENDERSON as she was climbing over a back fence.

LECLERC cautioned VAN BUREN and informed her of her right to counsel. VAN BUREN was transported to the downtown station where she was held in custody pending a bail hearing.

Officers searching HENDERSON's residence found a box of business cards and various stationery. Both had the name the Henderson Family Education Fund on them. As well, officers found a ledger with names, passwords, and monetary amounts listed in it. Esther VAN BUREN's name appeared on the list.

(Continued on the next page.)

FIGURE 16.2   Continued

[Witness Statements]

Name: Mark Peters   **Date of Birth:** April 30, 1970

Address: 198 Victoria St, Arnprior, ON K1Y 3P9

Business Address: 57 Main St., Arnprior, ON

Occupation: Furniture   **Telephone:** (613) 552-5480
Technician

Date: July 28, 2016   **Time Started:** 2:15 p.m.

                                 Time Completed: 3:00 p.m.

Officer Taking Statement: M. Leclerc #593

MARK PETERS will say

I am 46 years old. I live at 198 Victoria St., Arnprior, ON. I am employed as a furniture technician at Heritage Furniture Company. I have been employed there for 12 years. I live alone.

In mid-June of 2016, my mother called me to ask me about a banking concern she had. She told me the balance in her savings account was lower than it should be and that she saw several withdrawals that she did not remember making. She also told me that she had signed up to donate $200.00 a month to the Henderson Family Education Fund. She said she thought that maybe the bank had made an error in the frequency with which the withdrawals should occur.

I telephoned the bank, the Bank of Nova Scotia, to look into the matter. I have co-signing authority on my mother's savings account, so I was able to discuss the situation with a bank officer. My mother is of sound mind, but she dislikes banking and has relied on me to help her with it since my father passed away in December of 2009.

I was told that my mother's account looked fine. The withdrawals seemed to have been made by her or me, as the

(Continued on the next page.)

FIGURE 16.2 Continued

password had been used to access the account and withdraw funds.

After talking with the bank officer, I called the number on the card Henderson had given my mother. This was an out-of-service line.

I then called the bank back and closed the account, opened another, and transferred my mother's money to the new account.

I then contacted Ottawa Police to look into the matter.

Signed Mark Peters

28 July 2016

3:00 p.m.

(Continued on the next page.)

FIGURE 16.2 Continued

Name: Robert McKenzie

Date of Birth: April 30, 1967

Address: 57 Broadview Rd., Ottawa, ON K7S 2K8

Business Address: 487 Richmond Rd., Ottawa, ON

Occupation: Purchasing Manager, Loblaws

Telephone: (613) 555-2367

Date: August 1, 2016

Time Started: 10:15 a.m.

Time Completed: 10:50 a.m.

Officer Taking Statement: M. Leclerc #593

Robert McKenzie will say

I am 49 years old. I work as a purchasing manager at Loblaws and have been working there for 20 years. I live with my wife, Donna Smythe. We have been married for 14 years.

I have lived beside Esther Van Buren for 14 years. We have an amiable relationship. Sometime in mid-May of this year, 2016, I was approached at my front door by a door-to-door solicitor. She wanted me to sign up for some sort of charity for Somalian girls. My wife and I already sponsor two children in Africa, so I told the woman I was not interested. The woman was not pushy; she simply thanked me for my time and left.

On May 28, I was home with a head cold. I went out to the drug store to get some tissue, and when I arrived back home, I saw that my driveway was partially blocked by a small blue late-model hatchback car. I was annoyed because I had to drive over my lawn a bit to get into my driveway.

As I let myself into the house, I recalled seeing the car before and realized I had seen it parked in front of my house on the day I got the visit from the charity woman. I went outside and wrote down the licence plate number and a description of the car.

(Concluded on the next page.)

FIGURE 16.2 Concluded

This morning I had a visit from Constable Leclerc, who asked me about the charity woman. I told her about my visit with the woman in mid-May and about my incident with the car blocking my driveway. I was able to find the paper with the car's details on it and give it to Constable Leclerc. I told Constable Leclerc that I never did do anything with the information.

Signed Robert McKenzie

1 August 2016

10:50 a.m.

CHAPTER SUMMARY

The Crown brief is the report you are working toward from the moment you first attend a call and begin your notebook notes, until you arrest a suspect (or suspects). The Crown brief is the compilation of documents and evidence that detail your investigation, and it puts the prosecution process in motion. The Crown brief must be clear, complete, and correct in order to get the desired verdict.

As a new officer, you will not be tasked with writing a Crown brief, but all of the writing you do as you progress in your career will help prepare you for your duties as a senior investigator, not the least of which is writing the Crown brief. Keep this in mind every time you record information on the job, and you will develop a solid writing style that will guarantee you write excellent Crown briefs and earn the respect of the Crown prosecutors.

KEY TERMS

disclosure, 338
indictment, 339
subpoena, 339
synopsis, 339

Review and Reflection Questions

1. What are some of the documents that can accompany a Crown brief?

2. Why is it so critical that the Crown brief stand alone as a complete telling of a case from start to finish?

3. How will the witness statements help the Crown attorney prepare its prosecution plan?

4. Why is the summary of the brief written in the third person?

5. How can you prepare yourself for the task of writing Crown briefs?

17 The Written Communication Test*

---

* Permission acknowledged from Jo-Anne Procter, Associate Dean, Justice and Wellness, to use material in this chapter that was originally generated for Mohawk College.

Introduction

After you complete your studies, you may decide to apply for a position with a police service, or you may wish to enter the fields of private security, customs, or corrections. In most cases, you will be required to write the Written Communication Test (WCT) before you apply. The WCT tests your ability to sort out facts and to write an essay based on those facts.

The WCT is divided into two parts and includes detailed instructions. In the first part, you are given a scenario, usually concerning (but not necessarily) a traffic accident. The facts in this scenario are jumbled, and some are unnecessary to the final essay. Your task is to

1. eliminate unnecessary information
2. enter the facts of the scenario on a fact sheet under the headings *Who*, *When*, *Where*, and *What*

In the second part, you are asked to use your fact sheet to write an essay. The essay must relate the facts of the scenario in chronological order.

The Instructions

The instructions for the WCT are usually handed to applicants with the WCT scenario (see Figure 17.1). It is important that you read them carefully. There are a few things to note:

1. A sample grading sheet has been included with this material. There are various methods of marking the WCT, but one method is to mark the WCT out of 25 marks, with Information Provided worth 10 marks, Organization worth 5 marks, Conclusion worth 5 marks, and Writing Clarity worth 5 marks (see Figure 17.2).

2. You cannot achieve a passing grade on the WCT without a passing grade of 60 percent in each of the four sections. For example, an overall score of 19/25 on the test with a grade of 2/5 in the Information Provided section will result in a failure on the entire test.

3. Be sure to take the time to read the instructions carefully. One of the factors that influences a good grade on this test is your ability to follow instructions.

4. Use the information provided. Use the words, spelling, and grammar of the scenario whenever possible. This is not a creative writing exercise, and you won't be charged with plagiarism for using the wording of the original. In fact, using the wording from the scenario will help you avoid spelling and grammar errors.

5. Don't make assumptions. All the information you need is in the scenario. Don't add anything just because you feel that something is incomplete.

6. Irrelevant information is anything that doesn't contribute to the resolution of the scenario. There are usually only one or two irrelevant facts in any one scenario.

7. The conclusion, stating who or what was at fault in the scenario, is usually short and doesn't require the student to have a knowledge of the *Highway Traffic Act*. For example, it is sufficient to say something like, "Mr. Smith was at fault in this scenario. He was travelling too fast for the road conditions and lost control of his car."

8. If your handwriting is poor, print your answers. The material can't be graded if it can't be read. There should be plenty of time to print if you need to.

9. An hour should be adequate time to finish the WCT. Pace yourself. For example, spend 20 minutes on the fact sheet and 40 minutes on the essay. You'll get a better

idea of your personal time requirements as you review the sample scenarios later in this chapter and complete Exercise 3.

10. Don't panic. Read the scenario at least twice before starting to rearrange sentences. Remember, the WCT is merely a scenario with the facts jumbled. All you need to do is to arrange the facts in chronological order. Chronological order (or logical order or cause and effect) simply means that something had to happen before something else happened. For example, you cannot have damage to a vehicle until after an accident occurs.

FIGURE 17.1 Sample Instructions

INSTRUCTIONS

Your answer will be graded according to:

- Your fact sheet
- The organization of the essay
- Spelling and grammar
- Your ability to draw logical conclusions

Note: You must pass each of the 4 sections in order to pass the WCT.

Read all of the instructions carefully before proceeding. Part of your grade results from the ability to follow instructions, both verbal and written.

The Written Communication Test has two parts. Part 1 requires you to list the facts of a scenario in point form. Use the "4 Ws Fact Sheet" provided. Part 2 asks you to write an essay that describes what occurred in the scenario. Do not add new information that does not exist in the story. Do not change the facts or information. Use pen only. Don't forget to put your name and student number on the upper right-hand corner of each page.

1. Do not write or mark on the scenario page or this instruction page.
2. Examine the scenario carefully. In this scenario the information has not been organized. Some of the details are irrelevant.
3. On the "WCT Fact Sheet Guide" make a list of all of the relevant and important facts in the scenario. Important facts should include such things as time, date, location, witness statements, weather and road conditions, evidence, the chain of events in logical order as they occurred, assignment of responsibility for the incident. You must conclude who or what was at fault, based solely on the facts of the scenario.
4. Double-space your essay. Print if your handwriting is not legible.
5. A separate sheet of paper may be used for notes and diagrams. Label this page "Rough Notes." Put your name at the upper right-hand corner of this page.
6. You have one hour to complete the WCT. You will not be able to leave the room once the test has started. You will be given a few minutes before the test starts to read these instructions and to ask questions. No questions will be answered once the test has started.
7. When you are finished, staple your pages together with the fact sheet first, followed by your essay, which should be followed by any rough notes. A stapler will be provided. Turn your paper upside down and leave it in the designated area, usually on a table at the front of the room. You will not be allowed to take any papers with you when you leave the room.

FIGURE 17.2   Sample Grading Sheet

Written Communication Test (WCT) Marking Guide

(NOTE: Students must score at least 60% in each of the four sub-sections to pass.)

STUDENT'S NAME: _____

Overall Grade: A) *Information Provided*   /10
                   B) *Organization*   /5
                   C) *Conclusion*   /5
                   D) *Writing Clarity*   /5

                   Total   /25

A: Information Provided: Fact Sheet & Essay   /10

Information **must** appear on both the fact sheet and the essay to earn credit.

1. All relevant times and dates.   /1___
2. Full names of all affected parties and witnesses.   /1___
3. Complete addresses of all parties and witnesses.   /1___
4. Precise locations, particularly house numbers,
    streets, intersections and other landmarks, sides of
    streets, lanes, NESW, etc.   /1___
5. Colour, year, make, model, and licence plates of all motor vehicles. /1___
6. Damage and estimated cost of repair.   /1___
7. Injuries and action taken.   /1___
8. Visibility, weather, road conditions, etc.   /1___
9. All links in the chain of events start to finish.   /1___
10. Assignment of responsibility for the incident.   /1___

B: Organization: Fact Sheet & Essay   /5

Students must meet the following goals:

1. Followed instructions both oral and written, in all answers.   /1___
2. Organized the fact sheet using who, when, where, and what.   /1___
3. Provided a general introduction to the essay.   /1___
4. Organized the essay with a series of paragraphs.   /1___
5. Used logical order to establish the chain of events in the essay. /1___

C: Conclusion: Essay Only /5

The fact sheet should indicate and lead to a logical conclusion as to who was at fault, but only the essay must have a formal conclusion, which says **why** he/she was at fault:

1. Provided a formal conclusion. /1___
2. Indicated who was at fault. /1___
3. Supported the conclusion with information from the fact sheet. /1___
4. Drew the correct conclusion regarding the fault. /1___
5. Used appropriately objective language in assigned fault. /1___

D: Writing Clarity: Fact Sheet & Essay /5

Students must achieve clarity and accuracy in both the fact sheet and essay and avoid writing errors, which will affect their credibility as professional reporters:

1. Spelled names of all affected parties and witnesses correctly. /1___
2. Made five or fewer spelling errors, including apostrophes. /1___
3. Made two or fewer run-on sentences and sentence fragments.* /1___
4. Avoided all other major grammar errors that affect clarity (agreement, verb tenses, verb formation, etc.). /1___
5. Used professional, objective language throughout. /1___

_____

*   Please note: Point #3 does not apply to the fact sheet, which should be in point form.

The Fact Sheet

The blank fact sheet for the Written Communication Test is called the "WCT Fact Sheet Guide." Information from the scenario, minus irrelevant information, is written on this fact sheet in chronological order. In the end, *everything* in the scenario (minus irrelevant information) will be found somewhere on the fact sheet in point form. Everything on the fact sheet will be used to write the essay. A sample fact sheet is provided below in Figure 17.3.

FIGURE 17.3   Sample WCT Fact Sheet Guide

WCT Fact Sheet Guide

W4 = who, when, where, and what

Use this sheet to help you organize the information as you read the scenario.

WHO

WHEN

WHERE

WHAT

Before beginning to make entries on the fact sheet, thoroughly read the scenario at least twice. You will have time for this. Reading the scenario, even though the facts are jumbled, helps to give you an overall picture of what happened. Then, eliminate irrelevant material. Since you can't write on the scenario, you'll have to either keep this irrelevant information in your head or write it on your Rough Notes sheet. A sample scenario has been provided in Figure 17.4.

FIGURE 17.4 Sample Scenario

There was an amazingly wild ice storm, and the roads were ice-covered and slippery. At approximately 1002 hours, a green 2014 Ford Transit Connect, Ontario licence ANAP 277, was travelling southbound on Mainway Street, Mississauga, ON, approaching the stop sign on Mainway Street. The speed limit is 50 km/h on Gerrard Street East. On Wednesday, September 13, 2017, at approximately 0958 hours, a red 2015 Toyota Yaris, Ontario licence ADGR 308, was travelling westbound on Gerrard Street East in the curb lane at approximately 40 km/h. At approximately 1002 hours, the Ford slid into the side of the Toyota in the intersection of Gerrard Street East and Mainway Street, a T intersection. The driver of the Toyota was Jane Oliver of 56 Aylmer Blvd., Toronto, ON, d.o.b. August 8, 1994. Gerrard Street East is a four-lane highway, with two lanes each in the eastbound and westbound lanes. The weather was cold. Mr. Gulka couldn't stop at the stop sign due to the ice on the roadway. There were no leaves on the trees. Mainway Street is a two-lane roadway with one lane for southbound traffic and one lane for northbound traffic. There is a stop sign at Mainway Street and Gerrard Street East for traffic travelling southbound on Mainway Street. The driver of the Ford was Shaun Gulka of 297 Front St., Brantford, ON. The Toyota received damage to the front passenger door for an estimated damage of $2,000. The Transit Connect was travelling at approximately 50 km/h approaching the T intersection of Mainway Street and Gerrard Street East. Mr. Gulka's d.o.b. is March 23, 1993. Mr. Gulka started to apply his brakes when the Ford was approximately 5 metres from the stop sign. The drivers were not hurt. The Ford sustained damage to the front bumper and grill for an estimated damage of $600. The speed limit for Mainway Street is 50 km/hr.

From this scenario, there are two irrelevant statements:

1. "There was an amazingly wild ice storm."
2. "There were no leaves on the trees."

Neither of these statements is relevant. The fact that there was an amazingly wild ice storm is irrelevant since the necessary information about road conditions, that the roads were ice-covered and slippery, is stated. Likewise, the absence of leaves on the trees is irrelevant because visibility was not a factor in the accident—the cause of the accident was Gulka's failure to adjust his speed to suit the icy conditions.

Now that you have read the scenario carefully, and have eliminated irrelevant material, you can fill out the fact sheet. To help you complete the fact sheet, ask yourself the following questions:

WHO

Who is the officer?

Who is the victim/complainant (include address, phone number, date of birth, etc.)?

Who are the witnesses?

Who is the offender?

Who else assisted in the investigation (e.g., ambulance staff, fire department, coroner, youth bureau, etc.)?

WHEN (include time and date, chronologically)

When did the event take place?

When was the officer dispatched, detailed, flagged down?

When did the officer arrive?

When were witnesses and/or victim(s) interviewed?

When was someone arrested?

WHERE

Where did the offence occur (include address, general description of address, location of event within that address)?

WHAT

What were the road and weather conditions?

What type of occurrence was it? (For example, was it a motor vehicle accident or another type of occurrence?)

What happened? How did the occurrence take place?

What damage did the vehicles sustain? What injuries did the parties suffer?

What types of vehicles were involved? What were their licence numbers, etc.? What was the direction of travel?

What were the drivers doing leading up to the accident?

What emergency vehicles attended the scene? (For example, were there tow trucks, ambulances, Ministry of Transportation vehicles?)

One trick to putting information in the correct category is to fill in the *Who*, *When*, and *Where* categories first. The *Who* category will usually contain names, which are easy to pick out from the scenario. List the names in the order they appear in the scenario. The *When* category will contain the times and dates, in chronological order, when events occurred. Since times and dates are usually stated in the scenario, this category should also be easy to complete. Likewise, the *Where* category can be filled out by identifying the locations and addresses in the scenario. Anything not in these categories goes in the *What* category. Students are encouraged to draw a diagram on their Rough Notes sheet to assist in visualizing the accident scene and in putting events in chronological order.

Be sure that everything from the scenario, minus the irrelevant material, appears on the fact sheet (see Figure 17.5).

FIGURE 17.5   Completed Fact Sheet

WCT Fact Sheet Guide

W4 = who, when, where, and what

Use this sheet to help you organize the information as you read the scenario.

WHO

- Jane Oliver, d.o.b. August 8, 1994, of 56 Aylmer Blvd., Toronto, ON, driver of the Toyota Yaris.
- Shaun Gulka, d.o.b. March 23, 1993, of 297 Front St., Brantford, ON, driver of the Ford Transit Connect.

WHEN

0958   Toyota travelling westbound on Gerrard St. East.

1002   Ford travelling southbound on Mainway St.

1002   Ford approaching a stop sign.

1002   Collision occurred on Wednesday, September 13, 2017.

WHERE

- T intersection of Gerrard St. East and Mainway St., Mississauga, ON.
- Toyota travelling westbound on Gerrard St. East, Ford travelling southbound on Mainway St.

WHAT

- Motor vehicle accident involving property damage.
- Ice-covered roads, slippery, cold weather.
- Red Toyota Yaris Ontario licence ADGR 308 travelling westbound on Gerrard St. E. in curb lane at approx. 40 km/h. Gerrard E. has 4 lanes, 2 each way eastbound and westbound. Speed limit is 50 km/h.
- Green Ford Transit Connect Ontario licence ANAP 277 travelling southbound on Mainway St. at approx. 50 km/h, approaching stop sign at T intersection of Mainway and Gerrard. Mainway is a 2-lane road, one lane each way northbound and southbound. Stop sign is for southbound traffic. Speed limit on Mainway is 50 km/h.
- When Gulka was about 5 m from the stop sign he applied his brakes but couldn't stop because of ice on the road. He ran into the side of the Toyota.
- No injuries. Damage to Toyota — front passenger door — estimated damage $2,000. Damage to Ford — front bumper and grill — estimated damage $600.

The Essay

When the fact sheet has been completed, usually in 20 minutes or less of the hour allowed for the test, the next step is to write the essay. Everything contained in the fact sheet (and therefore everything contained in the scenario, minus the irrelevant material) will be found in the essay.

The essay relates, in chronological order, the background, facts, and conclusions of the scenario. Like any essay, it is divided into paragraphs, with each paragraph dealing with a specific topic. Use as many paragraphs as you feel are necessary. The WCT usually is written as a five-paragraph essay, but five paragraphs are a minimum; there can be more, such as in Figure 17.7. A typical essay outline is provided below:

First paragraph. The first paragraph should provide a general summary of the incident, chronologically, including what type of incident occurred, when it occurred, and where it happened. You don't have to be specific here; the summary gives general descriptions and information, while the specifics are found later in the essay. The road conditions and weather should also be included in this paragraph.

Second paragraph. The second paragraph should identify the first person involved in the incident, how the person identified himself or herself, his or her address, what that person said and did, and any other pertinent information about that person. Usually, the first person is the first individual to be mentioned in the scenario.

Third paragraph. The third paragraph should identify subsequent persons involved in the incident and provide pertinent information about them.

Fourth paragraph. The fourth paragraph should include other relevant information (all information that didn't appear in the paragraphs above), such as estimated damage to vehicles, other property damage, injuries, and witnesses. If there's a lot of information, break it up into separate but related paragraphs.

Final paragraph. The final paragraph should state who was at fault and explain the reason for assigning fault. Your conclusions should be based on the facts provided in the scenario, including any statements made by the parties involved or by witnesses, and descriptions of evidence at the scene.

Points to Remember

1. Write in the *third person*.
2. Write in the *past tense*.
3. Write events in *chronological order*. Begin at the beginning, and then describe what happens after that.
4. Record *times* for everything.
5. Write in *complete, simple sentences*, using the wording of the scenario whenever possible.
6. State the *facts*; opinions are not a part of the essay.
7. Draw a *conclusion* in the final paragraph on the basis of the *facts* presented in the scenario.

Two scenarios with sample essays are reproduced in Figures 17.6 and 17.7. Read both of them, noting how the essays demonstrate the essay format described above. After you have finished analyzing the essays, complete Exercises 1, 2, and 3. Exercises 1 and 2 are brief; Exercise 3 challenges you to a full-length WCT Exercise 1.

FIGURE 17.6 Scenario 1 and Sample Essay

Scenario 1

Miss Schwartz said the motorcycle tried to pass too close to her horse. Mrs. Marucci said she slowed down and moved well to the left to pass safely, but the horse had attacked her bike. Diamond Lil limped alone back to her stable. Stephanie Schwartz was on the gravel road directly north of the Chatham Horse Farm, 2478 Quarry Road, Chatham, ON, L0R 1H3. Miss Schwartz was riding eastbound on Quarry Road on her black four-year-old quarterhorse mare, Diamond Lil. The Schwartz animal was valued at $2,500. Vet fees were $250. The collision at noon on May 1, 2017 resulted in the death of a valuable horse and damage to an expensive motorcycle. Marcella Marucci of RR #3, Jonesville, ON, L8N 1J3, was riding her black 2015 Harley-Davidson. Mrs. Marucci was also eastbound on Quarry Road. Miss Schwartz was born on July 4, 1992. She lives at the Chatham Horse Farm, where her horse was stabled. Mrs. Marucci was born September 15, 1990. The road is marked with yellow and black signs warning the public of horse traffic. The personalized licence plate of the motorcycle is MI*HOG. Mrs. Marucci saw the horse and rider, slowed, and pulled into the centre of the road to pass. Later that day, Dr. Bill Davis of Chatham Animal Hospital examined the horse. He said her left hind leg was broken. He had to put her to sleep. As the motorcycle came by, the horse suddenly kicked wildly and struck the bike with its rear hooves. Mrs. Marucci lost control on the loose gravel. She and the bike slid 10 metres before coming to rest in the centre of the road. The Harley-Davidson had a broken windshield, damage to the front forks, and scratched paint. Mrs. Schwartz was also thrown to the ground. Neither person was hurt. Both identified themselves with Ontario driver's licences. Damage to the bike is estimated at $1,500. The weather was clear.

Sample Essay

A collision between a horse and a motorcycle occurred at noon on May 1, 2017 on a gravel road in Chatham, ON. The collision resulted in the death of the horse and damage to the motorcycle. The riders of the horse and the motorcycle were not injured. The weather was clear.

Stephanie Schwartz, d.o.b. July 4, 1992, was riding eastbound on her black four-year-old quarterhorse mare, Diamond Lil. She was on the gravel road directly north of the Chatham Horse Farm, 2478 Quarry Road, Chatham, ON, L0R 1H3, where the horse was stabled and Miss Schwartz lives. The road is marked with yellow and black signs warning the public of horse traffic.

Marcella Marucci of RR #3, Jonesville, ON, L8N 1J3, d.o.b. September 15, 1990, was riding her black 2015 Harley-Davidson motorcycle, licence MI*HOG. She was also heading eastbound on Quarry Road. She saw the horse and rider, slowed, and pulled into the centre of the road to pass.

As the motorcycle came by, the horse suddenly kicked wildly and struck the bike with its rear hooves. Mrs. Marucci lost control on the loose gravel.

She and the bike slid 10 metres before coming to rest in the centre of the road. Miss Schwartz was also thrown to the ground. Neither rider was hurt. Both women identified themselves with Ontario driver's licences. Diamond Lil limped alone back to her stable. Later that day, Dr. Bill Davis of Chatham Animal Hospital examined the horse. He said her left hind leg was broken. He had to put her to sleep. The Schwartz animal was valued at $2,500. Vet fees were $250. Mrs. Marucci's Harley-Davidson had a broken windshield, damage to the front forks, and scratched paint. Damage is estimated at $1,500. Miss Schwartz said the motorcycle tried to pass too close to her horse. Mrs. Marucci said she slowed down and moved well to the left to pass safely but the horse attacked her bike.

Mrs. Marucci was at fault for trying to pass too closely. Since the horse was able to reach the motorcycle with its hind legs, there was not enough room given to pass safely.

FIGURE 17.7 Scenario 2 and Sample Essay

Scenario 2

Damage to the Transit Connect exceeded $5,000. It will be sold for parts. Danielle Damphousse was driving eastbound about 8 metres behind the step van. The accident took place in front of Hamilton Financial Centre, 203 King St. West, Hamilton, ON. Financial Centre employees came rushing out to assist. It was raining heavily and visibility was poor. When the step van suddenly stopped, Miss Damphousse lost control of her vehicle, which slid into the rear of the step van, and was partly lodged under the step/bumper. It was a 2015 Ford Transit Connect minivan. At that point, King Street has one lane eastbound, one westbound, and spaces for metered parking along both sides. The speed limit is 50 km/h. The collision between the minivan and the delivery vehicle occurred at 1603 on March 5, 2017 in the busy downtown shopping district of Hamilton, ON. Miss Damphousse escaped injury. Patrick O'Reilly, d.o.b. July 4, 1990, was driving eastbound on King Street in a white 2014 GMC step van. He has a good record with his employer, Mohawk Courier Services, which owns the vehicle. Damage to the van was limited to the rear step/bumper and is estimated at $500. Its Ontario licence plate is SCS 200. The Ford is red. Its Ontario licence plate is AJXW 846. Mr. O'Reilly lives at apartment 1460, 400 Sixteenth St., Hamilton, ON, L0R 1S0. Mr. O'Reilly said that at the time of the collision, he had to make an emergency stop because "an old Volkswagen Beetle" pulled out of a parking space on his right and cut in front of him. Miss Damphousse is a Capricorn and was born on January 8, 1989. Though Mr. O'Reilly barely stopped in time, the Volkswagen did not remain on the scene, and there were no independent witnesses. Miss Damphousse lives at 198 King St., Hamilton, ON, L8N 1J3. Both drivers showed valid Ontario licences. Both said they were driving at about 40 km/h. O'Reilly was not injured.

Sample Essay

A collision between a delivery van and a Ford Transit Connect minivan occurred at 1603 on March 5, 2017, in the busy downtown shopping district of Hamilton, ON. It was raining heavily, and visibility was poor.

The accident took place in front of Hamilton Financial Centre, 203 King Street West, Hamilton. At that point, King St. has one lane eastbound, one westbound, and spaces for metered parking along both sides. The speed limit is 50 km/h.

Danielle Damphousse, d.o.b. January 8, 1989, lives at 198 King St., Hamilton, ON, L8N 1J3. She was driving eastbound at about 40 km/h about 8 metres behind the step van in her red 2015 Ford Transit Connect van, Ontario licence AJXW 846. She identified herself with a valid Ontario driver's licence.

When the step van suddenly stopped, Ms. Damphousse lost control of her vehicle, which slid into the rear of the step van and partially lodged under the step/bumper. Miss Damphousse escaped injury.

Patrick O'Reilly, d.o.b. July 4, 1990, lives at apartment 1460, 400 Sixteenth St., Hamilton, ON, L0R 1S0. He was driving eastbound at about 40 km/h on King Street in a white 2014 GMC step van, Ontario licence SCS 200, owned by his employer, Mohawk Courier Services. He identified himself with a valid Ontario driver's licence.

Mr. O'Reilly said that at the time of the collision, he had to make an emergency stop because "an old Volkswagen Beetle" pulled out of a parking space on his right and cut in front of him. Though Mr. O'Reilly barely stopped in time, the Volkswagen did not remain on the scene, and there were no independent witnesses. Mr. O'Reilly was not injured.

Damage to the Transit Connect exceeded $5,000. It will be sold for parts. Damage to the GMC was limited to the rear step/bumper and is estimated at $500.

Miss Damphousse was at fault for following too closely. She should have allowed more space between her vehicle and the van because of the wet weather. Posted speed limits are valid only in clear, dry weather, and a driver must adjust to adverse weather conditions.

EXERCISE 1 » Incident A: Practise Writing a Simple Fact Sheet

Create a fact sheet based on the following scenario.

The Ford F-150 was travelling northbound on Red Hill Creek Expressway in the passing lane at approximately 9:30 a.m. The roads were dry. The Chevrolet Volt was travelling at approximately 60 km/h. The Ford F-150 was estimated to have received approximately $1,200 in damages. The traffic flow was heavy, but it was moving at the posted speed of 60 km/h. The Volt has a Winnipeg Jets bumper sticker. The weather was clear. On Wednesday, March 23, 2016, at approximately 9:30 a.m. the Volt was travelling northbound on the Red Hill Creek Expressway in the curb lane. The Volt's licence is ANMB 341. At approximately 9:32 a.m., the Ford F-150 swerved from the passing lane into the curb lane and struck the Volt's front left fender with its right rear bumper. The F-150 was travelling at approximately 70 km/h when it approached the Chevrolet Volt. The Chevrolet Volt was estimated to have received approximately $800 in damages. The F-150's licence is AJBB 326.

EXERCISE 2 » Incident B: Practise Writing an Essay

Write an essay based on the following scenario.

Susan Coleman is the driver of the blue Toyota Corolla. Coleman was travelling east on Locke Street. There were no injuries. Grant attempted to stop her vehicle but the cars collided. The Honda received minor damages to the front bumper. There was damage estimated at $2,000 to the passenger's side door of the Toyota. A black Honda Civic driven by Carroll Grant was travelling north on Bay Street when he saw a blue Toyota Corolla enter the intersection. Two cars collided at the intersection of Bay Street and Locke Street in Mitchell's Bay at approximately 5:15 p.m. on October 12, 2016. Grant placed a cellphone call to Mitchell's Bay Police at 5:20 p.m. Grant was travelling at 60 km/h in a 40 km/h zone. Constable Lewis arrived at 5:24 p.m.

EXERCISE 3 » Writing a WCT Essay

Construct a fact sheet and essay based on the following scenario. (Use the blank "WCT Fact Sheet Guide" in Figure 17.3 to record your facts.)

Charlie Smith is employed as a delivery driver by Hampton Community Care. Damage to the front grill, hood, and windshield of the Mustang was extensive and is estimated to be $4,500. Mr. Smith said he did not see the Mustang until after the collision. Both drivers identified themselves with Ontario driver's licences. Mr. Shumaker said the van was a dangerous obstruction. He said it was barely moving and, although he braked hard, he had no time to avoid a collision. Mr. Shumaker said he is fed up with jokes linking him to the famous race car drivers. He says he travelled eastbound at the posted speed limit through the S bend in his red 2016 Mustang GT, Ontario licence 299 PFS. The collision between the delivery van and the automobile occurred at 1001 on May 26, 2017. Mr. Smith was born on January 8, 1954. He was driving the charity's white 2014 Ford panel van carrying a full load of donated furniture. Peter Shumaker lives at apartment 904, Queen Apartments, 4300 Queen St., Southam, ON, L8N 2S3. Mr. Shumaker says, as he exited the S bend, he saw the panel van. Mr. Smith lives at RR #3, Jonesville, ON, L0R 1J3. The van's Ontario licence is AAKN 201. Damage to the van's loading door and bumper was estimated at $1,100. Mr. Smith acknowledged that his fully loaded vehicle was travelling slowly up an incline. He said that, before the collision, he was travelling northbound on Twenty Road, stopped at the intersection with Regional Road 18, and checked the road in each direction. At the time of the collision, both vehicles were travelling eastbound on Regional Road 18, Hampton, ON, 20 metres east of the intersection with Twenty Road. Mr. Smith has an excellent employment record. He said it is not possible to see more than 30 metres west on Regional Road 18 from the intersection with Twenty Road, because of a blind S bend, a house, and trees. There were no injuries. The weather was clear. The speed limit through the S bend is 50 km/h. The car destroyed a sign posting a speed limit change to 70 km/h. Peter Shumaker was born February 5, 1990. When Mr. Smith was satisfied that the road was clear, he turned right, accelerating slowly up the incline in the eastbound lane of Regional Road 18. Replacement of the speed limit sign is estimated at $500. The front of the Mustang came into contact with the right rear of the Ford van. The car then slid into the ditch.

CHAPTER SUMMARY

The Written Communication Test is required for many positions in law enforcement. The WCT presents a scenario in which the facts are jumbled. You must eliminate irrelevant facts, arrange the remaining facts in chronological order on a fact sheet, and then write an essay based on those facts.

Review and Reflection Questions

1. What information should go in the introductory paragraph?

_____

_____

_____

2. What essential element must you create in the final paragraph of your test?

_____

_____

_____

3. If the test scenario seems to be missing information, how do you deal with this gap on your fact sheet and essay?

_____

_____

_____

4. On your fact sheet and essay, should you include all information provided in a test scenario?

_____

_____

_____

5. Do you think this type of test is a worthwhile evaluation for entry positions in law enforcement? Explain your answer.

_____

_____

_____

Glossary

absence report: a report written by officers requiring time off that will be submitted to superior officers and human resources.

acronym a word invented by putting together the first letters of several words. Sometimes vowels are added to make the acronym easy to pronounce. AWOL (absent without leave), VSA (vital signs absent), and LOL (laugh out loud) are examples of jargon created from using the first letters of words in a phrase.

ambiguity: vagueness or uncertainty.

ampersand: a typographical symbol meaning "and." It looks like this: &.

antonyms: words with opposite meanings.

arrest: to take control of a person—that is, to take a person into custody.

attachment: a document sent with your written communication. Indicate the number of attachments in your email or letter.

audience: the person or persons who watch your presentation. Your presentation is for the benefit of these participants; imagine their concerns when designing each aspect of the presentation.

bias: a strong opinion that influences a point of view.

briefing notes: written for officers who are addressing the media or other interested parties. Subjects for briefing notes include details about ongoing investigations or successful arrests, police initiatives such as a new hiring or equipment purchase, or any other police-related news the public should know about.

cause and effect: the relationship between an action and the resulting event. If a defendant *causes* harm to a victim and she is caught, the *effect* is incarceration.

citation: a reference to an original source.

clause: any group of words that contains a subject and a verb.

closed questions: limit choices when answering, as in "yes" or "no."

closed-ended questions: invite "yes" or "no" answers. They tend to shut down communication and can make a speaker feel defensive.

closing: in the closing of email and memos, type your title, name, and division; in letters, use a complimentary close such as "Yours truly" or "Sincerely."

comma splice: occurs when two independent clauses are joined together with a comma, but they are missing the essential conjunction or linking word. Commas do not join sentences.

complete subject: a subject consisting of more than one word.

concise: using as few words as possible to effectively describe something.

connotation: any additional impression a word carries with it. *See* denotation.

contradict: to disagree with something said or claimed. A witness can be contradictory on the stand by telling the Crown attorney that what the suspect said about his actions was untrue.

controlling idea: the attitude of the writer of the paragraph toward the topic identified in the topic sentence.

correction: a crossed-out error; both the witness and the officer should sign each correction.

credentials: qualifications that demonstrate a person has the appropriate background on a topic to give an opinion or argument about the topic with some authority.

credibility: a quality of believability. As an officer, keeping an accurate and complete notebook improves your credibility as a witness in court.

dangling modifiers: modifying words that don't logically modify anything in their sentence.

denotation: the dictionary meaning of a word.

dependent clause: a group of words containing a subject and a verb, but not a complete thought; therefore, it is not a complete sentence, and it needs something else to complete it.

direct order: a writing structure used to convey positive or neutral messages to the reader, such as good news or a request for information.

disclosure: the act of sharing or revealing information.

empathetic: being able to understand and be sensitive to another person's feelings or responses to experiences even though you may not have had similar feelings or experiences yourself.

enunciate: to pronounce clearly.

equipment maintenance report: a report in which officers are responsible for notifying the garage of any vehicle maintenance needed. Likewise, officers would notify equipment maintenance personnel if other pieces of equipment, such as radios, computers, guns, vests, or helmets, require maintenance.

exact statement: a verbatim account of the witness statement.

fact: verifiable and based on evidence.

fraudulent: to be dishonest, deceitful, or fake.

homographs: words that have the same spelling, but have different meanings or uses, such as *desert* (noun) and *desert* (verb).

homonyms: words that have the same pronunciation, but have different spellings and often different meanings, such as *brake/break* and *mail/male*.

homophones: words that sound the same but have different meanings, such as *hour* and *our*.

hot buttons: topics that trigger an emotional response based on attitudes and beliefs.

idioms: using language, usually figuratively, to express something in a creative way. Some common examples include "Cat got your tongue?" and "Hit the books."

independent clause: a complete thought containing a subject and a verb; therefore, these clauses are complete sentences.

indictable offences: serious crimes; examples of indictable offences include breaking and entering with intent (dwelling) (s. 348.1) and arson (s. 434).

indictment: a criminal charge before the court.

indirect order: a writing structure used to convey unwelcome news that will likely be met with resistance or negativity. It is also appropriate in cases where you expect a lack of interest. The indirect order is a "bad news approach."

inference: a conclusion drawn by making assumptions.

infinitives: the basic verb form without inflections to show person, number, or tense, as in the case of *to have*.

injury report: a report that must be filled out and filed with the human resources department and with insurance companies if an officer sustains an injury in the line of duty.

innuendo: comments that are suggestive about a person or situation but that are not necessarily factual. Innuendo is considered irrelevant material and should not be included in your notebook.

irregular verbs: verbs that involve adding words to change the tense.

irrelevant material: for the purpose of writing reports or testifying in court, information that is not connected, helpful, or useful to the investigation of the case. Irrelevant material should not be included in your notebook.

jargon: words or expressions that are commonly used by a select group of people and would usually be unfamiliar to others. Some better known examples include the use of *stat* in a hospital environment, or *10-4* between radio users.

job shadow reports: reports detailing the experiences of new recruits and officers in line for promotion, who will often shadow mentors.

leave report: a report written by officers requiring time off that will be submitted to superior officers and human resources.

lexicon: the body of vocabulary used by a person or group.

linking verbs: words that don't appear to be action words; the action isn't obvious, including forms of the verb *to be*.

listening: a complex communication skill and not simply a matter of hearing sound.

mechanics: the parts of a presentation that are not related to its content, such as volume, timing, and posture.

memo: short for *memorandum*. An informal written statement, usually brief and used for communicating within an organization. Today, the memo format is used when sending email. Also note that the memo format is now used for short informal reports containing headings, tables, and more.

misplaced modifiers: modifying words placed within a sentence in such a way that it is unclear what word they are meant to modify.

narrative: a story or a telling of events or occurrences.

necessities: for legal purposes, those things needed to maintain life, such as food, water, shelter, and safety.

non-verbal communication: includes visual elements, vocal elements, and spatial elements.

non-verbal cues: include body language and tone of voice.

open questions: questions that allow for information and elaboration.

open-ended questions: questions that invite respondents to say more about a topic. There are no limits imposed on answers to open-ended questions. Open-ended questions tend to draw out respondents and encourage them to speak more.

opinion: a point of view.

oral presentation: a presentation delivered through speech. Effective oral presentations have many purposes; in general, the purpose is to inform or persuade a group of listeners.

perception: awareness through the senses: seeing, hearing, touching, smelling, or tasting. Through perception, we collect basic facts.

preceded: to come before; for example, *a* precedes *b* in the alphabet.

précis: similar to a summary. In a précis, you condense the original text significantly, while capturing its main points in a concise, precise way.

precise: being precise means using as specific language as you can to effectively describe something.

reasonable grounds: facts or circumstances that would lead a reasonable, objective person to believe an offence has occurred.

regular verbs: verbs that can be changed from present to past tense by adding *-ed* to the present form of the word.

run-on sentence: two complete sentences joined together in an inappropriate way.

salutation: a greeting at the beginning of your communication. Use the receiver's given name and title, unless it is impossible to do so, such as in the automatic fields in email software.

sentence fragment: a group of words that is not a complete thought, or a group of words missing either a subject or a verb.

simple subject: a subject consisting of one word.

slang: an informal, common, but technically incorrect use of words. An example would be the use of *hanging out* to mean being somewhere for a while with no particular purpose.

stereotyping: to adopt an oversimplified idea of a person.

strategy: the method of presenting your point of view throughout the essay.

subject: the word or group of words that the sentence concerns.

subpoena: a legal summons that orders a person to attend court as a witness or a party in a legal proceeding.

substantiate: to provide proof that what you claim to be true is real or correct. An alibi substantiates a suspect's claim that he was not at the scene of the crime when it occurred.

suffixes: letters added to the end of a word to make a new form of the word; for example, adding the suffix "ed" to *walk* will make *walked*.

summarizing: capturing the main points of something larger in a briefer, concise way.

summary offence: a less serious crime; an officer might charge a person and release him or her using a promise to appear document.

supplementary report: an additional report following an original incident and further reporting relevant information about the investigation.

synonyms: words with similar meanings.

synopsis: a shortened summary of a larger work.

tense: refers to when the verb took place—in other words, its past, present, or future form.

thesis statement: a complete sentence expressing the writer's point of view on a topic.

topic: the subject of your presentation. Find a way to approach the topic so that it is interesting to you and your audience.

topic sentence: a sentence that includes two things: a *topic* and a *controlling idea*.

transitions: in transitions, transitional words and phrases are used to organize the paragraph better and to make the paragraph flow more smoothly.

trend analysis reports: can be filled out by officers or by civilian personnel tasked with trends analysis. These reports are used to plan special operations, hire more officers, or start special investigative units, such an elder abuse unit.

verb: the action word of a sentence.

verbatim: a direct quotation—the record of someone's statement with word-for-word accuracy.

visuals: aids meant to enhance a presentation, not to replace the speaker.

voice: the form of the verb that indicates whether the subject of a sentence is the instigator of the action or the receiver of the action. There are two voices: active and passive.

warrant: a court order giving authority to police to find and arrest a person; there are various kinds of warrants, including warrants to search, seize, enter, and arrest.

"will say": a phrase indicating that the witness will, in court, attest to the facts in the statement.

witness: someone with direct observations of facts in issue. A witness perceives something relevant to an incident.

Index

A

acronyms, 107
apostrophes, *see* grammar
arrest, *see* report writing; supplementary reports

B

bias, 24, 109, 289
body language, 5, 27, 203

C

citations, *see* research skills
clauses, *see* grammar
clichés, avoidance of, 104–105, 287
comma, *see* grammar
communication process
    ambiguity, 4
    barriers, 4
    disabilities, persons with, 10
    empathy, 4
    feedback, 4
    groups, 13, 15
    mentally challenged persons, 8–9
    multicultural society, in, *see* multicultural issues
    personal space, 14
    receiver, 4
    sender, 4
    team environment, 13, 15
    word choices, *see* words
communication theory, 4
community, 33, 192
conciseness, 113–114
connotation, 11
correspondence, general principles, *see also* email; letters; memoranda
    content organization, 134
    direct order writing structure, 135, 138
        letter example, 138
        memo example, 135
    indirect order writing structure, 135, 136–137, 139
        letter example, 139
        memo example, 136–137
    readability principle, 134
    spell checks, 134
    tone, 134
    "you" approach strategy, 134
Crown brief, *see also* report writing
    chronological order, application of, 352
    contents of, 339
    cover/title page, 339
    described, 338
    disclosure, rules of, 338
    documents included, 339
    exercises, 352, 253
    indictment, defined, 339
    individuals, identifying, 341
    introduction, 340
    parts, 339–340
    samples, 341–352, 354–364
    subpoena, defined, 339
    summary, 340
    synopsis, 339, 340
    third person voice, use of, 341
    witness list, 340

D

diagrams, 249–252
digital devices
    SceneDoc software, 226–227
    use of, 226

E

email, *see also* correspondence, general principles
    attachment, 127, 128
    body, 127
    closing, 127
    direct order writing structure, 126
    exercise, 140
    format of, elements, 125–126
    formatting, 128
    headings, 125
    indirect order writing structure, 126
    necessity for, 125
    purposes of, 125

email (cont.)
    replying
        caution re, 127
        context and clarity, 127
        described, 127
    salutation, 127
    style, 125
essay
    anatomy, 173–174
    audience, 166–167
    brainstorming subjects, 174–175
    checklist, 187–188
    conclusion, 184–185
    controlling idea, 170
    described, 173–174
    draft, first, 185
    information sources, 186
    organization of, 177–180
        body, 180
        introduction strategies, 178–179
        topics within, organizing, 180
    outline, 175, 184
    paragraph, 167, 169, 172
        strategies, 172
        topic sentence, 167, 169
        transition words/phrases, 180
        types of, 172
    purpose, 166
    research paper versus, 186
    structure, chart, 168
    subject, 174
    thesis statement, 170, 175–177
    topic, 170
    topic sentences, 167, 169, 171, 173
    writing strategies
        compare/contrast, 183
        description, 181
        exposition, 182
        narration, 181
        persuasion, 182

F

fact sheet, 371–372, 379
facts
    in issue, 270
    inferences versus, 110
    opinion versus, 28
factual language, 104

G

general occurrence reports, *see also* report writing
    active voice, use of, 291
    bias/subjectivity, editing for, 289
    cover page, 280, 282–284
    editing exercise, 292
    examples, 278, 281
    first versus third person voice exercise, 292
    fraudulent document reports, 280
    generally, 278
    narrative page, 280, 284–287
    necessities, 278
    requirement for, events, 279
    sample, 281
    slang/jargon/cliché, editing for, 287–288
    spelling exercise, 290
    supplementary reports, 279
    writing exercise, 293–296
grammar
    apostrophes
        contractions, 93
        exercise, 94
        possessives, 93
    capital letters, 98
    case, pronouns and, 86
    clauses
        dependent, 78
        described, 78
        independent, 78
    colons, 97
    comma splice, 82
    comma, use of
        exercises, 66, 92
        rules, 91–92
    contractions, 95
    correlative conjunctions, 89–90
    editing exercises, 69, 98–99
    exclamation points, 96
    importance of, 64
    modifiers
        dangling, 84
        described, 82
        misplaced, 82–83
    parallel structure
        described, 68, 88
        exercise, 89
    periods, 96
    pronouns
        ambiguous and indefinite, 87–88
        case and, 86
        described, 85
        exercise, 86
        personal, 85
    punctuation marks exercise, 67
    question marks, 96
    quotation marks, 96
    run-on sentences
        described, 80
        exercises, 66, 81

semicolons, 97
sentence, elements of
    subject, *see* grammar, subject
    verb, *see* grammar, verbs
sentence fragments
    clauses, 78–79
    described, 77–79
    exercise, 64
subject
    complete subject, 70–71
    generally, 70
    simple subject, 70
subject–verb agreement
    exercises, 64, 67, 77
    rules re, 74–76
subordination and coordination exercise, 65
verbs
    generally, 71
    infinitives, 73
    irregular, 72–73
    linking, 72
    regular, 72
    tense, 72, 74
    voice, 100
voice, active and passive, 100

H

handwriting versus word processing, 48

I

inferences, 110

J

jargon
    avoidance of, 5
    editing out, 387
    exercise, 108
    workplace versus communication use, 107

L

letters, *see also* correspondence, general principles
    closing, 130
    exercise, 140
    format, 130
    headings, 130
    purposes of, 129
    salutation, 130
    style, 130–133
        full block with open punctuation, 131
        modified block with modified open punctuation, 133
        traditional with closed punctuation, 132
lexicon, 106

listening
    acknowledgment and feedback, giving, 24–25
    advantages of, 23
    barriers to effective listening, 31, 34
    biased/stereotype listening, 24
    body language, 27
    community interaction, 33
    decision to listen, 23
    emotional response, control of, 29
    fact versus opinion/propaganda, distinguishing between, 28
    group exercises
        meaning, 36–37
        motivation, 36
    hot buttons, 29
    information assimilation, 30
    instructions, following, 33
    interviews, listening in, 37
    memory techniques, 32
    non-verbal cues, 27
    perceptions, 30
    questions
        appropriate, 25–26
        broadening, 26
        changing direction, 27
        clarifying/confirming, 27
    reflective listening, 25
    school, listening in, 35
    selective listening, avoidance of, 24
    self analysis, quizzes, 20–22
    self knowledge exercise, 31
    silence, 30
    skills
        need for, 20
        summary of, 33
    speaker's reality, interpreting, 30
    summary, agreement to, 30
    tone of voice, 28
    whole body listening, 28

M

memoranda, *see also* correspondence, general principles
    closing, 129
    exercise, 140
    format, 128
    headings, 129
    purposes of, 128
    style, 129
    subject line, 129
mobile devices, *see* digital devices
modifiers, *see* grammar
motor vehicle
    accident diagrams, 249–252
    accident statement, 324, 329
    collision report, 324, 330

multicultural issues
    body language, 5
    diversity training, 7
    enunciation, 5
    exercise examples, 14, 16
    idioms, use of, 5
    jargon, 5
    non-verbal communication, 5–6
    offensive/taboo behaviours, 6–7
    slang, use of, 5

N

non-verbal communication, 5–6, 27, 192, 202, 204
notebook, *see also* report writing
    accuracy, 258
    checklist, 258–259
    closed-ended questions, 243
    credibility, 246
    diagrams, 249–252
        motor vehicle accident example, 250–252
    entries, guidelines, 253–256
    generally, 242
    innuendo, 244
    irrelevant, 244, 245
    note-taking techniques, 244–249
    omissions, 249
    open-ended questions, 243
    organizing, exercise, 257
    question techniques, 243–244
    10-codes, 260
    use of notes in court, 249
    verbatim, 245

O

objectivity, *see* subjectivity and objectivity
occurrence reports, *see* general occurrence reports
oral presentation
    academic context, 192
    aggressive behaviour, dealing with, 206–207
    audience, 193
    body orientation, 203
    community outreach and, 192
    conferencing with peers, 207
    debating, 209
    defined, 192
    elements of, 195–197
    emphasis, 204
    exercise, 201
    eye contact, 202
    facial expression, 203
    gestures and posture, 203
    good impression, creating, 217
    impromptu speaking, 205

    information gathering, 194
    loudness, 203
    mechanics of, 198
    mock trial, example, 210–216
    nervousness, 199
    non-verbal communication, 192, 202, 204
    one-on-one communication with difficult person, 206–207
    organization, 197–198
    outline for, 197
    preparation for, 195
    purposes of, 193
    questions, answering, 198
    rate of speech, 203
    reading, avoidance of, 206
    research for, 194, 195
    special elements, 204
    topic, 193–194
    visual aids, 199–201
    visual elements, 202–203
    vocal elements, 203–204

P

paragraphs, *see* essay
paraphrase, *see* research skills
person, first/second/third, 115, 292, 341
perspective, *see* point of view
point of view
    changing, exercise, 116
    first person, 115, 292
    second person, 115
    third person, 115, 292, 341
    uses of, 115–116
preciseness, 113–114
pronouns, *see* grammar
public speaking, *see* oral presentation

Q

questions, *see* listening; notebook; oral presentation; witness statements
question marks, 96
quotation marks, 96–97

R

reference lists, *see* research skills, citations and reference lists
report writing
    arrest reports, 224
    briefing notes, 225
    cause and effect, 265
    chronological reporting, 267
    common errors, 271
    composition, 268
        simple report, example, 268

contradictory, 267
Crown briefs
    described, 224
        sample, 231–232
digital devices, use of, 226–227
equipment maintenance reports, 225
facts in issue, 270–271
general occurrence reports, 224, 230, 233, 238–239
general rules, 265–266
generally, 222, 264
injury reports, 225
irrelevant, 267
job shadow reports, 225
leave/absence reports, 225
notebooks
    described, 224
    sample entries, 228–230, 237
    transferring notes to report, 271
    writing reports from notes, exercises, 272–275
organization for, 266–268
outline, 267
parts of report, 264–265
    exercise, 269
    report narrative, 264
    summary page, 264
readers, 227–228, 264
    insurance companies, 228
    media, 228
    other enforcement agencies, 228
    peer personnel, 228
    prosecution personnel, 228
    supervisors, 227
report writing trail, chart, 222
sample scenarios, 223
SceneDoc software, 226–227
substantiate, 264
supplementary reports, 224, 230, 234–236
trend analysis reports, 225
types of reports, 224–225
writing process, 225–227
research paper, 186
research skills
ampersand, 155
author credentials, 144
citation, defined, 153
citations and reference lists
    APA style in-text citation, 153, 154–156
    APA style reference list, 156–158
    authoritative sources, 153
    MLA style, 153
    MLA style citations, 158
    resources, 161
credentials, 145
generally, 144
index cards, use of, 145–146

note taking, 145
paraphrase, 151–153
plagiarism, 145, 153
précis, 145
quotations, formatting, 159
reference lists, *see* research skills, citations and reference
    lists
research paper writing, exercise, 161
sources
    appropriate and credible, 144
    comparing, 145
summarizing, 146
summary, *see also* research skills, paraphrase
    direct speech, changing into indirect speech, 148–149
    exercise, 151
    samples, 150
    word counting, rules, 149
    wordy expressions, removal of, 147
    writing procedure, 146–147
works cited list, guidelines for, 159

S

sentences, *see* essay; grammar
slang, avoidance of, 5, 104, 106, 287
speaking, public, *see* oral presentation
spelling, *see also* vocabulary
    Canadian spelling, 56
    computer spell check, 48
    frequently misspelled words, list, 58
    generally, 40
    handwriting versus word processing, 48
    improvement tips, 41
    preceded, meaning of, 41
    plurals, 44–47
    rules, 41–44
    suffixes, 41
    troublesome words, chart, 42
subject, *see* grammar
subjectivity and objectivity
    bias avoidance, 109
    connotative language, 109
    described, 108
    editing exercise, 111
    editing for, 289
    field example, 112
    inferences versus facts, 110
summary, *see* research skills; supplementary reports
supplementary reports, *see also* report writing
    arrest
        documenting, 306
        indictable offences, arrest for, 306
        reasonable grounds for, 306
        statement from accused, 309–311, 314
        summary offences, arrest for, 306

supplementary reports (cont.)
  arrest powers, 306
  arrest report, 303–309
    exercises, 312–314
    sample, 307–309
  arrest warrant, 306
  blank report, sample, 305
  components of, 300
  cover page, 300
  exercise, 312–313
  general occurrence reports versus, 300
  generally, 300
  indictable, 306
  investigation exercise, 315
  linking reports, 301–303
  narrative content, 300
  Niagara Regional Police Services Reports, sample, 317–318
  outcome section, 303
  purposes of, 300
  reasonable grounds, 306
  sample, 304
  statement from accused, 309–311, 314
  summary, 306
  summary section, 302
  warrant, 306

T

10-codes, 260
test, *see* Written Communication Test

V

verbs, *see* grammar
vocabulary, *see also* spelling; words
  antonyms, 48
  choices, generally, 11
  correct word choice exercises, 53–56
  homographs, 48
  homonyms, 48
  homophones, 48
  legal profession words, list, 57
  misused words, list, 49–52
  synonyms, 48
voice
  active versus passive, 117–119, 291–292
  tone of, 28
  verb, 100

W

witness statements
  blank form, 327–328, 329
  corrections to, 324
  exact statement, defined, 320
  exercises, 333–334
  general rules, 322
  motor vehicle accident statement, 324, 329
  motor vehicle collision report, 324, 330
  Niagara Regional Police Services Reports, 331–332
  perception, defined, 320
  procedure, 324
  purpose of, 320
  questioning witness, guide, 322
  samples, 323, 325–327, 331–332
  types of, 320
  "will say," defined, 320
  witness, defined, 320
words, *see also* vocabulary
  connotation versus denotation, 11
  grammar, *see* grammar
  power of, 15
  semantics, 11–12
  spelling, *see* spelling
Written Communication Test
  described, 368
  essay, 376–380
  fact sheet, 371–372, 379
  fact sheet guide, 375
  instructions, 368–369
  sample grading sheet, 370–371
  sample scenario, 373–374
writing strategies, *see* essay
writing structure, *see* correspondence, general principles; email; essay